LANGUAGE DISORDERS IN CHILDREN
Real Families, Real Issues, and Real Interventions

ELLENMORRIS TIEGERMAN-FARBER
Adelphi University
Garden City, New York

CHRISTINE RADZIEWICZ
School for Language and Communication Development
Glen Cove, New York

PEARSON

Merrill
Prentice Hall

Upper Saddle River, New Jersey
Columbus, Ohio

Library of Congress Cataloging-in-Publication Data

Tiegerman-Farber, Ellenmorris.
  Language disorders in children : real families, real issues, and real interventions /
Ellenmorris Tiegerman-Farber, Christine Radziewicz.
    p. cm.
  Includes bibliographical references (p.).
  ISBN 0-13-091576-9
  Language disorders in children. I. Radziewicz, Christine II. Title.

RJ496.L35L364 2008
618.92'855—dc22   2006051585

Vice President and Executive Publisher: Jeffery W. Johnston
Executive Editor: Ann Castel Davis
Editorial Assistant: Penny S. Burleson
Senior Production Editor: Linda Hillis Bayma
Production Coordination: Linda Zuk, WordCraft, LLC
Design Coordinator: Diane C. Lorenzo
Photo Coordinator: Valerie Schultz
Cover Designer: Bryan Huber
Cover Image: Jupiter Images
Production Manager: Laura Messerly
Director of Marketing: David Gesell
Marketing Manager: Autumn Purdy
Marketing Coordinator: Brian Mounts

This book was set in Garamond by Carlisle Editorial Services. It was printed and bound by R.R. Donnelley & Sons
Company.
The cover was printed by R.R. Donnelley & Sons Company.

Photo Credits for Chapter Openers: Krista Greco/Merrill, p. 4; Anne Vega/Merrill, pp. 37, 132, 206; Patrick White/
Merrill, pp. 75, 111; Scott Cunningham/Merrill, pp. 160, 285; Barbara Schwartz/Merrill, p. 188; Ken Karp/PH College,
p. 226; Valerie Schultz/Merrill, pp. 260, 316; Karen Mancinelli/Pearson Learning Photo Studio, p. 342.

Pearson Education Ltd.
Pearson Education Singapore Pte. Ltd.
Pearson Education Canada, Ltd.
Pearson Education—Japan

Pearson Education Australia Pty. Ltd.
Pearson Education North Asia Ltd.
Pearson Educación de Mexico, S.A. de C.V.
Pearson Education Malaysia Pte. Ltd.

10 9 8 7 6 5 4 3 2 1
ISBN-13: 978-0-13-091576-4
ISBN-10:   0-13-091576-9

Preface

Special education became law (Public Law 94-142) in 1975; since that time, programs and services have evolved in state and local systems. Public Law 94-142 has been reauthorized several times by Congress and expanded to include children from birth to 5 years of age. A parallel process of change was also occurring in the field of speech-language pathology with the advent of child language theories. The theories in child language development precipitated dramatic changes in clinical practice, resulting in the creation of a new professional, the speech-language pathologist (SLP). The speech-language pathologist now works in homes, schools, hospitals, early intervention programs, and early childhood programs with children who have speech, language, and communication disorders. The clinical opportunities, work options, and areas of specialization have become more diverse and challenging. It is an exciting time for our profession as our clinical horizons expand.

It is not possible for any single textbook to present an in-depth discussion of every developmental disability in children. Our goal is to show how the role of the SLP has changed; what clinical intervention techniques are successfully being used today with children with different developmental disabilities; and what policies and procedures affect clinical practice. *Language Disorders in Children* introduces three families whose stories exemplify the challenges faced by families whose children have disabilities. Each of these families changes as their children grow and they learn to be effective advocates. Three developmental disabilities—autism, speech-language impairment, and hearing loss—are chosen as examples to highlight present-day language theories and clinical practices. To provide the reader with an in-depth understanding of the impact of a language disability on children and families, the textbook uses a developmental approach emphasized by six themes: language, children, diversity, educational systems, clinical practice, and strengths-based perspective.

Language. As children grow older, their language characteristics change. Children with disabilities do not remain static; their language changes and evolves. Their language and social behaviors are influenced by both internal and external factors. The fact that a child has a disability does not mean he does not learn. It does mean that a child approaches the social environment with a nonstandard organizational system that is different from the typical learner's system. This distinctive system provides the child with a disability with a framework to interact with communication partners within his or her environment, given his or her unique learning process. A child's language system affects what and how he or she acquires information, resulting in the following:

- The physical environment is perceived differently.
- Information is categorized and processed differently.

- The child acts and reacts differently with peers.
- The child develops different concepts about his or her social world.
- The child acquires different language and communication structures.

Early language problems result in long-term learning deficits that have academic implications in elementary school. Language problems can also create a negative emotional cycle affecting a child's self-esteem and social relationships with peers.

Children. *Language Disorders in Children* follows three children—José Martinez, Kaitlyn Whiteside, and Jeffrey St. James—from the point of initial diagnosis in early intervention to third grade in elementary school. We share the stories of these children and their families because they exemplify real experiences, and these families represent the largest ethnic groups of children being educated in the United States today. Our intention is not to stereotype, but rather to highlight the richness of ethnic diversity and examine how this diversity frames and enhances experiences. The problems these families face are their individual challenges and are not the problems of ethnic groups. We could have interchanged the stories, but we chose not to because our families agreed to describe their personal experiences and transitions. We could have erased their diversity, but that creates a stereotype of sameness. We know all families are not the same, and we make an egregious error when we ignore the contribution of diversity within and among families. These three families are diverse and demonstrate unique strengths. It is their own special set of differences that gives each family a resiliency that empowers them.

The children's changing language characteristics are described as they grow and develop. Their social problems, emotional frustrations, and educational needs are compared over time to highlight similarities and differences across the children. The children have an impact on their families, teachers, and peers. To appropriately meet their needs, parents and professionals must be trained to modify environmental factors around each child to facilitate learning. The ability of professionals to meet the individual needs of children with language disorders may be limited by institutional constraints. As speech-language pathologists, we need to be aware of the possible barriers to effective clinical practice to be able to advocate for the children and families whom we serve. The variables encountered by the speech-language pathologist in individual therapy are very different from those that must be altered by a classroom teacher. Because the children act differently from typical learners, they have different social experiences with peers and adults. It is important for SLPs to follow the sequence of language changes and behaviors in these children from their earliest points of origin. Language evolves in each child, with resulting language patterns that can be explained by the child's processing style.

Diversity. Three culturally and linguistically diverse families are described as their children are evaluated and treated in three separate special education systems. Cultural differences affect the ways in which families interact with professionals and develop expectations about their children's clinical treatment. Clinical practitioners and teachers need to become more sensitively aware of and attuned to the complex needs of diverse children and families. Effective communication between professionals and families becomes unlikely when there is little understanding of social values, family structures, belief systems, family stresses, and the meaning of interpersonal relationships in diverse cultures. Because cultural differences can create communication barriers that are as complicated as linguistic factors, such factors play an important role in the decision-making process for each family as they transition from one system to the next. These factors also affect how culturally diverse families are treated by professionals who have very different value systems.

Each family is introduced with a short family history to provide insight into how and why these parents make particular decisions. Each mother presents her own ideas and perceptions as she shares her experiences, concerns, and fears. The personal stories of these families are not only enlightening and powerful, they are memorable. Each family makes the "right" decision for their child based on their insights and cultural wisdom. All too often in education, the system collects data, and human experiences are not factored into policies and procedures. These three mothers describe their own journeys as they learn about their children's needs and how to interact with the various systems. The Martinez, Whiteside, and St. James families are discussed at different points in the chapters when their experiences are relevant to issues described within the text. Each mother shares her feelings and concerns about having a child with a disability, as well as explains how the child has affected family dynamics.

Educational Systems. The children transition through three distinctly different educational systems: early intervention, preschool, and elementary school. The systems are described in terms of their histories, policies, procedures, and problems. Special education has expanded over the past two decades to include more and more children and services. The cost of special education has also escalated, and policy makers, legislators, educators, and parents are expecting its effectiveness to be consistent with its related costs. Special-education law requires that children with disabilities be entitled to a free and appropriate education. What is an appropriate education? Nationwide there has been an emphasis on improving outcomes for special-needs learners. Reauthorization of the Individuals with Disabilities Act (IDEA) and the No Child Left Behind Act (NCLB) set in place educational mandates and expanded the role and responsibilities of the speech-language pathologist. NCLB mandates that by 2014 *all* children be proficient in literacy. Schools are working diligently to meet this goal. Children with special learning needs are included in "all."

Clinical Practice. *Language Disorders in Children* is divided into three parts to coincide with the three educational systems (early intervention, preschool, and elementary school) that provide services to children in the United States. Each part presents critical policies, procedures, and practices as the three families move from system to system. The mothers describe their experiences as they transition across the three systems. They describe how they interact with professionals and how each system defines their role as contributors. The role of the speech-language pathologist is highlighted because the SLP is the one professional who is consistently involved with children as they transition through the three educational systems. Speech-language pathologists are credentialed professionals who diagnose and provide treatment to children with communication disabilities and also advocate for them. They are certified by a national accrediting agency, the American Speech-Language-Hearing Association (ASHA) and often have state licenses as well.

The collaborative language assessment chapters describe differences in the evaluation process, as well as the changing interpersonal relationships between families and the professionals who provide individual home-based therapeutic services in early intervention to classroom-based educational instruction in elementary school. Problems related to linguistic and culturally biased assessments provide information on the complexities and limitations of clinical decision making. The chapters on intervention describe different intervention techniques that might be used by speech-language pathologists who practice across the developmental continuum and across the spectrum of developmental disorders.

Strengths-Based Perspective. *Language Disorders in Children* follows three children as their language patterns evolve over time. This provides readers with an opportunity to learn how changes in each child's language system create a distinct, nonstandard style of learning. Each child's personality is shaped by the interaction between his or her abilities to communicate and the environment's ability to respond supportively. Finally, it is important to work with families over time to better understand their life-cycle experiences, although systematic constraints limit clinical practice to sessions and weeks. Professionals can never have the family's perspective. The child with a developmental disability changes the dynamic social and emotional relationships of the entire family. There is a great resiliency in these families that develops as the children grow. We believe that it is important to approach the clinical process and interpersonal relationships with families and professional colleagues with a strengths-based perspective. The longitudinal organization of this textbook serves to underscore the diverse strengths of children and their families.

The individual and the environment interact in a complex fashion, rather than by means of a process of discrete stages (Berk, 1998; Boushel, 1998; Rutter, 2004). We recognize these complexities and lead the reader to focus on understanding how these complexities affect the process of educating special learners and the systems within which they live and learn. As educators, we believe a strengths-based approach creates opportunities for speech-language pathologists to learn from the children and families with whom they work. We hope to create a framework for the acquisition of knowledge that highlights the realities of language impairment, examines the ecological forces at work, and underscores intervention that is appropriate. For the students who use this text, we hope that we have given them a new perspective on children, families, and professionals, and, with this perspective, that they are able to integrate this information and create a firm base for their future professional development.

Acknowledgments

The authors wish to acknowledge the following reviewers for their kind and constructive commentaries, their critical analyses, and their insights during the development of *Language Disorders in Children*: Erika S. Armstrong, University of Texas at Dallas; Stephanie Beebe, University of Mississippi; Lewis A. Carter, Southern Illinois University, Carbondale; Sandra R. Ciocci, Bridgewater State College; D'Jaris Coles-White, Wayne State University; Stephanie Joyce, University of Mississippi; Charlotte Keefe, Texas Woman's University; Sheila M. Kennison, Oklahoma State University; Sara Elizabeth Runyan, James Madison University; Lillian N. Stiegler, Southeastern Louisiana; Carol Stoel-Gammon, University of Washington; and Diane T. Woodrum, Waynesburg College. Without their perspectives on clinical issues, the textbook would not have its current breadth and depth. During the development of any creative production there are always professional and/or clinical differences in opinion. Different viewpoints enrich our professional discipline. Those reviewers who understood this difficult long-term process with sensitivity and humor made the greatest impact on both of us as researchers and authors.

The completion of any textbook often results in a period of reflection. This textbook has taken a great deal of time, energy, and inspiration over the past two years. I do not think that I would have engaged in this process with the same commitment if I had been working with anyone other than my dearest friend and colleague, Dr. Christine Radziewicz. Even during the most stressful moments, there was never a word of disagreement between us. I have had the opportunity to work with many authors over the past 20 years during the creation of other books. This was my most challenging and enriching experience, both personally and professionally. I attribute the quality of the experience to my collaboration with Christine.

To my family, who has borne the brunt of this long-term creative process, I express my love, devotion, and appreciation.

To my husband, Joseph Farber, I owe many vacation days, dinners, and lots of chocolate chip cookies.

To my children, Jeremy, Jonathan, Andrew, Douglas, Dana, and Leslie, you have taught me about the most important aspect of life—motherhood. I am deeply grateful to have the six of you in my life.

To my grandchildren, Lindsey, Gabrielle, Brandon, and Olivia, you are my reminders about the miracle of child development and the gift of language.

To the parents at the School for Language and Communication Development, this book is about the timeless commitment of parents and their love for their children. Parents of children with disabilities face challenges and make extraordinary sacrifices. I believe that in working together we can have very high expectations for the success of SLCD's children. I also believe that we have identified the answer for our children and . . . **language is the key.**

To my parents, Morris and Rita Jacobs, I acknowledge that the gift from one generation to the next started with the two of you.

Ellenmorris Tiegerman-Farber

No one writes alone. The pages of this book reflect countless hours of conversations, lectures, and experiences with colleagues, friends, and family. It is difficult, therefore, to organize all of these events in order of importance. However, there is no doubt in my mind that collaborating with my colleague and dear friend Dr. Ellenmorris Tiegerman-Farber has been the primary reason that this book exists. Quiet yet earnest conversations related to our philosophies about the paramount importance of language as it relates to all aspects of an individual's functioning from birth through adulthood is the foundation of this text. Her insights and thoughtfulness are the blueprint that we followed.

To Tom, I send a multitude of thank-yous: for the dinners, for the understanding, and for the million and one ways you have helped me throughout the process of writing this book.

To my children, Alisa and Hank, and their spouses, Jule and Mindy, thank you for listening to me and allowing me to learn from each of you. The lessons are patience, perseverance, and kindness; these are the qualities that students must develop in order to become speech-language pathologists. My most enjoyable lessons have come from Ardyn and Lila, my grandchildren. Watching your first smiles and your first words reignited my love for the study of language development.

Finally, I thank my mother, Veronica. Now that the words do not come easily, you still have language. Your struggle has emphasized to me just how important language is and that it is the gift that every human being deserves.

Christine Radziewicz

To our initial editor, Allyson Sharp, and our current editor, Ann Davis, we express our deepest appreciation for your ongoing support, encouragement, and inspiration. We would also like to share that we both now believe in reincarnation: This book has had several lives since its inception.

Finally, this textbook could never have been completed without the extraordinary commitment and dedication of our administrative secretary, Jackie Cioni. We are deeply indebted and grateful to her for her daily help with this project.

Contents

NOTE: Every effort has been made to provide accurate and current Internet information in this book. However, the Internet and information posted on it are constantly changing, and it is inevitable that some of the Internet addresses listed in this textbook will change.

PART 1

Birth to Age 3:
A Family-Centered Approach

Meet the Martinez, Whiteside, and St. James Families

In this section we meet Maria Martinez, Katherine Whiteside, and Camille St. James who realize that their children are having learning difficulties. The three families are distinctly different from one another. Their family histories and backgrounds are described to provide insight into factors affecting their perceptions, behaviors, beliefs, and decisions and to show how they negotiate through the early intervention system.

Maria Martinez, a linguistically and culturally diverse parent, recently moved to a large U.S. city with her husband. Maria is overwhelmed by her new environment and her son Jose's nonsocial behavior and tantrums. Maria must come to terms with her own fears and concerns about the diagnosis of autism. She describes her experiences with professionals and her feelings about having a child with difficult behavioral problems. She provides an important perspective on the early intervention system's ability to identify linguistically and culturally diverse families in their communities by nontraditional communicative means.

Katherine Whiteside lives in a midwestern rural community in the United States. She is part of a closely knit family that has been in farming for many generations. She and her husband have faced financial and personal challenges. After her first child, Kaitlyn, was born her husband withdrew into himself. Kaitlyn is a premature baby with severe hearing loss. Her developmental disability was diagnosed early and services were provided through the early intervention system. Katherine feels that she is being pressured by the service coordinator to treat Kaitlyn in a particular way. This disturbs Katherine as she begins her journey into understanding the differences between the Deaf Community—its culture and language—and the hearing world. Katherine must decide about a cochlear implant for Kaitlyn and whether she should be placed in a school for the deaf.

In addition to Kaitlyn's problems and needs, Katherine's marriage is in turmoil. Her husband is abusing alcohol and the frequent arguments drain Katherine. Katherine has never been away from home or her family. Although she is afraid for herself and her marriage, she is more concerned about Kaitlyn.

Camille St. James is an African American mother from the southern section of the United States who dropped out of school to take care of her son, Jeffrey. She begins her journey into social service programs with Jeffrey in childcare. Camille works hard to support Jeffrey and attends night school. The child-care program recommends an evaluation through the early intervention system because of concerns about Jeffrey's aggressive behavior and speech delay. Camille cannot understand why Jeffrey is denied services. She believes that Jeffrey is frustrated by his inability to communicate effectively and that this explains his aggressive behavior. Camille's experiences are typical of many parents whose children are delayed, but who do not meet the eligibility criteria to warrant or receive therapeutic services. Camille knows that Jeffrey needs help, but she is not in a position financially to provide such services herself.

As the journey begins for each family, the reality of having a child with a disability evokes complex emotional feelings and reactions. It is a time of confusion and fear. What does disability mean? Will the child ever be normal? The families' experiences and interactions with professionals and programs shape their thinking and activism as advocates for their children.

Maria Martinez, Katherine Whiteside, and Camille St. James are three mothers struggling to gain control of their increasingly chaotic lives. Coming to terms with the reality of having a child with a disability involves a lifelong learning process for families. In some families, the child with a disability becomes the focus of everyone's attention, time, and energy. Other relationships—husband and wife, parent and child, sibling and sibling—are disrupted, to the detriment of the family's stability. For some families, interactional relationships remain intact as the family struggles to integrate the child with a disability into the family. The family unit must also continue to meet the emotional needs of all its members.

The role of the speech-language pathologist (SLP) is to help families understand the communication needs of the child with a disability, as well as their own. The SLP works with families during this formative period to identify and enhance their unique and specific strengths. Particularly during the early intervention period, family relationships are maintained and sustained by the effectiveness of the communication process.

As discussed in this part 1, the relationship between professionals and families is also affected by communication variables. Families describe qualitative factors, such as mutual respect, understanding, trust, and sensitivity to cultural differences, when they evaluate the effectiveness of systems that provide services. Of the three systems discussed in this textbook, parents describe the early intervention system in the most positive terms because of their relationships with its service providers. As you read part 1, consider how well the early intervention system meets the needs of children and whether it facilitates the development of language, which is the bedrock for all further learning.

Understanding Early Intervention for Infants and Toddlers

Chapter Objectives

After studying this chapter, you should be able to answer these questions:

1. What historical changes in federal legislation have resulted in changes in the provision of services to young children with disabilities?

2. What changes in legislation have affected the role and responsibilities of the speech language pathologist in developing therapeutic programs for infants and toddlers with disabilities?

3. Describe Public Laws (PLs) 94-142 and 99-457.

4. Describe the early intervention system and its mission.

With the developing national focus on early intervention, the role of the speech-language pathologist (SLP) has changed dramatically from a school-based-related service provider in elementary school to a primary-care provider and consultant in the early intervention system. Historically, early intervention meant programming and services provided to children below the age of 5 years (i.e., children not attending school-age programs). As the education law expanded to include children below the age of 5 years, the birth-to-5 population was separated into two groups of children and service delivery systems: infants and toddlers who are birth to 2 years, 11 months old receive services in the early intervention system, and preschoolers who are 3 to 5 years of age receive services in the preschool special education system. This chapter describes the early intervention system with its national program mission and services.

Many families begin the special education journey when their children enter the early intervention system. Families must deal with the realities of an initial diagnosis and the emotional, physical, and social changes that result from having a child with a disability. This is a frightening and overwhelming experience that is both complicated and time consuming (Doering, Moser, & Dracup, 2000).

Because language is the primary means of communicative exchange and often the first system that gives early warning signs of disability, the role of the SLP has changed most significantly over the past 25 years. The importance of language in early childhood development shifted the SLP's role from related-service provider to primary intervention specialist and classroom teacher in many programs.

Also, because children with disabilities are being identified much earlier, the SLP becomes involved with professional collaborative teams for infants and toddlers. As a result, the SLP is now more directly involved as a critical decision maker with more diverse responsibilities for collaborating and consulting with, training, and counseling parents, clinical specialists, special education teachers, and other primary-care providers. The SLP is also expected to function in the homes, schools, hospitals, and other settings that include children with critical care needs. This is a very exciting time for the field of speech-language pathology; our professional skills contribute to all aspects of early intervention and special education programming (Tiegerman-Farber, 2002b).

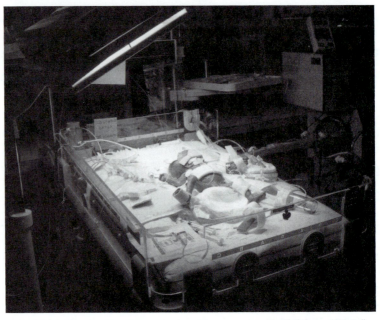

Smith Pedersen / PH College

The infant in a neonatal unit requires intensive medical monitoring from many different practitioners.

This chapter discusses some of the social, legal, and educational decisions that have influenced the development of the early intervention system for children in the United States and provides students with an understanding of how and why the early intervention system facilitates ongoing dynamic changes between policy and practice.

Finally, to provide students with an understanding of both a family systems approach to and an issue-based perspective on children and families across the educational continuum, each chapter provides information on family issues, developmental approach, diversity issues, and the family-centered approach.

Family Issues

Three families with different backgrounds, Martinez, Whiteside, and St. James, begin to deal with a common experience that changes the lives of everyone involved. The initial diagnosis of any person, let alone a child, with a disability or disorder is a traumatic experience for the family. Some families mobilize and find strength working together; others are shattered. Families describe a process of shock, denial, sadness, and, over time, acceptance of the difficult reality that their child will be different (Jackson, Ternestedt, & Schollin, 2003).

Initially, parents cannot fathom the inner strength required to love and support a child with a disability, and parents may experience guilt, feelings of victimization, and religious crisis. Most parents proceed through an existential crisis that changes both their view of the world and their priorities (Holditch-Davis & Miles, 2000). Few professionals can truly understand the depth and range of feelings experienced by families, but as professionals we can all learn a great deal about personal growth and commitment.

Our three mothers begin the process within different social and familial contexts, but they grapple with similar problems. They must find the inner courage needed to change their lives to effectively meet the needs of their children. The role of the SLP is to help families identify and support their strengths to enhance adaptive interactions. This perspective is referred to as a strengths-based approach that builds on family resources and capabilities. In this chapter, three mothers share their initial experiences, feelings, and thoughts about their children within the early intervention system.

Developmental Approach

This textbook utilizes a developmental approach to follow three children (José, Kaitlyn, and Jeffrey) and their families across three educational systems and time periods in the following ways:

1. The components assessed: cognition, physical perceptual, social–emotional, language, and motor
2. The types of developmental disabilities (categorical)
3. The children's core language behaviors

The children's educational progress is based on a series of decisions made by parents and professionals. The children's diagnostic labels and classifications are influenced by the assessment skills of professionals and the standardized measures available within the clinical field at the time. The types of services provided are a function of the early intervention system's ability to accommodate to the linguistic and cultural needs of the family and to the fiscal resources committed to the system. Finally, the interpersonal attitudes and beliefs of both professionals and parents are part of the decision-making process. To understand why José, Kaitlyn, and Jeffrey receive specific services, it is important to consider the factors contributing to a committee's placement decision.

Diversity Issues

The three families are representative of families with different attitudes and beliefs about life. An important part of the SLP's role involves family counseling as applied to a child's language and communication disorder. Given the ongoing changes in U.S. cultural and ethnic groups, more families within the early intervention system will be non-White.

There is general recognition within the field of speech language pathology about the importance of diversity-sensitive counseling and therapeutic intervention, but little attention has been given to what SLPs must actually do with clients to be diversity sensitive. It may not be enough for SLPs to study a cultural group and assume that the descriptive knowledge obtained will automatically translate into a more sensitive, helping relationship. Psychologists, social workers, and counselors have long discussed the issue of diversity-sensitive counseling theories and how they apply to culture-specific counseling approaches and strategies. But the counseling role, with its related responsibilities, has not been clearly defined for students or SLPs.

Although there is a wealth of clinical research from colleagues in other helping professions, only the field of speech-language pathology can answer the question. What does diversity-sensitive counseling include for the SLP? Students in academic training programs and other readers need to observe how diversity-sensitive SLPs counsel individuals with disabilities and their families.

Focus on Families

The family-centered approach represents the cornerstone of the early intervention system. Whereas the early intervention system is family centered, the preschool and school-age special-education systems are child centered. This philosophical difference has resulted in two distinctly contrasting service provision systems. As their child transitions from early intervention, parents often note that they have less involvement in and control of educational decisions. Students must understand how family-centered theory determines clinical practice. Although the social policy underlying early intervention is idealistic, practical problems create daily realities for families and children as the system is implemented. The Martinez, Whiteside, and St. James families describe their personal experiences within the early intervention system as they interact with professionals and attempt to access services.

Landmark Legislation for Individuals with Disabilities

Education has been facing dynamic legal requirements that ultimately result in programmatic changes at all levels for individuals with disabilities (Gallagher, 2000).

1973: Rehabilitation Act: The Rehabilitation Act, Public Law (PL) 93-112

1974: Rehabilitation Act Amendments, PL 93-516

1975: Education for All Handicapped Children Act, PL 94-142

1986: Education for All Handicapped Children Act Amendments, PL 99-457

1990: Individuals with Disabilities Education Act (IDEA), PL 101-476 (reauthorized and renamed as PL 94-142)

1990: Americans with Disabilities Act (ADA), PL 101-336

1997: Individuals with Disabilities Education Act (IDEA), amended and reauthorized

2001: No Child Left Behind (NCLB), PL 107-110

2004: Reauthorization of IDEA

Rehabilitation Act of 1973: Section 504

No otherwise qualified handicapped individual in the United States . . . shall, solely by reason of his handicap, be excluded from participation in, be denied the benefits of, or be subjected to discrimination under any program or activity receiving federal financial assistance.

(Section 504 of the Rehabilitation Act of 1973, as amended.)

The Rehabilitation Act of 1973 is enforced by the Office of Civil Rights under the guidelines of the Department of Education. This legislation protects the civil and constitutional rights of people with disabilities. It prohibits organizations that receive federal funds from discriminating against individuals with disabilities. In addition to school-age children who are eligible for special-education services, this includes persons with communicable diseases, chronic asthma, diabetes, physical disabilities, cancer, AIDS, multiple sclerosis, muscular dystrophy, cardiac diseases, arthritis, and the like. According to the Rehabilitation Act of 1973, Section 504, discrimination involves denying individuals with disabilities the opportunity to participate in or benefit from a service or activity provided to individuals without disabilities.

Although the Rehabilitation Act can be applied to educational settings, it is much broader in scope than the Education for All Handicapped Children Act, which followed in 1975. First, individuals with disabilities under the Rehabilitation Act may or may not have educational disabilities (e.g., cancer vs. autism). Second, the Rehabilitation Act includes issues such as refusing to hire a person with AIDS or denying a student with diabetes access to clubs. In its original version, the Rehabilitation Act applied to discrimination in the workplace; the individual with a disability was entitled to employment opportunities without regard to disability. The definition was expanded when it was amended under the Rehabilitation Act Amendments of 1974 (PL 93-516) to include education; individuals with disabilities were entitled to the same educational opportunities as those without disabilities.

Public Law 94-142

Public Law 94-142 is the primary legislation governing educational services for children with disabilities and was passed in 1975 as the Education for All Handicapped Children Act (EAHCA). It ensures that states provide all school-age children with a free and appropriate public education (FAPE). The EAHCA establishes the minimum requirements that must be complied with if states are to receive financial assistance from the federal government. Each state must develop "a policy that ensures all children with disabilities with the right to a free and appropriate public education (FAPE)" (20 USC Sec. 1412[1]) "and must develop a plan which details the policies and procedures which ensure that right" (Sec. 1412[2]). Each state must also establish procedural safeguards (Sec. 1412[5]) to ensure that local educational state agencies create the individualized educational programs (IEP) required (Sec. 1412[4]; i.e., referral procedures). In essence, before a state can receive federal funds, it must develop a formalized process for identifying and educating children with disabilities that is approved by the secretary of education. When it was passed, the EAHCA addressed a long-standing issue affecting the education of children with disabilities nationally; specifically, local school districts often excluded children with disabilities by preventing them from participating in regular school programs (Yell & Drasgow, 2000). Public Law 94-142 continues to be a primary force in maintaining the educational rights of children with disabilities. The legislation provides for four planning requirements:

1. Development of an individualized educational program (IEP)
2. The right to be educated in the least restrictive environment (LRE)
3. Provision of appropriate related services dependent on educational and developmental needs
4. Parental involvement

Public schools are required to follow specific procedures to develop special-education programs for school-age children with disabilities. Referral, evaluation, and placement procedures safeguard a child's right to a free and appropriate public education (FAPE) by requiring that parents are meaningfully involved in the development of their child's educational program. The procedures for every child suspected of having a disability establish a uniform system for all states. Such educational procedures define the formal parameters for all the stakeholders: parents, teachers, specialists, and administrators. The intent is to ensure that a child with a disability has the same right to a free and appropriate public education (FAPE) regardless of where she or he lives. The document detailing a child's individualized education program (IEP) is developed collaboratively by a multidisciplinary team of professionals with the involvement of parents. To determine if a child is receiving a FAPE, the IEP, which describes the program and services, often becomes the focus of review.

After PL 94-142 was passed, many researchers and educators argued that because the law did not mandate services for children from birth to 5 years it did not go far enough. Much clinical research related to early identification and intervention focused on the needs of infants, toddlers, and preschoolers with disabilities (Florian, 1995). But the technological and medical advances that enable an earlier diagnosis of many disorders were not followed by therapeutic intervention and services. Historically, services to infants, toddlers, and preschoolers were not mandated in public school settings, so voluntary agencies such as United Cerebral Palsy developed and expanded to address the needs of specific populations in some, but not all, communities. As a result, the types of services and the levels of service provided varied across the United States. Some communities provided extensive services, whereas some provided none for children below the age of 5. Clearly, identification requires intervention, but it was not until 1986 that PL 99-457 was passed.

Facts

- Schools must comply with both PL 94-142 (IDEA) and the Rehabilitation Act of 1973 (PL 93-112).
- Compliance with IDEA does not necessarily mean that a school district is in compliance with the Rehabilitation Act.
- One law does not take precedence over the other.
- IDEA lists categories of disabilities that negatively affect educational learning. A child can have a disability under the Rehabilitation Act but not qualify

for special education because the disability does not negatively affect his or her learning.

- The term *disability* under IDEA is qualified as educational disability; therefore, IDEA has a narrower definition of disability than the Rehabilitation Act.

Public Law 99-457

Essentially, PL 99-457 addresses two groups of children with disabilities. The first group consists of preschool children with disabilities who are 3 and 4 years of age. These children are guaranteed all the rights and protections currently provided to school-age children with disabilities (i.e., FAPE). Such requirements include an individualized education plan (IEP), adherence to least-restrictive environment guidelines (which must appear on the child's IEP), and due-process provisions (i.e., the parent's right to request an impartial hearing). Public Law 99-457 also provides for the development of early intervention services for infants and toddlers with disabilities and their families by means of a statewide, comprehensive, and coordinated interagency program (Gallagher, Harbin, Thomas, Clifford, & Wenger, 1998). The program intent is based on the substantial need within each state to accomplish the following:

1. Enhance the development of infants and toddlers who are developmentally delayed
2. Reduce educational costs to society, including our nation's schools, by minimizing the future need for special education and related services
3. Minimize the likelihood of institutionalization of children with disabilities and maximize their potential for independent living in society
4. Enhance the capacity of families to meet the special needs of their infants and toddlers with disabilities

Early intervention and preschool programs are not mandated. They are discretionary programs that states may choose to adopt. All 50 states have implemented programs for children below the age of 5. Once a state implements these programs, it must ensure access to appropriate services. The federal government through the Office of Special Education Programs monitors states and evaluates their compliance with the legal requirements and procedures (Brown & Conroy, 1999).

Facts

- All 50 states have implemented programs for infants and toddlers that vary in their eligibility requirements and services. To reduce programs and services, several states have limited state funding. Other states are considering the use of funding models that allow access to third-party reimbursement, including Medicaid, as well as parent fees for services.
- Only a few states have developed programs for at-risk children (i.e., children with a condition that has a high probability of resulting in a delay).

Americans with Disabilities Act of 1990 (ADA)

The Americans with Disabilities Act of 1990 (ADA) is the civil rights guarantee for individuals with disabilities in the United States. For these individuals, the ADA extends civil rights protections to employment in the public and private sectors, transportation, housing, public accommodations, commercial facilities, state and local governments, and telecommunications. The ADA also extends the standards for compliance indicated in the Rehabilitation Act of 1973 to institutions of higher education; this includes the entire range of university activities, including facilities, programs, athletics, and employment. Universities are responsible for having an established grievance procedure for students who feel their rights have been violated under ADA.

IDEA: Reauthorization

In 1990, the title of the education law was changed; the Education for All Handicapped Children Act became the Individuals with Disabilities Education Act (IDEA). IDEA was amended and reauthorized in 1997 and again in 2004. IDEA ensures that all children with disabilities have access to a continuum of services and programs from birth through age 21. IDEA has four major sections: Part A includes definitions and general provisions; Part B specifies how services are to be provided to preschool and school-age children; Part C specifies requirements for service provision to infants and toddlers and their families; and Part D includes provisions for supporting research, personnel preparation, technical assistance, and dissemination of information for improving the education of children with disabilities. To implement Part C of IDEA, many states have designated either their education agencies or health agencies as the lead agency to implement the requirements. Part C of IDEA (1997) requires states to provide services to infants and toddlers who:

1. are experiencing developmental delays, as measured by appropriate diagnostic instruments and procedures in one or more of the developmental areas: cognitive, physical, communication, social or emotional, and adaptive; or
2. have a diagnosed physical or mental condition that has a high probability of resulting in developmental delay (i.e., children who are at risk) (Sec. 632[5](a)).

The 2004 reauthorization signed by President George W. Bush and passed by the House and the Senate on November 19, 2004, became effective July 1, 2005. It eliminates the use of emergency temporary and provisional certification for related service providers, but gives states greater authority to establish professional qualifications in schools. This law eliminates the requirement that state education personnel standards meet the highest requirement for a profession or discipline in that state. Instead, it allows each state to set the qualifications for state-recognized certification or licensing. Several changes regarding IEPs were also passed. Parents and schools may agree to participate in IEP team and placement meetings via video, conferences, and conference calls. By using a responsible teacher or service provider, parents and school districts may amend or modify a child's current IEP without having to convene an IEP meeting. Parents and school districts may develop 3-year IEPs for students 18 years and older. This newly authorized law also gives school districts the option to eliminate the IQ discrepancy requirement, that is, a severe discrepancy between achievement and intellectual ability. Finally, this law authorizes, but does not mandate, full funding by 2011.

No Child Left Behind (NCLB)

The purpose of NCLB is to ensure that all children have an opportunity to obtain a high-quality education and achieve a minimum proficiency on state academic achievement standards and assessments (Furney, Hasazi, Clark-Keefe, & Hartnett, 2003). This purpose can be accomplished by the following:

1. Develop high-quality academic assessments, establish accountability systems, and provide teacher preparation and training
2. Meet the educational needs of low-achieving children
3. Close the achievement gap between high- and low-performing children
4. Hold schools, local educational agencies, and states accountable for improving academic achievement
5. Promote schoolwide reform and ensure access to scientifically based instructional strategies
6. Afford parents substantial and meaningful opportunities to participate in the education of their children (U.S. Department of Education, 2002)

Family-Centered Approach

Part C of IDEA emphasizes the need for involving families in the intervention process and empowering them to be advocates for their children. The early intervention program is family centered rather than child centered in its approach. The child-centered approach is the more traditional approach, in which the child is the focus of treatment. A family-centered approach focuses on helping families to understand their child's disability, to work collaboratively with service providers, and to support their personal choices (Brazy, Anderson, Becker, & Becker, 2001). Providing parents with information so that they are empowered to make their own decisions is the goal of a family-centered approach (Shannon, 2004).

Bilingual families are faced with language barriers that may interfere with a family-centered approach.

EMG *Education Management Group*

Although PL 94-142 mandated parental participation in the planning of the individualized education plan (IEP), the role of the parent in educational decision making remains rather limited. The passage of PL 94-142 introduced the concept of parent involvement, and PL 99-457 makes the role of the parent even more important in decision making for younger children. Preschool special education and the early intervention programs are, however, voluntary programs; as a result, the participation of parents is critical to the enrollment of the child (Bruder, 2000). If the parent does not trust the system, she or he is less likely to enter it or access services for the child.

States and school districts have a great deal of latitude in defining the role of parents, which changes from the early to the preschool to the school-age intervention systems. If the family becomes less involved in the decision-making process to determine a child's placement, the relationship with professionals will change qualitatively and quantitatively. Because the early intervention program focuses on parent advocacy, empowerment, and collaborative partnerships, this raises parent expectations (Taub, 2001). Having been trained to function at the policy and political levels in early intervention, parents want to continue their involvement as their child gets older and moves out of early intervention. Increasing tensions as the child transitions from system to system can result in cases of litigation in the preschool and elementary school systems.

Part C of IDEA was designed to determine the resources, priorities, and concerns of the family that are necessary to the development of the child. To achieve family centeredness, the interpersonal relationship between parents and professionals is critical. Good experiences are described by parents in terms of interpersonal characteristics within professional–family partnerships. Parents consider professionals family centered when they are responsive, supportive, caring, competent, and encouraging of parents' participation as team members (McWilliam, Tocci, & Harbin, 1998). The interpersonal relationship between the SLP and the parent provides the foundation for a successful therapeutic alliance. Clinical practitioners must learn how to attune themselves to the qualitative aspects of their relationship with parents. McWilliam et al. (1998) report that parents describe family-centered practice in terms of the therapist's ability to:

1. Focus on the needs of the entire family rather than just the child
2. Be positive and nonjudgmental about family issues
3. Be sensitive and understanding about parental differences and choices
4. Listen, attend, and take action when a parent expresses a need
5. Treat parents as partners, equals, and active contributors and friends

To appropriately use a family-centered approach, professionals need to remember that, although the infant or toddler evaluation is part of an entitlement program, it is still the family's decision to decide if an assessment should be performed. If families understand that they are respected members of the team and that their needs as well as their child's are considered to be important, the family is more likely to commit to the assessment process. Family-centered assessment identifies specific competencies in parents to facilitate their involvement in early intervention (Desjardin, 2003). In addition, assessment incorporates the family's description of the child's problem, his or her needs, and their goals. The family-centered approach expands the role of parents, because the parent plays a critical role in identifying contextual events that critically affect developmental changes for the child. Although the parent may not have a sophisticated level of clinical knowledge, his or her insights and intuitions can often provide valuable information for professionals to use to determine developmental objectives. As a member of the team, the parent becomes supportive of clinical decisions because he or she is a part of the process (Osborne, Garland, & Fisher, 2002).

The family-centered approach requires the use of a collaborative model in which the parent is viewed as an equal contributor. This model may be difficult for the psychologist, SLP, special educator, or parent to use initially, given traditional professional roles and expectations. Within a family-centered approach, the parent also serves as the primary caregiver and mediator of change for the child's home environment (Tiegerman-Farber, 1998). Figure 1.1 outlines the steps of the early intervention process.

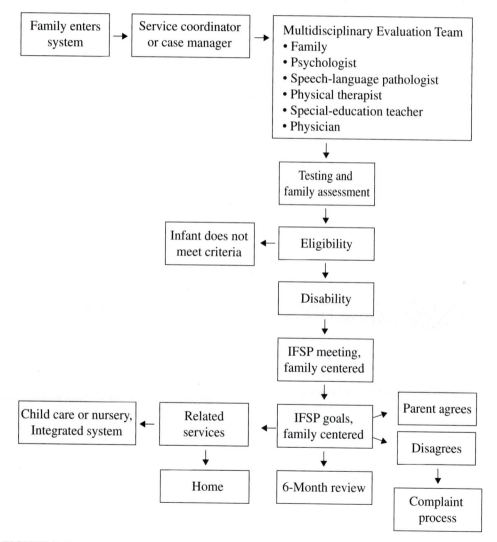

FIGURE 1.1

Early Intervention Process: The Family-Centered Approach

Individualized Family Service Plan

The result of the family-centered approach is the collaborative development of an individualized family service plan (IFSP). In Figure 1.2 the IFSP focuses on the family's needs and the goals that the family hopes to achieve through the early intervention program (Bruder, 2000). The IFSP is written in simple language so that the family can understand the program goals. The plan includes all the details about the early intervention services that the child and family will receive and when, where, and how often these services will be provided. The IFSP should be a document that is functionally useful to both parents and professionals. It should serve not only as a service plan, but also as the basis for the therapeutic curriculum. McWilliam et al. (1998) suggest the following guidelines when writing a family-centered IFSP: the writer of the IFSP should not be judgmental, should include positive statements with assessment outcomes, should use active voice when writing the IFSP, and should integrate the family's role in the goals and outcomes.

The IFSP is developed by means of collaborative decision making, with the initial service coordinator, the early intervention official, and the parents functioning as equal contributors. The IFSP meeting should be held in the primary language of the family. The IFSP document includes the following:

1. A statement of the child's present levels of physical, cognitive, communicative, and social or emotional and adaptive functioning
2. Information concerning the child's level of functioning or status based on professionally based objective data and criteria
3. A statement of the family's resources, priorities, and concerns related to enhancing the development of the child
4. A comprehensive picture of the child's total service needs (including the need for medical and health services, as well as the early intervention services)

Throughout the process of developing and implementing the IFSP, the family retains the ultimate decision in determining whether they will accept or decline services. Thus, collaboration and effective communication are critical components of the success of the early intervention system.

Service Coordination

IDEA requires that families be provided with service coordination within the early intervention system (Dinnebeil, Hale, & Rule, 1996; Roberts, Akers, & Behl, 1996; Romer & Umbreit, 1998). The service coordinator is the case manager who works directly with the family, coordinating services from the point of entry to the point of transition from the early intervention system to the preschool special-education system (Nolan, Young, Herbert, & Wilding, 2005). Service coordination should ensure that children and families receive continuous or uninterrupted services as they transition from system to system (Dinnebeil et al., 1996). Service coordination is also important because many children with disabilities require multiple services, which can be provided in the home, an early childhood center, or a natural setting. Service coordination is often one of the most challenging areas within early intervention because of the issues related to funding, cultural and linguistic diversity, and the systems' differences (Wesley, Buysse, & Tyndall, 1997).

The Individualized Family Service Plan (IFSP) is designed to help families get assistance they need so their children can grow and develop. It can open doors for families to new sources of support in everyday settings, and provide more opportunities for their child to play with other typically developing children. Children need to be children. They need to be part of the play of other young children in their family or neighborhood.

In the IFSP process you are an equal team member and the expert on your child's needs. This plan is designed to help you use skills you already have as well as develop new ones to meet the needs of your child.

FAMILY RESOURCES, CONCERNS, AND PRIORITIES

Child's Name: _José Martinez_

Tell me about your child. On most days what goes well?
José eats well. José finger feeds. He sometimes attempts to use the spoon. José is more interested in books now. José is very active. José runs and jumps. José does not know familiar people. José does not follow directions and commands. José basically gestures to communicate.

What are your concerns?
Mother would like José to have an audiological evaluation because she is concerned about José's language delay. Mother is concerned because of José's lack of language. Mother is concerned that José doesn't play with other kids.

Desired change or outcome:
Mother would like José to talk. Mother would like José to follow directions. Mother would like José to play with other children.

Transportation arrangements: [ ] Bus [ ] Parents [X]N/A –

Ideas and Activities (things we will do to make this happen):

Mother will start José in the Early Start Infant Program:
Speech therapy 5 × (45 minutes)
Family counseling 1 × (60 minutes)
Occupational therapy 2 × (30 minutes)
Special-education program:
Nutrition services 1 × (60 minutes)
Parent support group 1 × (60 minutes)

People working with child and family:

Parents, siblings
Speech therapist
Occupational therapist
Nurse
Psychologist
Social worker

IFSP Reviewed on: _9/17/07_ [X]6 mo. [ ]18 mo. [ ]30 mo. [ ]Amendment

[ ] Outcome(s) achieved

[X] Continue as above

[ ] Revised as above

Parent/Guardian's Signature: _M Martinez_

Early Intervention Official Signature: _Jane Doe, MSW_

Family, caregivers, and service providers will monitor progress and determine achievement of above outcomes. Measures of success: _José will understand "put in," "take out." José will say at least 20 words. José will ask for a cup. José will point to body parts. José will start putting words together. José will follow directions consistently. José will follow two-step commands._

FIGURE 1.2

Example of an Individualized Family Service Plan

The responsibilities of service coordinators may vary from state to state (Harbin et al., 1998). Service coordination can be provided by social workers, nurses, SLPs, and/or psychologists for children and families entering and continuing through the early intervention system (Hurth, 1998). Service coordinators may also have multiple functions in which they work as both a direct service provider and a coordinator. The service coordinator may also work only for an early intervention program or may also be responsible for preschool and school-age children. Few states have specific training programs for service coordinators, although the regulations describing the responsibilities of service coordinators are specific: parent intake, service plans and programs, mandated contacts with families, the coordination of child and family services, and identification of service providers (Farel, Shackelford, & Hurth, 1997; Malone, Straka, & Logan, 2000).

Infants and toddlers with disabilities often require the services of a variety of professionals from different agencies and practices. Because of this coordination, collaboration and communication may be problematic, given ongoing difficulties with scheduling, travel, illness, and distance (Bruder, 2000). Some working parents describe the problems related to scheduling various service providers in their home as the basis for their decision to refuse home-based services. Every family receiving early intervention services is assigned to a service coordinator when entering the system. The service coordinator helps the family:

1. To learn about the child's development and disabilities
2. To find resources and answers to questions concerning the child's medical condition

The coordinator also:

3. Identifies professionals and programs that offer support or help to meet the family's basic needs
4. Writes the individualized family service plan (IFSP) so that everyone involved with the family knows what the goals are
5. Coordinates services outlined in the IFSP to ensure that services are provided at the level and in the setting identified as appropriate
6. Ensures that the family knows its rights within the early intervention system

Family and Service Coordination

Some states conduct statewide forums or focus groups to acquire information from parents about their experiences within the early intervention system (see Figure 1.3). These forums provide information that can be used by state agencies to improve the service provision system to families (McWilliam & Young, 1996). Because they utilize different models of service coordination or case management, states need to develop a policy infrastructure to support the implementation of effective service coordination for families (Harbin et al., 2004).

Because the caseload for service coordinators is often so large that effective supervision is difficult, it is critical to the effectiveness of the early intervention system that professionals receive service coordination training to develop the necessary

Parent Expectations

1. Important for service coordinators to share information with families.
   - Need for service coordinator to review information in the *Parent Guide* with parents periodically: Initially and every 6 months.
     Not enough to hand the *Parent Guide* to parents.
   - Important to know how to help families:
     Long-term issues for some families; service coordinators must have information on financial and other programs and services.
     Work with counties to provide information to families.
     Parents generally don't have enough information to inform decision making; sense that "more is better."
   - Parents had an expectation that the service coordinator would be knowledgeable about the child's disability (Down syndrome, cerebral palsy, speech delays, etc.)
   - Some parents are not made aware of or not well-informed about choices available for early intervention services
2. After assignment of initial service coordinator:
   - Follow-up and monitoring.
   - Determine the skill level and/or expertise of the service coordinator when assigning to work with a family.
   - Case loads too large.
3. Parent comments
   - When service coordination worked, it was a "lifeline."
   - Most positive attribute of service coordination was responsiveness.
     No parent-to-parent support offered.
4. Ongoing service coordination
   - Parents reported the following related to choosing an ongoing service coordinator:
     Very hard to make a choice from the list of approved ongoing service coordinators; not enough information provided to inform the decision.
   - Ongoing service coordinator
     Initial service coordinators who can also function as ongoing service coordinators vary from county to county.
     Some counties are making a decision not to do ongoing service coordination.
5. Training Issues
   - Develop a checklist for initial service coordinators.
     Train service coordinators to be aware of services and supports available in the community; assist parent in how to access or make a connection.
   - Look at family structure.
   - Facilitate family identification of resources, concerns, and priorities.
   - Need for ongoing opportunities for service coordinators to enhance knowledge and skills.

Parent Suggestions

1. Include time frame of when or how information should be given to parents in service coordination training.
2. Develop a list of recommendations for parents on how to choose their ongoing service coordinator. Include a variety of different approaches that takes into account the diversity of parents and families in New York State.

FIGURE 1.3 *(continued)*

Service Coordination

Source: Summary of Regional Family Forums presented to the Early Intervention Coordinating Council on 5/10/2000 by the Parent Involvement Committee (New York State).

3. Have service coordinators who specialize (by disability, by specialty) so that parents don't have to spend so much time searching for information.
   • Develop a list of service coordinators and include information about qualifications and areas of expertise; provide contact information. Potentially have a profile of each service coordinator to help parents with making choices.
   • Provide more information for parents in the list developed of approved ongoing service coordinators, with the information on the organization they work for and what the initials next to the names mean.
4. Inform parents prior to the IFSP meeting as to choice of ongoing service coordinator; provide resources to parents at that time.
5. Service Coordinators need to:
   • Have knowledge of all available services: financial, emotional support.
   • Recognize the importance of parent and family support and assist parents to connect to other parents.
   • Accept to work within varying family situations; accept all family members.
   • Understand that parents need information before they can answer the question of what do they want.

FIGURE 1.3
(*continued*)

skills for effective collaborative interaction and communication (Malone, McKinsey, Thyer, & Straka, 2000). The service coordinator must be able to develop a cohesive program that translates family goals into the pragmatic realities of professionals providing services.

Dunst and Trivette (1989) have developed a service coordination model based on the premise that parents of infants and toddlers with developmental disabilities vary along a continuum of ability to make decisions independently. This specific ability allows parents to optimally utilize the resources available and make appropriate therapeutic decisions concerning their children. Professionals functioning as service coordinators require training in how to facilitate parents' abilities from the point of initiation along this dependence–independence continuum to a higher level of independent decision making (Dunst & Trivette, 1989).

In some states, the service coordinator remains the same throughout the family's involvement within the early intervention system. In others, an initial service coordinator is responsible for the IFSP, and then an ongoing service coordinator is assigned to the family. Many states have developed a manual or guidebook for parents that gives suggestions on how to choose an ongoing service coordinator. Service coordinators need to be knowledgeable about the early intervention system within the community and responsive to parents' phone calls. The family's work with the service coordinator will involve many intimate aspects of family programming, and so the family needs to feel comfortable with the service coordinator.

Local Interagency Coordinating Councils

IDEA provides for a comprehensive system that requires coordination to ensure implementation at the community level so that services are available to parents and children. The Local Interagency Coordinating Council (LICC) focuses on networking within a community so that the statewide comprehensive service delivery system is effectively implemented. The LICC attempts to accomplish the following:

- Ensure the delivery of needed early intervention services to children within the community in a timely manner
- Coordinate various eligibility requirements, including the definition of developmental delay
- Develop a public awareness program to focus on the importance and availability of early intervention services within the community
- Develop and disseminate a local central directory of providers and services, in addition to the state's central directory

Swan and Morgan (1994) note that the LICC utilizes the knowledge of local agency personnel and parents who understand the unique problems and idiosyncrasies of the local community system. They provide leadership to increase the responsiveness of the LICC to the needs of children with disabilities and their families. An LICC must incorporate cultural diversity into its planning to develop an efficient system of early intervention services, given specific needs and concerns within a community. An LICC is also in a position to develop and refine the infrastructure for existing community-based services. LICCs are generally active, effective, and successful in achieving their community mission because they include parents.

Variability in State Systems

Service delivery systems at the state and local levels vary from state to state and often from community to community (Spiker, Hebbeler, Wagner, Cameto, & McKenna, 2000). In some states three separate systems and governmental agencies may be responsible for children from birth to 21 years of age. Government officials agree on the need to coordinate services across agencies as a function of the educational continuum for children with disabilities (Danaher, Shackelford, & Harbin, 2004).

As of 2003, few states provided early intervention services to infants and toddlers who were at-risk (see Table 1.1). Children from at-risk families have a higher percentage of developmental disabilities (Guralnick, 2001). Poverty is an at-risk factor that many states do not consider. Culturally and linguistically diverse children are particularly vulnerable because many develop in a culture of poverty (Pearson, 2003). The United States is known to have one of the highest child poverty rates among developed countries. Children from birth to 5 years are highly vulnerable to deprivation, sickness, child abuse, substance abuse, and developmental disability. Poverty involves a level of economic status that does not allow families to meet adequate and basic living needs. Poverty creates values, beliefs, and behaviors that prevent people from accessing social and environmental opportunities to achieve economic independence (Wood, 2003). For children growing up in these environments, the risk is great that a generational pattern will be established because of hopelessness and social dependency (Heclo, 1997).

Over the past several years the number of infants and toddlers identified with disabilities has increased. Some states choose not to provide services to these at-risk children. As their number increased, the related costs (federal appropriations) also

TABLE 1.1 Number of At-Risk Infants and Toddlers Receiving Early Intervention Services Under Part C, December 1, 2003

State	0–1	1–2	2–3	Birth Through 2 (total)
California	404	669	936	2009
Hawaii	825	579	369	1773
Indiana	264	257	175	696
Massachusetts	111	156	154	421
New Hampshire	1	3	—	4
New Mexico	254	306	214	774
North Carolina	234	349	319	902
West Virginia	55	68	27	150
U.S. and Outlying Areas	2190	2433	2227	6850

Source: IDEA Part C Data Fact Sheet, www.ideadata.org/docs/cfactsheetcc.pdf

TABLE 1.2 Number of Infants and Toddlers Served Under Part C IDEA

Year	Number of Infants/Toddlers
1990–91	50,924
1991–92	145,313
1992–93	145,179
1993–94	152,287
1994–95	165,351
1995–96	177,286
1996–97	186,527
1997–98	197,625
1998–99	188,926
.	
.	
.	
2003–04	269,596

Source: IDEA Part C Data Fact Sheet, www.ideadata.org/docs/cfactsheetcc.pdf

increased (see Table 1.2). Although the research substantiates the need for and the efficacy of programs for children at-risk, prevention programs are not only of lowest priority, but are also the most vulnerable to legislative cuts (Guralnick, 2001). Because financial resources may be limited by economic changes, governmental decision making often focuses on an immediate crisis, emergency, or problem. Is it a priority to fund a prevention program when children do not yet have a problem?

Consider how increases in the number of children served in the early intervention program affect federal program costs. Then issues related to program effectiveness, accountability, and cost effectiveness are expressed more forcefully by governmental agencies (Barnett et al., 1999). Many public policy makers have recently raised the question of whether early intervention is worth the expense.

The various service-delivery models, curricula, and interventions vary along with interagency coordination, eligibility, and/or service coordination from state to state (Kleinhammer-Tramill & Rosenkoetter, 1994). Although these variations appear to be acceptable, given the parameters of the federal legislation, there is an obvious impact on the effectiveness of the services provided to children with disabilities. Over time, it has become difficult to evaluate the efficacy of clinical programs and systems across states when their service provision models vary (Roberts, Innocenti, & Goetze, 1999). Spiker et al. (2000) note that early intervention service-delivery systems are, for the most part, very dissimilar. There may be similarity among states on some system dimensions, but because the characteristics are assembled in so many different ways, the systems look very different. Some states vary not only in terms of their early intervention programs, but also in terms of the availability of services from one local area to another.

Table 1.3 shows that the number and percentage of infants and toddlers receiving services in an early intervention program vary dramatically from state to state. Note that, in general, the number of infants and toddlers identified increases as children get older, probably due to a number of related issues within states' early intervention programs:

1. The characteristics of disabilities become more apparent as children get older.
2. Primary-care practitioners are now more aware of developmental disabilities in younger children.
3. There is increased public awareness of the early intervention system and the services provided to young children.
4. More effective evaluative measures have recently been developed to appropriately assess developmental differences and disabilities in infants and toddlers.

Table 1.4 presents the percentage of infants and toddlers receiving early intervention services by race or ethnicity. When reviewing the data, consider the following:

1. In most states, the percentage of African American children served is higher than the percentage of White children. This overrepresentation may be due to the fact that the testing used to identify these children does not account for cultural differences and consequently overidentifies African American children.
2. In some states, representation of specific culturally and linguistically diverse groups is higher due to historical factors. In Hawaii, Asian–Pacific Islanders are significantly higher than African Americans, Hispanics, or Whites. In Iowa, Kentucky, and Maine, Native Americans represent the largest minority group.

The social, medical, and economic characteristics identified for groups indicate the following:

1. The need for *prevention*, as well as early intervention services, given the high-risk factors presented by many poor (White and diverse) families (Guralnick, 2001)
2. The high probability for the occurrence of developmental disabilities in children who are at-risk
3. The predictive validity of family risk factors

TABLE 1.3 Number and Percentage of Infants and Toddlers Receiving Early Intervention Services 2003

State	0–1 (*n*)	(%)	1–2 (*n*)	(%)	2–3 (*n*)	(%)	Total	Population	Percentage of Population
Alabama	216	10.03	730	33.91	1,207	56.06	2,153	179,557	1.2
Alaska	90	14.04	219	34.17	332	51.79	641	29,588	2.17
Arizona	491	13.18	1,266	33.99	1,968	52.83	3,725	267,139	1.39
Arkansas	260	9.38	846	30.52	1,666	60.10	2,772	112,886	2.46
California	5,562	20.23	9,275	33.73	12,659	46.04	27,496	1,564,154	1.76
Colorado	444	14.10	1,034	32.85	1,670	53.05	3,148	201,711	1.56
Connecticut	419	11.32	1,088	29.40	2,194	59.28	3,701	125,072	2.96
Delaware	192	20.10	315	32.98	448	46.91	955	32,881	2.9
District of Columbia	24	9.56	75	29.88	152	60.56	251	22,234	1.13
Florida	2,219	15.08	4,525	30.74	7,975	54.18	14,719	644,833	2.28
Georgia	690	14.26	1,571	32.46	2,579	53.29	4,840	407,295	1.19
Hawaii	1,386	33.17	1,395	33.39	1,397	33.44	4,178	54,256	7.7
Idaho	272	18.26	457	30.67	761	51.07	1,490	61,149	2.44
Illinois	1,675	12.75	4,055	30.86	7,410	56.39	13,140	542,634	2.42
Indiana	1,585	17.10	3,002	32.38	4,683	50.52	9,270	256,084	3.62
Iowa	323	15.12	684	32.02	1,129	52.86	2,136	109,492	1.95
Kansas	413	15.02	805	28.28	1,531	55.69	2,749	114,498	2.4
Kentucky	320	8.23	1,214	31.24	2,352	60.52	3,886	163,880	2.37
Louisiana	460	13.15	1,088	31.10	1,950	55.75	3,498	199,678	1.75
Maine	98	8.87	304	27.51	703	63.62	1,105	39,831	2.77
Maryland	763	13.21	1,851	32.06	3,160	54.73	5,774	222,035	2.6
Massachusetts	2,391	16.60	4,569	31.71	7,447	51.69	14,407	243,241	5.92
Michigan	1,320	16.08	2,631	32.05	4,259	51.88	8,210	385,835	2.13
Minnesota	472	13.48	1,027	29.33	2,003	57.20	3,502	196,886	1.78
Mississippi	1,062	53.77	631	31.95	282	14.28	1,975	129,200	1.53
Missouri	465	20.86	1,067	34.87	1,891	44.27	3,423	226,097	1.51

Montana	131	13.97	219	29.68	278	56.35	628	32,261	1.95
Nebraska	176	13.97	374	29.68	710	56.35	1,260	74,108	1.7
Nevada	113	12.15	346	37.20	471	50.65	930	98,798	0.94
New Hampshire	155	13.53	329	28.71	662	57.77	1,146	43,959	2.61
New Jersey	688	8.50	2,382	29.44	5,021	62.06	8,091	343,154	2.36
New Mexico	455	19.55	804	34.55	1,068	45.90	2,327	80,568	2.89
New York	2,640	7.99	9,500	28.77	20,886	63.24	33,026	746,410	4.42
North Carolina	735	12.34	1,938	32.53	3,284	55.13	5,957	359,233	1.66
North Dakota	86	18.07	166	34.87	224	47.06	476	22,381	2.13
Ohio	1,233	15.21	2,641	32.59	4,230	52.20	8,104	446,806	1.81
Oklahoma	652	19.47	1,222	36.50	1,474	44.03	3,348	149,495	2.24
Oregon	184	10.01	591	32.15	1,063	57.83	1,838	133,203	1.38
Pennsylvania	2,009	16.16	4,000	32.18	6,420	51.65	12,429	422,550	2.94
Puerto Rico	187	7.52	749	30.13	1,550	62.35	2,486	—	—
Rhode Island	227	17.71	372	29.02	683	53.28	1,282	36,822	3.48
South Carolina	284	16.33	570	32.78	885	50.89	1,739	168,010	1.04
South Dakota	70	8.43	270	32.53	490	59.04	830	31,183	2.66
Tennessee	552	13.10	1,386	32.88	2,277	54.02	4,215	233,187	1.81
Texas	2,654	13.12	6,436	31.81	11,145	55.08	20,235	1,119,161	1.81
Utah	341	14.32	734	30.81	1,307	54.87	2,382	141,350	1.69
Vermont	64	10.29	171	27.49	387	62.22	622	18,161	3.42
Virginia	579	13.77	1,561	37.13	2,064	49.10	4,204	299,461	1.4
Washington	349	9.62	1,133	31.24	2,145	59.14	3,627	232,643	1.56
West Virginia	352	19.50	581	34.85	761	45.65	1,667	61,008	2.73
Wisconsin	607	11.21	1,554	28.69	3,256	60.11	5,417	203,426	2.66
Wyoming	100	14.88	214	31.85	358	53.27	672	18,826	3.57
50 States and D.C.	39,021	14.47	85,218	31.61	145,357	53.92	269,596	12,048,310	2.24

Source: U.S. Department of Education, Office of Special Education Programs, Data Analysis System (DANS), OMB# 1820-0557 Infants and Toddlers Receiving Early Intervention Services in Accordance with Part C, 2005. Data updated as of July 17, 2006.

TABLE 1.4   Number and Percentage of Infants and Toddlers Ages Birth Through 2 Served Under IDEA, Part C, by Race or Ethnicity December 1, 2003

State	Black		Hispanic		White	
	(*n*)	%	(*n*)	%	(*n*)	%
Alabama	834	1.39	54	0.83	1,244	1.11
Alaska	34	3.25	37	1.55	341	1.93
Arizona	164	2.18	1,345	1.18	1,852	1.50
Arkansas	1053	4.35	101	1.31	1,594	2.01
California	2534	2.54	12,560	1.60	10,122	1.99
Colorado	116	1.44	804	1.34	2,133	1.68
Connecticut	412	2.75	665	3.27	2,514	2.96
Delaware	241	2.93	109	3.30	579	2.84
District of Columbia	160	1.10	55	1.99	34	0.77
Florida	3100	2.05	3,341	2.11	8,088	2.52
Georgia	1667	1.21	492	1.05	2,577	1.21
Hawaii	83	4.21	124	1.28	407	3.88
Idaho	13	7.10	222	2.65	1,211	2.36
Illinois	2582	2.54	2,767	2.29	7,439	2.49
Indiana	924	3.32	478	2.78	7,718	3.71
Iowa	74	2.37	154	2.35	1,866	1.92
Kansas	230	3.01	349	2.38	2,098	2.37
Kentucky	426	2.94	103	2.34	3,270	2.28
Louisiana	1566	1.82	45	0.89	1,850	1.76
Maine	5	1.82	7	1.30	1,080	2.82
Maryland	1897	2.53	368	2.28	3,292	2.72
Massachusetts	1055	5.39	2,021	6.21	10,691	6.02
Michigan	1236	1.78	442	2.00	6,340	2.24
Minnesota	275	2.13	208	1.60	2,845	1.80
Mississippi	1033	1.72	23	1.07	911	1.39
Missouri	419	1.23	103	1.18	2,824	1.58
Montana	8	10.00	21	1.87	464	1.73
Nebraska	56	1.42	147	1.69	1,009	1.71
Nevada	90	1.21	294	0.85	496	0.97
New Hampshire	25	6.48	26	1.64	1,061	2.60
New Jersey	1016	1.76	1,128	1.54	5,497	2.97
New Mexico	61	4.86	1,242	3.00	676	2.60
New York	4376	3.04	7,769	4.49	19,470	5.17
North Carolina	1852	2.06	657	1.56	3,269	1.52
North Dakota	15	6.88	6	1.37	385	2.01
Ohio	1559	2.31	385	2.82	6,008	1.68
Oklahoma	370	2.68	424	2.90	2,229	2.15
Oregon	35	1.56	336	1.42	1,387	1.38
Pennsylvania	1828	3.08	801	3.26	9,533	2.91
Puerto Rico	0	—	2,485	—	1	—

TABLE 1.4   (*continued*)

State	Black (*n*)	%	Hispanic (*n*)	%	White (*n*)	%
Rhode Island	63	2.21	232	3.57	949	3.66
South Carolina	717	1.19	88	1.02	918	0.95
South Dakota	18	7.79	14	1.67	581	2.37
Tennessee	935	1.83	200	1.79	3,004	1.79
Texas	2298	1.78	9,175	1.74	8,271	1.93
Utah	44	5.92	301	1.54	1,925	1.65
Vermont	15	22.06	13	10.66	572	3.23
Virginia	1054	1.51	351	1.26	2,666	1.42
Washington	130	1.53	572	1.58	2,383	1.42
West Virginia	69	3.66	14	5.58	1,576	2.69
Wisconsin	752	3.94	518	3.45	3,961	2.46
Wyoming	12	7.32	71	3.97	528	3.30

Source: U.S. Department of Education, Office of Special Education Programs, Data Analysis System (DANS). Infants and Toddlers Receiving Early Intervention Services in Accordance with Part C, 2005.

CW 1.1

Use the Companion Website to help you answer the following questions:

1. How would you respond to the statement that there are too many culturally and linguistically diverse children in the early intervention system?

2. Describe what happens to the number of children served when eligibility criteria shift from mild to moderate to severe disabilities. Discuss whether states should limit services to children with mild or moderate disabilities. Explain your answer.

3. What are the benefits of serving infants and toddlers who are at-risk? Why is early intervention so important for younger children? Explain.

Eligibility Differences

The federal law stipulates the general parameters for states to use when defining their eligibility criteria for children to receive early intervention services. However, each state has some discretion in determining the criteria and in defining what they mean by developmental disability and/or developmental delay (Brown & Conroy, 1999).

CW 1.2

Use the Companion Website to help you answer the following questions:

1. Describe the service coordination process in your state and local community.

2. What are the responsibilities of service coordinators in your state and local community?

As a result, states may vary in terms of their categories for classification and criteria for entrance to the service-delivery system (Harbin & Danaher, 1994), and some may use general definitions of developmental delay and/or severe disability.

Some states use specific criteria such as months of delay and/or standard deviations (SDs) related to delay on standardized evaluative instruments (see Table 1.5). As a result of the variation in definitions from one state to another, children who are eligible for services in one state may not be eligible in another (Bailey, 2000). For example, a 3-year-old who has an 11-month delay would be eligible to receive services in Arkansas but not in Arizona. States vary in terms of the following:

1. Percentage of delay required to determine eligibility
2. Use of categorical (etiological cause) versus noncategorical classification systems
3. Threshold for eligibility (Mississippi: 25% delay in two areas) versus different thresholds as children get older (Arizona: 11 months at age 3, 14 months at age 4, and 18 months at age 5)

The Children's Journeys Begin

The Martinez Family

Raul Martinez arrives first in the United States, leaving his family behind in El Salvador. He works as a landscaper for 2 years and then brings his wife, Maria, and children Rosita (5 years), Manuel (4 years), and José (2 years) to the United States. Raul applies for a green card because he wants to become a U.S. citizen. Because he does not yet have a social security number, his family is not eligible for many social services. Spanish is the primary language in the home, and this language difference creates a barrier that interferes with the family's ability to access services. The Martinez family lives in an apartment with extended family members, who reside with them for a short term when they arrive from El Salvador. The Martinez children are immediately enrolled in a parochial school and preschool in the neighborhood parish. They receive food, clothing, and religious services through church-based organizations. There are a large Latino community and network of services in this urban

TABLE 1.5 Summary Chart of Eligibility Criteria Under Part C of IDEA

Selected States	Level of Developmental Delay Required for Eligibility[1]	Serving At-Risk	Comments
Arizona	50% delay in one or more areas	No	If child is not eligible after evaluation, offer continued tracking of child's development with the Ages and Stages Questionnaire and assist family to identify needed community resources.
Arkansas[2]	25% delay in one or more areas	No	
Illinois[2]	30% delay in one or more areas; informed clinical opinion by MDT including clinical observations	No	List of established medical conditions and parent participation
Indiana	1.5 SD in one area or 20% below chronological age; 1 SD in two areas or 15% below chronological age in two areas; informed clinical opinion	Yes (biological)	Eight biological risk factors defined; only one risk factor necessary for eligibility
Louisiana	Delay in one or more areas, determined by MDT, including family, based on multisource data: team decision making	No	List of established conditions
New York	12-month delay in one area; or 33% delay in one area, 25% delay in two areas; 2 SD in one area or 1.5 SD in two areas; or informed clinical opinion by MDT	No	
South Dakota	25% below normal age range or 6-month delay; or demonstrating at least a 1.5-SD delay in one or more areas	No	
Tennessee	25% delay in two or more areas; 40% delay in one area; informed clinical opinion	No	List of established conditions

Source: Survey of Part C Coordinators; definition from most recent Office of Children with Special Needs-approved application; IDEA Part B Data, www.ideadata.org/partbdata.asp

Note: Diagnosed physical or mental condition with high probability of resulting in developmental delay, commonly referred to as *established conditions,* is an eligibility category required under Part C and thus is not included in this table.

1. Areas refers to the five developmental areas (physical, communication, cognitive, social or emotional, and adaptive) that are cited in the law.
2. This state's or jurisdiction's eligibility definition has changed significantly since January 1998.

area, so the Martinez family feels a strong sense of connection to other Latino families in their church. Maria and Raul Martinez do not take their children to a primary-care specialist on a regular basis, so José's problem is not diagnosed for several months. Because of this, José misses months of services that he is entitled to receive.

Linguistic and cultural diversity increases the probability that families will either learn about early intervention services late or not at all. The benefit of an early intervention system is a direct function of public awareness and information that is disseminated in the primary language of the family. This family is profiled because in large metropolitan cities this lack of information is a common occurrence. The social and educational problems resulting for millions of immigrants are complex. The Martinez family's personal experiences in advocating for their child are presented in Box 1.1 to provide students with an understanding of the barriers faced by culturally and linguistically diverse families.

The Whiteside Family

Katherine and Connor Whiteside live in a rural part of the midwestern United States. They are proud of their heritage and can trace their lineage all the way back to communities in Scotland. Although families in their community are few and geographically far apart, they are closely involved with each other. The Whitesides see themselves as self-sufficient and quietly religious people. They firmly believe that problems should remain within the confines of the family and must be resolved by family members.

Connor Whiteside tends to drink frequently. Katherine speaks to her family and they tell her that Connor is under a great deal of pressure managing their farm. Connor's explosive temper frightens Katherine, but she cannot make him stop drinking. When she prematurely gives birth to Kaitlyn, Connor does not want to talk about any possible at-risk factors related to the birth. Although Kaitlyn is eventually diagnosed with a hearing loss, Connor remains uninvolved. Katherine makes all the important decisions herself. Katherine's and Connor's families deny that there are serious problems that need to be addressed.

Katherine learns about the early intervention system from a nurse when Kaitlyn is in the neonatal intensive-care unit of the hospital (Association of Women's Health, Obstetric, and Neonatal Nurses, 1990). Katherine and Connor are uncomfortable with the intrusion of social workers, counselors, and speech-language pathologists who want to provide services in their home. It takes a long time for professionals to gain their trust and cooperation once Kaitlyn is diagnosed with a hearing loss. Katherine Whiteside does not like her service coordinator and feels that all the professionals are being too directive in their interactions with her. She does not appreciate being told "what is good or appropriate for Kaitlyn." She is also concerned that once county officials and professionals are involved, if she disagrees with their advice, she could be accused of being a neglectful parent.

Because Katherine respects her audiologist and pediatric neurologist, she goes back to see them. They suggest that she contact the Mission School for the Deaf, which utilizes a total communication (sign language and speech) approach, and the

BOX 1.1

My name is Maria and my son, José, is now 30 months of age and has autism. I live in an apartment in a very large city with my mother, my husband, and two other children. José is my youngest child, and I learned about early intervention services from a nurse practitioner at a local community clinic. José is not talking or acting like my other children. I was concerned and asked the teacher in the church's nursery school if he has a problem. She said that boys develop more slowly than girls and not to worry. When I asked her about José months later, she said José is not talking because he is learning two languages at the same time. Finally, at 30 months she told me to take José to a local clinic. I told the nurse that José is having terrible tantrums. He doesn't play with his sister and brother. He stares at nothing as though he doesn't hear or recognize us. He doesn't always respond to his name and rocks back and forth in his crib. The nurse told me that a service coordinator from the early intervention program would call me to evaluate José. A bilingual service coordinator then came to my home to talk to me about a multidisciplinary family assessment and individual family service plan. After José's assessment, I was told that he has autism and that services can be provided in my home. I chose to take José to a local infant stimulation program. The Early Start Infant Program provides medical services, nutritional services, counseling, parent–infant groups, occupational therapy, physical therapy, and language therapy. I feel strongly that scheduling services and therapists in my home would be difficult and disruptive to my family. One difficulty for Latino families is that there aren't enough bilingual professionals. Very often an interpreter is not available and important medical information or clinical advice is misunderstood. I like the fact that José can receive all his services in one place. I can speak to his therapists and they can talk to each other. The Early Start Infant Program has parent support groups with other Spanish-speaking parents. I want to talk to other parents because I feel very alone and isolated at home. The infant program also has a service coordinator that I talk to every week. I take José everyday by bus to the program, and by the end of the week I am exhausted. José is a very needy child, and at times it is impossible for me to take care of my other children. While I am at the program, my mother helps out with my other children, Rosita and Manuel. My husband Raul works two jobs and I don't see him much during the week. Raul is frustrated about work and our living conditions at home. It's crowded and noisy in our apartment. It's hard for Raul to get any rest when he gets home. It's also hard to take José out of the house. Raul takes Rosita and Manuel to the park or to friends. I'm very grateful for the services José receives and all the caring specialists that I have met through early intervention. My life seems to revolve around taking care of José. I miss being a family. We were all so very close. It's hard for us to get a babysitter who can deal with José's behavior and for us to do things as a family. I want to spend some time with my husband, but my mother can't take care of José by herself. I know José wouldn't receive these services in my country. I'm afraid José will never be normal.

Maria Martinez

Use the Companion Website to help you answer the following questions:

1. How does the family's bilingual background create a barrier to the provision of services?

2. What special accommodations are made in your state for bilingual families?

3. How would you evaluate Maria Martinez's experiences in early intervention?

4. What kinds of services could José receive in your state? What other services would be helpful to this family?

5. Discuss what family-centered programming might mean in the Latino community. Identify several issues to which speech-language pathologists need to be sensitive when working with linguistically and culturally diverse families.

Carlyle School for the Deaf, which utilizes an aural–oral communication approach. When she visits both programs, she notices that in the Mission School some of the parents are deaf and in the Carlyle School most of the parents are hearing. At both schools the intake evaluators speak to her about developing the quality of the interaction between her and Kaitlyn. Their overall goals for Kaitlyn are also the same, to develop her language, speech, intellectual abilities, and social–emotional growth. She and Kaitlyn could participate in individual sessions with teachers several times a week; there would also be home visits in both programs. Instructional play groups for parents and infants are also provided on a weekly basis along with parent workshops. Although the teachers at the Carlyle School are certified educators of the deaf, at the Mission School two of the teachers have hearing losses themselves. Katherine feels that this is an important difference.

The St. James Family

Camille St. James grew up in a small town in the southern part of the United States. Her parents are a hard working African American family who attend the local church, which is a pivotal part of the family's activities. Camille is the youngest of five children, and all the St. James children, except Camille, have graduated from high school and either attend a trade school or college. As a result, it is a shock to the family when Camille informs her parents that she is pregnant. Of all the St. James children, Mrs. Tarsha Washington indicates that Camille is her brightest child with the greatest potential for success. This is also a particularly difficult problem for Camille's parents, because they are the first generation to achieve middle-class status within their community. Given the religious convictions of the family, Camille is encouraged to have and to keep the baby.

At this point, Camille drops out of school because an alternative high school program for pregnant teenagers is not available. Camille's parents insist that she find a

BOX 1.2

My name is Katherine and I live in a rural community on a farm; my family has been farmers for many generations. My daughter Kaitlyn was a premature baby (32 weeks) and she is my first child. I went into labor early and had an emergency cesarean section, and for days we did not know if Kaitlyn was going to live. When Kaitlyn was in the neonatal unit, the nurse told me about the early intervention system. When I contacted the Public Health Department, I was told that eligibility for at-risk infants was a birth weight below 1501 grams or a gestational age of less than 33 weeks. Kaitlyn was eligible to receive services. After extensive testing I discovered that Kaitlyn had a severe bilateral hearing loss. Everyone in my family is devastated. I want the best for Kaitlyn. When I travel to meet with various medical specialists, I often stay in a hotel overnight. Instead of helping my husband, parents, and brothers with the farm, I am away for days at a time. I am emotionally overwhelmed by the reality of Kaitlyn's disability. As a hearing parent, I'm not sure if I want Kaitlyn in a program with hearing children or children with hearing losses. The service coordinator encourages us to accept services in our home and develops an infant stimulation program. The service coordinator feels that the natural environment for Kaitlyn is with hearing peers and that we should use an aural–oral method. We really don't understand the difference between the aural–oral and total communication approaches. I'm not sure what's right for Kaitlyn, so I decided to do some research on my own. After several interviews with professionals, I finally understand that the primary difference between the programs is the inclusion of and emphasis on sign language in a total communication program versus no sign language in an aural–oral program.

Katherine Whiteside

Use the Companion Website to help you answer the following questions:

1. How does Katherine Whiteside's background contribute to her perceptions and expectations?

2. Does your state have an infant screening program? Describe its outreach procedures.

3. Discuss Katherine Whiteside's concerns about Kaitlyn's hearing loss and the kinds of programs available to children with hearing loss.

4. Critically reflect on whether Katherine Whiteside has had a family-centered experience. How would you evaluate her experience?

5. How do you think Katherine Whiteside might describe her family-centered experience?

job after the baby is born and complete her education by taking night classes. Camille's pregnancy and delivery are uneventful, and the baby (Jeffrey) remains at home for the first 3 months with his grandmother while Camille works at a local retail store. Camille attends classes two nights a week and is committed to completing her education.

Camille contacts the Department of Social Services requesting child-care support so that she can continue working. Jeffrey is placed in an early childhood program from 7 a.m. to 5 p.m. until he is 24 months of age. Jeffrey's developmental milestones are slightly delayed, and the director of the early childhood center recommends an early intervention evaluation through the Public Health Department. Camille is told by Jeffrey's child-care teacher that he can be aggressive during play, particularly when other children approach him, and that he is not a verbal child. A service coordinator from the Public Health Department schedules a family assessment, as well as the related developmental evaluations. During the IFSP meeting Camille is informed that Jeffrey has a mild delay in his communication skills. Because there are no other developmental delays, Jeffrey is not eligible for early intervention services. During the next several months, Jeffrey's communication skills are monitored by a speech-language pathologist. The SLP and the early childhood teacher both note that Jeffrey's behavior with his peers has become progressively worse. Eventually, Jeffrey is expelled from the program because he is biting and hitting other children. The early childhood teacher meets with Camille to explain that the program does not have a psychologist on staff or an individual aide to work directly with Jeffrey. Camille describes her first encounter with the system in Box 1.3.

BOX 1.3

My name is Camille and my son Jeffrey has problems in his child-care program. I contact a service coordinator at the Public Health Department to tell her that Jeffrey needs help because of his behavior. The evaluations are done in my home and I take off from work. The psychologist says Jeffrey is normal, but he's impulsive and distractible. The speech-language pathologist says Jeffrey is delayed in both speech and language development, but he's not eligible to receive therapy services. I'm frightened and frustrated because Jeffrey can be difficult to manage. He seems to understand what we're telling him, but he doesn't obey. Jeffrey must go to child care because I've got to work. I'm told to contact the Department of Social Services because the Public Health Department only assists families whose children are eligible for early intervention services. This isn't helpful and I'm frustrated. Jeffrey is delayed. What's the difference if it's 5, 6, or 7 months? Delayed is delayed. Jeffrey's delay isn't going away. I just don't understand the system. For the next several months a social worker from Social Services attempts to find a program for Jeffrey so that I can work. She says that Jeffrey might be eligible for preschool special education services when he turns 3. Why do I have to wait until then?

I always seem to find out about programs and services after I need them. It would've been helpful if one social worker told me about all the programs. If someone doesn't tell me, I don't know what's available or who to call. I just can't understand how teachers can expel a 2-year-old child because he can't be managed. Jeffrey can be managed—he's not retarded. If all those professionals give up, how can they expect a parent to do better?

Camille St. James

Use the Companion Website to help you answer the following questions:

1. How does the family's cultural background play a role in determining Camille St. James's perceptions and expectations?

2. How would you have addressed Camille St. James's questions?

3. How do you think Camille St. James might describe her family-centered experience?

4. What else could have been done for this family in your state and local community? What is your reaction to the fact that Jeffrey is not eligible?

5. What issues should SLPs be aware of when working with African American families?

6. Can you find how many African American SLPs, psychologists, special educators, occupational therapists, and physical therapists are licensed in your state and work in your community (Special Education Personnel Report, 1999)?

7. Compare the service coordination issues for the three families.

8. How has your state evaluated its early intervention program?

SUMMARY

As the early intervention and preschool systems have expanded to include an increasing number of children, issues of program efficacy and cost effectiveness have been raised more frequently. When the early intervention system was new, the primary issue was child identification. Now, after a decade of service provision, policy makers, administrators, and legislators are debating about who should receive services and whether the programs are too expensive. In the next several years, accountability will be defined in terms of outcome measures (Barnett et al., 1999). The question of whether early intervention works may not be answered in terms of child change and progress. One criterion determining program success relates to the number or percentage of children exiting the system. The transition from early intervention to preschool special education provides the opportunity for each state to indicate the percentage of infants and toddlers exiting early intervention versus those who are eligible for Part B (IDEA) preschool special education. These percentages are impressive as indicators that the early intervention system on a national level is effective. By comparing the early intervention system to the preschool and school-age systems, the exit data indicate that fewer children leave special education as their age increases. Several factors explain this phenomenon:

- The earlier a child receives services, the better the prognosis.
- Eligibility criteria in early intervention may be too stringent. So infants and toddlers who are not considered "disabled enough" do not meet the eligibility criteria, remain unserved, and appear later in the preschool or elementary school systems. To understand this issue, we need longitudinal data.
- The early intervention system does not identify every infant or toddler who *should* receive services because linguistically and culturally diverse families are often underserved.

When children are not eligible to receive services, it does not mean they do *not* have a problem. Jeffrey St. James presents a profile of a child whose delay is not severe enough at 18, 24, or 30 months for him to receive services. This does not mean that his delay will disappear or that he will be able to catch up developmentally when placed in a setting with typical peers. Recently, it has been shown that language impairment is not necessarily identified by low scores on standardized tests (Spaulding, Plante, & Farinella, 2006). Forty-three commercially available tests of child language were analyzed to determine whether evidence existed to support their use in identifying language impairment. The data review failed to support the assumption that children with language impairment will routinely score at the low end of a test's normative distribution and thereby meet eligibility criteria for services. If a delay is not serious enough for services, professionals cannot provide parents with assurances that a delay will not become more severe as the child gets older. Data indicate that, when children with disabilities remain unserved or underserved, children do more poorly in school as they get older. Some states serve a lower percentage of infants and toddlers. The percentages increase when children enter elementary school.

A great deal of discussion concerns the methodology related to program assessment. Differences are reported in the literature in attempts to measure program effectiveness in terms of child-based changes. The method, measures, data analyses, and dependent variables may vary, but the investigatory intentions are all the same (Bailey, Aytch, Odoms, Symons, & Wolery, 1999; Bailey et al., 1998; Hebbeler et al., 2001). How do professionals substantiate that a program works and that a child is learning? The concern has also been expressed that, even when the child changes, learning outcomes may not justify the educational costs. In 1986, the moral dilemma related to the fact that children needed services and programs. Today, the moral dilemma raises the issue that costs related to children's services and programs are increasing.

The responsibility of legislators is to create a balance between what is necessary and appropriate and the costs involved. Once this balance is achieved, children will receive the services they require.

Language Disorders in Infants and Toddlers

Chapter Objectives

After studying this chapter, you should be able to answer the following questions:

1. What is the difference between a language delay and a language disorder?

2. What is a strengths-based approach?

3. What is a deficit-based approach?

4. Define and describe autism.

5. What is the role of the speech-language pathologist (SLP) in the early intervention system?

6. What is a specific language impairment (SLI)?

The Families Speak

Jeffrey goes to childcare while I am at work. He was an alert, happy baby who smiled and cooed in response to me. His child-care teacher, Miss Burke, told me that he was developing well. He learned to crawl, sit, and stand just like all the other kids. He loved songs and games like Pat-A-Cake, So-Big, Peek-A-Boo, and Itsy Bitsy Spider. He learned to say "No" and push things away that he did not want. He said "Mama" at 1 year and he could imitate animal sounds. At 18 months Jeffrey could say about 30 to 40 words, or what sounded like words. He could understand a lot more than he could say. I know he understands just about everything. When Jeffrey was 2 years old he would use gestures with speech sounds and actions. He liked to be with other kids and would speak to them. But he began to get frustrated when the other children didn't understand him. He does better with adults. His attention span is not long, and he

The communicative interaction between parent and children is critical to language development.

Anne Vega / Merrill

can become impatient when he doesn't get what he wants. He will tantrum and even bite and hit. Miss Burke told me that because of his biting and hitting he will not be able to stay at childcare.

The speech and language pathologist who evaluated Jeffrey through the early intervention system observed him in childcare. She told me that Jeffrey's vowel productions are limited to earlier forms (a, ʌ, e, i), and his consonant productions remain restricted (b, k, d, p, d, m). Jeffrey speaks like a younger child, and he omits and substitutes many sounds. He can't say the "s" sound, and he doesn't use plural "s" or past tense. He is intelligible about 30% to 40% of the time, and he doesn't always try to imitate speech.

Camille St. James

When Kaitlyn was just an infant, she made sounds just like any baby. I couldn't tell the difference anyway. What did I know about normal development or deaf speech? Kaitlyn was cooing and crying. How did I know she didn't hear? The other confusing problem was that Kaitlyn was so responsive to anything she could see. When Kaitlyn did not respond to sudden noises, I became suspicious. She did smile and react to familiar objects and people. Kaitlyn developed a differentiated cry (hungry, tired, uncomfortable, etc.). Because there was limited sound feedback, her cooing began to decrease, but by this time we knew. Whereas vocalization patterns increase in a hearing baby to include a greater variety of sounds, hers did not. Kaitlyn responded when I appeared with a bottle; she recognized my facial expressions and physical games that were repetitive and visually based. So Pat-A-Cake was not a game that worked with Kaitlyn; she could not hear the vocal sound patterns and rhyming. But interactional games that relied on gestures and pop-up toys resulted in gaze, vocal, and gestural responses. Kailtyn was alert, highly responsive, and happy. Kaitlyn's developmental motor milestones (rolling over, sitting, reaching, pointing) were slightly delayed. Kaitlyn was fascinated by her crib mobile, which she hit repeatedly to make it move over and over again. She usually tracked anything that moved and watched complicated patterns of colors and designs on the "baby" videotapes that I got for her. Kaitlyn was social and enjoyed being with other babies. When Kaitlyn was 18 months old, we decided that she should have a cochlear implant (CI). With the implant, Kaitlyn was exposed to environmental sounds and speech. I enrolled Kaitlyn at the Mission School for the Deaf and I learned sign language. I was just amazed by how quickly Kaitlyn picked up the signs and used them with us and other people. With the cochlear implant, Kaitlyn's speech began to develop, but her sounds were different. The cochlear implant made a tremendous difference, but it was not so simple to take care of. I was shocked to find that the issue of cochlear implants in the Deaf Community was controversial (New cochlear implant, 2006). Persons within the Deaf Community feel that once children with deafness are implanted they are rejecting the Deaf Community and stepping into the hearing world. In the years before IDEA, persons who were deaf were considered ineligible for various professions and were cut off from mainstream society. In fact, some states made it difficult for persons with deafness to become teachers of the deaf. In response, a Deaf Culture community developed that instilled pride in its members. Cochlear implants are a recently new method of treatment for deafness, and many people in the Deaf Community are not CI users and see no reason for their use. I felt Kaitlyn has an advantage with her cochlear implant and by learning sign language. Kaitlyn understands 500 words, and she can answer simple who, what, and where questions. She can point to pictures when named. She signs to herself while playing, and she vocalizes during play as well. She has a very long attention span; she can follow a signed story for many minutes. She asks simple questions, and we can have a simple conversation. She refers to herself and everyone else by name. She also names objects and pictures. Kaitlyn plays at cooking, cleaning, and washing activities with her

During infancy it is often difficult for practitioners to appropriately diagnose language and communication disorders.

toys and dolls. She plays with blocks and builds things. She is very imitative; if she sees me do something once, she can imitate it. I think Kaitlyn's as smart as any hearing child.

Katherine Whiteside

I don't know who this boy is. At times when he is screaming and banging his head, I don't know what to do to stop him. When I have to take him out of the apartment, I carry all the food and candy that I know he likes. If I don't give him the candy when he starts to act up, he bites his hands and sometimes slaps himself in the face. People stop and stare; God knows what they think. How much candy can I give him? José gets sick later and throws up at night. Sometimes I can't make him stop screaming and hitting. If he has a tantrum at home, I do the best I can to calm him. José has punched, kicked, and bitten me. I am afraid of these behaviors. How can José go to school like this? I am afraid he will hurt himself or another child. We only leave the apartment if José needs to go to therapy or to the pediatrician.

Maria Martinez

Many infants and toddlers with language disorders are also classified with medical or etiological labels. However, these labels are not necessary for a child from birth through age 2 years to receive services in the early intervention program. What qualifies a child is a delay in an area of development, such as cognitive, motor, or language development. This noncategorical approach is effective and efficient when considering children with language disorders, because many children who evidence early delays do not have any medical diagnoses. Furthermore, a noncategorical approach reflects an emphasis within IDEA's reauthorization plan to focus on children's strengths and the services they need to make progress. Whereas a categorical approach relies on a static set of descriptive characteristics for a disorder, a noncategorical approach allows for an understanding of a disorder based on its changing characteristics as a child grows older. This chapter will discuss concepts such as language delay, disorder, and difference. It will explore the impact of a language disorder in children who have very different etiological classifications. However, the presence of that language disorder affects multiple aspects of their social and educational experiences, and it is language that provides a methodological framework to systematically compare different developmental disabilities.

Delay versus Disorder

Many states refer to the child's developmental difference as a delay below the age of 5 and as a disability above the age of 5. The term *delay* implies that the child can catch up with his peers given the appropriate intervention. This presents a problem in evaluating the efficacy of early intervention programs (Barnett & Pepiton, 1999). The hope of parents is often painfully shattered when they are presented with the possibility and then the reality of their child's disorder. In the attempt not to label a disorder "too soon," the system has shifted to understating the lifelong needs of many young children with disabilities. Owens (2002) has argued that the term *delay* has a "short shelf life" and becomes meaningless when the difference continues to increase as the child ages. To describe a developmental difference of 10 years as a delay is definitely stretching the concept of delay as it relates to typical development. "After a mental age of 10, the developmental paths seem to deviate, and the language of the two groups shows qualitative differences as well as quantitative differences" (Owens, p. 379).

In explaining the difference between delay and disorder, the developmental pattern presented by children with autism is often described. When compared to children of similar mental age and language level, the child with autism presents a different pattern of social and language behaviors than the typical child. In many cases, functional language does not develop at all. Verbal language, when it does develop, is usually rigid, ritualistic, and stereotypical. Language level, mental age, and IQ cannot account for the child's interactional deficits (Loveland, Landry, Hughes, Hall, & McEvoy, 1998). The term *delay* also suggests that the child with a disability appears to be developing a more typical *sequence* of behaviors, but more slowly. In contrast, the term *disorder* suggests that the child with a disability appears to be developing an idiosyncratic or atypical sequence of behaviors. For instance, the child with a language delay acquires language forms in the same order as a typically developing child; however, these forms are acquired at a slower rate and later than for the typical language learner. However, the child with a language disorder may never acquire competency levels across language components.

Deficit versus Strengths-Based Approach

Most educational and mental health disciplines evaluate a child's functioning within a deficit framework (Reid, Epstein, Pastor, & Ryser, 2000). Inherent within this model or approach is the reference standard of *normalcy* or *typicalness*. Developmental norms are standardized by evaluating thousands of children at specific age levels. Based on these maturational milestones, children who are suspected of having a delay can be compared linguistically, cognitively, socially, and motorically to typically developing children of the same chronological age. When a difference has been identified in one of these areas, the significance of the difference will determine whether the child receives intervention services (Salvia & Ysseldyke, 1991). A practitioner's perspective provides the framework for decision making, so it is important to understand how a theoretical model determines not only the clinical–educational intervention practices used by the SLP, but also the goals and activities developed for the child. With a deficit-based model the practitioner assumes the following:

- Developmental differences between a child and his or her peers reflect deficiencies–disorders in functioning.
- Deficits in the child need to be addressed so that he or she functions like typical peers.
- Goals and instructional methodologies are based on what the child cannot do.

Strengths-Based Approach

A strengths-based approach provides a perspective of children's developmental differences based on diversity theory that establishes ethnically sensitive practices and acknowledges alternative life-style choices in culturally and linguistically different families. This model proposes that it is important for the SLP to interact with parents, given a nonpathologic and nonjudgmental perspective, and focus on the adaptive aspects of the family's interactional system (Brink, 2002; Shulman, 1999). Race, culture, ethnicity, and gender establish different perceptions, which often become impermeable boundaries and immovable barriers where miscommunication and negative experiences occur with professionals. Davis and Proctor (1989) suggest that racial and cultural differences should be acknowledged and not ignored by professionals.

By viewing the child and family from a strengths perspective, the SLP identifies the family's resources, capabilities, and support systems to be used to address their problems. When the speech pathologist acknowledges the ethnocultural primacy of the parent's needs, values, and perceptions when establishing therapeutic objectives, she also acknowledges the nonstandard integrity of the child's communicative system. Applied to a child with a disability, the strengths-based model shifts the focus from disordered to different, which is a significant change in thinking for most clinical disciplines.

Presently, educational and clinical communities, training methodologies, and intervention systems are based on a pathology model in which children are labeled, categorized, described, and treated in terms of their deficits (Fewster, 2002; Friedman, Leone, & Friedman, 1999). In fact, it is difficult to describe a child with autism without referring to her or his deficits. Although we discuss the generalizability of a strengths-based model to children with disabilities, its clinical application may be more readily accepted by clinical practitioners working with linguistically and culturally diverse families; the strengths-based model underscores the centrality of ethnically sensitive practice when working with these family members. The changes in thinking from the family-centered to the relationship-based to the strengths-based approaches represent natural transitions in facilitating empowerment skills in families (Atkins-Burnett & Allen-Meares, 2000).

Different versus Disordered

Rather than viewing a child's behaviors as the result of a disordered system, behaviors can be viewed as a result of an operational system that has its own integrity but is functioning differently. The strengths-based model requires the practitioner to view the child from a culturally sensitive perspective.

- The child is developing skills and knowledge by means of a developmental system that is different, not deviant.
- The cultural system is responsible for the child's behavioral patterns and is responsive to contextual factors.
- To understand a child's learning system, one must analyze the child's language behaviors within social contexts.
- When intervention techniques are not effective, SLPs should use a learning model based on the sequence of language acquisition presented by nonstandard learners, such as children with autism. We may find that children along the autism spectrum continuum have a language-acquisition pattern that is uniquely distinct and different from that of typical children.
- The theoretical approach proposed for bilingual–biliterate learners may be helpful in teaching nonstandard learners; their systems are different, not deficient. To teach the bilingual–biliterate child, practitioners need to understand that their language-acquisition process is different. We should begin instruction with the perception that the monolingual model may not be applicable to the bilingual child; the same applies to the nonstandard learner.
- Alternative assessments are needed to determine the rules governing the nonstandard learner's communicative and linguistic interactions in order to design a program based on these rules (Reid et al., 2000).
- Instead of focusing on typical behaviors, professionals need to analyze how the child's system functions to serve his or her needs without negative judgments.

Children with language disorders change the life-cycle continuum for families. Parents are often overwhelmed by fear of and then the reality of the initial diagnosis. Professionals need to be aware of and sensitive to the range of emotions that parents typically experience. To help the parent, the SLP must understand the family's emotional journey, validate its feelings, and support its goals. Part of the role of the SLP includes helping parents to achieve the following:

- Define their needs for support services
- Integrate the child with a disability into the family structure
- Maintain a balance to meet the social–emotional needs of all family members—parents, siblings, and extended members
- Identify the family's strengths and values that will help the child with a disability as well as each other
- Identify intrafamilial resources
- Identify community-based resources
- Maintain the family's characteristic attributes as linguistically and culturally diverse members of society

CW 2.1

Use the Companion Website to help you answer the following questions:

1. How can a strengths-based approach be used to meet the diverse needs of children and families?

2. How can a strengths-based approach be used in the development of intervention goals for children and families?

3. If special education does not rehabilitate a child to average or mainstream functioning, does that mean it is not effective?

4. When does a developmental difference become a delay (3, 4, 5, or 6 months)?

5. When does a developmental delay become diagnostically significant enough to warrant clinical intervention services?

6. As an SLP, would you rather see more false positives or false negatives in determining eligibility for services?

- Teach family members techniques to support the child with a disability within the home environment
- Understand early intervention procedures, requirements, and teaming
- Advocate for their child's needs, especially during transitions to the next system
- Understand the long-term care needs of the child

Speech-language pathologists need specialized knowledge and training to provide services to infants and their families. Historically, the field of speech-language pathology has focused on developing a generalist practitioner who could work with any population depending on his or her personal interests. The reality of clinical research in the field has highlighted the need for both specialized training and expertise in specific areas of practice. Some practitioners and parents propose that specialized skills are also needed to work with specific types of disabilities.

Definitional Differences Across States

A language-based model provides SLPs with a common professional language that becomes a powerful methodological tool, especially when educational systems are different. In some states, a child needs to have a 33% delay or disability in one component or a 25% delay or disability in two areas to be eligible for early intervention services. Can a child have a significant delay in one of the other component areas (i.e., cognition, social–emotional, motor) and not have a language disorder? The answer is yes, but more often no; usually, children who have a disability in one of the other component areas also have a language disorder. However, many children who are identified as having language disorders do not have physical, cognitive, and/or motor

CW 2.2

Use the Companion Website to help you discuss the following:

1. Review ASHA's definition and discuss the implications for the use in class of the different terms.

2. Describe several issues related to children with language disorders about which ASHA is advocating on a national level.

3. Discuss the statistics presented in this section and explain what they mean in terms of services provided in your state to children with speech or language impairments.

disorders; these children are described as having a specific language impairment (SLI). The American Speech-Language-Hearing Association (*www.asha.org*) provides the following demographic information:

- Case histories indicate that between 28% and 60% of the children with a speech and language deficit have a family member who also has a problem (Fox, Dodd, & Howard, 2002).
- Services provided for children with speech or language impairment showed an overall increase of 9.5% between 1991 and 2001 (U.S. Department of Education, 2002).
- Moderate to severe language problems are predictive of long-term educational difficulties (Laing, Law, Levin, & Logan, 2002).

A significant problem within special education is the interchangeable use of the terms *speech* or *communication*, rather than *language disorder*. At the present time there are many definitional differences across states when referring to children with language disorders.

Autism Spectrum Disorders: José

The autism spectrum disorder (ASD) continuum includes such a broad range of children who evidence language, cognitive, communicative, behavioral, and social learning problems that many researchers suggest it is not a single group with a single etiological cause. A review of autism research, more than research concerning any other population of children with disabilities, reveals the many theoretical and therapeutic changes that have occurred in the area of child language acquisition.

Children with autism have distinctive language characteristics that are also evident in the language patterns of other children with language disorders. The language continuum in this population presents a range of abilities, with severe social deficits shared by all children. Primary-care providers have been more effective in identifying children with autism at the earlier ages of 12 to 18 months in recent years. Although hundreds of research studies support the efficacy of language-intervention therapy, the treatment of choice in many states remains applied behavioral analysis (ABA). The primary treatment approach reflects a focus on managing behavior in individual therapeutic sessions and not on facilitating language in social contexts (Tiegerman-Farber, 2002a).

Maria Martinez

It is important for the SLP to identify relevant information when working with culturally diverse families. A lack of understanding of cultural differences can result in misinterpretations of a family's behaviors, attitudes, and beliefs. The pathologist needs to consider how diversity issues may affect interpersonal relationships and clinical practice. In addition to the cultural differences between the pathologist and the client, specific family and client factors should be recognized.

The use of a *culturagram* provides a mechanism for assessing and empowering culturally diverse families (Congress, 1994). Figure 2.1 presents a model that can be used by the SLP to identify relevant group-, family-, and client-specific factors. The culturagram could include reasons for immigration, legal status, spoken language, family structure, social relationships, holidays, home life, traumatic events, and crises. Review the information that might be incorporated into an ecological model to strengthen culturally or ethnically sensitive practice (Congress, 1994; Gutheil, 1992; Shulman, 1999; Tracy & Whittaker, 1990).

All diverse groups who come to the United States face issues related to acculturation (Henry, Stiles, & Biran, 2005). The process of acculturating into mainstream society is difficult and complex for first- and second-generation family members. Identification with the mainstream dominant group creates acculturative stress in adults and ongoing value-based conflicts between parents and children (Goodman & Silverstein, 2005). From an ecological perspective, acculturation occurs as individuals socialized in one cultural context adapt and modify their behavior to improve the person–environment fit (Gitterman, 1996). Acculturation has been linked to mental health problems when mainstream identification leads to alienation and isolation from traditional supports, values, and relationships (Bratter & Eschbach, 2005; Kim, Brian, & Omizo, 2005). Latinos in the United States have a lower socioeconomic status (SES) profile, which is associated with poorer overall health (Abraido-Lanza, Chao, & Florez, 2005).

The Martinez family is struggling to survive and maintain the connection to their cultural values. Maria cannot work, given José's needs, but she does have a social support system, including an extended family and friends within the Latino community. Every member of the Martinez family is affected by José's behaviors. Maria's attention shifts from her husband and two other children to José. The balance of relationships within the family has been disrupted by José, who becomes the focus of Maria's affections and energies. The older siblings do not understand why José receives so much of their mother's attention and at times express their frustrations emotionally. Although she can return home to El Salvador, Maria recognizes that comprehensive services for children with disabilities are not available in her country. Maria's religious faith and her love for José propel her to learn a new language and to learn about a complicated educational system; this is one of Maria's strengths.

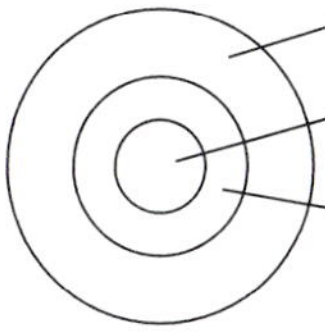

Micro issues
• Description of child _____
• Parents' concerns about child _____
• Important events related to the child_____
• When problem was identified_____
• How problem was identified _____

Mezzo issues
• Family's reactions to child_____
• Parents' relations with other children _____
• Family members_____
• Spousal status _____
• Quality of spousal relationship _____
• Evidence of child abuse_____
• Parental expectations for child _____
• Home environment (number of people, personal space, noise, privacy)_____
• Family resources (work, finances, health care, reason for immigration) _____
• Family supports (friends, extended family, neighbors)_____
• Family beliefs and values (holidays, religion, organizational membership)_____
• Domestic violence _____
• Education level _____
• Language spoken in the home_____
• English language proficiency_____
• Substance abuse _____
• Family values_____
• Specific family concerns _____

Macro issues
• Cultural roles and responsibilities_____
• Gender issues_____
• Major cultural events _____
• Community resources_____
• Cultural practices _____
• Cultural expectations _____
• Unique cultural factors _____

Other factors
• _____
• _____
• _____

FIGURE 2.1
Culturagram for Immigrant Latino Family

CW 2.3

Use the Companion Website to help you answer the following:

1. Research the Latino immigrant experience and fill in the information about the Martinez family based on the material that you have read.
2. Compare the culturagrams in class and discuss their differences.
3. Identify some ways of strengthening culturally sensitive practice.
4. Identify several issues unique to immigrant families.
5. How is the child with a disability integrated into the Latino community?
6. How would a child with a language disorder be affected by family factors such as poverty and cultural diversity?
7. What changes need to be made within the system to ensure that diverse families are identified?

José is diagnosed with autism, but he misses many months of early intervention services. Consider some factors that affect José's identification as a child with autism:

- Certain behaviors trigger the diagnosis of autism.
- Maria lives in a Latino community.
- Maria is a parent who knows nothing about autism.
- José is exposed to Spanish and English.
- José's developmental differences need to be separated from his language differences. It is difficult to evaluate a bilingual child.
- There are not enough qualified bilingual evaluators and SLPs, psychologists, and special-education teachers trained to work with autism spectrum disorders.
- It is difficult for systems and professionals to reach immigrants in linguistically and culturally diverse communities.

Micro issues for the child: language delay attributed to bilingual environment

Mezzo issues for the family: limited English proficiency, inexperienced parent

Macro issues for the system: difficult to reach undocumented community members, limited bilingual professionals, limited professionals with expertise on training with ASD

Defining Autism Spectrum Disorders

Autism is a disability specifically defined in the Individuals with Disabilities Education Act (IDEA). IDEA, which uses the term *autism*, defines the disorder as "a developmental disability significantly affecting verbal and nonverbal communication and social interaction, usually evident before age 3, that adversely affects a child's educational performance." Other characteristics often associated with autism are engagement in repetitive activities and stereotyped movements, resistance to environmental change or change in daily routines, and unusual responses to sensory experience. Autism is one of a number of developmental disorders (autism spectrum disorders: ASD) that influences social, cognitive, and language behaviors under the broader heading of pervasive developmental disability: Asperger's syndrome, Rett's disorder, and childhood disintegrative disorder.

Incidence

ASD occurs in approximately 1 in 250 births, it is four times more common in boys than girls, and the causes of ASD are unknown. Currently, researchers are investigating areas such as neurological deficits, biochemical imbalance, and genetic factors; autism spectrum disorders are not caused by psychological factors (Blackwell & Niederhauser, 2003).

Characteristics

Some or all of the following characteristics may be observed along a continuum of severity: communication problems; difficulty in relating to people, objects, and events; unusual play with toys and other objects; difficulty with changes in routine or familiar surroundings; and stereotypical behavioral patterns. Children with ASD vary widely in abilities, intelligence, and behaviors. Some children do not speak; others have limited language that often includes repeated phrases or conversations. Children with more advanced language skills tend to talk about a limited number of topics, have difficulty with abstract concepts, and have limited knowledge-based interests (Gerber, 2003). Despite the ability to use more sophisticated language forms and functions, their social interactions and emotional skills are not commensurate. José is diagnosed with autism, and ultimately he will develop the ability to recognize social and emotional differences within himself that he cannot regulate.

Pragmatic Abilities

Children with autism evidence severe deficits in communicative functions that contribute to their rigid and socially limited use of language. As an infant and toddler, José does not produce or understand gestural and communicative behaviors. He is not able to develop the earliest communicative interactions (vocal, gaze, and gestural behaviors), all of which provide the underpinnings for interactional patterns of behavior (Klinger & Renner, 2000). For example, when there is some kind of extended reaching, it usually signals José's request for an object, rather than an indication of the object's location or existence. José's inability to determine his own limitations in space (i.e., awareness of physical self) interferes with the development of pointing. Children with autism may not develop the following behaviors (Blackwell & Niederhauser, 2003; Woods & Wetherby, 2003):

1. Prototypical behaviors such as protodeclaratives or protoimperatives by 12 months
2. Attention and joint action schemes by 12 months
3. Awareness of agent, action, or object contingencies by 18 months

4. Turn-taking or reciprocal action skills by 12 months
5. Gestural or imitative behaviors by 12 months
6. Babbling by 12 months
7. Single words by 16 months
8. Two-word combinations by 24 months

Because José's prelinguistic behaviors, such as pointing, showing, or turn-taking, are not present, the development of communicative behaviors is different from the acquisition sequence that occurs in typical children. In addition, José is nonresponsive to his peers' verbalizations and social and gestural behaviors. When other children approach, he flaps his hands and moves away. If left alone, José moves about a playroom, avoiding social contacts. He rocks back and forth, spinning and/or twirling objects when he is left alone. Attempts by Maria to get José to look at her are met with physical resistance. José tends to turn his head and body away from a communication partner and to emit infrequent, fleeting gazes from the corners of his eyes.

Semantic and Syntactic Abilities

During the first 36 months, José, like many children with autism, is mute; he emits only perseverative noises, as described by Charman (2004). José did not develop the extensive vocabulary present in typical children of this age because the preintentional and prelinguistic stages were severely limited. Gerber (2003) suggests that the underlying semantic deficits in children with autism relate to an inability to establish meaningful and relevant perceptual–conceptual categories. Unlike typically developing children, José is not able to relate agents, actions, and objects to one another. He is not able to make cohesive and consistent sense of stimuli and experiences within an environment that is continually novel and changing. These conceptual abilities provide the means for typical children to organize their physical experiences into manageable and related categories (Tiegerman-Farber, 2002a).

Mutism includes a range of behavior, from periods of total silence to the production of meaningless sounds (i.e., used for self-stimulatory rather than communicative purposes). Most, if not all, children with autism progress through a period of mutism. Some autistic children remain mute all their lives. Eisenberg (1956) posits a critical speech period and proposes that if functional speech is not developed by 6 years of age there is little probability of it developing thereafter.

Perceptual Abilities

Little is known about how children with autism perceive their environments. Assumptions are made on the basis of their patterns of interaction, that is, the way in which they relate to agents, actions, and objects. José's behavioral characteristics provide some indication of his internal operations and his reactions to the impinging world. Words, voices, faces, and gestures are no more than rapidly changing stimuli, like changes in color, that are transient and difficult to grasp. Adults handle José and do things to him; what are all these people doing? All the faces and changing expressions; what do they mean? From moment to moment the environment is changing (Tiegerman-Farber, 2002a). José struggles to maintain a ritualized and ordered environment. His tantrums are the result of frustration and confusion. José's self-stimulation, which is typical of children with autism, can be seen as an attempt to reestablish sameness (Tiegerman-Farber, 2002a). Maria notes that José exhibits self-stimulatory behaviors when he is presented with a new situation or when an unanticipated change occurs during an activity.

Cognitive and Play Abilities

It is generally acknowledged that play is important to the development of adaptability, learning, cognition, and social behavior (Weisler & McCall, 1976). The function of play is to exercise and develop manipulative and interactional strategies that children later integrate into more sophisticated task-oriented sequences (Terpstra, Higgins, & Pierce, 2002a). A more general theory suggests that in play children learn to affect and control activities they are unable to execute or dominate in other contexts. Thus, play has a cognitive, social, and integrative function in development.

The process of play that naturally results in the integration of new knowledge and the application of learned behavior to new situations does not occur in José. Once José fixates on one kind of object performance, such as spinning objects, he retains this primitive manipulative pattern as a mode of manipulation. Buschbacher and Fox (2003) documented how autistic children learn to manipulate by means of temper tantrums and disruptive behaviors. José evidences these behaviors. Withdrawal from the environment also makes it difficult to determine if he does not know how to play, if he lacks the opportunity to play, or both. There is a cyclical relationship between José's bizarre ritualistic performances and his inability to integrate experiences within the environment, causing even further withdrawal.

Tiegerman-Farber (2002a) states that the child with autism attempts to create an inner world to establish and maintain an internal order that cannot be controlled externally. Self-stimulatory and ritualistic behaviors are the result of José's distorted perceptions of his environment. José sits for hours rocking back and forth. Some researchers suggest that sensory, perceptual, and intellectual pathways are pathologically involved, limiting sensory and motor development and thereby resulting in this type of behavior (Teitelbaum, Teitelbaum, Nye, Fryman, & Maurer, 1998). Basic skills, such as banging, shaking, rolling, or throwing, do not become progressively more complex, as would be expected (Tiegerman-Farber, 2002a).

Social and Emotional Abilities

José's interpersonal deficits manifest themselves in his lack of gaze interactions and physical contacts, as well as in severe limitations in cooperative play and social interactions. José withdraws from the approach and touch of others and becomes rigid or stiff when he is held or cuddled. When José does not respond to or withdraws from others, is there a feeling of frustration and/or rejection? Consider how José's mother and Jeremy (a $2\frac{1}{2}$-year-old typical peer) describe their interactions with José.

MARIA: It is difficult to get close to a child who always pushes you away; interacting with José is not reinforcing.

JEREMY: José no like me.

Njiokiktjien and colleagues (2001) indicate that social and affective deficits are the most salient characteristics of children with autism. Although described as withdrawn and unresponsive to other people, children with autism are not uniformly aloof and isolated. The repertoire of behaviors José uses with his mother is not the same as that used with strangers. The difference in behavioral responsiveness can be considered as evidence of José's attachment to his mother.

Adolphs, Sears, and Piven (2001) report that children with autism display specific deficits in the area of affective expression. Their results contradict the common perception that children with autism have a flat affective response pattern and that their affective responses are always inappropriate and unrelated to the social context. The children in their study display smiling and laughing behaviors that appear to be appropriately related to the interactional situation. By means of his negative reactions, José also shows an ability to differentially respond to various partners.

Temper Tantrums

Temper tantrums can be either self-abusive or aggressive in form. The self-abusive and aggressive behaviors José exhibits include the following: pulling hair, biting, scratching, head banging, pinching, head butting, and hitting. The difference between self-abusive and aggressive behaviors is the direction of the behavior, whether it is toward self or toward others (Tiegerman-Farber, 2002a). One difficulty related to José's temper tantrums is the intensity of his reactions to even a minute change in the environment. José's mother fears that the older and bigger he gets, the harder it will be for her to manage his behaviors.

Blackwell and Niederhauser (2003) have documented the unpredictableness of tantrums in children with autism. Sometimes only a tiny—or what seems to be tiny—change occurs (e.g., putting the Snoopy cup in a different place). Contributing to Maria's anxiety is her inability to identify what has precipitated a temper tantrum. Mirenda (1997) notes that contextual "escape" explains 63% of a child's aggressive behaviors. Another difficulty is that José is not easily comforted, and his tantrums last for an extended period of time. Maria often notes that it is almost impossible to make him stop once he has started: "He's like a train coming down a hill." McCracken (2002) notes that tantrums can also include self-injurious behaviors. José screams uncontrollably once a tantrum has started; he may bite his hands and bang his head on the floor. Since the tantrums are sudden, José's mother does everything she can to avoid them, including staying at home. Maria feels trapped, and José is further isolated from experiencing real-world social experiences.

Ritualistic Behavior

José exhibits several ritualized sequences in the same way, in the same order, repeatedly. He drinks from a certain cup at home and puts his cup in a specific place on the table. When changes are made in José's environment, he attempts to reorganize the context to return objects to specific places. José's behaviors are generally part of a ritualized pattern that serves to further limit his exploratory experiences within a social environment.

Self-Stimulatory Behavior

Self-stimulation includes high-frequency behaviors traditionally described as noncommunicative and noninteractional (Dempsey & Foreman, 2001). José emits these behaviors when he wants to withdraw from the environment. This usually occurs when he cannot cope with direct input from teaching or instruction. Because José's self-stimulatory behaviors are nonprogressive, they interfere with his learning. Behavioral approaches to training children with autism have been used more frequently to decrease the frequency of such behaviors by changing the environmental consequences that follow. José appears to use self-stimulatory behaviors as a means of either reducing his anxiety in a new situation or withdrawing from something he does not want to do.

Erratic Responses to Stimuli

José often places his hands over his eyes and ears to block out the slightest changes in light or sound. He runs to a corner to rock back and forth; this heightened or excessive sensitivity to stimuli is called *hypersensitivity*. At other times, a child may not react to loud noises or respond to his name being called; this is called *hyposensitivity* to stimulation, which has been discussed in the research of Baranek, Foster, and Berkson (1997) and Dawson and Watling (2000). Maria indicates that at those moments "José was someplace else."

Strengths-Based Description

Instead of describing José's deficits during this period of development, consider Box 2.1, which was written by a speech-language pathologist as an alternative description within her toddler classroom report.

BOX 2.1

José responds differentially within various contexts, given his familiarity with that context. He is able to indicate his preferences for the food items he likes and dislikes. He approaches peers and adults when a preferred food item is offered, and he remains engaged as long as the item is available. When he does not want an object or to engage in an activity, he indicates his rejection by pushing the object away, walking away, or flapping his hands. He is interested in manipulating objects that can be twirled, shaken, or turned on and off. He is able to signal his interest in an object by approaching the person who has it or the person who can get it for him. When José wants physical contact, he will move close and/or attempt to sit in the person's lap. He indicates his awareness of people by interacting differently with various communicators. He approaches adults more frequently than he approaches his peers. José indicates his awareness of object relationships within an environment by rearranging objects to maintain their organizational placement. José's ability to reorganize objects highlights his ability to remember and to retrieve information. When José is overwhelmed by ongoing social activities, he withdraws to a separate area to reduce his anxiety level. José attends for long periods of time to music and computer games. He is able to look for a desired object with a search pattern that indicates he remembers the object's past placement. José seems to enjoy climbing, children's rides, roller skating, playground activities, and flashing colored lights. He readily approaches animals and shows an interest in following the animal around the room. He has extraordinary mechanical skills and enjoys taking things apart and putting them back together again. José has the ability to attend to and to maintain an activity that he likes for long periods of time without being distracted by external stimuli.

Use the Companion Website to help you discuss the following:

1. Discuss the importance of observing a child such as José with members of his family, at home, and in a variety of social settings.

2. José has not developed linguistic skills, but he uses conventional and unconventional behaviors to interact. Develop a profile of José and describe these behaviors within a social setting with peers.

3. Discuss the arguments related to the behavioral management of high-frequency, self-stimulatory behaviors and temper tantrums. What is the role of the SLP in managing these behaviors?

Specific Language Impairment: Jeffrey

Many children who exhibit an early language delay do not have physical, sensory, emotional, or cognitive difficulties. Although they do not show gross neurological signs of dysfunction, organizational and processing deficits are characteristics related to language development. In addition, children with specific language impairment (SLI) may demonstrate concomitant emotional and behavioral disorders. Historically, identification of children with SLI has been one of exclusion by ruling out other developmental disabilities as explanations for the child's delays in language development. When differential diagnosis involves an analysis of subtle developmental characteristics, children with specific language impairment may be misdiagnosed or diagnosed later in their development.

Another issue involves the importance of accurately identifying children with early language disorders. A high percentage of children identified in the early intervention system nationally are referred because of concerns about slow language development. Several studies describe a high percentage of these children as late talkers who have a better outcome than toddlers with SLI. Rescorla (2002) believes that these late talkers are a subset of children with SLI and have a predisposition for slower language acquisition (Thal & Katich, 1996; Whitehurst, Fischel, Arnold, & Lonigan, 1992). The inability to accurately distinguish transient from persistent language difficulties heightens concerns about escalating costs and services to late-talking toddlers. As a result, early intervention criteria may require a delay of services for 12 months or more for children whose developmental difference is less than 2 standard deviations (SDs) below the mean.

Finally, there have been attempts to uncover a genetic basis for SLI. Bishop, Price, Dale, and Plomin (2003) suggest that, if there is a family history of language difficulties, there is a greater likelihood of persistent language difficulties.

Because of the history of slavery and the oppression that followed this period, African American families are more likely to be poorer than White families (Kirst-Ashman & Hull, 2001). Educational gaps and employment rates indicate significant differences between African Americans and Whites (Daly, Jennings, Beckett, & Leashore, 1995). Many African American families have a substantial extended family network with flexible roles. Both men and women assume supportive roles, creating both a greater interchange between adults and marital relationships that tend to be egalitarian. Within the African American culture, the church represents the organizational center for the community and family. Historically, church groups have been involved in social and political advocacy to advance the social causes that would increase economic opportunities for African Americans. The church has provided spiritual growth, emotional support, social services, and community activism. About 22% of African American families live in poverty (U.S. Census Bureau, 2005). Poverty rates are significantly worse for families headed by women of color (Stout & McPhail, 1998).

Camille St. James

Camille St. James faces difficult circumstances in raising her child as a single parent without a high school education. To complicate matters, Jeffrey is initially viewed as an oppositionally defiant child. When he is evaluated, he does not meet the criteria to receive early intervention services. Jeffrey is perceived to be and treated as a child with emotional and behavioral disorders, rather than as a child with a specific language impairment. Consider some of the factors that affect Jeffrey's experiences within the early intervention system:

- Behaviors that trigger the diagnosis of specific language impairment are subtle and may not be identified until 3 or 4 years of age, depending on the severity of the problem.
- A lack of consensus exists within the clinical field about the mechanism underlying specific language impairment.
- There is poor predictability concerning transient versus persistent language difficulties.
- Jeffrey's verbal expressive skills are limited, but his nonverbal skills appear to be age appropriate.
- Camille is a young, inexperienced mother and a single parent.
- Jeffrey's pragmatic problems are viewed as social–emotional problems.
- Jeffrey's phonological difficulties are identified as a speech or articulation problem and are not serious enough to warrant services.
- Jeffrey's lexical and morphosyntactic deficits are not evaluated extensively.
- Once identified with an emotional–behavioral disorder (EBD), this description will follow him from program to program.
- Jeffrey's social and emotional problems mask the specific language impairment.

- Early childhood and child-care teachers are not trained to discriminate between pragmatic and behavioral problems; they have limited knowledge of the characteristics of specific language impairment.
- Jeffrey is at risk for rejection by peers.
- The system teaches Jeffrey that negative behaviors effectively get someone's attention.
- Hindsight teaches us that the more subtle the specific language impairment, is, the more likely the diagnosis will be attributable to an emotional–behavioral explanation.

Micro issues for the child: subtle signs of disability, behavioral problems

Mezzo issues for the family: single parent, teenager, inexperienced parent

Macro issues for the system: social–racial prejudice about oppositional behavior in boys; early label EBD follows child

Figure 2.2 lists the family, child, and social factors that are affecting Jeffrey.

Incidence

Estimates of the number of children with specific language impairment vary widely by age and may be much higher than 1% to 3% (Tallal, 1987).

Characteristics

Leonard (1998) notes that "the category of SLI is little more than a terminological way station for groups of children until such time as finer diagnostic categories can be identified" (p. 23). Montgomery (2002) defines SLI children as those who, in the absence of developmental disability, hearing loss, and cognitive deficits, demonstrate

CW 2.4

Use the Companion Website to help you discuss the following:

1. Research the African American experience and adolescent pregnancy to fill in the information on the St. James family.
2. Identify ways of strengthening ethnically sensitive practice.
3. Identify several issues unique to teenage mothers.
4. How is the child with a disability integrated into the African American community?
5. How would a child with a language disorder be affected by family factors such as racism and adolescent parenting?
6. What changes need to be made within the early intervention system to ensure that children with early language disorders are appropriately identified?

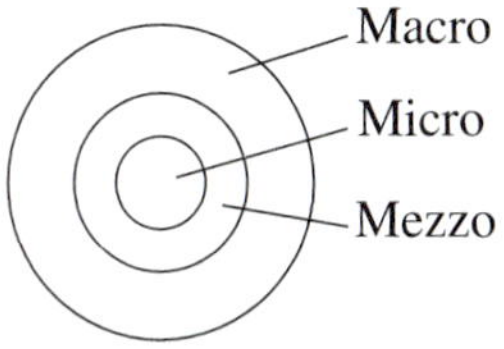

Micro issues
• Description of child _____
• Parents' concerns about child _____
• Important events related to the child _____
• When problem was identified _____
• How problem was identified _____

Mezzo issues
• Family's reactions to child _____
• Parents' relations with other children _____
• Family members_____
• Spousal status _____
• Quality of spousal relationship _____
• Evidence of child abuse_____
• Parental expectations for child _____
• Home environment (number of people, personal space, noise, privacy)_____
• Family resources (work, finances, health care, reason for immigration)_____
• Family supports (friends, extended family, neighbors)_____
• Family beliefs and values (holidays, religion, organizational membership)_____
• Domestic violence _____
• Education level _____
• Language spoken in the home_____
• English language proficiency_____
• Substance abuse _____
• Family values_____
• Specific family concerns _____

Macro issues
• Cultural roles and responsibilities_____
• Gender issues_____
• Major cultural events _____
• Community resources_____
• Cultural practices _____
• Cultural expectations _____
• Unique cultural factors _____

Other factors
• _____
• _____
• _____

FIGURE 2.2
Culturagram for African American Family with Teenage Mother

marked receptive and/or expressive language-learning and performance difficulties. Children with SLI are part of a diverse group whose language deficits may be attributable to a number of factors: generalized deficits in processing capacity, information-processing deficits, phonological working-memory deficits, slower and less efficient linguistic processing, and poor phonological processing.

Children with a specific language impairment may show primary deficits in language production, language comprehension, or both production and comprehension; these characteristics may occur along a continuum of severity. Like children with autism, children with SLI vary widely in abilities, intelligence, and social–emotional behaviors. Recent studies continue to underscore subtle linguistic deficits, pragmatic difficulties, semantic difficulties, auditory-processing deficits, and figurative and metaphorical language difficulties in children with SLI. Jeffrey experiences early and repeated rejections by peers. His poor pragmatic skills result in his teachers perceiving him as socially problematic. They assume that he has a socialization problem, rather than a communication problem. A child such as Jeffrey may continue in a child-care center for several years until his social–emotional problems result in a referral for an evaluation.

Pragmatic Abilities

Whereas José fails to produce or to understand gestural–communicative behaviors, Jeffrey expresses information in sophisticated gesture form more often than his typically developing peers. This use of gestures is described by Evans, Alibali, and McNeil (2001) and reflects the difficulty for many SLI children of organizing acoustic information in speech. Jeffrey does not develop a stable phonological representation of the language system that he hears. He focuses on other forms of communication, such as gesture and movement, along with nonlinguistic contextual cues. This provides Jeffrey with critical information to link linguistic information to communicative interactions. Over time, Jeffrey relies on the input modalities that are not impaired.

In typical children, gestures and speech are integrated to enhance communicative meaning (McNeill, 1992). Similar to the learning process in children who have hearing loss (e.g., Kaitlyn), acoustic information is replaced by alternative forms of communication, and contextual, behavioral, and social information that is not acoustically based. As a visual learner, Jeffrey is highly imitative and gestural in his interactions with his peers. He acquires intentional communication by combining vocal, gaze, and gestural behaviors that provide the underpinnings for social interactional patterns.

Semantic Abilities

Evans, Alibali, and McNeil (2001) note that the acoustic pattern of a word is linked to its meaning (semantics). Since Jeffrey has difficulty developing a phonological representation of the acoustic pattern, he acquires knowledge based on visual, motor–movement, and physical stimuli. Initially, typical children acquire semantic knowledge based on information that can be represented nonverbally. Although, Jeffrey is having difficulty processing acoustic input, he does not appear to be different from other infants and toddlers. Between 12 and 24 months, phonological representations evolve in typical children through repeated patterns of speech that take the form of words. To the extent that Jeffrey can disambiguate communicative exchanges from perceptually based information, he appears to be a typical learner. Jeffrey is unable to transform nonverbal information into verbalized forms. He does not acquire new words readily. Jeffrey's vocabulary is highly restricted and the "naming explosion" that is distinctive for this period occurs only in a limited way for Jeffrey.

Jeffrey's mother, Camille, completes a vocabulary checklist, the Language Development Survey (Rescorla, 1989), when he is 24 months old. The LDS contains 310 words arranged within semantic categories. Camille indicates whether the words listed are either present or absent in Jeffrey's lexicon. At 24 months Jeffrey presents a pattern similar to the late talkers in the Rescorla, Alley, and Christine (2001) study; he has a depressed vocabulary and limited word combinations. Although a child's vocabulary may improve by 36 months, his morphosyntactic skills may still remain impaired. Dale, Price, Bishop, and Plomin (2003) document this pattern of behavior in SLI children.

Jeffrey is in a child-care program and he looks and acts like a typical child except for his behavior. His child-care worker expresses concerns about Jeffrey's behavior, not about his semantic difficulties. Although Jeffrey is evaluated through the early intervention system, he does not present a 33% delay in communication. He plays well with peers, he follows the routines, and he appears to understand verbal directives. At this point there is not enough of a developmental difference, enough of a delay, for Jeffrey to be classified as developmentally delayed so that he can receive services. Jeffrey's compensatory and gestural skills are deceiving; the language assessments used do not accurately reflect his problem between 12 and 30 months.

Syntactic Abilities

Children's phonological deficits also affect the acquisition of morphosyntactic skills (Fey, Long, & Finestack, 2003). Jeffrey's productions are limited to a sequence of simple words, rather than a combination of words indicating emerging sentence structure. Children with SLI reduce syntactic complexity to simple, active, declarative structures that are accompanied by gestures and nonverbal behaviors (Perkins, 2001). Jeffrey's language productions are often reduced to word repetitions and/or gestures. When he feels pressured to communicate, he becomes easily frustrated with peers who do not respond readily to his initiatives. At 36 months, Jeffrey's syntactic level of production is similar to that of a younger peer of 24 months.

Phonological Abilities

Phonological awareness is defined as the ability to reflect on and manipulate the sound structure of words (Ellis, 1993). During the first 36 months of life, ongoing exposure to the acoustic system results in the recognition of meaningful units of sound that are finite and repeated to create word forms. Jeffrey does not follow the typical developmental pattern for the acquisition of phonological skills. He does not appear to have oromotor difficulties, so verbal apraxia is not a complicating factor. Children learn that specific phonological rules determine which phonetic structures are possible in different word positions and combinations. The rules that describe the phonological constructions of words are referred to as phonotactic constraints (Trask, 1996). Given phonological processing problems, variables such as prosody, word length, and syllable structure also affect lexical acquisition (Storkel & Rogers, 2000). Jeffrey does not do the following:

1. Play with the sounds of speech in real and nonsense words
2. Develop representational patterns for phoneme categories
3. Readily develop novel words
4. Perceive word boundaries or syllable configurations

For the first 36 months, Jeffrey's gestural and nonverbal skills compensate for his phonological and semantic delays. The speech and language evaluation performed through the early intervention system measures comprehension ability in terms of lexical acquisition. The SLP provides the phonological form of the word, and Jeffrey points to the related referent, given a number of possibilities. If testing had required Jeffrey to identify the lexical item by phonological production as well, his processing deficits, particularly in novel word forms, would have indicated the following:

1. If he had a fully developed phonological system, given his age
2. His ability to reproduce nonword forms, given early versus later phonemes
3. His production of phonemes in various word positions: initial, middle, and final (Stoel-Gammon, 1998; Storkel & Rogers, 2000)

For children with SLI, early identification is affected by the professional's awareness of the relationship between phonological development and lexical acquisition. In this case, the early intervention team recommends *monitoring* for Jeffrey because he appears to be a late talker. The relationship between phonology and semantics needs to be emphasized to professionals, the early childhood teachers, psychologists, and special educators who might assume that the late-talking toddler will catch up in 6 months. The ability to distinguish between transient and persistent language difficulties in late talkers has critical implications for children (Paul, 2000). The lack of valid formal assessments leaves decision making about high-risk children, particularly for those who are linguistically and culturally diverse, to parent questionnaires and/or professional judgments. Price, Bishop, and Plomin (2003) believe that some children who evidence delay in the acquisition of language milestones may possibly experience a persistent disorder that will affect communication and academic achievement.

Cognitive Abilities

By definition, children with SLI are identified by means of a process of exclusion. They do not develop age-appropriate linguistic skills, although they perform within the typical range on standardized nonverbal tests of intelligence. Thus, deficits in emotional, cognitive, neurological, and perceptual areas are ruled out prior to the diagnosis of SLI (Montgomery, 2002). Several studies indicate that linguistic deficits are a function of processing difficulties: phonological working memory, verbal working memory, functional working memory, articulatory planning, and phonological coding (Catts,

2001; Chiat, 2001; Crosbie, Dodd, & Howard, 2002; Felton & Pepper, 1995; Orsolini, Sechi, Maronato, Bonvino, & Corcelli, 2001).

Bishop (1997) believes there is a relationship between the range of variation in cognitive deficits and the specific production and comprehension problems in children with SLI. This relationship is not clearly defined and needs to be examined more clearly. Jeffrey acquires his physical knowledge experientially. He interacts with toys and objects in his environment by manipulating materials and pieces appropriately. He is able to engage in symbolic play by using a plate for a hat and in pretend play by using miniature plastic kitchen furniture. Jeffrey is able to play by himself with puzzles, blocks, and books. He plays cooperatively with other children in group activities that are directed by an adult and dyadically when the activity involves creative arts and crafts projects. He also engages in playground games with peers. He sits during circle time and responds appropriately to verbal and nonverbal cues; he *appears* to understand his teacher's directions and instructions.

Social and Emotional Abilities

Because some children with SLI are not identified until elementary school, children's emotional frustrations may be expressed behaviorally (Fujiki, Brinton, & Clarke, 2002). Jeffrey has difficulty expressing his feelings along with communicating his needs. Socially, a child with SLI may be perceived by his teachers as difficult, rather than as a child with difficulty in communicating and therefore in need of contextual modifications and supports. Jeffrey is treated as a child who has behavioral and emotional problems that are attributed to family factors such as low SES, poor parenting, and lack of supervision. Jeffrey's typical peers are often frightened by his outbursts and temper tantrums. The strategy in the child-care program is to remove Jeffrey when he becomes difficult, and over time his peers separate themselves from him when he starts to act inappropriately. The social process becomes a vicious cycle of Jeffrey inappropriately expressing his frustration, followed by negative reactions from peers and adults who systematically isolate him for greater periods of time. He is a social failure when he is suspended from childcare, and his record precedes him from this point forward.

Jeffrey's social experiences are not positive. Over time, without appropriate intervention, he will become what he is perceived to be, a child with an emotional–behavioral disorder (EBD), rather than a child with a specific language impairment (SLI). Jeffrey understands the negative reactions from peers: Don't like him. . . . Don't play with Jeffrey. He bites. Go away. As a result, Jeffrey is generally left alone, playing by himself or seeking out the company of adults. By the time Jeffrey is 36 months, he has acquired a repertoire of negative behaviors that work to get the attention of adults and peers, but result in repeated rejection. Jeffrey learns to function on the outside of his peer group with other children who have poor social skills. He accepts the rejection and watches other children play together. Children with SLI may become increasingly anxious about social situations and transitional changes, given their negative experiences (Webster-Stratton & Reid, 2004). Jeffrey is deprived of the opportunities to learn about the rules of social interaction and to apply his language skills to the conversational exchanges that would become a foundation for more sophisticated and formalized social activities in elementary school.

Strengths-Based Description

Instead of describing Jeffrey's deficits during this period of development, consider the descriptive profile in Box 2.2.

BOX 2.2

Jeffrey is communicative and gestural with peers and adults. He has strong motor skills and enjoys blocks, puzzles, and complex manipulative toys. He can sit for long periods of time with activities such as coloring, Lego blocks, computer games, picture books, trucks, and trains. He enjoys watching other children play and socialize. He can follow complex routines and has an excellent memory for games and puzzles. He has advanced gross- and fine-motor skills. He can manipulate, categorize, and organize smaller objects. He can complete activities by watching other children perform a task. He has strong visual–spatial and incidental learning skills. He is highly imitative and presents an early talent for musical instruments and drawing. He can identify colors, shapes, and numbers even at this early age.

 Use the Companion Website to help you discuss the following:

1. Discuss the importance of observing a child such as Jeffrey with members of his family, at home, and in a variety of social settings. What information could be critical to the process of differential diagnosis?

2. Describe Jeffrey's speech and compare his phonological development to José's.

3. Discuss the ethical issues related to the use of management techniques with children who have behavioral and emotional problems. Are SLPs and child-care workers adequately trained to use such techniques? Do some research to answer this question and discuss your position on the issue.

4. Describe several theoretical models related to specific language impairment.

5. Discuss the controversy related to the issue of late talkers.

Hearing Loss: Kaitlyn

Along with other minority groups, the Deaf Community has experienced discriminatory practices for many years. This discrimination has been compounded by their hearing and language differences. Deaf persons have functioned separately and apart from mainstream society for decades (Reisler, 2003). The use of sign language, which was eventually recognized as a formal language with its own syntax, has been the primary factor unifying the Deaf Community. Sign language is responsible for the development of Deaf Culture, group identity, and educational practices within separate schools for children. The sense of pride for their culture, along with effective group advocacy, has created a rich history of narrative tradition, social values, and creative arts in the Deaf Community.

Many members of the Deaf Community do not perceive themselves as having a disability that requires reconstructive repair (deHalleux & Poncelet, 2001). With advances in technology, however, the cochlear implant is now used by many young children. This has fueled a debate between hearing and deaf adults about the implant's negative effect on Deaf Culture and language. Both the number of children with severe hearing loss and enrollment in schools for the deaf have been declining (Johnston, 2004). An increasing number of children with hearing loss who benefit from implant technology are now included in general-education classes in public schools. As the number of children enrolled in schools for the deaf declines, what will happen to Deaf Culture and language when the primary social identification becomes the mainstream hearing world? Many researchers describe the campaign by hearing educators to "conquer deafness" as offensive to members of the Deaf Community (Tolson, 1999).

Katherine Whiteside

Katherine's mother and mother-in-law are very helpful, but Connor's drinking problem has gotten worse. Although Kaitlyn is diagnosed with a hearing loss, Connor remains uninvolved. Katherine makes all the important decisions about Kaitlyn. Kaitlyn is diagnosed with a hearing loss, and the primary issue for Kaitlyn involves the least restrictive environment. Kaitlyn undergoes surgery for a cochlear implant and is placed in an early intervention program for children who are deaf. Consider some factors that affect Kaitlyn's experiences within the early intervention system:

- The severity of Kaitlyn's hearing loss is easy to identify once an audiological evaluation is performed.
- There are conflicting educational philosophies about the least restrictive environment for children who are deaf or hard of hearing.
- There is disagreement within the Deaf Community about the role of cochlear implants.
- There are conflicting educational methodologies: the total communication approach versus the aural–oral approach.
- Clinical practitioners pressure Katherine to provide Kaitlyn with a cochlear implant and place her in an early childhood program with hearing children.
- Katherine makes a difficult decision, realizing that the Deaf Community does not really accept her and that she may be communicatively and socially separated from Kaitlyn as she gets older.
- Hearing parents must accept that their child's integration within the Deaf Community is separation from the hearing world.
- Members of the Deaf Community do not see themselves as having a disability.
- Katherine learns to sign, but she will never learn the metaphoric–inferential aspects of American Sign Language, which is the language of the Deaf Community.

CW 2.5

Use the Companion Website to help you discuss the following:

1. Identify several issues that are unique to deaf children who have hearing rather than deaf parents.

2. How is the child who is deaf integrated into the hearing world and the Deaf Community?

3. How would a child with a language disorder be affected by these family factors?

- In the hearing world, Kaitlyn is viewed as having a disability.
- In the Deaf Community, Kaitlyn is viewed as a typical child. Katherine feels that Kaitlyn's self-esteem is important to her emotional growth.
- Katherine wants Kaitlyn to have friends.
- The Whiteside family lives in a rural farming community where access to services is difficult.

Micro issues for the child: hearing loss, cochlear implant

Mezzo issues for the family: isolated rural community, parents must learn sign language

Macro issues for the system: limited services, extensive travel to access services, pressure to keep child who is deaf in hearing world

Definition of Hearing Loss

Hearing loss is a classification that includes a broad range of hearing disorders. It should be considered in terms of type, classification, and degree. There are three types of hearing loss: conductive, sensorineural, and mixed.

Incidence

The overall estimates of congenital hearing loss in the United States are 1 to 6 per 1000 births (Cunningham & Cox, 2003; Kemper Downs, 2000).

Conductive Hearing Loss

Conductive hearing loss refers to the impedance of sound either in the outer ear or middle ear (Martin & Clark, 2000), with the inner ear functioning normally. Conductive hearing losses have a limit of 60 decibels (dB) and are often medically treatable. Otitis media is a common cause of a temporary conductive hearing loss and occurs most frequently during the first 3 years of life. It is generally caused by eustachian tube dysfunction (Stach, 1997), which is secondary to upper respiratory infection and results in acute otitis media.

Acute otitis media is an active inflammation and an infection of the middle-ear space. It usually lasts up to 5 weeks. Subacute otitis media begins at 6 weeks and lasts up to 11 weeks, and chronic otitis media is from 12 weeks onward (Pashley, 1984).

Otitis can be painful and develop quickly. When the middle-ear space begins to fill with fluid, the fluid can be either serous, which is thin, watery, and clear, or purulent, which is a thick pus. If the buildup of fluid is rapid and intense, the tympanic membrane can rupture. Many times treatment of chronic otitis media includes the insertion of a small tube through the tympanic membrane.

Other causes of conductive hearing loss are atresia, stenosis, complete stapes fixation, ossicular discontinuity, or accumulation of ear wax or cerumen that becomes impacted. In addition, cholesteatoma is another cause of conductive hearing loss. A cholesteatoma is a cyst that is lined internally with squamous epithelium (scalelike skin). The cyst originates from the upper part of the tympanic membrane and forms a pouch. Eventually, this cyst can cause perforation of the tympanic membrane and erode the ossicles of the middle ear. Generally, children with conductive hearing loss are not candidates for special-education programs designed specifically for children who are deaf.

Sensorineural Hearing Loss

A sensorineural hearing loss is caused by a damaged sensory end organ, the cochlear hair cells, or the auditory nerve. The damage may have occurred during fetal development or from injury or infection. Hearing loss is often genetically linked; consequently, when children are born into a family with a history of hearing loss, the newborn infant is considered to be at risk for hearing loss. Sensorineural hearing losses are not medically treatable and are generally irreversible (Radziewicz & Antonellis, 2002).

Mixed Hearing Loss

A mixed hearing loss is one that involves both a sensorineural and conductive hearing-loss component. Consequently, both the conductive and sensorineural mechanisms are involved. Young children often suffer from otitis media, which can result in a conductive hearing loss.

Degree of Hearing Loss

Martin and Clark (2000) provide an audiometric scale in Table 2.1 to classify hearing-loss severity. This scale refers to the ANSI 1996 standards, and decibels (dB) are a measure of sound intensity. The pure tone average is the average of thresholds of 500, 1000, and 2000 hertz (Hz), respectively. These three frequencies are called the *speech frequencies*.

Pragmatic Abilities

Children with severe hearing loss communicate early on by using prelinguistic communicative functions such as gestures. Indeed, they can often express a wide range of pragmatic intentions through nonverbal means. By age 2, the pragmatic functions of the child with hearing loss are equal to the pragmatic abilities of the hearing child. However, specific semantic functions develop at a slower rate for the child with hearing loss. Because of the hearing loss, the child uses nonverbal behavior more frequently than verbal behavior, and it is extremely difficult to code meaning through nonlinguistic means (Curtis, Prutting, & Lowell, 1979). Children with hearing loss develop the same semantic categories and communicative intentions as do young normal-hearing children, although development of their linguistic semantic abilities occurs at a slower rate. This is

TABLE 2.1   Audiometric Scale

Pure Tone Average (dB)	Degree of Hearing Loss
−10–15	None
16–25	Slight
26–40	Mild
41–55	Moderate
56–70	Moderately severe
71–90	Severe
91+	Profound

Source: Martin and Clark, 2000.

true for young children who are in either an aural–oral environment or a total communication environment. Kaitlyn is very good at producing and understanding gestural communicative behaviors. She is often better at expressing information in gesture than typically developing peers. Because Kaitlyn is in an environment that utilizes signs, her semantic development begins to catch up with her pragmatic development. She attaches sign words to her protoimperatives. For example, at age 13 months, when she finishes eating a cookie, she executes the sign for "more" while pointing to the cookie box.

Semantic Abilities

Semantic development in Kaitlyn begins when she attaches meaning to signs. Because she is deaf, she does not have the acoustic information on which to attach meaning to a spoken word (acoustic pattern). Instead, she attaches meaning to a visual representation of a word. Kaitlyn's early exposure to sign language enables her to develop a signed linguistic system that mirrors that of hearing toddlers. She first signs single words, such as "more," "doggie," or "want." Eventually, as her sign vocabulary expands, she puts two signs together: "cookie more," "want go." Kaitlyn's sign words are powerful because she uses them to express her wants. Kaitlyn is learning how to communicate effectively and efficiently with signs. Often, children who are exposed to sign language early on develop receptive and expressive single-word-sign vocabularies that are commensurate with their hearing peers. Kaitlyn enjoys going to the Mission School for the Deaf because she can easily interact with other children who also sign.

Syntactic Abilities

Syntactic development in children with hearing loss depends on the same variables as do other aspects of language development. Degree of hearing loss, age of onset of loss, and time of amplification significantly affect the development of syntax. One cannot address the subject of syntax without discussing the mode of communication used by the child. If a child is taught using an aural–oral approach, the syntax that develops is spoken-English syntax.

Several factors have been linked to the development of spoken language. Mussulmen and Kircacli-Iftar (1996) describe the following as important factors supporting language development: early use of binaural ear-level aids, more highly educated mothers, auditory–verbal or auditory–oral instruction, reliance on spoken language as a method of communication, individualized instruction, integration, and structured teaching by parents and a high commitment to their child's spoken language. Yoshinaga-Itano (2003) indicates that, for children who are deaf or hard of hearing and who have hearing parents, the predictors of successful developmental outcomes are the age of identification of the hearing loss and the age of initiation of intervention services.

Kaitlyn is in a total communication environment that includes signing and speech. By 30 months of age she is signing sentences such as "I want ball" and "Give me cookie." Her syntax is developing like that of hearing children. When Kaitlyn receives her implant, she continues to use sign language. However, it is expected that eventually she will rely more on her hearing to enable her to approximate speech more accurately. Implantation gives Kaitlyn a greater range of acoustic information on which to map meaning.

Cognitive Abilities

The cognitive development of the child with hearing loss has been examined and measured from 1900 to the present (Pinter, Eisenson, & Stanton, 1941; Pinter & Patterson, 1916; Pinter & Reamer, 1920). In the 1960s and 1970s, it was determined that there is very little difference between the cognitive abilities of the deaf and hearing populations (Furth, 1966; Furth, 1973; Furth & Youniss, 1965; Vernon, 1967). Meadow (1980) notes that children with hearing loss score within the normal range on intelligence tests when the tests are administered with nonverbal instructions and when the children do not have to respond verbally. Hence, intelligence tests such as the *Test of Non Verbal Intelligence*, Third Edition (TONI-3) (Brown, Sherbonou, & Johnsen, 1997) are appropriate for use with children with hearing loss. Furthermore, such children learn concepts in the same manner and in the same sequence as hearing children. However, the rate of concept development is somewhat delayed when compared with hearing children because of the secondary effects of auditory and experiential deprivation. Kaitlyn learns quickly. Signs enable her to understand what is happening around her and she develops basic concepts. For example, she learns the signs for "in," "off," "up," "down," "between," "over." These sign words are used in school and therapy, and Katherine Whiteside uses them at home. By the time Kaitlyn is 3 years old, she has acquired the same basic concepts as the hearing child.

Phonological Abilities

The phonological development of children with hearing loss is generally dictated by the amount of residual hearing, the onset of the hearing loss, and the time of amplification fitting. The type of amplification, whether hearing aid or cochlear implant, also goes into the mix. If a child has a severe hearing loss in the high frequencies, it is very unlikely that high-frequency sounds will become part of the child's spoken repertoire. Since the vowels are the most easily heard, vowels emerge early on before the consonants. However, the "visible" consonants, those that are more readily seen on the lips, can be acquired. Some visible sounds are /p/, /f/, and /m/. These are early developing phonemes for normal-hearing children. Dunn and Newton (1986) indicate in a literature review on the speech development of children with hearing loss that development is generally described in terms of speech errors. Most errors are similar to those of younger, normal-hearing children. The speech of the child with hearing loss is marked by multiple deletions and substitutions, and often final consonants are deleted. In addition, the supersegmentals of speech are also deviant. Speech rate is slow and stress is inappropriate. Vocal resonance is disordered, with either hypernasality or hyponasality. Vowels are often distorted because of tongue movement and positioning restrictions (Ling, 1976). Often vowels tend to be neutralized.

Furthermore, idiosyncratic errors also impair speech intelligibility (Levitt & Stromberg, 1983; Stoel-Gammon, 1987), which is affected by several factors; the degree of hearing loss is the predominant one. There is negative correlation between hearing level and speech intelligibility (Boothroyd, 1969). Smith (1975) indicates that children with severe to profound hearing loss with measurable thresholds up to 3000 Hz have better speech intelligibility than children with hearing thresholds below 3000 Hz. Monsen (1978) indicates that children with hearing loss who have hearing levels better than 90 dB have better speech intelligibility than children whose hearing loss is greater than 90 dB.

Today, with cochlear implants being provided to more deaf children, the outcomes for speech intelligibility are changing. The implant makes available to the child a greater range of acoustic information than can be provided by conventional hearing aids (Tyler, Davis, & Lansing, 1987). With this expanded auditory information the child can more readily approximate normal speech and many times does. Furthermore, increased auditory stimuli enable the child to access the phonological code of English and become more prepared to learn to read and write. Before the implant, Kaitlyn's phonological development was delayed. She produced few consonants, and most of her early vocalizations were vowel sounds. After the implant, more consonants and vowels became part of her phonological repertoire.

Hearing Loss and Language Development

Hearing loss has an enormous negative impact on language development. The brain responds to auditory stimulation even when the fetus is in utero. The normal-hearing newborn child's brain is bombarded with sounds. All this auditory stimulation is critical to the development of language. When an infant has a hearing loss, several variables determine the effect that hearing loss will have on language development:

- Degree of hearing loss
- Age of onset of loss
- Slope or configuration of hearing loss
- Age of identification of hearing loss
- Age of habilitation
- Amount of habilitation
- Type of habilitation (Quigley & Kretschmer, 1982)

Identification

Because language development begins even before birth, an organized infant screening procedure should be in place to identify those infants who may have hearing losses.

Infant screening is different from a hearing evaluation. These screenings identify children who *may* have a hearing loss. Infant screenings do not identify the type or degree of hearing loss. In addition, they give a certain percentage of false negative results (i.e., the results indicate no hearing loss when there is) and false positive results (i.e., the results indicate hearing loss when there is no loss). In spite of this, newborn hearing screenings are valuable, and ASHA has lobbied diligently for universal newborn screenings.

In 1997, the National Institute on Deafness and Other Communication Disorders' (NIDCD) Workshop on Universal Newborn Hearing Screening recommended that these screenings be conducted in the United States. To date, over three quarters of the states have enacted legislation that provides such screening to newborns. If newborn children are screened for hearing loss in hospital nurseries before discharge, there is a greater likelihood that a child with a hearing loss will experience academic, social, and vocational success (NIH, 1997).

Yoshinaga-Itano and Apuzzo (1998a) conducted a study in Colorado and found that language development is significantly delayed when a hearing loss is not identified until after a child is 6 months of age. If infants do not receive hearing screenings shortly after birth while still in the hospital, it is likely that a hearing loss, if present, will not be identified until long after 6 months of age. These authors found that children who are identified with a hearing loss before 6 months of age and who receive early home intervention perform significantly better in measurements of expressive language, comprehension of language, and development of concepts than children who are identified after 6 months of age (Yoshinaga-Itano & Apuzzo, 1998b).

Amplification

Once a child is found to have a hearing loss, the audiologist must work with the family to determine the type of amplification to be used. In the past the main option was a hearing aid. However, today the cochlear implant is available worldwide. Today approximately 50,000 infants and children have been implanted. Hearing aids come in many types, and the audiologist and family work together to fit the child with an appropriate device.

Cochlear Implants

Cochlear implantation is the most recent and exciting treatment for deafness. Originally, cochlear implants were performed on adults only, but today children as young as 12 months are being implanted. Research on children with cochlear implants shows that such children progress more rapidly and have higher reading achievement than children using conventional hearing aids (Spencer, Tomblin, & Gantz, 1997; Tomblin, Spencer, Flock, Tyler, & Gantz, 1999).

Cochlear implants typically consist of internal and external components. The microphone, processor, and transmitter are the external components. The electrode array and receiver stimulator are the internal components. Originally, only single-channel, single-electrode devices were used. Later, multichannel systems with multiple electrodes inserted along the cochlea were implanted, resulting in improved speech recognition (Hedley-Williams, Sladen, & Tharpe, 2003).

Cochlear Implant Candidacy

Although cochlear implants have been shown to be effective and integral to the rehabilitation of children with hearing loss, not all infants are candidates for these devices. The FDA suggests that children who have bilateral profound sensorineural hearing loss and receive little or no benefit from hearing aids are likely candidates. However, these criteria are very broad, and because implantation involves irreversible surgery and intense habilitation, other considerations need to be factored into the candidacy process:

- **Age.** Children older than 10 years have a poorer prognosis.
- **Duration of deafness.** Less than 4 years, no concern; more than 8 years, great concern.
- **Cochlea.** Normal cochlea, no concern; congenital anomalies, more concern.
- **Functional hearing.** The amount of preimplantation hearing aid use; the more hearing aid use, the better the prognosis.
- **Language.** The linguistic system; the higher the level at preimplant, the better the prognosis. (Nevins & Chute, 1997)

Cochlear implantation does not mean that the child will hear normally and immediately develop good speech. Realistic outcomes and the means to such outcomes must be discussed before the cochlea is implanted.

Recently, Most and Zaidman-Zait (2003) examined the needs of the parents of children who were implant candidates or current implant users. They found that optimal intervention for families must involve a team of professionals, such as audiologist, surgeon, speech-language pathologist, social worker, and psychologist. Information about medical, educational, technical, and communication issues needs to be provided, and emotional support by way of speaking to parents of other implanted children is critical. This intervention needs to occur not only during the assessment period, but also throughout the first year of implantation.

Intervention with Infants and Toddlers

Early on, parents must decide the approach to be used with their child. If the family chooses an aural–oral approach, no sign language is used in the intervention process. If the family prefers the inclusion of sign language in the intervention process, a total communication approach is used. Both approaches are successful, and in many instances one approach is tried and then the family decides on the other. Whatever the approach, the overall goals of intervention are the same: improve the communicative abilities of the child and develop a language system.

Speech and Language Acquisition

The normal-hearing infant is predisposed to language learning, and early sensory input provides the material necessary for the infant to internally organize language. The young child learns how to monitor and control his or her language if given early feedback. The social–emotional and intellectual growth of a child is proportional to a child's ability to relate to others and therefore is contingent on early language training. All the above are true for the young child with a hearing loss as well. The ability to acquire language, either spoken or signed, decreases with age (Emmorey, Belligi, Frederici, & Horn, 1995; Johnson & Newport, 1989; Mayberry & Eichen, 1991; Newport, 1990).

A complex relationship among outcomes with the cochlear implant includes age at implantation and communication teaching strategy. It has been shown that children who receive their implant before the age of 5 attain significant improvement in receptive spoken vocabulary, expressive spoken and/or signed vocabulary, and consonant-production accuracy, regardless of the communication teaching strategy used (aural–oral communication only or total communication), and they develop adequate language skills.

However, for children who receive their implants during early or middle elementary school (between 5 and 10 years), those children in aural–oral-only programs appear to achieve higher expected speech scores and rates of growth in scores over time (Connor, Herber, Arts, & Zwolan, 2000). Other variables also affect outcomes, such as the quality of the educational program (Eccles, Wigfield, & Schiefele, 1998). In addition, family, school, and community variables that influence long-term outcomes for cochlear implant use are more important than the teaching method employed (Bronfenbrenner, 1986).

Interestingly, cochlear implants have both social and academic and communication implications. It has been shown that cochlear implant use has the potential to improve the child's relationships with hearing peers, in spite of the fact that communication obstacles still exist for the cochlear implant user (Bat-Chava & Deignan, 2001).

Social and Emotional Abilities

Because Kaitlyn learns signs early, she is able to communicate with other persons in her environment who sign. Katherine works diligently to use signs whenever she is in Kaitlyn's presence. When Kaitlyn attends the Mission School, she is placed in a small group of signing children where she learns how to use her signs to communicate with peers. Early socialization with peers is the foundation for Kaitlyn's self-esteem. She is learning how to communicate and identify with other children who are deaf. Her cultural identity as a child who is deaf is being developed. Participating in small groups enables Kaitlyn to learn the social rules of communication.

The SLP and teacher make more salient the subtleties of social behavior that Kaitlyn needs to learn. For example, when Kaitlyn and her peers pass the bean bag during circle time, she learns to take turns by waiting for a nod or eye contact. By the time Kaitlyn receives her cochlear implant, she is well on her way to becoming an effective communicator. However, other challenges meet Kaitlyn after she is implanted.

Strengths-Based Description

Kaitlyn is an adequate communicator with adults and peers. She utilizes signs, gestures, vocalizations, and a few words to communicate. Frustration tantrums have decreased. Her attention appears to be good, and she enjoys all the activities that typical children do. Her visual–spatial skills are strong as she readily acquires new signed words. She is very imitative and has copied many things she sees her mother do, such

Scott Cunningham / Merrill

The multidisciplinary team meets to collaboratively interpret clinical data.

as putting a telephone to her ear, putting her finger up to her mouth to indicate "quiet," and shaking her finger at her dog to indicate "no." Kaitlyn will also carefully look at a speaker's face and even turn a person's face toward her when she wants to communicate. Kaitlyn enjoys socializing with adults and peers. She appears to have good indicators that her communicative abilities will continue to develop. See Box 2.3.

BOX 2.3

After Kaitlyn was implanted I realized there are more decisions to be made. Some people suggest that since she can "hear" she should be placed in regular preschool so that she can learn from typical children. I feel that Kaitlyn is still a deaf child, even though she now has a cochlear implant. After the operation she still functions the same way, although I notice that she has become more aware of environmental sounds like our doorbell or the dog barking in the next room, and she is producing some different speech sounds. I was told by the cochlear implant team that she still needs a great deal of speech–language training in order to make maximal use of her implant. This is why I made the decision to keep Kaitlyn in the Mission School for the Deaf. My special-education committee is trying to encourage a less restrictive environment. Kaitlyn is still deaf; she requires an environment where she can continue to develop cognitively, socially, and communicatively all day long. I believe that a continuation in a total communication environment is the *only* appropriate setting for her.

Katherine Whiteside

Use the Companion Website to help you discuss the following:

1. Describe the three different types of hearing loss.

2. What are the positive outcomes of infant screenings?

3. Describe the different types of amplification that can be used with children with hearing loss.

4. Describe the profile of a child who would be a good candidate for a cochlear implant.

5. Why is family structure an important consideration in the postimplant rehabilitation process?

6. How does the use of sign language affect the child who has a cochlear implant? Explain your position on sign language use with children who either have or are considering an implant.

7. Compare and contrast Kaitlyn's early language development with that of Jeffrey's and José's.

8. Many children who are deaf or hard of hearing are born to hearing parents. What factors are integral to positive language outcomes for these children?

9. For those children who are deaf or hard of hearing and born to deaf or hearing-impaired parents, what factors contribute to positive language outcomes?

SUMMARY

In this chapter we describe the early developmental patterns of three children who are different language learners. Children with language disorders are often misdiagnosed because their developmental differences are perceived as being secondary to other problems. States have not developed a uniform definition for language disorders, and the result is great variability in diagnosis and treatment for children with language disorders. As our profession evolves, speech-language pathologists are more interested in identifying signs of developmental differences in younger and younger children. Early identification links the child to the intervention strategies that present the greatest opportunity for language acquisition. It also enables families to be proactive and take the actions necessary to enhance development in their children.

Speech-language pathologists need to be aware of the fact that they are providing services to families and that the child is embedded within the context of the family. Family members provide the means to enhance changes in the child that will generalize to natural social environments. The SLP can help the family recognize and accept behaviors associated with their child's language difference by providing information about language development and facilitation at home.

The SLP also helps parents understand their child's pattern of development. The speech-language pathologist teaches families to recognize their child's learning

FIGURE 2.3

Early Intervention Services Provided, December 2002, 50 states, the District of Columbia, and Puerto Rico

Occupational therapy:	94,155
Physical therapy:	95,008
Speech-language therapy:	140,217
Psychology:	9,225
Family training counseling and home visits:	54,957
Special instruction:	125,934

Source: IDEA Part C Data Fact Sheet, www.ideadata.org/docs/cfactsheetcc.pdf

strengths. The child with autism may respond well to music and be interested in computers. He may be able to take things apart and reassemble them quickly. The child with hearing loss may have good visual memory and be able to interpret facial, social, and contextual cues readily and efficiently. The child with specific language impairment may have exceptional visual–spatial and gross- and fine-motor skills. He may develop early number concepts and excel in math.

Issues such as delay, difference, and deficit-based approaches influence the relationship between the SLP and parents within the therapeutic alliance. The speech-language pathologist works with the family and other members of the collaborative intervention team to incorporate family strengths by means of culturally and ethnically sensitive practices. Most professionals do not receive specific or extensive training on how to engage in such practices. The problem of diversity is further exacerbated by the insufficient number of professionals who are members of various minority groups. Early intervention service coordinators and providers need to be either members of the minority groups with which they work or very knowledgeable and well trained about the diversity groups with whom they work. It is important for SLPs along with other service providers to focus on the family's strengths in developing a therapeutic alliance based on mutual respect. Finally, when children are denied early intervention services, there is a likelihood for later school-based learning problems. With SLPs providing more early intervention services than any other service provider, the significance of our profession within the early intervention system is confirmed (see Figure 2.3).

CHAPTER

3

Collaborative Language Assessment and Decision Making for Infants and Toddlers

Chapter Objectives

After studying this chapter, you should be able to answer the following questions:

1. How has assessment changed since the implementation of Part C of PL 99-457?

2. What are cultural differences and what are the implications for assessment?

3. What are different types of assessment?

4. What factors place a child at risk?

5. What is ecological validity?

6. What areas are assessed when evaluating children from birth to 3?

7. Who are the various stakeholders in collaborative decision making?

8. What is a match–mismatch model?

9. What kinds of modifications need to be made to meet the needs of linguistically and culturally diverse families in a family-centered assessment?

The Families Speak

I don't understand José's problem. No one in my family or community has a problem like this. My husband and I are trying hard to learn English. It is hard enough for José to talk; Spanish and English at home must be very confusing. I feel guilty about José missing so much. If I had spoken English, he would have received services earlier. I don't like working with José, I'm his mother not his teacher. When the therapists watch me, I get uncomfortable. I'm afraid of doing the wrong thing. I don't want anyone to think that I'm not a good mother.

Maria Martinez

I am feeling overwhelmed and indecisive. I have spoken to the speech-language pathologist at the Mission School for the Deaf about the emotional conflicts concerning language and communication development in a family with a deaf child. When I spoke to the evaluator from the Carlyle School, she described Kaitlyn as a child with a hearing loss who fits the criteria for a cochlear implant. She stressed that the goal of the Carlyle School is to maximize Kaitlyn's hearing and teach her to speak so that she functions in a hearing world. She also indicated that, as hearing parents, we will be able to talk to Kaitlyn when she learns speech. If Kaitlyn were to go to a school for the deaf, such as the Mission School, we will have to learn sign language and communication will be harder for us. Also, Kaitlyn will become a part of the Deaf Community, which we will never really be a part of. I guess my husband and I need to talk about Kaitlyn's future. It's hard to think about it now since she's just a baby. Where do we want Kaitlyn to live? What do we want Kaitlyn to be? The decision is made that Kaitlyn will attend the Mission School where sign language is used. I want Kaitlyn to use whatever hearing she has to help her learn in school. I've contacted several specialists to determine whether a cochlear *implant is appropriate for Kaitlyn. Some members of the Deaf Community feel the implant undermines their language and culture. I work hard to learn signing, but it is difficult. My husband and I will always be hearing parents of a deaf child. Although my husband and I are never going to fit in the Deaf Community, Kaitlyn will, so it's worth it. Kaitlyn is learning everything a normal hearing infant learns and more. I bought a TTY machine so I can call the parents and teachers who are deaf at school. One of Kaitlyn's teachers is deaf. I feel that deaf children should have teachers who are deaf.*

Katherine Whiteside

The service coordinator, the child-care teacher, and the evaluators say Jeffrey has problems. Although we know about his behavior problems, nothing is done and no one works with you unless your child is eligible. I need someone to help me and Jeffrey. If Jeffrey's problem is not serious enough for him to get services, why can't someone help me teach him? Really, I know I can do it myself. I just don't know what to do or what's right. If you're not in the system, your problems and your child don't exist. After the IFSP meeting, I was told to come back in 6 months to see if it gets worse. No one is able to help me get services through another agency. Why can't a service coordinator help me get services from another agency so that I can get Jeffrey some kind of help?

Camille St. James

This chapter discusses the process of collaborative assessment and decision making and how parents feel when information about the child is presented. Diversity factors can contribute to communicative misunderstanding and misinterpretations. The clinical goal involves enhancing the family's ability to address the child's needs. This goal can only be accomplished if a therapeutic alliance is developed between the SLP and the family. The alliance involves a relationship based on reciprocal interaction and mutual trust.

The mechanism to establish this therapeutic alliance is collaboration, a process that requires professional self-reflection and self-evaluation. Just as few academic courses and training experiences focus on counseling theory for SLPs, even fewer describe the self-reflection and self-evaluation process. The traditional thinking within our profession has relegated counseling to psychologists and mental health practitioners.

With the expanding and changing role of the SLP, the profession must define the parameters of counseling, given our clinical practice relationships with families. Counseling is an important part of the SLP's clinical relationship with parents and clients. These pathologists need to define what counseling means for our profession, and universities need to develop courses to train preprofessionals about the counseling process.

Collaboration

Provision of early intervention services includes the parents. Assessment procedures view the child in relation to the family (Bailey, 1991). In the past, the evaluation of the child did not include parent–child interactional variables. The typical evaluation focused on assessing the child alone, without seeing the child and the parents together. Today, we recognize that family assessment must be an integral part of the evaluation of an infant suspected of having developmental delays. Furthermore, collaboration is a creative partnership that can be used by professionals and parents to achieve early intervention programming in the least restrictive environment for infants and toddlers. The collaborative process is a therapeutic or clinical model that involves a learning process in which parents and clinical practitioners need to learn how to engage in shared decision making.

> *Collaboration consultation is an interactive process that enables people with diverse expertise to generate creative solutions to mutually defined problems. The outcome is enhanced, altered and produces solutions that are different from those the individual team members could produce independently.* (Idole, Paolucci-Whitecomb, & Nevin, 1986)

The Role of the Speech-Language Pathologist

When PL 99-457 introduced programs for infants and toddlers, language development became a critical component in the evaluation and treatment of young children with disabilities, because most children with developmental disabilities have language and communication disorders (Tiegerman-Farber & Radziewicz, 1998). The importance of language in early childhood development has shifted the role of the SLP from a related-service provider to a teacher consultant and a parent educator in many programs. The family-centered approach, which is the cornerstone of early intervention, has facilitated the development of different interactive models.

With the increased emphasis on more naturalistic programming, the SLP is required to utilize interactive models to meet the needs of culturally and linguistically diverse children and families in a variety of community-based settings (Cavallaro & Ballard-Rosa, 1998). The SLP provides comprehensive services to infants and toddlers, specialists, and parents across a continuum of settings, from therapy room to special education or early childhood classroom to home setting (Meyer, 1997).

Understanding diversity is also a critical part of the required professional competencies of the SLP. The complex needs of diverse families require the development of early intervention courses and preservice training for SLPs, along with other professionals. Many academic programs in universities have developed courses on early intervention and collaboration within undergraduate and graduate curricula (Jones & Blendinger, 1994).

For professionals already within the field of early intervention and special education, new competencies and skills need to be acquired by alternative training means. This creates significant difficulties for clinical teams and early intervention programs attempting to use a collaborative model. At the present time, the SLP works with other professionals in diverse settings outside the traditional therapy room without prior training. As a result, early intervention and early childhood programs often focus on staff development to address clinical issues related to diversity (Little & Robinson, 1997).

Diversity

Multiculturalism is "a principle, an approach, or a set of rules of conduct that guides the interactions and influences the perceptions, beliefs, attitudes and behaviors of people from diverse cultural backgrounds" (Fu, Stremmel, & Treppte, 1993, p. 40).

CW 3.1

Use the Companion Website to help you answer the following questions:

1. Find the ASHA Website and identify the different types of disabilities with which SLPs work.

2. Describe the settings within which SLPs work.

3. Identify some of the issues that ASHA is attempting to address related to early intervention. What is ASHA's position on early intervention?

4. Identify some of the diversity issues that ASHA is attempting to address. What position does ASHA take on competency skills of professionals working with diverse families?

5. Can you find any position statements on family diversity generated by ASHA that were sent to Congress and to the Office of Special Education Programs?

To effectively work with diverse families, professionals need to examine their own cultural beliefs and be willing to accept the cultural beliefs of others in our pluralistic society. The United States is rich in cultural and racial diversity. Approximately 29% of the population are culturally and linguistically diverse, and it is expected that by 2030 50% of the population will consist of culturally and linguistically diverse persons (Seibert, Stridh-Igo, & Zimmerman, 2002).

In today's society, children from diverse cultural communities are frequently identified as having language disorders. It is important that bilingual evaluators and interpreters be included when these children are evaluated. However, once these children are identified, it is imperative that the parents and professionals participate when developing individualized education plans (IEPs) and individualized family service plans (IFSPs). When large differences, such as socioeconomic status and differences in values and beliefs, exist between families and professionals, this collaborative partnership becomes more fragile and poses challenges to all team members. A study by DeGangi, Wietlisbach, Poissoon, Stein, and Royeen (1994) identifies the challenges to family–professional collaboration related to diversity and socioeconomic status (SES). It was found that families from lower SES and educational backgrounds are concerned with basic survival needs and often defer to professional judgments when setting goals, have difficulty identifying their child's needs, and show reluctance in sharing information.

Seibert et al. (2002) use a checklist to facilitate cultural awareness. This checklist of 10 points highlights the need to recognize language barriers, to provide interpreters whenever necessary, to understand a person's culture and religious beliefs, to develop a trusting relationship with the family, to check that the family comprehends a situation, to conduct assessments with cultural sensitivity in mind, to consider culture-specific dietary considerations, to make sure the family has realistic views about the process of treatment, and for professionals to recognize their own biases.

Professionals Who Collaborate or Consult and What They Do

Several professionals are involved in the early intervention process.

The Service Coordinator

Usually, the service coordinator is a social worker who functions as a case worker for the family. The service coordinator is usually the first professional representative from the early intervention system that the parent meets. The service coordinator informs parents of their rights and their entitlement to various services that do not involve any financial costs to the family and also schedules and facilitates the IFSP meeting. Malone, McKinsey, Thyer, and Straka (2000) note that social workers need specific course work and internship training to develop the appropriate competency skills to work in early intervention. The issue of preparedness, given the specialized needs of early intervention families, is problematic in many clinical areas. See the description in Box 3.1.

BOX 3.1

I have been a social worker for many years. I have worked in mental health and specialize in family practice. I function as a director, organizer, supporter, and negotiator with families and professionals. The process of coordinating people's schedules and paperwork to meet timelines and deadlines is difficult. It is also difficult to find certified and licensed professionals who will travel to the family's home. Professionals most often complain about the travel time and the isolation; we rarely meet after the IFSP meeting to discuss problems that arise during therapy sessions. At times my caseload is so large that I only meet with parents and therapists during the annual meeting. I do call parents on a regular basis to determine if services are being provided as indicated on the IFSP, and I hear from parents when there are interpersonal or clinical problems with therapists. Once in a while, parents will ask to change to another service provider because of interpersonal differences. I enjoy working with families who have young children. I feel that infants and toddlers benefit tremendously from early intervention services. I often keep in touch with families as they move into the preschool special education system. They don't like preschool as much because they don't get the same level of emotional support and nurturing.

Candice Burton, MSW

Use the Companion Website to help you answer the following questions:

1. What special skills does a service coordinator need to have to support families?

2. Why did the service coordination services fail Camille St. James?

The Psychologist

The psychologist administers developmental assessments to determine the psychosocial functioning of the child. In some states, psychologists also perform a family assessment, which provides cultural information about dynamic family issues affecting the child. The psychologist may perform these evaluations in the home, child-care program, or developmental center. The psychologist reviews the results of the assessments with the parent, incorporates any concerns expressed by the parent, and works with the parent to develop social and cognitive goals. He or she attends the IFSP meeting with the parent and other professionals to develop a clinical protocol that the parent feels reflects her needs and her child's needs. See the discussion in Box 3.2.

The Speech-Language Pathologist

The SLP administers speech and language assessments in the home, child-care program, or developmental center. She or he reviews the results of the assessments with

BOX 3.2

I just graduated from a doctoral program in school psychology. Working with parents in early intervention is significantly different from dealing with parents in elementary school. I do not meet often with parents in elementary school. In early intervention, the family-centered approach establishes a consultation relationship between the psychologist and the parent. The consultative relationship targets either the parent or the child as the client. When the parent is the consultee, I focus on developing appropriate management skills and parenting behaviors. These strategies will generalize into the home environment when the parent works directly with the child on IFSP goals. When the parent is the client, I work on stress-related problems within the family in counseling or parent-support groups. It is my professional opinion that a parent who is emotionally centered and secure about his or her parenting abilities will deal with daily family conflicts, disappointments, and problems more effectively. The consultation model allows me to have a much larger caseload than when I am working directly with parents or children. This model is more cost effective in terms of the delivery of services, particularly within large urban communities. I also believe that the consultation model works well with other professionals. Instead of working directly with a child, I can advise and train teachers so that they can implement learning strategies in their classroom. I find the family-centered approach challenging because the interpersonal relationships with parents and professionals create a working bond that does not develop in elementary school.

Suzanne Pollino, PhD
School Psychologist

Use the Companion Website to help you answer the following questions:

1. How would a consultation model be used with each of the three families?

2. Given the needs of the three families how effective is the consultation model with each?

the parent, incorporates any concerns expressed by the parent, and works with the parent to develop communication and language goals. The SLP attends the IFSP meeting with the parent and other professionals to develop a clinical protocol that trains the parent to communicate effectively with the child. This family-centered approach supports the parent's goals for the family and the child by enhancing her or his abilities to meet these goals. So there are many opportunities for collaboration and consultation between the SLP and the parent (see Figure 3.1). See Box 3.3.

Collaboration

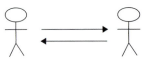

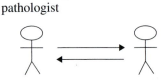

Speech-language pathologist	Parent	Speech-language pathologist	Parent

Speech-language pathologist evaluates the child with the parent's information and suggestions.

Together speech-language pathologist and parent generate communication goals and recommendations for services.

Consultation

Speech-language pathologist	Parent	Child

Speech-language pathologist teaches the parent about communication techniques and strategies.

Parent uses these strategies at home with the child.

Consultation

Speech-language pathologist	Teacher

Speech-language pathologist teaches the child-care teacher about communication techniques and strategies.

Child-care teacher uses these strategies in early childhood group with the child.

FIGURE 3.1
Speech-Language Pathologist

BOX 3.3

I was very uncomfortable when I first started to work with infants and toddlers. When I took courses in graduate school 15 years ago, there were no courses or internship training experiences in early intervention programs. I've worked with children who have disabilities in elementary school. Several years ago, I started to work for an early intervention agency after school. The speech and language services were all provided in the home, and there was a great deal of traveling, which became problematic in the winter. In rural communities, it is not unusual for therapists to travel 50 or 60 miles. With these distances, I can only see two children per day after school. But the travel is worth it when I see the children improve.

Patricia Carpenter, MS, CCC

Use the Companion Website to help you answer the following questions:

1. The focus of early intervention is the provision of services in a natural environment. How did this focus affect provision of services for each of the families?

2. How did the parents feel about services being provided in their homes? What were their issues?

At the IFSP meeting, the service coordinator, psychologist, and SLP present and review their results as an interactive team. The IFSP goals and therapeutic services for the family and the child are generated by consensus (see Figure 3.2). The IFSP meeting embodies shared decision making because parents and professionals function as equal contributors. The collaborative process underscores the team's shared responsibility to develop a common vision for the family.

Interactive Process

Collaborators as agents of change must agree to change their traditional roles and responsibilities. Chess (1986) describes a *goodness of fit* concept that can be used as a starting point when a collaborative team needs to make decisions about assessment, learning goals, and instructional techniques and strategies for children and families. The goodness of fit model requires that members of the collaborative team consider and incorporate the perceptions of other members of the team (see Figure 3.3).

Common Goals

The interactional process should reflect a set of short-term goals that describe developmental changes and achievements that professionals and parents will work toward (Farlow, 1996). Common goals provide an opportunity for all members of the team to address the same objectives, often by means of different therapeutic

Service coordinator   Parent

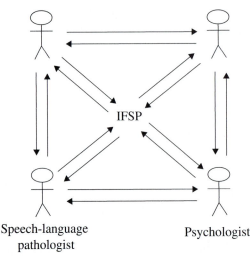

Speech-language   Psychologist
pathologist

The collaboration model defines the manner in which
team members interact with one another; equal roles and
shared decision making are the hallmark of collaboration.

FIGURE 3.2
The Team

techniques and procedures. The following list of SLP responsibilities was compiled
by ASHA (2001):

- Provide parent training and/or education classes about development and
  disabilities
- Work directly with a parent to facilitate parent–child interactions
- Counsel fathers, siblings, and extended family members at home or in groups
  about language and communication techniques to generalize appropriate behaviors to other settings and agents of change
- Develop a staff development program or seminar to educate and/or train other
  professionals on language-acquisition milestones and therapy techniques
- Work with families in a variety of settings and travel much greater distances:
  home, hospital, early child center, clinic, and anywhere that parents can be
  reached
- Help parents understand developmentally appropriate behaviors during evaluations and IFSP team meetings
- Serve as a case manager and a service-delivery coordinator
- Train, supervise, and manage speech-language pathology assistants and other
  support personnel

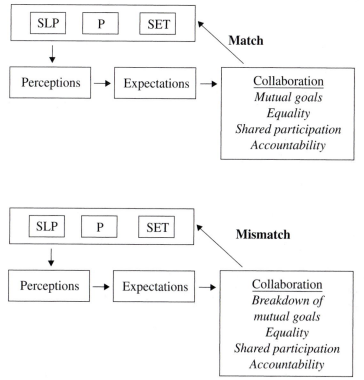

Note:

Match, consonance; Mismatch, dissonance; SLP, speech-language pathologist; SET, special education teacher; P, parent or guardian

FIGURE 3.3

The Collaborative Decision-Making Process: Developing a Shared Perspective

Source: Tiegerman-Farber, Ellenmorris; Radziewicz, Christine, *Collaborative Decision Making: The Pathway to Inclusion*, © 1998, p. 69. Adapted by permission of Pearson Education, Inc., Upper Saddle River, NJ.

- Advocate at the local, state, and national levels for access to and funding for services to remediate language disorders
- Foster public awareness of speech and language disorders and their treatment
- Promote healthy life-style practices for the prevention of language disorders and their treatment
- Recognize the special needs of diverse populations by providing services that are free of potential biases, including selection and/or adaptation of materials to ensure ethnic and linguistic sensitivity (ASHA, 2001)

Family Assessment

For an assessment to be complete, the team must acknowledge the importance of the family and conduct a family-focused assessment, in which both family and professionals consider the child's functioning within the family.

Effective Communication

Changes in federal law have provided a mechanism for parents to change their role in the educational system (Yanok, 1986). Perhaps healthier transactions will occur as parents learn to assert their role in the early intervention system (Briggs, 1991). Just as parents have attitudes about professionals, professionals also have attitudes about parents. Table 3.1 details some of the negative attitudes on both sides. Negative attitudes need to change. Clearly, each side has concerns about the other. Many parents are sensitive about not being respected for their efforts and their dreams. Many professionals believe that parents need to show up, generalize learning, and listen to instructions. If parents are going to be partners in the process, then they and the professionals need to develop effective communication strategies that embrace mutual respect, competence, and commitment.

TABLE 3.1   Parental and Professional Attitudes

Parental Attitudes	Professional Attitudes
No two professionals agree.	Parents are not appreciative. They just complain and complain.
Professionals focus only on my child's deficits and disabilities—my child never has any strengths.	Parents do not work hard enough and are not committed to change.
Professionals do not understand that I have to do other things in my life than toilet-train my child six times a day. I have other children, a husband, and a household.	Parents are inconsistent and lazy.
Professionals do not understand that I am a single parent and it is my child who has a disability—not me.	Parents do not spend enough time with their children.
I find that professionals are impatient and intolerant; they see things only from their own vantage point.	Parents expect miracles. They want you to fix their children.
I find that professionals do not understand that there is a long-term issue with a child who has a disability. They are too narrow in their focus and too short-term in their viewpoint.	Parents are never satisfied; the only thing they want is a normal child. Whatever you give them, it's never enough.
Professionals do not go home with a child who has a disability.	Parents cannot accept the child as she or he is.

Factors to Consider

Several factors must be considered when shifting the focus from child-centered assessment to family assessment. Although assessment is provided under the law, it is up to the family to decide if they want an assessment. If the family understands that they are respected by the professional team and that both their needs and their child's needs are considered important, they are more likely to be committed to the assessment process. The assessment identifies and incorporates the family's objectives with the family's description of its resources, priorities, and concerns.

Assessing Family Standards and Values

Family values are standards; families make decisions based on these standards. Family structure is the organizational framework of the family (i.e., the individual roles of family members). Family functioning describes how the family works to achieve or accomplish goals. The professional must identify those areas of functioning that require support or help. Several scales can be used to determine family needs. *The Coping–Health Inventory for Parents* (Gallagher, Scharfman, & Bristol, 1984), a measure of role performance in the family, identifies who is currently responsible for most child care and is most helpful when considering intervention strategies and IFSP goals. Another measure of family functioning, the *Family Adjustment Survey* (Abbott & Meredith, 1986), determines a family's coping style and its strengths and support systems. Each scale provides insights into the unique style and structure of special-needs families.

Several important questions need to be considered before the assessment process begins. What strategies should be used in this assessment process? When is the best time for a family assessment to be done? How can the team prevent the family from viewing the assessment process as intrusive? Who should perform the family assessment? What if the team identifies a family need that the family does not recognize? Why is an assessment of family strengths important? These questions need to be considered when conducting an assessment.

The Parent's Perspective

The perceptions of the parent should provide the parameters for decisions about services and program activities.

- Have the family's perceptions of the child's needs been identified?
- Have the family's goals for achievement been reflected in the team's decisions?
- Does the family feel that the collaborative process has enhanced their ability to support their child?
- Does the family feel supported?
- Does the family agree with the team's decisions?
- How has each team member's beliefs created specific expectations about the following?
  a. The family's needs
  b. The child's needs

c. The required services

d. The appropriate clinical setting

e. The supports that will enhance child growth and development

f. The long-term achievements of the child

When perceptions and expectations match, there is a synchrony or confluence that flows from perception to expectation to clinical agreement. Alternatively, when there is a *mismatch* between perceptions, expectations, and the parent's expressed needs, disagreement and misunderstanding can result (see Figure 3.4).

The SLP, along with other professionals in early intervention, must learn to translate their differences in educational training into family-focused themes (Watkins, 1999). Utilizing a family-focused approach facilitates the generation of goals that parents will accept as appropriate to enhancing the needs of their child. One way to determine the effectiveness of collaborative teams is to have the family provide feedback about their satisfaction with the family-centered process (see Figure 3.5).

Parent evaluations can provide feedback about (1) how parents feel about their personal experiences and treatment by professionals and (2) the information they

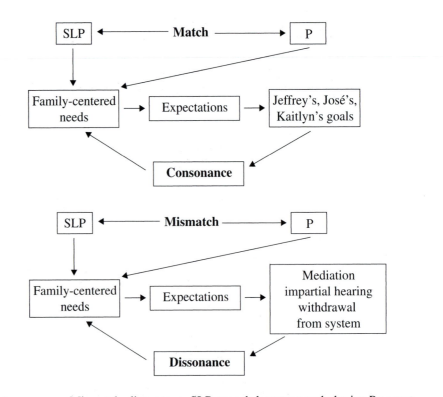

Note:

Match, consonance; Mismatch, dissonance; SLP, speech-language pathologist; P, parent or guardian

FIGURE 3.4

Working from the Parent's Perspective

Source: Tiegerman-Farber, Ellenmorris; Radziewicz, Christine, *Collaborative Decision Making: The Pathway to Inclusion,* © 1998, p. 90. Adapted by permission of Pearson Education, Inc., Upper Saddle River, NJ.

Sample Questions:

	Yes	No
1. The team asked me to describe my child's and family's needs	____	____
2. The team made me feel comfortable about expressing my opinions and ideas.	____	____
3. The team encouraged me to ask questions and seek explanations of technical words.	____	____
4. The team explained the family assessment process and eligibility, and described the programs and services available in the early intervention programs.	____	____
5. The team explained my rights and responsibilities as a parent.	____	____
6. The team explained confidentiality and what written consent means.	____	____
7. The team explained that I have the right to disagree with the team and the due-process procedures that must be followed.	____	____
8. The team explained my right to access my child's reports and evaluations.	____	____
9. The team explained that I have the right to change my decision at any time about having my child screened and/or evaluated and/or serviced.	____	____

FIGURE 3.5
Parent Satisfaction Survey

received about required procedures. Parent surveys can be used as a monitoring mechanism, and it would be beneficial if they were used by counties or states (McNaughton, 1994).

Formal Assessment Instruments

There are a variety of formal family assessment instruments; see Table 3.2 for a sampling. The purpose of these instruments is to measure areas such as stress, support, and parent interaction in families; they are usually administered by a professional, such as a social worker or a psychologist. In addition to administering scales and questionnaires, professionals working in the early intervention system must also understand families from a systems perspective, use effective listening and interviewing techniques, negotiate values and priorities to provide quality services to children, and be able to function as case managers to match family needs with community resources (Bailey, 1987). When working with families whose dominant language is not English, every attempt should be made to identify personnel who can speak the language of the family. However, if this is not possible, an interpreter

TABLE 3.2 Family Assessment Instruments

Assessment Instrument	Publisher or Source
Critical Events Checklist (Bailey et al., 1986)	*Journal of Early Childhood*, 10(2), 156–171
Family Support Scale (Dunst & Jenkins, 1983)	Western Carolina Center, Morganton, NC 28655
Parenting Stress Index (PSI) (Abidin, 1983)	Pediatric Psychology Press, 2915 Idlewood Drive, Charlottesville, VA 22901
Survey of Family Needs (Bailey & Simeonsson, 1985)	Families Project, Frank Porter Graham Child Development Center, University of North Carolina, Chapel Hill, NC 27514

should be available to aid the professional in the administration of the assessment instruments.

Another important area of assessment for the SLP is parent–child interaction. There are basically four types of parent–child interaction assessments: rating scales, checklists, parent reports, and observational coding. Previous research has identified parent–child social interactions as bidirectional and homeostatic (Lewis & Rosenblum, 1974; Bell & Harper, 1977; Brazelton, 1982; Tronick & Ganino, 1986). Thus, during a communicative interaction between parent and child, each is an active member of the interaction and each makes adaptations to the other's behavior. When the parent interacts with the infant, she facilitates organization of the child's behavior and bears most of the responsibility for the interaction. As the child becomes older, he shares more responsibility for the interaction and learns to interact in a communicative style that matches the style of the parent. In optimal circumstances, there is a good fit or match so that parent–child interchanges are pleasant and sustaining (Thomas & Chess, 1977).

Assessment of parent–child interactions can be performed by means of observational techniques, in combination with parent–child interactional scales. Table 3.3 presents a list of several scales that would be useful to the SLP.

The proper use of some of these scales requires recording equipment. These scales are effective in identifying strengths and weaknesses in the parent–child interactive dyad. The information then provides the SLP with communicative data to help the family understand its interactive style in relation to the child's. When analyzing parent–child interactions in families from diverse cultures, always take into account the cultural rules and styles of the family. Never identify a custom or parenting style as a weakness. It is the responsibility of the SLP to respect the difference while gently shaping and modifying interactions to facilitate language development. Highlighting the behaviors that enhance communication empowers parents to become more effective teachers, models, and communication partners.

TABLE 3.3 Parent–Child Interaction Assessment

Assessment Instrument	Publisher or Source
Social Interaction Assessment/Intervention	McCollum & Stayton (1985). *Journal of the Division for Early Childhood*, 9(2), 125–135
Interaction Rating Scales	Clark & Siefer (1985). *Infant Mental Health Journal*, 6, 214–225
Teaching Skills Inventory	Rosenberg, Robinson, & Beckman (1994). *Journal of the Division for Early Childhood*, 8, 107–113
Parent/Caregiver Involvement Scale	Farran et al. (1987). In T. Tamer (Ed.), *Stimulation and Intervention in Infant Development*. London: Freund Publishing
Maternal Behavior Rating	Mahoney (1992). Available from G. Mahoney, Family Child Learning Center, 143 Northwest Ave. (Bldg A), Talmadge, OH 44278
Parent–Caregiver Involvement Scale (PCIS)	Farran, Kasari, Comfort, & Jay (1986). Available from Dale Farran, Department of Child Development and Family Relations, University of North Carolina at Greensboro, Greensboro, NC 27412
Mother–Child Rating Scales (M-CRS)	Crawley & Spiker (1982). Mother–Child Rating Scale. Chicago: University of Illinois (available from ERIC Document Reproduction Service No. ED221978)
Maternal Behavior Rating Scale (MBRS)	Roach (1989). Mother/Infant Communication Screening (M/ICS). Schaumburg, IL: Community Therapy Services. (Available from Community Therapy Services, P.O. Box 68484, 975 E. Nerge Road, Suite 130, Schaumberg, IL 60168-0484.

The SLP's educational training and background equip her to work with parents and include familiarity with areas such as prespeech, language, play, social routines, gestures, intentions, and parent–child interactions. Mahoney and Spiker (1996) caution professionals regarding the use of parent–child interaction assessments to keep in mind that most of these scales are not standardized on culturally and linguistically diverse families.

All the information gained from observations, interviews, and parent–infant assessment scales can readily be translated into intervention goals by the SLP. Crais and Roberts (1991) developed a decision-making framework for early intervention that they refer to as *decision trees*. This framework is appropriate for children from 3 months to 5 years and is an alternative to standardized testing. The decision trees include a sequenced set of questions followed by available response choices; they assess social interaction, comprehension, and production.

Figures 3.6 and 3.7 represent a social interaction tree and a comprehension tree for a child at the one-word utterance stage.

Challenges of Family Centeredness During Assessment

The professional literature is replete with information about utilizing strategies and procedures designed to promote infant development by enhancing and supporting patterns of parent–child interaction (Dawson et al., 1990; Mahoney & Powell, 1988; Seifer, Clark, & Sameroff, 1991; Tannock, Girolametto, & Siegel, 1992). Relationship-based approaches are now considered more effective, because service delivery emphasizes the relationships between parents and child, parents and providers, and child and providers (Atkins-Burnett & Allen-Meares, 2000). With this new perspective, the professional is challenged to evaluate his or her relationship with families and other professionals. Each professional must assimilate knowledge from the other team members and from the family (Foley, 1990; Rosetti, 1990). Team members must communicate honestly and be willing to dedicate time to the communication process. Families and professionals learn to work together to facilitate and integrate skill development into the child's daily functioning. The SLP is still working to help the child meet developmental milestones, but more importantly she or he is developing relationships with the other members of the team and enabling others to utilize discipline-specific strategies that enhance child development.

Most early intervention services are provided in the home. Helping the family to anticipate settings, situations, and behaviors that are unsafe; assisting the family in selecting play materials; helping the family to organize play environments; helping the parent to promote positive social interactions through play; and helping parents establish daily schedules for conducting household caregiving routines are all important offshoots and supports of family-centered intervention (Lubech & Chandler, 1990). Table 3.4 lists some home environment assessments that will help the SLP assess the home environment.

The Association for the Care of Children's Health (1988) defined a family-centered service delivery model as one in which the family is recognized as the constant in the child's life, with service systems recognized as temporary and fluctuating. Parents and professionals who collaborate and participate in a partnership respect each other and are committed to each other. Professionals must share complete information with parents about their child, must implement policies and programs that provide emotional and financial support to meet the needs of the family, and must recognize family strengths and respect the family's coping mechanisms.

Assessment Questions		Intervention Activities

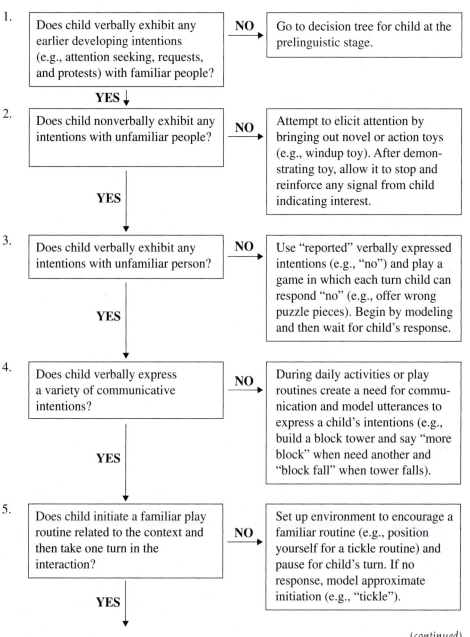

1. Does child verbally exhibit any earlier developing intentions (e.g., attention seeking, requests, and protests) with familiar people? — **NO** → Go to decision tree for child at the prelinguistic stage.

YES ↓

2. Does child nonverbally exhibit any intentions with unfamiliar people? — **NO** → Attempt to elicit attention by bringing out novel or action toys (e.g., windup toy). After demonstrating toy, allow it to stop and reinforce any signal from child indicating interest.

YES

3. Does child verbally exhibit any intentions with unfamiliar person? — **NO** → Use "reported" verbally expressed intentions (e.g., "no") and play a game in which each turn child can respond "no" (e.g., offer wrong puzzle pieces). Begin by modeling and then wait for child's response.

YES

4. Does child verbally express a variety of communicative intentions? — **NO** → During daily activities or play routines create a need for communication and model utterances to express a child's intentions (e.g., build a block tower and say "more block" when need another and "block fall" when tower falls).

YES

5. Does child initiate a familiar play routine related to the context and then take one turn in the interaction? — **NO** → Set up environment to encourage a familiar routine (e.g., position yourself for a tickle routine) and pause for child's turn. If no response, model approximate initiation (e.g., "tickle").

YES

(continued)

FIGURE 3.6

Decision Tree for a Child at the One-Word Utterance Stage, Social Interaction Tree

Source: Crais, E. R., & Roberts, J. E. (1991). Decision making in assessment and early intervention planning. *Speech and Hearing Services in Schools*, 22(2), 19–30. Copyright American Speech-Language-Hearing Association. Reprinted by permission.

Assessment Questions	Intervention Activities

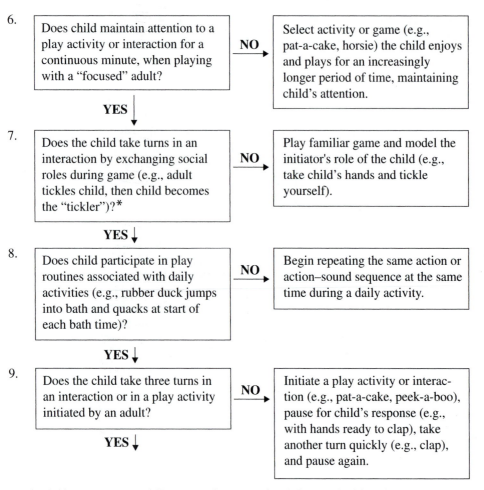

6. Does child maintain attention to a play activity or interaction for a continuous minute, when playing with a "focused" adult? — **NO** → Select activity or game (e.g., pat-a-cake, horsie) the child enjoys and plays for an increasingly longer period of time, maintaining child's attention.

YES ↓

7. Does the child take turns in an interaction by exchanging social roles during game (e.g., adult tickles child, then child becomes the "tickler")?* — **NO** → Play familiar game and model the initiator's role of the child (e.g., take child's hands and tickle yourself).

YES ↓

8. Does child participate in play routines associated with daily activities (e.g., rubber duck jumps into bath and quacks at start of each bath time)? — **NO** → Begin repeating the same action or action–sound sequence at the same time during a daily activity.

YES ↓

9. Does the child take three turns in an interaction or in a play activity initiated by an adult? — **NO** → Initiate a play activity or interaction (e.g., pat-a-cake, peek-a-boo), pause for child's response (e.g., with hands ready to clap), take another turn quickly (e.g., clap), and pause again.

YES ↓

*As the child's communicative skills improve, these turn-taking behaviors should first be seen vocally and later verbally.

FIGURE 3.6

(*continued*)

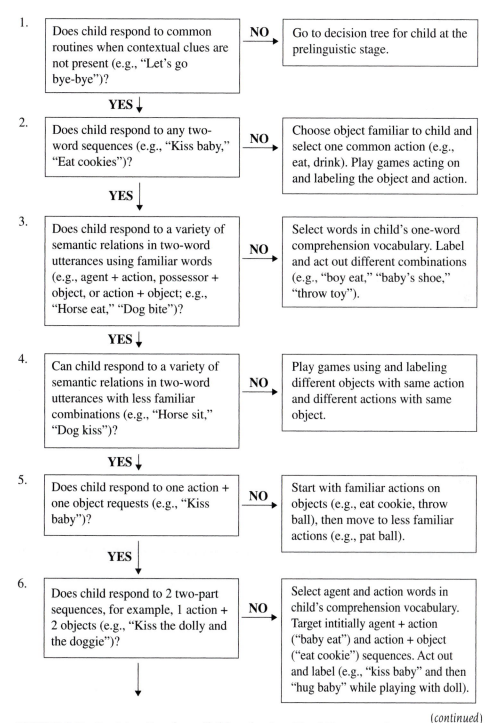

1. Does child respond to common routines when contextual clues are not present (e.g., "Let's go bye-bye")?

NO → Go to decision tree for child at the prelinguistic stage.

YES ↓

2. Does child respond to any two-word sequences (e.g., "Kiss baby," "Eat cookies")?

NO → Choose object familiar to child and select one common action (e.g., eat, drink). Play games acting on and labeling the object and action.

YES ↓

3. Does child respond to a variety of semantic relations in two-word utterances using familiar words (e.g., agent + action, possessor + object, or action + object; e.g., "Horse eat," "Dog bite")?

NO → Select words in child's one-word comprehension vocabulary. Label and act out different combinations (e.g., "boy eat," "baby's shoe," "throw toy").

YES ↓

4. Can child respond to a variety of semantic relations in two-word utterances with less familiar combinations (e.g., "Horse sit," "Dog kiss")?

NO → Play games using and labeling different objects with same action and different actions with same object.

YES ↓

5. Does child respond to one action + one object requests (e.g., "Kiss baby")?

NO → Start with familiar actions on objects (e.g., eat cookie, throw ball), then move to less familiar actions (e.g., pat ball).

YES ↓

6. Does child respond to 2 two-part sequences, for example, 1 action + 2 objects (e.g., "Kiss the dolly and the doggie")?

NO → Select agent and action words in child's comprehension vocabulary. Target intitially agent + action ("baby eat") and action + object ("eat cookie") sequences. Act out and label (e.g., "kiss baby" and then "hug baby" while playing with doll).

↓

(continued)

FIGURE 3.7 Decision Tree for a Child at the One-Word Utterance Stage, Comprehension Tree

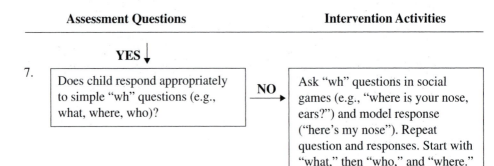

Assessment Questions	Intervention Activities

FIGURE 3.7

(*continued*)

Source: Crais, E.R., & Roberts. J.E. (1991). Decision making in assessment and early intervention planning. *Speech and Hearing Services in Schools*, 22(2), 19–30. Copyright American Speech Language-Hearing Association. Reprinted with permission.

TABLE 3.4 Home Environment Assessments

Assessment Instrument	Description
Early Childhood Environment Rating Scale	Clifford & Harms (1980). New York: Teachers College Press.
Home Observation for Measurement of the Environment	Caldwell & Bradley (1984). University of Arkansas at Little Rock.
Purdue Home Stimulation Inventory	Wachs, Frances, & McQuiston (1978). Psychological dimensions of the infant's physical environment. *Merrill-Palmer Quarterly*, 24, 3–41.

Child Assessment

Child assessment is best achieved through both formal and informal assessment techniques. Formal assessment instruments are either standardized norm-referenced instruments or standardized criterion-referenced instruments. Norm-referenced tests compare a single child's performance to a representative sample of the performance of other children of the same age. Norm-referenced tests must be valid and reliable and can render scores in the form of developmental age scores, developmental quotients, standard scores, and percentile ranks.

Criterion-referenced tests measure a child's performance on a predetermined set of skills that relate either to academic performance or to daily living (Bailey & Wolery, 1989). The skills tested in a criterion-referenced test are generally listed in a developmental sequence. This allows the test giver to determine the level at which the child is functioning and to measure the child's progress from one point in time to another.

Consequently, criterion-referenced tests are well designed to measure small changes in a child's development and lend themselves to facilitate programming (Harbin, 1977).

When assessing culturally and linguistically diverse children, the SLP needs to perform a nonbiased assessment. We must always consider whether the language used in testing is the primary language of the child and the cultural relevance of the assessment instrument (Anderson, 1994). We must examine the population sample of the test and determine the percentage of the sample children that match the culture of the child we are testing. For example, if we are testing a child whose family is Colombian and speaks Spanish, there is no guarantee that the Latino population in the normalization sample matches that of our Colombian child (Crowley, 2003).

Using a dynamic assessment approach to testing is one method of ensuring that a language difference is not identified as a language disorder. The dynamic assessment approach emphasizes the ability of the child to make changes after short-term teaching occurs. If linguistically diverse children can make these changes, they most likely do not have a language disorder. Best practice dictates that if a child comes from a bilingual environment, the child should be assessed in both English and the language of the family to determine the dominant language of the child and whether a delay exists.

Goldstein (2000) describes several nonlinguistic factors that can affect assessment, such as degree of acculturation, procedures that do not match a child's cognitive style, culturally different nonverbal behaviors (i.e., body language, eye contact, facial expressions, proximity, touching, gestures, silence), country of birth, and family's attitude toward English and English speakers (Goldstein, 2000).

Behavioral Observations

Behavioral observation is a critical diagnostic skill, and it is imperative that it be performed in as natural a context as possible. It is useful to record behavior so that it can be analyzed later. When assessing a child, the SLP needs to establish a rapport, use a variety of toys, schedule appointments during the best time of day for the child, assess on more than one occasion, and assess in an environment that is natural and comfortable for the child. It is also a good idea to observe the child interacting with caregivers to determine the interactive styles of both and to extract critical elements that either positively or negatively affect communicative interactions. During these observations interactive elements such as physical proximity, eye gaze behavior, types of games played, use of toys, and types of verbalizations of parent and child can be observed and analyzed.

Bailey and Wolery (1984) recommend measuring specific behaviors as they occur in one of two ways: frequency counts or durations of event recordings. For example, the clinician could analyze a 30-minute parent–child interaction in terms of number and type of communicative acts, such as requesting or showing. A frequency of occurrence count could be gathered for communicative functions (regulation, calling attention to self, etc.). This information would allow the clinician to analyze the child's communicative style and pattern and would also reveal the caregiver's responsiveness to the child's communicative and noncommunicative acts. As part of an assessment, the interview is a critical element. Background information on the developmental history of the child can be gathered, and important information regarding medical history, hearing, vision, motor development, and speech-language development can be determined.

Assessment Instruments for Children from Birth to 3 Years

A number of assessment instruments are available for the child from birth to 3 years. The items listed in Table 3.5 include those scales or assessments that test across multiple domains, such as motor, language, cognitive, communicative, and play development.

TABLE 3.5   Child Assessment Instruments

Assessment Instrument	Description
Autism Diagnostic Interview, Revised (ADI-R), Lord, 1994.	A semistructured interview that focuses on three key areas which define autism: reciprocal social interaction, communication and language, repetitive stereotyped behaviors; can be used with children as young as 2 years.
Autism Screen Instrument for Educational Planning—Second Edition, Krug et al., 1980.	Consists of five components to provide information on aspects of behavior such as vocal behavior, interaction, communication, etc., for ages 18 months through adulthood.
Childhood Autism Rating Scale (CARS), Schopler et al., 1988.	Standardized instrument to aid in the diagnosis of autism; can be used with children 2 years of age and older.
Pre-Linguistic Autism Diagnostic Observation Schedule (PL-ADOS), Lord et al., 1989.	Assesses four social behaviors and four communicative behaviors; it can be used with children under 6 years of age.
Clinical Linguistic Auditory Milestone Scale (CLAMS), Pro-Ed, 1998.	Screens for language delays in young children between birth and 3 years.
Early Language Milestone Scale (ELM)— Second Edition (ELM-2), Coplan, 1993.	Screens children's language abilities; for children birth to 36 months.
Expressive One-Word Picture Vocabulary Test-R, Brownell, 2000.	Measures expressive vocabulary. It is appropriate for children 2 to 11.11 years. It is available in English and Spanish.
Receptive One-Word Picture Vocabulary Test-R, Brownell, 2000.	Measures a child's single-word receptive vocabulary. It is appropriate for children 2 to 11.11 years. It is available in English and Spanish 2 to 9 years.
Test of Early Language Development, 3rd ed., Hresko, Reid, & Hammell, 1999.	Measures the understanding and expression of grammatical forms, language content, and semantic knowledge.

TABLE 3.5 (*continued*)

Assessment Instrument	Description
Receptive-Expressive Emergent Language Scale 3rd ed., Bzoch & League, 2003.	Identifies infants and toddlers with language impairments or other disabilities that affect language development.
Rossetti Infant Toddler Language Scale, Rossetti, 1990.	Measures communication and interaction skills for children birth through 3 years. It looks at areas such as play, interaction attachment, pragmatics, gestures, language comprehension, and expression.
Scales of Early Communication Skills for Hearing Impaired Children, Moog & Geers, 1975.	Designed to assess speech and language development in children with hearing impairments ages 2 to 8 years.
Grammatical Analysis of Elicited Language, Moog & Geers, 1979.	Assesses the development of grammatic forms in children who have hearing impairments 2 years to 9 years.
Infant-Toddler Meaningful Auditory Integration Scale (IT-MAIS) (This is used specifically for children who have received a cochlear implant) Zimmerman-Phillips, Osberger, & Robbins, 1997.	
Hodson Assessment of Phonological Patterns, 3rd ed., Hodson, 2004.	Assesses intelligibility in children 2 years to 8 years.
Reynell Developmental Language Scales, Reynell & Gruber, 1990.	Measures language skills in young children ages 1 to 6.11 years.
Clinical Assessment of Articulation and Phonology, Secord & Donahue, 2002.	Assesses the articulation and phonology of children 2.6 to 8.11 years.
Sequenced Inventory of Communicative Development-Revised (SICD-R), Hedrick, Prother, Tobin, 1984.	Assesses language skills such as sound awareness, and comprehension and verbal expression in children 4 months to 4 years.
Goldman–Fristoe Test of Articulation-2, Goldman & Fristoe, American Guidance Service, 2000.	Measures a child's articulation of consonant sounds. It is appropriate for children 2 years old.
Khan–Lewis Phonological Analysis, Khan & Lewis, 2000.	Measures phonological development. It is used in conjunction with the Goldman–Fristoe Test of Articulation and is appropriate for children 2.6 to 5 years old.
Peabody Picture Vocabulary Test-III, Dunn & Dunn, 2001.	Assesses receptive vocabulary in children ages 2.6 years to adult (available in English and Spanish).

(*continued*)

TABLE 3.5 *(continued)*

Assessment Instrument	Description
Preschool Language Scale-4 (PLS-4), Zimmerman, Steiner, & Pond, 2002.	Assesses auditory comprehension and verbal language for children birth to 6-11 years (available in English and Spanish).
MacArthur–Bates Communicative Development Inventories: Words and Sentences (CDI:WS), Fenson et al., 1993.	A parent report instrument for measuring early vocabulary and syntax.
The Language Development Survey: A Screening Tool for Delayed Language in Toddlers, Rescorla, 1989.	A screening tool for the identification of language delay in toddlers.
Naturalistic Observation of Newborn Behavior (Preterm and Full-term), Als, 1985.	For children in the neonatal intensive-care unit of a hospital.
Assessment of Preterm Infant Behavior, Als, Lester, Tronick, & Brazelton, 1982.	For children in the neonatal intensive-care unit of a hospital.
Neonatal Behavioral Assessment Scale, Brazelton & Nugent, 1995.	For children in the neonatal intensive-care unit of a hospital.
The Neonatal Neurological Examination, Sheridan-Pereira, Ellison, & Helgesen, 1991.	For children in the neonatal intensive-care unit of a hospital.
The Neurological Assessment of the Preterm and Full-Term Newborn Infant, Dubowitz, Dubowitz, & Mercuri, 1999.	For children in the neonatal intensive-care unit of a hospital.
Stages of Normal Noncry Vocal Development in Infancy: A Protocol for Assessment, Proctor, 1989.	For infants birth to 1 year.

An integral part the of assessment of children from birth to 3 is a language sample; indeed, it is the cornerstone of the assessment process for young children. A language sample can be gathered when a parent is interacting with the child or when the speech-language pathologist is interacting with the child. Stickler (1987) suggests the following guidelines:

1. Always begin the interaction with parallel play. For the child at the one-word stage, imitate the child's vocalizations, make animal sounds, noises, and the like. If the child is 2 years or older, talk about what you are doing (e.g., "I'm going to put the mommy and the baby in the car").
2. Restrict your questions to approximately one question for every four speaking turns.
3. Always follow the child's interactional lead.

4. Use alternative questions (e.g., "Should we play with the doll house or the gas station?").
5. Allow for interactional pauses because they are a natural aspect of communication exchange.
6. Keep your utterances relatively short.
7. Have available a diverse group of materials and toys.

Recording of child–adult interaction is best done during one session of anywhere from 60 to 90 minutes. The goal is to gather 100 child utterances and then transcribe and analyze the sample.

Besides determining an MLU (mean length of utterance), other linguistic information can be determined, such as the semantic categories used (e.g., action, locative), grammatical categories (e.g., negation, attribute), and conversational devices (e.g., attention, interjection "oh," affirmation "okay"). The child's syntactic level of functioning can also be determined from the language sample. Does the child use the "–ing" form, the plural "-s," or regular past "-ed"? This information assists the SLP with the development of targeted appropriate speech-language goals.

Looking at children's narratives is another important focus of child assessments. Narratives and conversations are two types of discourse. Narratives begin to emerge at 2 years when children look at picture books and retell stories they have heard many times before. In the beginning, narratives are just collections of unrelated ideas (Huston-Nechkash, 1990). The young child turns the pages of a book and comments on what she sees: "House and flowers" and "Doggie jumps." Hedberg and Stoel-Gammon (1986) have devised an assessment of narratives that can be used with children whose MLU is greater than 3. Narratives are critical to development of preacademic and social skills. As narratives develop, children become more effective at organizing information and communicating it to the listener. Somewhere between the ages of 2 and 3 years, children's narratives take the form of sequences (Westby, 1984).

Cognitive Development

Piaget (1952) developed a model of cognitive development that extends from birth to 14 years. This model is particularly interesting to educators in planning intervention techniques (see Table 3.6). Also of interest and use to the assessment team are scales that assess the earliest cognitive skills. Several such scales have been developed that utilize this Piagetian framework. Uzgiris and Hunt (1975) developed six scales that pertain to the six branches of psychological development of infants.

TABLE 3.6 Piagetian Stages of Cognitive Development

	Stage	Chronological Age
I	Sensorimotor period	Birth to 24 months
II	Preoperational period	2 to 7 years
III	Concrete operation period	7 to 11 years
IV	Formal operations period	11 to 14 years

Another useful theory of cognitive development for assessing young children is information-processing theory. Information-processing theorists propose that mental operations such as thinking require mental hardware and software (Klahr & MacWhinney, 1998). Information-processing psychologists believe that children have special mental software that allows them to learn to read and to problem solve. As children develop, they acquire strategies to process information more rapidly and efficiently (Shrager & Siegler, 1998). The complex system is described in terms of mental processes that enable the child to problem solve and process cognition.

Play Development

Play is the child's domain. Assessment of play gives the evaluation team valuable information about how a child interacts with his or her environment. Westby (1980) developed a scale that describes symbolic play and integrates Piaget's stages of cognitive development with play. Another play-assessment instrument that looks at social play is Howes' *Peer Play Scale* (1980), which considers five developmental levels of play and allows the examiner to determine at what level the child is functioning based on observations of play.

Motor Development

Normal motor development is well documented (Chandler, 1979; Knoblock & Passamanick, 1974); children pass through motor-development milestones in sequential fashion. Consequently, assessment of motor development is easily managed and is typically divided into fine- and gross-motor skills. The areas that should be considered when conducting a motor assessment include muscle tone, reflexes and reaction, movement and posture patterns, and functional abilities (Smith, 1989).

Recently, much research has centered on the development of oral-motor skill in the infant. Oral-motor functioning includes reflexive oral-motor abilities such as sucking and swallowing; assessment of feeding is especially important when working with a child who has suspected motor disabilities. In addition, the study of the early vocal behaviors of the infant is of particular interest to the SLP. The chronology of oral-motor feeding patterns is as follows:

Birth to 6 Months

Suckling: extension–retraction of tongue, up and down jaw movement, loose lip-approximation

Sucking: rhythmic up and down jaw movements with tongue-tip elevation, tight approximation of the lips

Rooting: head turns in response to tactile stimulation of lips or mouth

Phasic bite reflex: rhythmic bite and release pattern when gums are stimulated

Six to 24 Months

Munching: earliest level of chewing in which the tongue is flat and the jaw moves up and down

Chewing: food is propelled between the teeth through spreading and rolling movements of tongue

Tongue lateralization: the tongue moves to the sides of the mouth and propels food between teeth for chewing

Rotary jaw movements: integration of vertical, lateral, diagonal, and circular movements of the jaw during chewing

Controlled bite: easy closure of teeth on food with easy release of food for chewing (Jaffe, 1989)

One important responsibility of the SLP when working with infants is an evaluation of feeding and swallowing and the development of an intervention plan when needed. The SLP must diagnose suckling–swallowing disorders and determine if abnormal anatomy and physiology are associated with the disorders. This type of assessment is highly specialized and requires understanding of developmentally and functionally appropriate nonnutritive and nutritive sucking and swallowing. It is the SLP who determines infant readiness for oral feeding. This requires a breast-feeding and/or a bottle-feeding assessment. Table 3.7 lists the assessments that are commonly used. One assessment, *The Feeding Assessment*, has English and Spanish versions. Many times children with suckling–swallowing difficulties require instrumental evaluations such as videofluoroscopic swallow study, endoscopic assessment, and ultrasonography. These assessments are performed by other professionals, but it is the responsibility of the SLP to develop appropriate intervention plans based on these assessments.

The normally developing infant learns to shape vocalizations into sound productions that approximate words and, eventually, multiword productions. Although there are no norms for articulatory and acoustic data on noncry vocal behaviors in infancy, research studies have examined infant vocalizations (Delack & Fowlow, 1978; Oller,

TABLE 3.7   Feeding Assessment Instruments

Assessment Instrument	Authors
The Feeding Assessment (English and Spanish versions are available)	Morris & Klein, 1987
The Pre-Speech Assessment Scale	Morris, 1982
Oral Motor Assessment	Sleight & Niman, 1984
Systematic Assessment of the Infant at Breast (SAIB)	Association of Women's Health, Obstetric, and Neonatal Nurses, 1990
Preterm Infant Breast-Feeding Behavior Scale (PIBBS)	Nyqvist, Rubertsson, Ewald, & Sjoden, 1996
Neonatal Oral Motor Assessment Scale (NOMAS)	Palmer, Crawley, & Blanco, 1993
Infant Feeding Evaluation	Swigert, 1998

1980, 1986). Proctor (1989) delineates five stages of vocal development and has developed a vocal assessment form:

Stage 1: More crying sounds than noncrying sounds; noncrying sounds are mostly vegetative

Stage 2: Less crying; predominance of vocalic sounds, CV productions

Stage 3: Increased consonant productions; varied vowel productions; consistent CV syllables; varied intonation contours

Stage 4: Reduplicated babbling in the form of CV or CVC structures; consistent variations in intonation contours

Stage 5: Variety of CV and CVC combinations with sentence-like intonation; approximations of meaningful single words

Utilization of a protocol such as Proctor's enables the SLP to determine the level of vocal development, compare it with oral-motor-feeding skill development, and plan therapeutic intervention strategies.

Stoel-Gammon (1987) states that by 2 years of age the normally developing child produces words using CV, CVC, CVCV, and CVCVC forms; produces a few consonant clusters; matches the consonant phonemes of adult words with 70% correctness; produces 9 or 10 different consonants in initial position; and produces 5 or 6 different consonants in the final position.

The Martinez Family

A bilingual SLP evaluates José Martinez. The family assessment instrument selected is the *Parenting Stress Index* (Abidin, 1983). The parent–child interaction assessment instrument selected is the *Parent/Caregiver Involvement Scale* (Farran, Kasari, et al., 1987). These two instruments highlight the areas in which Maria needs support. She has feelings of being overwhelmed and worries a good deal about José. She does not understand why he is not developing at the same rate as her other two children, and she does not have anyone with whom to share these feelings. She utilizes many questions and physical manipulations when interacting with José. She does not know how to get José to look at her or pay attention, and she feels that he is happy when he watches certain television programs.

In addition to these two assessments, other language and communication assessments are administered: the *Bzoch–League–Brown Receptive Expressive Emergent Language Scale* 3rd edition (REEL-3), the Preschool Language Scale-4 (PLS-4) (Zimmerman, Steiner, & Pond, 2002), and the Childhood Autism Rating Scale (CARS) (Schopler, Reichler, & Renmen, 1988).

Other professionals also evaluate José. These professionals are the psychologist, who assesses the social–emotional and cognitive areas, the occupational therapist, who assesses José's physical motor development, and the special-education teacher, who assesses his play. After their evaluations are completed, their findings are reviewed by the early intervention official, as well as the other evaluators. José presents as a child with autism, and several services are recommended.

IFSP Recommendations for José

Individual special education services 5 times a week for 60 minutes

Individual speech-language therapy 5 times a week for 45 minutes

Individual occupational therapy 2 times a week for 30 minutes

Family counseling 1 time a week for 60 minutes

Nutrition services 1 time a week for 60 minutes

Parent support group 1 time a week for 60 minutes

Parent training group 1 time a week for 60 minutes

Individual physical therapy 2 times a week for 30 minutes

At the Individual Family Service Plan (IFSP) meeting, several statements or outcomes are generated. These statements reflect Maria's priorities and concerns for José. The following are some of the outcome statements on José's IFSP:

José will look at his mother when she talks to him.

José will play pat-a-cake with his mother.

José will hold a spoon to eat applesauce.

José will assemble a 5-piece foam board puzzle.

In addition to these outcome statements, strategy statements are also developed. For example,

Outcome: José will hold a spoon to eat applesauce.

Strategy: Use a special adaptive spoon. Use hand over hand guidance to practice scooping food with a spoon.

Maria Martinez requests that all his services be provided at the Early Start Infant Program (ESIP). Because José is nearing 3 years of age, it will soon be time to transition him from the early intervention program to the preschool program. This will mean more testing for José, and it is likely that a center-based special-education preschool will be recommended because José evidences severe developmental delays.

Maria Martinez benefits from parent training classes that help her to understand José's learning needs. Once she understands more about autism, she feels more comfortable about making daily decisions for José. A parent support group is provided for Maria so that she can share her hopes, dreams, and fears about José with other parents of children with developmental disabilities. Knowing that other families are also faced with challenges provides enormous comfort and support to Maria. The SLP explains her training procedures to ensure that Maria understands how to facilitate José's social behaviors and interactions. Maria is fortunate to be working with a bilingual SLP who can answer her questions about José's therapy sessions. Because some service providers do not speak Spanish, an interpreter is present during their therapy sessions so that Maria is able to participate in the therapy sessions: ask questions, seek clarification, and learn how to carry out the therapy goals.

CW 3.2

Use the Companion Website to help you answer the following questions:

1. Would you administer a family assessment to the Martinez family? If so, which would you select?

2. What other assessments would you administer and why?

3. What special needs do you think this family has?

4. Using the Social Interaction Tree (Figure 3.6), identify at what level you believe José Martinez is functioning.

5. How does diversity affect the family-centered approach?

6. Should José have been taught in English, Spanish, or both? Find research articles that discuss this issue.

7. Go to the ASHA Website to find 8/26/05 updates on assessing culturally and linguistically diverse children.

The Whiteside Family

When Kaitlyn is born, there is no universal hearing screening program in her state. Kaitlyn is several months old before Katherine realizes that Kaitlyn is not responding to the sounds around her. Kaitlyn's pediatrician recommends a hearing test–assessment, which requires several visits. At first, the family is shocked, and it takes a while for them to accept that she has a hearing loss. Eventually, the family must make decisions about Kaitlyn's educational training. Bilateral hearing aids are recommended, and Kaitlyn receives early intervention services at the Mission School. Katherine chooses this program because she believes that if Kaitlyn learns signs early she will develop language faster. Consequently, as Kaitlyn learns to use signs to communicate, so too does Katherine. The Whitesides accept Kaitlyn as a child with a hearing loss and are prepared to support her development.

Although Kaitlyn is fitted early on with hearing aids, her loss is such that she does not seem to make much progress or show much benefit from the aids. When Kaitlyn is 22 months old, Katherine decides to have her evaluated for a cochlear implant. Luckily, there is a regional center a few hours from their home, and it is determined that Kaitlyn meets the FDA criteria for implantation.

Prior to her implantation, Kaitlyn is assessed by the implant center. The center establishes that she does not have any abnormalities of the cochlea or any other handicapping conditions. In addition, the family's ability to provide Kaitlyn with consistent support and training after the implant is also assessed.

Once Kaitlyn is implanted, she continues with her therapy services at the Mission School for the Deaf. Kaitlyn continues to learn sign language as she is beginning to approximate words. By the time she turns 3 years old, she has a spoken vocabulary of 15 to 20 words. However, she is much more developed in her signing skills, and she can make her needs known by signing 100 to 150 words and stringing two signs together to generate sign phrases.

The Whiteside family is well aware that, although Kaitlyn has been implanted, the device does not give her normal hearing, and Kaitlyn is still functioning like a child with a severe hearing loss. After the implant, the implant center educational consultant works closely with Kaitlyn's speech pathologist and Katherine to make sure that the device is functioning properly and that Kaitlyn is making the kind of progress expected from the implant.

The clinical program developed for the Whiteside family at the IFSP consists of the following:

1. **Collaboration:** The SLP, with the teacher of the deaf, the psychologist, the audiologist, and the parent, will discuss developmentally appropriate activities.
2. **Direct services:** Speech and language therapy (4 × per week, individual, and 1 × group).
3. **Consultation:** The SLP will work with the parents to teach them sign language and how to facilitate language in the home (4 × per week).
4. **Consultation:** The SLP and the psychologist will work with the parents in a support group to discuss emotional difficulties arising within the family as a result of their child's communication problems (2 × per week group).

The St. James Family

The problems presented by Jeffrey raise concerns about the need for at-risk programs, the reliability of infant assessment measures, and the predictability of their results.

CW 3.3

Use the Companion Website to help you answer the following questions:

1. What parent–child interaction assessment would be appropriate for the Whiteside family?
2. What child assessment instruments would you administer? Why?
3. Do you think Kaitlyn is evidencing a language difference or a language delay? Why?
4. Are all children with hearing loss good candidates for a cochlear implant? Why or why not?
5. Describe the issues presented by parents in the Deaf Community about Deaf Culture.
6. Find out about the effectiveness of cochlear implants in younger versus older children with hearing loss.
7. See what you can find on the Internet about schools for the deaf or hard of hearing in your state. What do hearing parents say about Deaf Culture and cochlear implants?

Camille's frustration is relevant because every system utilizes eligibility criteria as a threshold for the provision of services. At 24 months, Jeffrey presents with a delay. How valid are the infant evaluation measures? What is the standard deviation for error on assessments for infants and toddlers? These questions are critical, because Jeffrey is a child from a family with at-risk characteristics. Despite these characteristics, Jeffrey and Camille are denied early intervention services because he does not meet the eligibility criteria for the state's definition of delay. Camille's frustration is expressed by many parents; "If there is a recognizable delay, why take the risk and wait to see if it gets worse?"

When Jeffrey is evaluated through the Public Health Department, several standardized instruments are used. Specifically, the Preschool Language Scale-4 (PLS-4) and the Receptive Expressive Emergent Language Test 3 (REEL-3) address Jeffrey's auditory comprehension of language and his expressive language. The Parenting Stress Index is also administered to determine what circumstances in the family situation might negatively affect Jeffrey's development. This instrument highlights several areas of stress; however, the only program or mechanism in place to address these factors is the Department of Social Services Childcare Program. Of course adequate child care is of extreme importance in meeting the needs of at-risk children and families.

Camille has other needs that cannot be addressed through the early intervention system. For instance, Jeffrey and his mother live at home with Camille's parents. When Camille's mother becomes ill, the family structure changes. Camille's mother cannot take care of Jeffrey. Camille is often exhausted from her full-time job and educational pursuits. Jeffrey becomes more demanding, and Camille is not able to meet his needs. Although Camille is a loving parent, she is inexperienced in dealing with Jeffrey's behavioral challenges. Jeffrey is a bright little boy who is feeling the impact of family stressors, and his behaviors reflect his anxieties.

By the time Jeffrey turns 3 years of age, his behaviors have worsened. In addition, his speech, language, and communication behaviors are not commensurate with his chronological age. Specifically, his understanding of certain syntactic constructions, his articulation, and his expression of ideas and concepts are delayed. Jeffrey's receptive single-word vocabulary and expressive single-word vocabulary are age appropriate. In addition, Jeffrey's play centers around action figures who are fighting with very little expressive and descriptive language. Other evaluations performed by the occupational therapist and psychologist show Jeffrey's motor and cognitive skills to be age appropriate.

Rescorla and Schwartz (1990) note that identifying language delay at age 3 or 4 is prognostically significant. However, there is little empirical research regarding the identification of language delay at age 2, even though from the period of 2 to 3 years parents are most likely told that their child will outgrow the delay. The question that remains is how likely is it that the 2-year-old, language-delayed child will outgrow the slow language development by age 3. In 1996, Paul's research recommended a policy of "watch and see," based on her data that children who present expressive language delays early in life often get better without any help. Van Kleeck, Gillam, and Davis (1997) return to this issue of late talkers, indicating that the issue is still not resolved and question the policy of "watch and see." They believe that such a policy can only be based on unambiguous evidence, which is not yet available.

CW 3.4

Use the Companion Website to help you answer the following questions:

1. What additional assessment instruments could have been used when Jeffrey and his family were initially assessed in the early intervention system?

2. Would you consider Jeffrey to be a child at-risk or a child with a delay when he is under the age of 3 years?

3. Would Jeffrey's cultural background require any specific knowledge by the evaluators and therapists working with him?

4. By the time Jeffrey is 3 years old, he is described as a child with emotional problems. Do you agree with this label? Why or why not?

5. Identify research studies that describe children who have transient versus persistent language problems.

6. Should Jeffrey have received early intervention services? If so, what kinds of services might have been helpful to Camille St. James and Jeffrey?

Some practitioners have embraced this idea of "watch and see," although it is still controversial within our field. This perspective has resulted in a delay of services to some children with communication disorders. If a percentage of children with a delay of less than 33% in the area of communication catch up later, the state has saved hundreds of thousands of dollars in early intervention services.

To parents, the decision to "wait and see" is just too risky. The other misconception related to communication disorders is that many infants and toddlers just have a communication problem. When a state utilizes restrictive eligibility criteria and does not provide programming for at-risk children, a "wait and see" policy can present serious problems, particularly for linguistically and culturally diverse children who need services.

In Jeffrey's case, the communication delay presents as the earliest indicator of a developmental problem, but it is not considered significant enough to warrant early intervention services. Jeffrey's communication difficulties exacerbate his social problems. How important is the relationship between language and social–emotional development? Because Jeffrey does not meet the eligibility criteria for early intervention services, Camille does not have the opportunity to benefit from family-centered programming.

SUMMARY

Inherent in the term *early intervention* are concepts such as flexibility, sensitivity, respect, collaboration, nontraditional, and creativity. Inherent in the term *early childhood service providers* are concepts such as listener, teacher, partner, and friend. To meet the challenge of early intervention, practitioners must revolutionize their thinking. Speech-language pathologists are no longer simply teachers or diagnosticians. They are partners in a collaborative relationship that is based on trust and respect. Just as PL 99-457 expanded the boundaries of special education, so too does it expand our professional horizons; thus SLPs must expand their thinking about professional roles and practices.

The speech-language pathologist no longer provides services only to the child. Instead, SLPs work with the family and the child to facilitate development in multiple areas, such as communication, play, and social interaction. SLPs model strategies for the parent while the parent is interacting with the child. Parent collaboration is the cornerstone of the early intervention system. By identifying family strengths, the SLP recognizes the relationship of culture and language. SLPs use a variety of standardized assessment instruments to determine how a child performs in relation to peers; observations, questionnaires, and interviews determine how the child functions in the home environment and what the expectations are for the child in this environment. SLPs modify the assessment process when necessary to perform nonbiased evaluations of children from different linguistic and cultural communities. Therapy goals are based on data gathered from the family, observations and testing, and the assessments of other professionals. Therapy goals cross disciplines to meet the family's and the child's needs. Public Law 99-457 has challenged the field of speech-language pathology to look into its therapy mirrors and to go beyond what is—to enter into what can be.

Language Interventions for Infants and Toddlers

Chapter Objectives

After studying this chapter, you should be able to answer the following questions:

1. What are some intervention approaches?

2. How can treatment strategies be modified within a natural environment?

3. How can parents be trained to facilitate language development?

4. What should the content of a parent-training program include?

5. What modifications need to be made when working with linguistically and culturally diverse families?

I n this chapter, language-intervention techniques are described within a family-centered model. The majority of early intervention services are provided in the home, which lends itself to both parent and child training. There are two primary issues in the training process. The first issue involves *how* to teach parents to function as facilitators. What methods are used to train parents? What are some techniques presently being used in parent-training programs? The second issue involves *what* to teach parents. Clearly, this is the content component of the program. What are parents going to be trained to do? How much information can parents be given and what topics are discussed? Can parents be taught facilitative techniques without understanding developmental theory? The significant advantage to early intervention is the family-centered approach, which is inclusive of siblings and extended family members. In this clinical approach, the parent is the consultee. The speech-language pathologist works directly with the child to provide the parent with an interactional model.

The Role of the Speech-Language Pathologist

When SLPs work with infants, specific roles and responsibilities have been delineated by the American Speech Language Hearing Association (1997). These responsibilities include the following:

- Communication evaluation and intervention in the context of developmentally supportive and family-focused care
- Feeding and swallowing evaluation and intervention
- Parent–caregiver education and counseling
- Staff–team education and collaboration

Communication evaluation involves the use of developmentally appropriate assessments of prelinguistic and sociocommunication interactions. The intervention plan must enhance the development of social, interactive communication. This plan also must be culturally appropriate for the family. Furthermore, the intervention plan must allow for either direct or indirect care, with indirect care being facilitated through caregiver education.

The Role of the Caregiver

Several studies emphasize the role of the parent, particularly the mother, as a language facilitator, in terms of the regulated input (motherese) provided during early development (Cross, 1977; Snow, Midkiff-Borunda, Small, & Proctor, 1984). There is no question that parents require help in learning how to teach their language-delayed children to talk. One such program that has had good success is the Hanen Early Language Program. The Hanen philosophy embraces the notion that parents are facilitators of language development. In the parent-training program, parents are taught to recognize their children's attempts to communicate; follow their children's lead; respond appropriately to their children's communicative attempts; and learn how to take turns, prompt, and incorporate appropriate activities and games for learning. Throughout the training program, parents learn how to use books, art activities, and music activities as vehicles for learning. This program was initiated in 1975, and there are updated revisions (Monolson, 1992; Watson, 1993). It continues to serve well the families of young children with special needs.

More recently (Dobson & Henderson, 1998), Hanen has been used as a training program for teacher assistants in early childhood classrooms and is considered effective and useful. Snow (1986) stresses the highly individualized communicative relationship between parent and child. Maternal input that is *language rich* is directly related to the child's vocal, verbal, and nonverbal behavior approximately 70% of the time. Thus, what the mother is speaking about to the infant is concrete and present.

Motherese was coined to describe the language produced by a mother when she regulates and attunes her input to her child's level of comprehension. Mothers talk about what the child is doing and saying. This level of child-centered and child-oriented input decreases as the child's language system develops and the parent's assumptions change about the communication process. During the first 3 years of life, the mother functions as an active, ongoing, highly responsive listener. She assumes that there is a need for the following:

- For repetition: "Want juice? Juice? Want juice? Juice"
- To talk about what is happening in the immediate context
- To be present when talking to the child; making eye contact, pointing, and providing gestures that are important to the communication process
- To regulate the level of her language complexity (i.e., up and down) to ensure that the child understands her and she understands the child

The mother's assumption that the child understands is critical to the entire process. Tiegerman-Farber and Siperstein (1982, 1984) note a breakdown in the communication interaction between mothers and children who are language disordered. Their studies indicate that the communication process between mother and child is not reciprocal because the child does not respond. As a result, mothers do not receive feedback from their children, which deprives them of the information needed to appropriately regulate their input.

The authors' results highlight two aspects of the communication exchange between mothers and their children with language disorders that are significantly different from those of mothers of typical language learners. First, mothers are semantically related 11% rather than 70% of the time. Thus, what the mother is speaking about to the infant is concrete and present only 11% of the time. For example, asking the child if he is hungry while giving him some food is semantically related. Second, the content of the input consists mainly of questions that mothers ask and then answer. Mothers indicate that they are frustrated because they do not know how to facilitate, let alone respond to, their nonresponsive children. This disruption in communication exchange between mother and child inhibits the language-learning process.

To facilitate a more naturalistic interactional experience, mothers can be taught to use a semantic approach at home. This approach incorporates the belief that it is important to talk about the "here and now" of what children experience. For example, when giving the child a plush toy animal to play with, the parent names the animal, makes the sound of the animal, and rubs it near the child's face while saying "Oh so soft." Some parents can be trained to collect data during the week and keep an anecdotal log. The SLP can *model* the appropriate technique for the parent and then observe the parent while she interacts with the child. Some parents have the skills to learn from text materials, but most parents require guidance, explanations, and emotional support as they learn. The SLP needs to understand the learning requirements of both the parent and the child.

Program Content

A semantic learning approach teaches parents that the input to their child should be a direct function of what she is doing and saying in the immediate context. Parents are taught the following:

1. To focus on the child
2. To stay on topic and follow the child in terms of his verbalizations and actions
3. To talk about the immediate context
4. To provide an ongoing commentary by naturally linking words with events
5. To regulate their language to the child's level of comprehension
6. To bridge between the child's level of performance and a more developmentally appropriate production
7. To use daily routines and natural experiences as language lessons

Establishing routines at home and talking about routines, particularly when unanticipated events occur, tends to be very difficult for mothers of children with language disorders because the dyadic interactional exchange takes a long time to develop. The mother is not going to be naturally reinforced when her child is unresponsive. She will have to accept limited gaze, gestural, and vocal responses.

Part of the training involves teaching mothers what to expect and what to accept, given the child's level of functioning. Parents can be trained about categories of semantic relatedness (see Table 4.1).

Depending on the parent's level of motivation and sophistication, one or more semantic categories can be modeled by the SLP. Each week the parent is given a worksheet to be completed by the parent during a play activity with the child (see Figure 4.1). The parent's job is to practice using the semantic strategies targeted by the SLP. During

TABLE 4.1   Coding Key and Category Definitions: Semantic Relatedness (Analysis I)

Code	Category Definition
RNVA	Maternal statement related to *child's nonverbal activity* (to what child is looking at, pointing to, action he or she is performing)
ERNVA*	Maternal *elicitation related to child's nonverbal activity* (question or statement whose purpose is to elicit verbal information from child)
NRNVA	Maternal utterances *not related* to child's nonverbal activity
RNVV	Maternal utterance *related* to child's nonverbal vocalizations (includes imitations, interpretation, and elicitations)
NRNVV	Maternal utterance *not related* to child's nonverbal vocalization
Imit.	Maternal *imitations* related to child's utterance (imitations may be partial or complete)
Exp.	Maternal *expansion* of the child's utterance (filling in omitted function words and grammatical markers)
Ext.	Maternal *extension* of the child's utterance (new information and grammatical markers are added)
Elicit.	Maternal *elicitation* of words related to child's utterance (questions and/or statements)
Other	Maternal utterances related to child's verbal activity that are acknowledgments (e.g., "ok," "very good," "yes")
NRVA	Maternal utterances *not related* to child's verbal activity (previous utterance)
NC*	*Nonclassifiable* (maternal and/or child statements that are *unintelligible*)
NS*	*Nonscorable*; any disagreement in coding a particular nonverbal or verbal interaction

Source: Snow, 1986.
*Additional categories not utilized by Snow.

| Type of Session: | | Child Number: | | Page: |
| Type of Number: | | Parent Name: | | |

Context:			**Semantic Category**
	Child	Adult	
Verbal			
Nonverbal			

Context:			**Semantic Category**
	Child	Adult	
Verbal			
Nonverbal			

Context:			**Semantic Category**
	Child	Adult	
Verbal			
Nonverbal			

Context:			**Semantic Category**
	Child	Adult	
Verbal			
Nonverbal			

FIGURE 4.1

Semantic Relatedness

this unstructured play period, the parent records the parent–child interactions. The SLP then reviews the worksheet with the mother to determine the ease of facilitation and/or specific child-related problems that require further explanation or clarification. The mother's data collection provides a long-term written record that is reviewed to determine mother–child interactional progress. The data-collection process is an invaluable tool that is reinforcing to the mother and the SLP. So a parent-training program should be designed with the following goals in mind:

1. The language analysis of the mother–child interaction identifies communication differences that interfere with the development of a dyadic exchange process. The language-learning needs of the child are analyzed within a communicative social framework (McLean & Vincent, 1984).
2. To reinforce language development at home, parents are trained to facilitate language. The generalization process is ensured when parents are actively involved in language-based activities.
3. The content of the training program focuses the parent's attention to specific language-learning variables in the child. Parents need to know specifically *what* to do and *how* to do it. Model the technique or the semantic relation, and minimize written descriptions and verbal explanations.

Group therapy sessions for parents are useful. This establishes networking opportunities for parents to talk to other parents with similar problems and experiences at home. The group sessions also give parents an opportunity to share information about and solutions to problems they have resolved. In parent–child therapy groups, parents can observe and help one another. Parent–parent interaction is as important for parents as it is for children. Group interventions usually involve a professional working with two or more children who have similar developmental characteristics and clinical needs. The size of the group may vary as a function of the children's needs, abilities, and the type of therapeutic procedures required.

Group interventions may occur in a variety of clinical, educational, and community settings. Language-intervention approaches can focus specifically on the child (direct intervention) or on teaching intervention skills to the parent or primary caretaker, who then works with a child (indirect intervention). When intervention focuses directly on the child, sometimes the SLP works with a child individually in a separate therapy room (pull-out services) or in an early childhood setting with typical peers (push-in service). The decisions concerning therapy setting and direct versus indirect interventions depend on a number of factors:

- Needs of the child and his family
- Child's physical age and developmental level of functioning
- Type of disability
- Severity of the child's disability
- Cultural values and beliefs of the family
- Primary language used in the home

Program Procedures

Once a theoretical framework is established, parents can be shown how to apply their knowledge at home with their children. Parent training reinforces the idea that they play a primary role in the language facilitation of their children. Parent classes train parents at various levels.

Parent as Student

Parent-education classes provide an excellent forum for teaching parents about developmental disabilities and educational decision making (Kaiser et al., 1990; McDade & Simpson, 1984). The topics presented in the classes range in diversity from normal developmental issues to management techniques to IFSP goals. Such classes provide definitions of technical terms so that parents can more competently contribute to educational exchange and more adequately understand reports and evaluations. Classes also provide developmental charts and materials so that parents can understand their child's level of functioning in relation to typical patterns. Professionals from different disciplines (psychology, physical therapy, occupational therapy, etc.) lecture on goals and therapeutic instructional techniques. Parents learn about the educational process, philosophy, and integration of related services and are taught how to work with their children at home. Specifically, the procedural techniques used with parents can facilitate long-term developmental changes achieved in children. The development of parents' knowledge is regulated to the parents' level of understanding, motivation, diversity, and needs. At no time should parents be made to feel that the material is being watered down or that there is an expectation that they will not utilize this knowledge.

The intent and motivation of professionals is very clear; parents must understand that if they are going to function effectively with their children they need to know what to do. These classes can require readings, simple examinations, and parent assignments. Parent lectures are helpful in getting parents to utilize their knowledge in class with other parents. This is an excellent exercise; eventually, parents will need to be able to contribute as members of multidisciplinary teams. When parents receive educational instruction, the child's language training is expanded and broadened. When parents are taught as students, they acquire an understanding of what the child is progressing through, because he or she is also a student. Classroom instruction for parents involves teaching them how to teach—how to facilitate interactive language behavior in the child.

Parents learn about being agents of change; they also learn what must be changed in the home environment. They become sensitively attuned to the child's language-learning needs. Parent programming formalizes the educational process with the family. It is obvious that, as part of this programming, a curriculum for parent education must be developed, implemented, and evaluated over time (Fitzgerald & Karnes, 1987). Success with such a curriculum will obviously be a function of many different variables, and these variables must be discussed during parent training.

Parent as Observer

If children are enrolled in group early intervention programs, parents can participate in the groups with their children on a weekly basis. In this case, SLPs provide the appropriate models for interaction, and parents have an opportunity to observe the instructional activities that set the occasion for social communication and to learn by seeing how it is done. They learn how to interact with their children in ways that facilitate communication.

If the therapy rooms have closed-circuit video systems, parents can observe frequently. This nonintrusive mechanism allows them to watch the child in learning contexts without interfering with the instruction. At these times, parents often see their children interacting and behaving in ways that are different from when just the parent and child are together.

Parent as Child Facilitator

Moran and Whitman (1985) suggest taping parents during play interactions with their children and analyzing the videotapes to determine the forms and communicative aspects of the adult–child interaction. The form in Figure 4.1, which is used to transcribe parent–child conversational utterances, also allows the parents to categorize the semantic function of the linguistic input provided to the child. They can also determine the number of communicative turns that occur on each topic: the greater the number of turns, the more knowledge the child has about the topic or object.

Based on the analysis, parents are provided with prescriptive training on how and what to facilitate. Parents can be trained to transcribe and analyze language samples as a means of monitoring ongoing adult–child communication and language changes at home. Adult–child videotapes can also be used for parent-training and parent–child assessment purposes.

Parent as Child Advocate

The process of becoming partners in the educational process encourages parents to become more assertive and more independent (Parks & Smeriglio, 1986; Schaefer, 1989). This is a challenge to the educational system and to professionals. As parents become more sophisticated, they naturally become more involved and more demanding in terms of decision making. The educational system cannot do it all from 9:00 a.m. to 3:00 p.m. Parents are a resource; they must be educated to function in the system. Part of the challenge of involvement is advocacy (Healy, Keesee, & Smith, 1989). Sophisticated and knowledgeable parents question. They challenge the decisions of professionals, multidisciplinary teams, and committees on preschool special education. They can advocate for their children's needs in a way that no professional team ever can. Parents have an investment in their children and their short- and long-term growth. One issue in education involves an understanding of educational policy, legislation, and law. Part of the parent-training experience should be devoted specifically to advocacy issues so that parents do not step into team meetings without a firm understanding of process, procedure, and protocol.

Parents who understand their role know what to expect and how to contribute effectively to the decision-making process of the educational team (Yell & Espin, 1990). Parents who "know" about their children can understand their needs, explain IFSP goals, and contribute to team decision making. It is important to understand that professionals see the child for a limited amount of time in a rather artificial setting, whereas parents can present a set of long-term observations and issues.

Early intervention programs can have a long-term impact on parent education by including advocacy training. Learning to advocate for the child is an invaluable gift and skill that the parent will use as the child grows and enters the preschool and school-age educational programs. Early intervention programs begin the process of training parents to function effectively as advocates for their children.

Program Process

Cultural Background

Parent-training programs must take into consideration the various backgrounds of parents and families. Obviously, cultural differences will affect the parent-education process. Parents will have different attitudes and concerns about their child's education and their role as facilitators.

Economic Level

The financial factors that influence the family also affect the child. Single parents or working parents are already stressed by social, economic, familial, and child-based issues. During the day, it might be difficult to reach the parents, and it will be difficult for them to attend parent-education classes. The early intervention system must make a commitment to these families and provide alternative training sessions on weekends and evenings. A single parent who is struggling to support her children may give priority to her job. SLPs must learn to take into account the factors that affect the ecological health and welfare of the family.

Involvement with the Child

Traditionally, mothers have been much more involved in the rearing and nurturance of young children. The infant with a language delay or disorder presents a significant stress on family dynamics and interactions. When fathers are less involved, the presence of an infant with a disability makes it even more difficult for the father to assume responsibilities when the mother is not around. Fathers often have different issues than mothers as far as children are concerned.

Figure 4.2 describes some of the differing attitudes that mothers and fathers present at the beginning of parent training. Sparling, Berger, and Biller (1992) offer specific suggestions for enhancing the father's commitment to the education of his child with special needs:

- Recognize the unique role of the father; he can provide support and advice.
- Recognize culture, tradition, and unique paternal perspectives and schedules. With these in mind, plan for father-support meetings, father–child play interactions, and therapist or teacher consultations.
- Recognize and accept the male role of fathers with culturally different perceptions. In patriarchal cultures, the father manages the relationships of family members with the outside world. Be sure to direct questions to the father when initially working with the family to arrange for services.
- Visit the family to determine the preferences and roles the father has in the education of the child.
- Determine paternal perceptions through the interview process.

Mothers

I feel totally overwhelmed with my child.

I do not have any time to spend with my other children or my husband.

I do not have any time for myself, and I am stressed out.

My husband feels that along with housekeeping, washing, cleaning, and disciplining, my child is my problem and responsibility.

I am very concerned that my husband is afraid of our child.

Fathers

I work. That is my primary responsibility. My wife takes care of the kids.

I try to help my wife, but she is much more effective in managing our son.

My son with disabilities listens to his mother more than he listens to me.

After working all day, I really don't want to be bothered with the noisy havoc in the house.

I need to go to work in the morning. I can't stand the confusion, the screaming, and the mess.

FIGURE 4.2

Parents' Attitudes Prior to Parent Training

Scott Cunningham / Merrill

Parents need to learn effective strategies in order to facilitate language development in the home.

The more effectively parents work together in supporting each other and working with the infant, the greater the chance for the family to function as a unit and for each adult to provide respite for the other. Time together and time alone are very important issues in any family, but they are especially important in a family that includes an infant with a disability.

The Effectiveness of Instruction

Over time, parent education and programming will change. The program should be evaluated annually. Figure 4.3 provides an example of a questionnaire to be filled out by parents who have been through the program. At the end of the year, short- and long-term evaluations are helpful in providing a feedback mechanism to fine-tune procedures and content.

Language Intervention in the Home

To facilitate communication and language development in the home, the professional who works with the family must recognize that his or her role has changed. The consultation model has a long and successful history in fields such as psychology and social work. Social work and counseling also can be very successful in early intervention. In the psychological literature, consultation is defined as an indirect problem-solving process (Coleman, Buysse, Scalise-Smith, & Schute, 1991).

In early intervention the consultant (early interventionist) and the consultee (parent or caregiver) work together to achieve specific goals. The consultee does most of the direct work, and the consultant directly helps the child by working with the consultee. Consultation is a problem-solving process with several common steps: problem identification, problem analysis, plan implementation, and problem evaluation (Coleman et al., 1991). When the SLP interviews the family, he or she identifies the problem in terms of the family's perspective. The SLP then works together with the family to develop a plan of action to resolve the problem.

For instance, the parents of a developmentally disabled infant are concerned that she does not look at them when they talk to her. The SLP (consultant) and the parent (consultee) discuss what the child does do and then determine that a good plan would be as follows. When the child is seated in the high chair and ready to eat, the mother puts the spoon near her face or eyes, says something, such as, "Here comes the applesauce," and then feeds the child. The goal is that at each feeding the mother uses this technique to establish eye contact at least 10 times. The mother takes a count of the number of times it is successful and then discusses it with the SLP at the next visit. If it is not successful, another strategy is decided on, one that both the parent and SLP plan together.

In this type of model, the parent is an equal partner and planner in the intervention process. The parent identifies the area of concern and then works out an achievable plan with the consultant. The parent is more likely to be invested in the intervention, and there is greater likelihood that it will be successful. Furthermore, the parent feels successful because she has helped develop and implement the plan in which the child has been successful.

Therapeutic Approaches: Directive and Naturalistic

One cannot consider early intervention strategies without a discussion of behaviorism. Recently, a substantial growth in the incidence of pervasive developmental disorders (PDD), a broad diagnostic category that includes autism and autismlike disorders, has been documented.

Please circle: Male

                        Female

Please fill out the following questionnaire. Rate your responses according to the following:

1 ———— 2 ———— 3 ———— 4 ———— 5

Strongly Agree (SA)	Agree (A)	Don't Know (?)	Disagree (D)	Strongly Disagree (SD)

	Questions	SA 1	A 2	? 3	D 4	SD 5
1	My child's problem is so serious I can't deal with it.					
2	My child is unmanageable.					
3	I'm a better manager than my spouse.					
4	I don't like that my child has behavior problems.					
5	I'm embarrassed by my child's behavior problems.					
6	I would describe my child's behavior problem as serious.					
7	I'm embarrassed my child has a disabling condition.					
8	My family does not understand my child's behavior problems.					
9	I don't understand why my child acts out.					
10	I feel I did something wrong.					
11	My other children don't understand why my child acts out.					
12	My child is difficult to interact with.					
13	My child is not typical, so I do not talk to him or her the same way I would talk to another child.					
14	My child acts out all the time.					
15	I can only manage my child by being physical.					
16	I can only manage my child by yelling.					
17	I can only manage my child by putting him or her in his or her room.					
18	My child cannot play with other children.					
19	I am frustrated managing my child.					
20	I wish my child would listen.					
21	In managing my child, my other children are ignored.					
22	My spouse and I argue about how to manage our child.					
23	There is conflict between my spouse and me because we have a child with a disability.					

FIGURE 4.3
Parent Attitudinal Scale

(continued)

	Questions	SA 1	A 2	? 3	D 4	SD 5
24	My spouse leaves the management of our child to me.					
25	This course has taught me how to manage my child's problem.					
26	I feel better about myself.					
27	I understand my child's needs better.					
28	I understand that as my child's language increases his behavior will improve.					
29	I think every parent needs to take a parent-training course.					
30	Parent education is just as important as a child's education.					
31	This parent-training class has improved my relationship with my other children.					
32	This parent-training class has improved my relationship with my spouse.					
33	Parent training has improved my self-confidence.					
34	I am willing to change my behavior to meet my child's needs.					
35	I know how to change my behavior to meet my child's needs.					
36	I feel I can adequately advocate for my child's needs.					
37	I have the power to make decisions related to my child.					
38	I am comfortable with the role I have in my child's education.					
39	I am responsible for learning what my child's needs and rights are.					
Comments:						

FIGURE 4.3
(*continued*)

Because of the severity of the impact this disorder has on the overall functioning of children, some states have developed clinical guidelines for effective diagnosis and treatment of autism. These guidelines recommend intensive intervention programs using a systematic behavioral approach, which includes principles of applied behavior analysis (ABA) and behavior intervention strategies:

- Systematic use of behavioral teaching techniques and intervention procedures
- Intensive direct instruction, usually on a one-to-one basis
- Extensive parent training so that parents can provide additional hours of intervention

This type of program may be provided for a minimum of 20 hours per week. More recently, the American Academy of Pediatrics, the American Academy of Child and Adolescent Psychiatry, the surgeon general, and the National Academy of Sciences recommended a minimum of 25 hours of therapy per week for children who are autistic. A behavioral program is considered a form of directive intervention in that the SLP provides situations in which she controls the motivators and the reinforcers. Specific techniques, such as modeling and prompting, are utilized to elicit specific targets for outcomes. Modeling takes the form of the SLP modeling the target behavior and then prompting the child to respond with that behavior. For example, the SLP wants the child to say the word "head." The SLP touches her own head and says "head" and then prompts the child to touch his head and say "head." In an ABA paradigm the programming is strictly delineated and the SLP follows the plan very strictly. Data are also carefully gathered. Figure 4.4 delineates a specific program for a training session.

In contrast to the behavioral approach, the developmental individual difference relationship (DIR) model (Greenspan & Wieder, 1997) is employed when working with children who have pervasive developmental delays. The focus of the DIR is to increase the child's ability for social interactions with the parent. An integral part of therapy is spent with the parent and child sitting on the floor for 20 to 30 minutes at a time, 6 to 10 times a day, and interacting. This approach is a more naturalistic, experiential approach and has also been referred to as "floor time." Naturalistic approaches:

- Generally use the child's day-to-day environment as an opportunity for learning
- Are more child directed in that the child's interest or focus is capitalized on
- Utilize reinforcers that are a natural consequence of a social communication experience, such as hugs and kisses

In a naturalistic approach the SLP arranges materials in the environment to generate specific responses from the child and train the parent to do the same (New York State Department of Health, 1999). No one approach or technique is best for all children. It is up to the collaborative team, and most importantly the family, to decide on the approach to be used. Once this decision is made, the family can be trained to facilitate development using appropriate techniques, given the approach selected. When making this decision, several factors need to be considered, such as the availability of the parents and child to receive intensive programming, the child's level of language development, and the individual characteristics of the child.

Ecological Foundation of Early Intervention

The ecological approach to early intervention seeks to identify "ecologies" that are meaningful to parents and SLPs and that will target goals for intervention. The use of this approach requires ecobehavioral consultation whereby activities that are problematic within specific settings are identified and analyzed into meaningful ecological units. These units are considered in terms of physical and social features, and a program of useful activities is developed from the analyses. In this approach, ecological principles are merged.

NAME: Tommy Q

TARGET BEHAVIOR: To imitate actions with objects.

LONG-TERM GOAL: To improve imitation skills.

LONG-TERM OBJECTIVE: Upon delivery of the instruction "do this," the trainer will model an action with an object, and Tommy will perform 1 through 20 of the appropriate actions with the objects, with 80% accuracy or better over three consecutive sessions.

SHORT-TERM OBJECTIVE 1: Upon delivery of the instruction "do this," the trainer will model an action with an object, and Tommy will perform 1 through 5 of the appropriate actions with the objects, with 80% accuracy or better over two consecutive sessions.

SHORT-TERM OBJECTIVE 2: Upon delivery of the instruction "do this," the trainer will model an action with an object, and Tommy will perform 6 through 10 of the appropriate actions with the objects, with 80% accuracy or better over two consecutive sessions.

SHORT-TERM OBJECTIVE 3: Upon delivery of the instruction, "do this," the trainer will model an action with an object, and Tommy will perform 11 through 15 of the appropriate actions with the objects, with 80% accuracy or better over two consecutive sessions.

DEFINITION OF TARGET BEHAVIOR: Correct responses are defined as Tommy appropriately modeling the trainer's actions with various objects.

SETTING, TIME, AND ACTIVITY FOR TEACHING: During direct teaching trials at a desk.

MATERIALS NEEDED: Objects for the actions.

REINFORCERS IDENTIFIED: Reinforcer assessments will be conducted on a daily basis. Verbal praise, chips, toy horse, big bird, bristle blocks, tickles, and hugs have been identified as potential reinforcers.

MEASUREMENT SYSTEM: The percentage of correct trials.

PROGRAM PROCEDURE: Trainer will place two identical objects on the table. Trainer will sit across the table facing Tommy. Establish attending. Present the instruction "do this" while simultaneously modeling an action with one of the objects. Prompt Tommy to perform the action with the other object and reinforce the response. Fade prompts over subsequent trials. Differentially reinforce response with the lowest level of prompting; only reinforce correct unprompted responses.

LANGUAGE COMPONENT: While the trainer is modeling the correct actions for an appropriate response, record data on the response at that moment. After the trial is executed and data are taken, the trainer will illicit "wh" questions to facilitate both receptive and expressive language skills from Tommy. For example, you would utilize the object that Tommy is working on and facilitate "wh" questions regarding the object Tommy is performing the action with.

FIGURE 4.4
Specific Program for a Training Session

The ecological approach is very useful when interactions between the child and parent are unsatisfactory and do not meet developmental goals (Barnett & Lentz, 1997). By examining planned parent–child interactions and determining what problem responses occur (crying, hitting) and what other environmental conditions are in place (other persons, toys, TV playing), the SLP gains insight into how to modify ecologies for more effective interactions. These modifications are intervention plans that incorporate the parents' goals for specific settings and activities.

Often the parents' plans or goals for their children include social and personal competence and mastery. The SLP must then develop activities that take into account the reality of the parental situation and a program of activity-based intervention that is child directed and relates to parenting skills, preacademics, language development, and social competence. The process of assessing behavioral interactions within social contexts involves interviews with parents and caregivers, as well as several planned observations of parent– and caregiver–child interactions (Martens & Witt, 1988; Willems, 1977).

SUMMARY

This chapter discusses the need for formalized parent education. The issues faced by families of children with disabilities are real issues faced by all parents whose children attend school. The problems in the American family are very similar to problems faced by teachers in schools. It is critical to understand that today's student will be the teacher of tomorrow, who must face these challenges and understand the history and the basis for parent empowerment and child advocacy. Let us look forward and view these changes as a positive movement; the realignment of parent and professional presents a great opportunity and potential for education. Let us look forward to a time when parents and professionals can share in the decision-making process; the ultimate investment is the product of both—the child.

PART 2

Preschool:
A Child-Centered Approach

In Part 2, Maria Martinez, Katherine Whiteside, and Camille St. James deal with the daily realities of having a child who is developmentally different from typical peers. The social and language differences are becoming more evident in natural settings such as playgrounds, restaurants, family parties, and neighborhood events.

Maria Martinez is struggling with family and work issues aside from her concerns about José. Maria is learning English and trying to understand what is being done in preschool because there is only one person who speaks Spanish. José has started to talk, but repeats everything he hears. He has an excellent memory, but his routines of keeping objects in the same place and following certain steps to complete activities have become quite problematic. It is difficult for Maria to visit José's school. Teachers and specialists use a notebook in which information is translated into Spanish. Although the professionals are supportive, Maria feels isolated from José's learning experiences. She misses the contact with her service coordinator from the early intervention program. Maria has not had a conversation with José. She has not heard, "Mommy, I love you," "Mommy, I'm sick," or "Mommy, are we there yet?" Maria wonders about what José is thinking and feeling.

Katherine Whiteside is very pleased with Kaitlyn's progress at the Mission School for the Deaf—she receives sign-language training, aural rehabilitation services, and speech-language therapy. Katherine attends every training class, support group, and education workshop provided to parents. She establishes close relationships with Kaitlyn's teachers and works with Kaitlyn at home on a daily basis. Kaitlyn has become a "mission" for Katherine. The family problems have been put aside so that Katherine can focus all her time and energy on Kaitlyn.

Some families whose children attend the school are part of the Deaf Community. Katherine wants to learn as much as she can about deafness and wishes that she were closer to the families who are deaf. Katherine feels different and alone. The parents who are deaf are polite, but it is not always easy for them to communicate with Katherine. Katherine cannot maintain a conversation with these parents, and she misses all the subtle humor and interpersonal interactions. Often the signing is just too fast, and she does not feel comfortable telling everyone else to slow down.

Katherine practices her signs but she thinks in words, which tends to slow her down. No one is deliberately leaving her out, but she does not have a hearing loss. The other parents have a shared experience that facilitates a social connection and bond. When Katherine watches Kaitlyn, she realizes that there is also a difference between the two of them. Kaitlyn is becoming a part of a community within which Katherine will never feel comfortable. Kaitlyn will speak a language that the two of them will share only on a superficial level. Katherine realizes that her daughter is growing up in another social world, one that does not easily include her as a hearing person. Katherine feels strongly about Kaitlyn's separate schooling. In the Deaf Community, Kaitlyn will not be perceived as being different or having a disability. Katherine is preparing herself to ensure Kaitlyn's right to remain in a separate school.

Camille St. James realizes that Jeffrey has behavioral problems that are affecting his ability to socialize with typical peers. She does not think that Jeffrey is emotionally disturbed. Camille is beginning to understand that Jeffrey's problems are directly linked to his speech and language skills. Camille is advocating for Jeffrey's services by herself. She feels that she is at a serious disadvantage, because she does not have the knowledge to effectively discuss Jeffrey's need for services with professionals. Although Jeffrey could benefit from interactions with typical peers, his aggressive behaviors limit their willingness to play with him. As a child with a disability, Jeffrey does not know how to modify his own behavior to adapt to his social environment. Over time, Jeffrey becomes more isolated in the general-education early childhood classroom.

Each child's language characteristics evolve during the preschool years and highlight the damaging consequences of early language delays. The language differences affect all the other areas that are also developing at the same time. It is important to track how the children's language problems influence how they think, behave, and feel about others, as well as themselves. The developmental systems are interactive and interdependent. Delays in vocabulary development result in a continuum of cognitive, social, and affective problems, ranging from José's obvious social deficits to Kaitlyn's subtle communication differences. The fact that Jeffrey could verbalize was not an advantage in a system that utilizes quantitative measures, such as a 33% delay criterion, to determine eligibility for services. Often the child with specific language impairment is perceived as not being severe enough to receive special-education services. Within the field of education, a misunderstanding remains about the relationship between speech and language. This confusion results in the perception that children with a speech impairment do not have a disability as severe as children with cognitive deficits. It is here that the role of the speech-language pathologist as an advocate becomes important to both the development of public awareness and the protection of services to children and families.

CHAPTER

5

Understanding Early Childhood Education

Chapter Objectives

After studying this chapter, you should be able to answer the following questions:

1. How would you describe the preschool special-education system from early referral to special-education programming?

2. What are the responsibilities of the preschool special-education committee (PSEC) and of its decision-making process?

3. What issues are related to cultural and linguistic diversity for families and children in the preschool system?

4. What are the problems for children, parents, and professionals as related to early childhood inclusion?

5. What are the legal and definitional difficulties related to the concept of free and appropriate education?

The purpose of this chapter is to review the preschool special-education system as a function of changing federal legislation since the passage of PL 94-142. The systemic differences within and across states can be problematic for many families. The preschool special-education system is different from the early intervention system and does not always provide a seamless transition experience for families and children (Prendeville & Ross-Allen, 2002). Successful transition from early intervention to preschool special education requires both interagency and professional collaboration (Dimes, Merritt, & Culatta, 1998; Gallagher, Harbin, Thomas, Clifford, & Wenger, 1998; Gallagher & Desimone, 1995; Garrett & Thorp, 1998; Gallagher, Harbin, Eckland, & Clifford, 1994).

Preschool special education as a system of services is influenced by its own unique structural, procedural, and interpersonal relationships (Kaczmarek, Goldstein, Floreg, Carter, & Cannon, 2004). The result is that the experiences of families and children with language disorders are affected by each system's ability to evaluate and change its service provision system to meet the families' unique cultural and linguistic needs (Holditch-Davis & Miles, 2000). Bureaucratic systems are often difficult to change because of their histories and long-standing procedures that determine the decision-making process. Systemic changes require administrators to view service provision from a different perspective and professionals to create collaborative partnerships with each other and with parents (Buck, Cox, Shannon, & Hash, 2001). Many families have not found transition from early intervention to preschool special education to be an easy transition (Shogren & Turnbull, 2006).

Family Concerns

In this chapter, the three families describe their experiences as their children transition into the preschool special-education system. The families face their first major obstacle when they realize that the preschool system "works differently." Each family describes concerns that occur for many parents at preschool special-education committee meetings.

Child-Centered Approach

The child-centered approach represents the critical difference between the preschool special-education and early intervention systems. The change to a child-centered committee approach is difficult even in the best of circumstances. Since the preschool special-education system is not family centered, the needs of the family are not a primary concern of professionals. It is important to keep in mind that theory underlies practice, so the shift from family centered to child centered creates a completely different service-delivery system (Shannon, 2004; Romer & Umbreit, 1998). Within the child-centered approach, the family role changes. Parents frequently complain that there are fewer opportunities for families and professionals to work together, and fewer opportunities for involvement with teachers and therapists in the preschool special-education classroom.

Diversity Issues

Some preschool special-education teachers and early childhood teachers have not received training about the complex problems facing linguistically and culturally diverse children and families, so they may not be sensitively attuned to their unique differences and needs. This becomes a much more complicated issue in the preschool special-education system; where parents and professionals tend to interact less frequently, given the educational constraints. The result is an increase in opportunities for miscommunication between families and professionals and a sense of frustration about the communication process.

Preschool Special Education

In the United States, special-education teachers are the primary specialists certified to provide services to preschool children with disabilities. States have different certifications that are either specific (teacher of the mentally retarded, teacher of the autistic, teacher of the learning disabled) or general (teacher of special education) that cover all populations of children with disabilities. Whatever the certification, special education over the past several decades has become highly specialized and separate from general education, thus creating two parallel systems.

This division is particularly evident and problematic for the preschool special-education system that mandates services for children with disabilities between 3 and 5 years old in a voluntary system. Parents of preschool children with disabilities do not have to accept special-education services, because education is not compulsory in the United States until children turn 6 years of age. The other issue involves the lack of a national early childhood initiative that supports child-care programs that could provide inclusion opportunities for preschool children with disabilities. Thus, if the special-education program does not also provide services to typical preschoolers as part of a separate program, inclusion opportunities are limited.

The statewide preschool system may regulate child-care programs, but only families receiving social services can access these programs at no cost or at a reduced fee. The philosophical notion or underlying premise of special education is that children with developmental disabilities require both different instructional techniques and highly specialized educational curricula. Thus children with developmental disabilities have both *qualitative* and *quantitative* learning differences. There has been an expansion in the number and type of special-education programs and an increase in the number of children served since the passage of PL 99-457 in 1986. Three different populations of children and families have been entering the preschool special-education system since this law was passed:

1. Group 1 received early intervention services and transitioned into preschool with an IFSP. Parents in this group had experiences with the assessment and intervention requirements of a service delivery system. They had worked with many professionals and generally have a positive attitude about the family-centered approach.

2. Group 2 did not receive early intervention services because they were not eligible. Some parents in this group had experiences with the early intervention assessment process, but were informed at an IFSP meeting that their children did not meet the eligibility requirements to receive services. Some parents did not accept the decision of the IFSP team and paid for therapeutic services themselves or through private insurance carriers. When their children are reevaluated by preschool special-education committees, they are then found eligible for services.

3. Group 3 did not receive early intervention services because parents were either unaware of the program or of their children's developmental disability. The preschool special-education system is their point of entry, and the initial assessment and diagnostic process can be emotionally overwhelming.

Special and Separate Education

The special-education system has been criticized as a separate system that is too restrictive in its options for children with disabilities (Fitch, 2003). Terms such as *segregated* education, rather than self-contained education, are used to highlight the issue of separate special-education programming for children with disabilities. Because children with developmental disabilities present highly individualized learning dynamics, they are often placed in specialized classrooms with children who either have the same developmental disability or different categorical labels, but similar learning needs. Madelline Wills (Matthews, 1994), assistant secretary for special education and rehabilitation in the U.S. Department of Education, advocated for a change in the way that children with developmental disabilities are educated within the public schools. She proposed that children with developmental disabilities should not be placed in separate settings, classrooms, or schools, but rather in classrooms with typical peers. Some parent groups advocate that preschool children with disabilities need to experience a normal learning environment with typical peers.

Inclusion Concept

Inclusion conceptually means the integration of children with and without disabilities. In its purest form, it is the belief that children with disabilities should be integrated into general education regardless of their type or level of disability. However, questions arise about the following:

1. When inclusion should be provided to a child with a disability
2. How inclusion should be accomplished within general education
3. Whether inclusion is appropriate for *all* children with disabilities

Preschool education is not compulsory in the United States; typical children are not entitled to early childhood programming "at no cost to families." So, when parents want their typical children to attend early childhood (nursery school or child-care) programs, they must pay for it. When the federal government reauthorized IDEA in the 1990s, the push to provide inclusive programming escalated (Harbin & Kameny, 2000; Harbin & Salisbury, 2000; Sandall, McLean, & Smith, 2000). Whereas typical children are readily available in elementary school to facilitate the development of inclusive classrooms, they are not available below the age of 5 years. The result is a complicated situation for parents and preschool special-education program providers.

1. Many early childhood and child-care programs do not have staff trained to work with preschool children with disabilities, so they may refuse to accept them.
2. Preschool special-education programs that attempt to integrate their programs are faced with financial and public-relations problems. Parents of children with and without disabilities need to be convinced that their children's development will not be negatively affected by integrated experiences. Parents of typical preschoolers may remove their children if their concerns and fears are not addressed.
3. It is more expensive for programs to hire certified special-education teachers than child-care workers. Who should pay for the additional staff costs? Preschool programs and governmental agencies cannot use special-education funds to create inclusive programs or provide incentives for parents of typical children to participate in such programs (Federal Register, 1998). As a result, many inclusive preschools consist of children with disabilities and economically disadvantaged children whose tuition is paid through social service agencies. Parents who can afford to pay for child care often choose preschools that use academic-centered programs and do not include children with special needs.
4. Some preschool special-education committees inform parents of children with disabilities that, if their child is high functioning enough to benefit from an early childhood program, the schools are not responsible for the child-care or nursery school costs. The parents can privately enroll their child into the

typical early childhood program, and then only related services will be at no cost to the families.

State Variations: Eligibility

Table 5.1 compares the percentage of children in early intervention to the percentage in preschool special education within various states. All 50 states have implemented programs for preschool children 3 to 5 years of age. To better understand fluctuations in the children identified and served, the early intervention and preschool systems

TABLE 5.1   Comparison of Children Receiving Services by Number and Percentage, December 2003

State	Birth–2 Total	Percentage of Population	Ages 3 to 5	Percentage of Population
Alabama	2,153	1.2	7,843	4.44
Alaska	641	2.17	1,968	6.86
Arizona	3,725	1.39	11,952	4.74
Arakansas	2,772	2.46	10,670	9.7
California	27,496	1.76	61,950	4.2
Colorado	3,148	1.56	9,673	5.16
Connecticut	3,701	2.96	8,135	6.24
Delaware	955	2.9	2,031	6.43
District of Columbia	251	1.13	301	1.77
Florida	14,719	2.28	35,258	5.73
Georgia	4,840	1.19	20,260	5.4
Hawaii	4,178	7.7	2,284	4.96
Idaho	1,490	2.44	3,807	6.31
Illinois	13,140	2.42	32,718	6.34
Indiana	9,270	3.62	18,439	7.06
Iowa	2,136	1.95	5,985	5.51
Kansas	2,749	2.4	9,190	8.21
Kentucky	3,886	2.37	20,219	12.58
Louisiana	3,498	1.75	11,386	6.09
Maine	1,105	2.77	4,647	11.18
Maryland	5,774	2.6	12,105	5.67
Massachusetts	14,407	5.92	14,822	6.37
Michigan	8,210	2.13	23,465	5.93
Minneosta	3,502	1.78	12,987	6.69
Mississippi	1,975	1.53	7,994	6.56
Missouri	3,423	1.51	15,140	6.85
Montana	628	1.95	1,798	5.62
Nebraska	1,260	1.7	4,445	6.37
Nevada	930	0.94	4,933	5.1
New Hampshire	1,146	2.61	2,586	5.78

(*continued*)

TABLE 5.1　*(continued)*

State	Birth–2 Total	Percentage of Population	Ages 3 to 5	Percentage of Population
New Jersey	8,091	2.36	18,545	5.48
New Mexico	2,327	2.89	5,656	7.16
New York	33,026	4.42	55,588	7.9
North Carolina	5,957	1.66	21,018	6.12
North Dakota	476	2.13	1,501	6.76
Ohio	8,104	1.81	19,659	4.44
Oklahoma	3,348	2.24	7,769	5.46
Oregon	1,838	1.38	7,453	5.48
Pennsylvania	12,429	2.94	24,459	5.74
Puerto Rico	2,486		8,806	
Rhode Island	1,282	3.48	2,930	7.81
South Carolina	1,739	1.04	11,818	7.25
South Dakota	830	2.66	2,540	9.34
Tennessee	4,215	1.81	11,121	4.97
Texas	20,235	1.81	40,607	3.96
Utah	2,382	1.69	6,733	5.13
Vermont	622	3.42	1,378	7.05
Virginia	4,204	1.4	16,422	5.72
Washington	3,627	1.56	13,010	5.49
West Virginia	1,667	2.73	5,604	9.25
Wisconsin	5,417	2.66	15,393	7.53
Wyoming	672	3.57	2,211	12.05
	269,596	2.24	679,212	5.78

Source: IDEA Part C Data Fact Sheet, www.ideadata.org/docs/cfactsheetcc.pdf

should be evaluated as a seamless or single system. When separate governmental agencies collect and report data differently, systematic comparisons become difficult (Harbin, Kochanek, McWilliam, et al., 1998; Bailey, McWilliam, Darkes, et al., 1998; Kochanek & Buka, 1998; Roberts, Innocenti, & Goetze, 1999). Provocative statements that one system has too many children with disabilities cannot be methodically substantiated and can be viewed as politically charged and motivated. Shackelford (1998) and Harbin and Danahar (1994) indicate that the infants and toddlers in a specific state who are eligible under the early intervention program may not be eligible under the preschool special-education program within the same state (see Table 5.2). This occurs because of the use of the following:

- A noncategorical approach (e.g., preschooler with a disability) in the identification of preschool children and a categorical approach (e.g., autistic or cerebral palsy) in the identification of infants

TABLE 5.2   Eligibility Criteria for Preschool Special-Education Programs

States	Early Intervention Criteria	Preschool Criteria
Arizona	50% Delay in one or more areas	Preschool moderately delayed (1.5 SD in two areas) Preschool severely delayed (3.0 SD in one area)
Alaska	50% Delay in one area	Early childhood developmentally delayed (2 SD or 25% delay in one area; 1.7 SD or 20% in two areas)
Indiana	1.5 SD in one area or 20% below chronological age	Developmental delay (2 SD in one area or 1.5 SD in two areas)
Michigan	Informed clinical judgment of MDT and parents	Preprimary impaired (50% delay in one area)
Minnesota	1.5 SD in one area	Developmental delay (medically diagnosed syndrome or condition)
Missouri	50% Delay in one area 25% Delay in two areas	Young child with a developmental delay (2 SD in one area or 1.5 SD in two areas)
New Jersey	33% Delay in one area 25% Delay in two areas	Preschool disabled identified disabling condition or measurable developmental impairment
New Mexico	25% Delay in one area	Developmentally delayed (2 SD or 30% delay in one area)
North Carolina	1.5 SD in one area or 20% delay	Developmentally delayed (2 SD or 30% delay in one area; 1.5 SD or 25% in two areas)
North Dakota	50% Delay in one area 25% Delay in two areas	Noncategorical delay (2 SD or 30% in one area; 1.5 SD or 25% in two areas; or syndromes)

(continued)

TABLE 5.2 *(continued)*

States	Early Intervention Criteria	Preschool Criteria
Ohio	Child has not reached developmental milestones (measurable delay)	"Preschool child with a Disability" 2 SD in one area 1 SD in two areas
Vermont	Clearly observable and measurable delay in one or more areas; must substantiate that the child's future success in school, home, or community cannot be assured without provision of early intervention	Eligible for essential early education (40% delay in one area or medical condition)

Source: IDEA Part C Data Fact Sheet, www.ideadata.org/docs/cfactsheetcc.pdf

- Different categories or definitions for categories in the identification of preschoolers and infants
- A quantitative level of delay for eligibility that is greater for preschoolers (e.g., Indiana's 2 SDs in one area) than for infants

As a function of the variations in definitions from one state to another, children who are eligible for services in one state may not be eligible in another (Bailey, 2000). For example, a 3-year-old who has a 25% delay in one area is eligible to receive services in New Mexico, but not in Arizona or New Jersey. States also vary in terms of the following:

- Percentage of delay required to determine eligibility
- Use of categorical versus noncategorical classification systems
- Measures used to determine delay and disorder

Finally, problems related to eligibility are particularly troublesome for children with language disorders. Many states and school districts have utilized more restrictive eligibility criteria for speech and language services. When a categorical system is utilized, children classified as speech impaired are often not considered to be as developmentally disabled as a child with mental retardation. In this type of system, children with categorical labels may be ranked as more or less severe.

When this occurs, children with speech impairments and learning disabilities may be considered to have mild disabilities when compared to children with autism and mental retardation. With this misconception, a preschool special-education committee may take the position that a child with a language disorder requires fewer services than a child with mental retardation. So, at a time when resources are contracting, children with language disorders may not receive preschool special-education services because they are not considered "handicapped enough," or they may receive only related services without special-education programming.

Problems of Diversity

Keep in mind that most states do not provide services to children who are at-risk for abuse, neglect, sickness, or future delay. Many at-risk children come from impoverished

CW 5.1

Use the Companion Website to help you answer the following questions:

1. Compare the eligibility criteria for the early intervention and preschool programs in the state you reside in.

2. What kinds of services would José, Kaitlyn, and Jeffrey be eligible to receive in your state?

3. How might the family of a child with special needs feel about an inclusion preschool classroom? How would the family of a typical preschool child feel about an inclusion classroom?

family and social environments. Data analyzed by race and ethnicity indicate that poverty in America has been "feminized"; there are more women in poverty than men (see Table 5.3).

Notice that 28% of the families living in poverty are headed by a woman. The percentage of individuals below the poverty level is presented by state. Next to that is information about poverty in families and racial and ethnic groups. The percentages are overwhelmingly higher in culturally diverse groups. Also notice that there is a much higher percentage of Blacks, women, and children in poverty. Consequently, we must be aware of these social issues and be attuned to the specific needs of these families.

Table 5.4 indicates that there is a much lower percentage of Black and Latino preschool children (individually or combined) than White children receiving preschool special-education services in most states (Jenkins, 2005). So, although there is a higher percentage of culturally diverse children in poverty, a lower percentage of these children are served in preschool special education.

Table 5.5 presents a nationwide trend showing that the number of children receiving services increases as children get older for all disability categories.

Table 5.6 presents a racial and ethnic breakdown of children classified with speech or language impairments. The majority of these children are White in most states. California, New Mexico, and Puerto Rico have a higher percentage of Latino children classified with speech or language impairments. If diverse students are *underserved* due to linguistic and cultural barriers in preschool special-education programs, a much higher percentage of diverse children in elementary school will receive special-education services. Let's consider some conclusions based on demographic data:

- More children are in the preschool system than in the early intervention system.
- Because states have different eligibility criteria for services, some states provide more services to preschoolers than other states do.
- Poverty puts children at risk for developmental delays. A higher percentage of families living in poverty are culturally and linguistically diverse or are single-parent families headed by a woman.

TABLE 5.3 People and Families in Poverty

Percentage of Poverty by State (3-Year Average, 2001–2003)			
United States	12.1	Missouri	10.1
Alabama	15.1	Montana	14.0
Alaska	9.0	Nebraska	9.9
Arizona	13.9	Nevada	9.0
Arkansas	18.5	New Hampshire	6.0
California	12.9	New Jersey	8.2
Colorado	9.4	New Mexico	18.0
Connecticut	7.9	New York	14.2
Delaware	7.7	North Carolina	14.2
District of Columbia	17.3	North Dakota	11.7
Florida	12.7	Ohio	10.4
Georgia	12.0	Oklahoma	14.0
Hawaii	10.7	Oregon	11.7
Idaho	11.0	Pennsylvania	9.9
Illinois	11.8	Rhode Island	10.7
Indiana	9.2	South Carolina	14.0
Iowa	8.5	South Dakota	10.9
Kansas	10.3	Tennessee	14.3
Kentucky	13.7	Texas	15.8
Louisiana	16.9	Utah	9.8
Maine	11.8	Vermont	9.4
Maryland	7.7	Virginia	9.3
Massachusetts	9.7	Washington	11.4
Michigan	10.8	West Virginia	16.9
Minnesota	7.1	Wisconsin	8.8
Mississippi	17.9	Wyoming	9.1

Characteristics	2003 Below Poverty	
	No.	%
People	35,861	12.5
Family status		
In families	25,684	10.8
Related children under 6	4,654	19.8
Race and Hispanic origin		
White alone	24,272	10.5
Black alone	8,781	24.4
Asian alone	1,401	11.8
Hispanic only (of any race)	9,051	22.5

(continued)

TABLE 5.3 (continued)

Residence		
Inside metropolitan areas	28,367	12.1
Inside central cities	14,551	17.5
Outside metropolitan areas	7,495	14.2
Outside central cities	13,816	9.1
Type of family		
Married couple	3,115	5.4
Female household, no husband present	3,856	28
Male household, no wife present	636	13.5

Source: U.S. Census Bureau, *Income, Poverty, and Health Insurance Coverage in the United States: 2005.*

TABLE 5.4 Number and Percentage of Children Ages 3–5 Served Under IDEA, Part C, by Race or Ethnicity, December 1, 2003, All Disabilities

State	Black		Hispanic		White	
	Number	%	Number	%	Number	%
Alabama	2,466	31.44	89	1.13	5,195	66.24
Alaska	90	4.57	86	4.37	1,082	54.98
Arizona	540	4.52	4,242	35.49	6,169	51.61
Arkansas	2,949	27.64	373	3.50	7,242	97.87
California	4,770	7.70	27,695	44.71	24,379	39.35
Colorado	492	5.09	2,400	24.81	6,425	66.24
Connecticut	1,014	12.46	1,307	16.07	5,611	68.97
Delaware	584	28.75	156	7.68	1,243	61.20
District of Columbia	226	75.08	37	12.29	34	11.30
Florida	8,235	23.36	7,024	19.92	19,391	55.00
Georgia	6,752	33.33	947	4.67	12,268	60.55
Hawaii	113	4.95	95	4.16	454	19.88
Idaho	36	0.95	490	12.87	3,196	83.95
Illinois	4,553	13.85	4,154	12.70	23,352	71.37
Indiana	1,688	9.15	614	3.33	15,978	86.65
Iowa	251	4.19	255	4.26	5,396	90.16
Kansas	756	8.23	590	9.68	7,316	79.61
Kentucky	1,862	9.21	271	1.34	17,931	88.68
Louisiana	4,671	41.02	152	1.33	6,410	56.30
Maine	36	0.77	22	0.47	4,530	97.48

(continued)

TABLE 5.4 *(continued)*

State	Black		Hispanic		White	
	Number	%	Number	%	Number	%
Maryland	3,941	32.56	630	5.20	7,075	58.45
Massachusetts	1,072	7.23	1,710	11.54	11,488	77.51
Michigan	3,291	14.03	827	3.52	18,696	79.68
Minnesota	1,077	8.29	672	5.17	10,550	81.24
Mississippi	3,246	40.61	53	0.66	4,658	58.27
Missouri	1,902	12.56	282	1.86	12,793	84.50
Montana	20	1.11	38	2.11	1,512	84.09
Nebraska	238	5.35	411	9.25	3,631	81.69
Nevada	544	11.03	1,297	26.29	2,779	56.33
New Hampshire	34	1.31	61	2.36	2,437	94.24
New Jersey	2,499	13.48	2,836	15.29	12,358	66.64
New Mexico	125	2.21	2,862	50.60	1,982	35.04
New York	8,518	15.32	10,220	18.39	35,158	63.25
North Carolina	6,651	31.64	1,124	5.35	12,490	59.43
North Dakota	28	1.87	33	2.20	1,294	86.21
Ohio	2,367	12.04	450	2.29	16,631	84.60
Oklahoma	689	8.87	433	5.57	5,282	67.99
Oregon	216	2.90	1,087	14.58	5,796	77.77
Pennsylvania	3,360	13.74	1,378	5.63	19,388	79.27
Puerto Rico	9	0.10	8,796	99.89	1	0.01
Rhode Island	195	6.66	403	13.75	2,270	77.47
South Carolina	5,310	44.93	224	1.90	6,163	52.15
South Dakota	67	2.64	51	2.01	1,902	74.88
Tennessee	2,102	18.90	217	1.95	8,715	78.37
Texas	4,823	11.88	16,209	39.92	18,612	45.83
Utah	58	0.86	520	7.72	5,935	88.15
Vermont	18	1.31	12	0.87	1,335	96.88
Virginia	3,927	23.91	963	5.86	11,026	67.14
Washington	688	5.29	1,875	14.41	9,490	72.94
West Virginia	180	3.21	23	0.41	5,384	96.07
Wisconsin	1,396	9.07	876	5.69	12,689	82.43
Wyoming	21	0.95	221	10.00	1,846	83.49
50 States, D.C., P.R.	100,676	14.82	108,093	15.91	444,968	65.51

Source: IDEA Part C Data Fact Sheet, www.ideadata.org/docs/cfactsheetcc.pdf

- Although more children live in poverty who are culturally and linguistically diverse and are more at risk for developmental delays, a lower percentage of these children receive preschool special-education services.
- As children grow older, they are identified more readily as having disabilities. This may be a function of assessment instruments, expected academic readiness for kindergarten, or increased awareness of adults in recognizing signs of communication and other difficulties in children.

TABLE 5.5   Number of Children Ages 3–5 Served Under IDEA, Part B, by Disability and Age, 2003

	3 Years Old	4 Years Old	5 Years Old
Specific learning disabilities	1,969	3,484	8,707
Speech or language impairments	57,699	107,676	165,948
Mental retardation	4,453	6,505	11,405
Emotional disturbance	819	1,539	3,455
Multiple disabilities	1,962	2,446	4,049
Hearing impairments	1,972	2,446	3,056
Orthopedic impairments	2,412	2,955	3,673
Other health impairments	3,332	4,295	7,190
Visual impairments	899	1,080	1,282
Autism	5,029	7,221	10,501
Deafness or blindness	81	76	94
Traumatic brain injury	198	301	448
Developmental delay	68,726	114,808	55,951
All disabilities	149,551	254,832	275,759

Source: IDEA Part C Data Fact Sheet, www.ideadata.org/docs/cfactsheetcc.pdf

TABLE 5.6   Number and Percentage of Children Ages 3–5 Served Under IDEA, Part B, by Race or Ethnicity, December 1, 2003, Speech or Language Impairments

State	Black		Hispanic		White	
	Number	%	Number	%	Number	%
Alabama	1,469	27.51	54	1.01	3,750	70.24
Alaska	19	3.20	17	2.87	316	53.69
Arizona	120	4.42	979	36.09	1,392	51.31
Arkansas	77	18.22	78	1.84	3,331	78.52
California	2,936	7.15	17,927	43.65	17,241	41.98
Colorado	155	3.55	971	22.25	3,073	70.42
Connecticut	282	9.13	359	11.62	2,375	76.89
Delaware	117	17.78	20	3.04	509	77.36
District of Columbia	124	76.07	22	13.50	14	8.59
Florida	3,414	19.83	2,749	15.97	10,764	62.54
Georgia	3,233	27.43	398	3.38	8,036	68.17
Hawaii	15	6.76	8	3.60	68	30.63
Idaho	8	0.61	99	7.58	1,179	90.28
Illinois	2,206	11.13	2,327	11.74	14,953	75.42
Indiana	934	7.57	364	2.95	10,952	88.77

(*continued*)

TABLE 5.6 (*continued*)

State	Black		Hispanic		White	
	Number	%	Number	%	Number	%
Iowa	48	3.76	43	3.36	1,175	91.94
Kansas	459	7.69	433	7.25	4,946	82.82
Kentucky	700	6.82	123	1.20	9,370	91.28
Louisiana	1,909	32.71	62	1.06	3,805	65.20
Maine	22	1.00	9	0.41	2,137	96.74
Maryland	1,947	26.69	336	4.61	4,780	65.52
Massachusetts	303	5.05	622	10.36	4,876	81.25
Michigan	1,876	11.90	505	3.20	12,975	82.29
Minnesota	220	4.46	200	4.06	4,290	86.98
Mississippi	1,913	35.30	22	0.41	3,469	64.04
Missouri	353	7.12	67	1.35	4,503	90.84
Montana	20	1.21	36	2.17	1,401	84.55
Nebraska	105	4.03	239	9.17	2,163	83.03
Nevada	103	7.89	239	18.30	891	68.22
New Hampshire	16	1.16	30	2.18	1,302	94.42
New Jersey	416	10.30	476	11.48	3,066	73.93
New Mexico	41	2.25	849	46.55	748	41.01
New York	0	.	0	.	0	.
North Carolina	3,042	25.96	424	3.62	7,743	66.07
North Dakota	16	1.64	23	2.35	835	85.38
Ohio	717	12.04	136	2.28	5,040	84.61
Oklahoma	140	7.96	110	6.25	1,124	63.90
Oregon	96	2.30	657	15.77	3,240	77.77
Pennsylvania	1,031	9.07	472	4.15	9,750	85.77
Puerto Rico	8	0.12	6,876	99.87	1	0.01
Rhode Island	94	6.52	205	14.22	1,114	77.25
South Carolina	3,594	43.16	128	1.54	4,532	54.42
South Dakota	9	0.83	15	1.39	866	80.04
Tennessee	1,395	18.14	120	1.56	6,122	79.60
Texas	3,647	11.27	12,679	39.19	15,299	47.29
Utah	14	0.52	147	5.45	2,464	91.29
Vermont	1	1.11	0	0.00	89	98.89
Virginia	1,363	17.57	341	4.40	5,903	76.11
Washington	153	4.67	401	12.25	2,505	76.51
West Virginia	87	2.69	14	0.43	3,130	96.60
Wisconsin	712	6.71	601	5.67	9,026	85.12
Wyoming	16	0.92	176	10.14	1,449	83.47
50 States, D.C., P.R.	42,391	12.81	54,188	16.38	224,082	67.72

Source: IDEA Part C Data Fact Sheet, www.ideadata.org/docs/cfactsheetcc.pdf

CW 5.2

Use the Companion Website to help you answer the following questions:

1. What information can you find about your community and state concerning children raised in poverty?

2. If families in poverty have a higher percentage of children with disabilities, what factors would influence the children's early identification?

3. What kinds of outreach programs would you develop to ensure that linguistically and culturally diverse families know about the preschool system?

4. Find information on the racial and ethnic breakdown for other disability categories, and consider whether there are implications for discriminatory practices and cultural profiling of children.

Least Restrictive Environment

The passage of PL 99-457 mandated a free and appropriate public education (FAPE) for preschool children with disabilities. The extension of the regular education initiative (REI) to preschool children means that the least restrictive environment (LRE) is an early childhood classroom with typical peers. The least restrictive environment concept is based on the assumption that the opportunity for interaction with typical children is not only beneficial, but developmentally appropriate. Some educators argue that the preschool special-education classroom is too restrictive and that the early childhood classroom is preferable for preschool children with disabilities. Furthermore, they believe that when preschool children are placed in classrooms with typical peers they will learn from these peers.

Unfortunately, there is nothing magical about placing a child with a disability in an early childhood program. Questions remain: Is the preschool child with a disability ready to be in a classroom with 9, 12, or 15 peers? How, specifically, will the preschool child with a disability benefit from interaction with typical peers? Have early childhood teachers been adequately prepared to work with preschool children with disabilities? Many parents of preschool children with disabilities have concerns regarding these questions. They are not convinced that their children will learn by merely being exposed to or within the same environment as typical peers. The LRE is not an educational fad; it is a legal mandate. It directly relates to the emphasis on another educational model, full inclusion, described later in the chapter.

Presently, many educators express the concern that, if educational decisions are based on anything other than the individual needs of the child, educational programming for children with and without disabilities will be compromised. They question the hierarchal progression of decision making and the emphasis on LRE. They are concerned that LRE will be the primary factor for a child's placement, with not enough consideration of the individual learning needs and style of the child. Clearly, a balance must be met between the LRE and the needs of the child. Good placement decisions are achieved when this balance occurs.

Preschool versus Early Intervention

Many preschool special-education systems are under the jurisdiction of state education departments; as a result, the child-centered approach has been "rolled down" from the school-age to the preschool system. States and school districts have a great deal of latitude in defining the role of parents under the preschool special-education system, so there is a great deal of variability in the role of parents from state to state and district to district. A comparison of systemic differences in early intervention and preschool reveals some differences in the role of parents:

- For parents, being a partner means being listened to and being respected (Attride-Stirling, Davis, Markless, Sclare, & Day, 2001). The early intervention program incorporates the views of parents by means of a collaborative approach that is reflected in the child's goals (Christenson, 1999; Freund, Boone, Barlow, & Lim, 2005). As children transition into the preschool special-education system, the role of parents changes, creating a transitional process that is not always seamless (see Figure 5.1). The family-centered approach in early intervention becomes a parent–teacher partnership in preschool (Watkins, 1999).
- The early intervention program focuses on parent advocacy, empowerment, and family needs, which raises parental expectations about preschool special education. Parents who have been trained to function at the policy and political levels in early intervention recognize the ambiguities of partnership in the preschool system.
- The early intervention program provides a range of clinical and therapeutic services that focuses on the needs of linguistically and culturally diverse families, because the parent is recognized as the primary facilitator (Dinnebeil, Hale, & Rule, 1996). The parent–child relationship provides the foundation for clinical goals and intervention. In preschool special education, the parent is important but not primary. The parent–child relationship is replaced by the therapist–child relationship, without the need for the parent to be present during therapeutic intervention.
- In early intervention, the family-centered approach enhances the parent's ability to facilitate the child's development (Taub, 2001). As a result, services are provided to parents and siblings, giving a more holistic and ecological approach. In comparison, the preschool special-education system is child-centered, so family support and counseling services are not provided; goals are not developed with a focus on family enhancement.
- In early intervention, the natural environment is the home. In preschool special education, the concept of natural environment is replaced by least restrictive environment (LRE).

1. The systems are so different that the transition process was overwhelming. Why isn't there a seamless system?
2. By the time I learned about the procedures in early intervention, it was time for my child to transition into the preschool system, which has very different procedures.
3. My role as a parent was different when my child was in the early intervention system than when he was in the preschool system.
4. I thought there was going to be transition planning that was part of the IFSP process. No one helped me as my child transitioned from system to system. There is not a service coordinator that works directly with either the local public schools or private preschool programs. My service coordinator's responsibility ended very abruptly and I was handed over to the preschool committee on special education.
5. No one sat down to tell me about the procedural differences in the preschool system.
6. Once my child left early intervention, I could no longer get home-based services. If I knew that earlier, I would have looked for a program before my preschool committee met. In the end, I didn't know what was available, so I just accepted what they gave me.
7. The transition process needs to start earlier to give parents a chance to adjust psychologically to the changes ahead. The transition was so abrupt that I felt shoved out of one system and into another.
8. Where is the parent guidebook? There is a parent guidebook that talks about the transition process. Parents need to know about transition during their first IFSP meeting.
9. I was shocked to find out that, although my child was eligible to receive services in early intervention, he is not eligible to receive services in preschool because he is not "handicapped enough." I was told that my child doesn't have a severe developmental disability. I am now paying for his related services.
10. What does parent involvement mean? Is it just lip service? My experience over the past several years is that bureaucracies do not share power and relinquish control to parents.
11. Why can't parents talk to parents? It would be very helpful if there was a parent directory that provided names and telephone numbers of other parents who are in the system.

FIGURE 5.1

Transition Issues from the Early Intervention System to the Preschool
Special-Education System
Data collected during exit interviews with parents, 1999–2000.

- In early intervention, most services are provided in the home. In preschool special education, most children attend special-education or early childhood programs.
- In early intervention, most children receive individual therapy services, rather than group services. In preschool special education, the classroom with other children is the primary setting.

Individualized Educational Plan

Under the requirements of IDEA, each local school district establishes a multidisciplinary team of professionals that evaluates children with suspected disabilities to determine their eligibility for preschool special-education services (see Figure 5.2).

ABC SCHOOL DISTRICT
INDIVIDUALIZED EDUCATION PROGRAM
2001–2002

STUDENT INFORMATION

Student Name: José Martinez
Date of Birth: 08/06/96

Sex: Male

Parent/Guardian: Raul & Maria Martinez
Address: 123 Number Street
City, St, ZIP CODE
Home Phone: (123) 456–7890
Home Language(s): Spanish/English

Meeting Date: 09/14/99
Meeting Type: Preschool Special Education Committee
Purpose of Meeting: Initial Referral—from EI
Projected Annual Review: 6/2002
Triennial: 9/2003
Dominant Lang. Student: Spanish
Interpreter Needed: Yes [X] No [ ]

CURRENT PRIMARY PLACEMENT DATA

Program Initiation Date: 10/20/98
Classification: Autism

Early Intervention Program

RECOMMENDATION PRIMARY PLACEMENT DATA—PRESENT SCHOOL SESSION

Program Initiation Date: 01/01/00
Classification: Autism
Program: Early Start Infant Program
Transportation: Door to Door

Testing Modifications: No
Case Manager: Joan Parker
Grade: Preschool
Extended School Year: Yes [X] No [ ]

SPECIAL MEDICAL ALERTS

José has no physical or medical problems that affect education or require special alerts.

PROGRAM MODIFICATIONS—STAFF SUPPORT

Program modifications or supports for school staff that will be provided on behalf of José to address the annual goals and participation in general education curricula and activities.

MEETING PARTICIPANTS

CPSE Committee: Chairperson:

Edward Frye, Director of CPSE
Parent Member, Waived
Parent of Child, Maria Martinez
Sherry Tellers, Speech-Language Pathologist
Mary Tomson, Special-Education Teacher

PRESENT LEVELS OF PERFORMANCE AND INDIVIDUAL NEEDS

SOCIAL DEVELOPMENT   Social Development: Considering José's disabilities, needs to help him relate appropriately to adults and/or peers are as follows:
José requires a special-education setting to learn social interactional.
José requires a structured approach to learning.
José requires short, goal-oriented tasks for built-in success.
José requires carefully presented materials to reduce frustration.
José will learn to function in a group situation.

FIGURE 5.2
ABC School District Individualized Education Program, 2001–2002

(continued)

PHYSICAL DEVELOPMENT	Physical Development: José has no physical and/or medical problems that will interfere with his education. José does not need any special equipment and/or adaptive devices.
MANAGEMENT NEEDS	Management Needs: José requires additional support in order to function within the educational setting. José requires a highly structured ABA approach to learning. José requires an individual aide. José requires small-group instruction. José requires teacher reinforcement in order to stay on task.

PRESCHOOL LEARNING STYLES

José will benefit from a visual kinesthetic approach to learning that is age/developmentally appropriate. José will benefit from a variety of activities utilizing a range of textures and sensory experiences (sand, pudding, clay, etc.) to increase the acquisition of information/skills presented.

RECOMMENDED RELATED SERVICES–INTEGRATED CLASS

Related Service	Max. Grp. Freq.	Duration	Staff	Start Date	End Date
Recommended:					
Speech (Pull Out)	1:1	5/W	30 Mins	07/01/01–06/30/02	
O.T. (Pull Out)	1:1	3/W	30 Mins	07/01/01–06/30/02	
A.B.A.	1:1	5/W	60 Mins	07/01/01–06/30/02	

COMMENTS

Initial Meeting: Student referred by EI Service coordinator. Reason: Consider student's eligibility for services. Current instructional program/interventions are therapeutic services in an early intervention program. Therapists and staff indicate the effect of intervention has been minimal development in speech and language areas. José's social development is also limited. Evaluations conducted and significant previous history indicate that child is significantly speech and language delayed. Parent comment/concerns presented to the preschool committee were that child does not talk and socialize with peers. Preschool committee has determined that student is eligible for special-education services. Parent agrees with recommendations. The recommended LRE is an integrated early childhood classroom. Preschool committee accepted goals/objectives from EI program.

CLASSROOM ACCOMMODATIONS

Given the student's functional level, the student requires classroom accommodations of an individual aide to have an equal opportunity to learn.

FIGURE 5.2
(*continued*)

The preschool special-education committee (PSEC) has specific mandated responsibilities for the following:

1. Evaluating a preschool child who is suspected of having a disability
2. Classifying and labeling a preschool child with a disability
3. Identifying an appropriate educational program to meet the child's individual needs

CW 5.3

Use the Companion Website to help you answer the following questions:

1. What kinds of services are available in the preschool system in your state?
2. Compare the average costs per child in the early intervention and preschool special-education programs. What does this indicate?
3. How does your state provide opportunities for children with disabilities to interact with typical peers?

4. Generating an individualized educational program (IEP) for the preschool child with a disability and reviewing that plan on an annual basis
5. Determining the appropriate types and levels of services to meet the child's developmental needs
6. Satisfying the least restrictive environment (LRE) requirements

Figure 5.2 is an example of an IEP. Note that this IEP fulfills the LRE requirement in that José will be educated in an integrated preschool classroom that includes typical peers. As a function of the multidisciplinary evaluation, the educational team can recommend a range of services for preschool children with disabilities, from self-contained to integrated programming and stand-alone related services. The IEP summarizes the child's current skills and abilities, identifies educational goals, and describes the program components necessary to meet the child's individual needs. The IEP functions in the same way as the IFSP by providing the basis for the child's educational instruction.

The IEP, like the IFSP, serves as a contract between the parent and the program, because it specifies the services that will be provided. Classroom lessons and activities should relate specifically to short- and long-term goals identified on the IEP. For as long as the child remains in preschool special education, the IEP is reviewed and modified by the preschool committee on an annual basis to determine the child's ongoing eligibility within the special-education system and her or his need for specific services.

Continuum of Services

The IEP for a preschool child can be implemented in a variety of settings or placements. The preschool committee considers whether the child can benefit from a placement in the least restrictive environment (LRE) and identifies the appropriate placement that meets the individual needs of the preschool child. The preschool child may be educated in any of the following placements depending on his educational needs: (1) an early childhood classroom, (2) a special-education classroom, and (3) at home or in the hospital. If the preschool committee decides that a program is appropriate, an early childhood program with typical peers is considered to be the least restrictive setting. If the preschool child requires (1) more intensive individualized instruction, and/or (2) rehabilitative services, and/or (3) a highly structured classroom environment, and/or (4) a smaller class size, and/or (5) a modified curriculum, then a special-education preschool classroom is considered.

Maria Martinez and the Preschool System

Maria Martinez is very pleased with the nurturance and support she receives in the early intervention system. The family-centered approach provides Maria with a service coordinator who functions as a troubleshooter. Although the language barrier creates communication problems, the service coordinator is able to identify resources for the family in the community. The transition to preschool is difficult for Maria Martinez and her family. Maria Martinez is surprised and distressed that the preschool system has different procedures and requirements. In addition, Maria is very anxious about her preschool meeting with the new professionals who she does not know. Her concerns are expressed in Box 5.1.

Due Process

Due process describes the procedures used to ensure that the preschool child with a disability is provided with a free and appropriate public education (FAPE). Due process consists of several assurances concerning parental rights:

1. To be fully informed about the actions to be taken concerning the child
2. To participate in the determination of decisions through attendance at meetings
3. To give or withhold consent
4. To challenge the committee's decision by requesting mediation or an impartial hearing
5. To appeal the decisions of an impartial hearing officer

These due-process rights are not only entitlements, but the responsibility of parents. Federal law requires states to establish procedures to ensure that parents

BOX 5.1

I just got used to the early intervention program and now I have to leave. I don't want to change. Everyone is so nice in the Early Start Infant Program. Everyone treats me like a special person. Everyone calls me and works with me. I can work with the therapists in their rooms. I can watch. I really feel like I am part of the team. I am not happy about this new system. I did not like the preschool meeting. No one was concerned about family services for me or my other children. They told me that I wouldn't get services anymore. Only José would get services. I don't understand why my family is not important anymore. Our family problems haven't changed. Things are harder at home because José is bigger. I asked them to help me. I want to keep my family services and my service coordinator, but the committee said they're not part of the preschool system. They didn't ask me what I wanted; they told me what services José would get. I must trust that what they recommend is good for José. I really miss my service coordinator. I'm not treated the same.

Maria Martinez

of children with disabilities are appropriately informed and given the opportunity to participate in the decision-making process. This informing usually takes the form of a handbook that is given to the parents by the preschool committee to read. It is available in several languages. Unfortunately, no one reviews the information with the families. The Office of Special Education Programs in the federal Department of Education monitors states every 6 or 7 years, and violations of parental rights are reviewed on a case by case basis when a complaint is filed by a parent against a state education department or a school district. School districts work hard to meet all the due-process rights of parents. However, only so much time and so many personnel are available to address all the needs and concerns of parents. Many parents who are linguistically and culturally diverse, economically disadvantaged, and/or developmentally disabled may need a community advocacy group to represent their children's interests if they believe their child is not receiving appropriate services.

Mediation

In an attempt to assist preschool committees and parents to resolve disputes without resorting to impartial hearings, some states have implemented a mediation process that provides an interim step (see Figure 5.3). Mediation offsets the time and legal expenses resulting from an impartial hearing. It provides a mechanism for parents and professionals to clarify issues and areas of agreement and disagreement so that a negotiated resolution can be reached about the child's special-education program. If the mediation process does not result in mutual agreement, nothing prevents the parent from then requesting an impartial hearing. Mediation often takes place at a community dispute resolution center (CDRC) that has personnel who are trained to address issues related to the rights and educational needs of children with disabilities in an environment that fosters and facilitates negotiation. The goal is always to achieve appropriate services for children, and not to determine who is right or wrong.

Impartial Hearing

The impartial hearing is a quasi-legal proceeding that provides a mechanism to hear both sides of the issues and resolve the dispute through a third party, the impartial hearing officer (IHO). This officer must not be an employee of the school district. In some states the IHO is paid by the district or state. Safeguards are in place to ensure nonbiased decision making by the impartial hearing officer. Any person who is an appointed hearing officer must be qualified as follows:

1. Not have any personal or professional interest that would negatively affect his or her objectivity
2. Not have been involved in the original preschool committee's recommendations
3. Be certified as a hearing officer and have fulfilled all state education requirements for such a position

The impartial hearing is conducted like a court proceeding with an IHO, who functions as a judge, and a court stenographer. The school district and the parents are

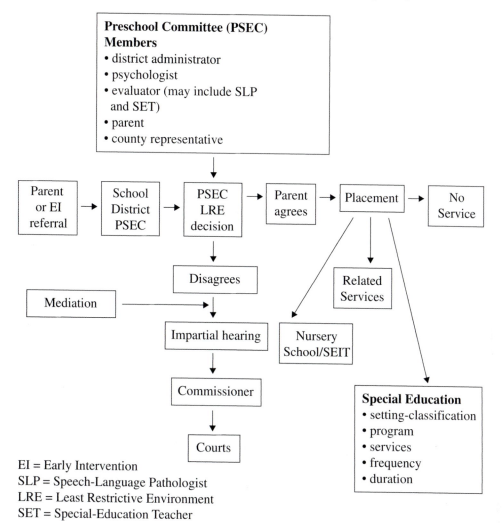

Preschool Committee (PSEC)
Members
• district administrator
• psychologist
• evaluator (may include SLP
  and SET)
• parent
• county representative

Parent or EI referral → School District PSEC → PSEC LRE decision → Parent agrees → Placement → No Service

PSEC LRE decision → Disagrees

Mediation → Impartial hearing

Impartial hearing → Commissioner → Courts

Placement → Nursery School/SEIT

Placement → Related Services

Placement → **Special Education**
• setting-classification
• program
• services
• frequency
• duration

EI = Early Intervention
SLP = Speech-Language Pathologist
LRE = Least Restrictive Environment
SET = Special-Education Teacher

FIGURE 5.3
The Preschool Process: Three to Five Years

often represented by attorneys. The cost of legal representation is high; impartial hearings can range in cost from $10,000 to $30,000 depending on the length of the hearing. Many parents who cannot pay such legal fees often seek the assistance of low-cost advocacy groups. Often these groups have long waiting lists of parents requesting their services. The hearing process requires expert witnesses and cross-examination by both the school district and the parent or advocate. The hearing officer's decision is based on the information presented during the hearing and includes the reasons and the basis for the decision. The decision states that each party maintains the right to appeal the impartial hearing officer's decision to the commissioner of education within the state.

Katherine Whiteside and the Preschool System

Katherine Whiteside has her own ideas about Kaitlyn's needs. She is an articulate parent who does her own research and who accepts professional judgment only after careful consideration. Although the service coordinator from early intervention provides information on the transition process to preschool special education, Katherine prefers to make all the calls herself. She also calls the state education department to determine if there is a handbook for parents describing preschool procedures and her parental rights. She reads everything before the preschool committee meeting and contacts the school district's Special-Education Parents–Teachers Association (SEPTA). Katherine is clear about what she wants for Kaitlyn and, in anticipation of potential difficulties, contacts a local advocacy group. Katherine does not want Kaitlyn in a typical early childhood program. She wants her daughter to receive special-education services with a teacher trained to work with children who are deaf. She purchases an audiocassette player to record the meeting in case she needs to request an impartial hearing. Katherine describes her concerns in Box 5.2.

Preschool committees must decide whether a child with a hearing loss can be appropriately served in a natural environment.

Scott Cunningham / Merrill

BOX 5.2

The bureaucratic structure of the preschool special-education committee is stifling. They listen and are polite, but it is clear that they make the decision about Kaitlyn as a committee and I do not feel like an equal partner on this committee. They keep their professional roles and tell me what's appropriate for Kaitlyn. They acknowledge my opinion by nodding their heads. They recommend what they feel is appropriate and give me assurances that Kaitlyn will benefit from her interactions with typical peers. How can they tell me that Kaitlyn will benefit? They met with Kaitlyn for several hours to do evaluations in a totally unnatural situation. I've lived with her day in and day out. How do they know? What if they're wrong? I vote as a member of the committee, but I am outvoted by the committee. This system is child-centered and not family-centered. I found the family-centered approach much more parent friendly. I can really understand why parents go to impartial hearings. They think they know more than I do about what Kaitlyn needs and this is just mind-boggling. I must decide to either accept their decision or fight it.

Katherine Whiteside

Parental Choice

Some parents have expectations about the preschool special-education system based on their experiences in early intervention. So it is not surprising that some parents are frustrated by the procedural complexity as they try to negotiate their way through the unfamiliar preschool special-education rules. This is further complicated by the fact that the structure of families is clearly changing in U.S. society. The traditional family can no longer be defined by a working father and a mother who remains at home with the children. Diversity needs and the increasing number of nontraditional families require organizational changes in the public school system nationally.

Camille St. James and the Preschool System

Jeffrey has been suspended from several child-care programs because of behavioral problems. He is identified as a late talker. Unlike José or Kaitlyn, his speech and language delays are not severe enough for him to receive early intervention services. In

Tom Watson / Merrill

Children from diverse cultural backgrounds may be underserved within the preschool system.

BOX 5.3

All this time, I complained that Jeffrey is having problems getting along with other children, but the early intervention service coordinator said that his problem is not serious enough. Now, after Jeffrey has been expelled from two different child-cares, I'm being told that he needs to be evaluated again. I took Jeffrey to school to arrange for more evaluations because the ones from early intervention are too old. He will need another psychology and speech evaluation. I chose an evaluation center, so I have to take off from work. Jeffrey has a lot of difficulty. He doesn't listen to the psychologist, and he doesn't want to go in the room with her. The psychologist tells me that preschool has different services than early intervention. She says, if Jeffrey wasn't eligible for early intervention services, chances are he won't be eligible for preschool services. Jeffrey should've gotten early intervention services. This time I'm supposed to meet with a committee. If no one listened to me last time, why should a committee listen to me now? I don't like meetings with committees. Why can't I just meet with one person? I feel very uncomfortable when someone tells me about Jeffrey. Why is there another system? What's wrong with the early intervention system? This is very confusing and upsetting. I feel like I'm in pieces. Different agencies take a particular part of me. Nobody takes care of all of me and Jeffrey. For my job, I go to one agency. When Jeffrey gets sick, I go to the health center. And for Jeffrey it's another agency. No one helps me find my way.

Camille St. James

CW 5.4

Use the Companion Website to help you answer the following questions:

1. What kind of integrated programs are provided in your state for children with disabilities?

2. Identify three local child-care programs and find out if they accept children with disabilities. What kind of children with disabilities are accepted?

3. Identify various groups in your community that advocate for children. What are their specific missions as not-for-profit agencies? What are their eligibility criteria in determining which families receive advocacy support and/or legal representation? How are these agencies funded?

4. What do you think happens to families who cannot find advocates to represent their needs?

the third child-care program, the social worker helps Camille St. James contact her local school district for an evaluation when Jeffrey turns 3 years of age. Camille's problems are described in Box 5.3.

SUMMARY

Data on the preschool special-education system have consistently shown an increase in the number of children receiving services over the past decade. In many states, preschool special-education programs are vulnerable to political issues. Preschool special education may not be part of the public school system, and as educational costs increase in elementary schools, state legislators focus on the efficacy of preschool programs in relation to their costs. This requires states and local communities to raise taxes and rely more heavily on the practice of privatization, which has spread to other sectors of human service as well.

Privatization refers to the shift of government responsibility for the funding and provision of services to nongovernmental agencies (Gibelman, 1998). The trend in the last several years has been the promotion of linkages between public- and private-sector groups. The political theme to downsize government spending focuses on concerns about systemic abuses in social services programs and the belief that private groups can provide more cost-effective and efficient services, such as Head Start (Moore, 1998). The movement to localize and privatize services has facilitated the growth of nonprofit and nongovernmental organizations (NGOs) in many human service sectors, including early intervention and preschool special education. These contracted agencies are resource dependent on governmental bureaucracies and funds (Kramer, 1994). Governmental agencies focus on measurable short-term performance changes, as well as on the process by which services are provided (Gibelman, 2000). Early intervention and preschool programs are expected to produce these measurable outcomes.

CHAPTER

6

Language Differences in Preschool

Chapter Objectives

After studying this chapter, you should be able to answer the following questions:

1. What language characteristics differentiate the three children during the preschool period?

2. What social and behavioral characteristics are important to the process of differential diagnosis?

3. What is the difference between verbal and nonverbal abilities in each child?

4. Identify several learning problems presented by the three children.

This is the second chapter on language disorders; it describes each of the children during his or her preschool years and the differences that exist among their language systems and those of typical language learners. The specific profiles of each of these children and the information about their patterns of development can be extrapolated and applied to other children with language-learning differences who do not carry the specific labels of these three children.

A central issue for preschool children involves the developmental changes that occur when children present nonstandard characteristics in social environments with typical peers. For example, what happens when a child with autism such as José does not develop the prelinguistic behaviors of pointing, showing, turn-taking, and joint attention? When expected behaviors do not appear, what influence does this have on other communicators and the social learning process? Developmental behaviors are progressive and occur synchronously along a continuum in typical children. How are skills such as conversation and narration affected when early communicative behaviors do not develop? Early development creates a foundation for later learning; if the foundation is weak, the blueprint will not be completed as planned.

Children with different language behaviors follow separately evolving paths. Therefore, the language-learning processes for José, Kaitlyn, and Jeffrey will be different. The preschool period is not just a transitional stage of development; it is a time of language integration and consolidation. The foundation for literacy and meta-learning is laid brick by brick between the ages of 3 and 5 years. A child's academic success has its genesis in the prerequisite language skills developed during this period.

Autism Spectrum Disorders: José

The description of the language-development process for typical learners is based on the acquisition of a single language. What happens when children are exposed to two

Children with autism are often isolated from their peers because of severe communication and socialization deficits.

Dan Floss/Merrill

or more languages? What happens if the child has a disability and the family speaks a language that is different from the mainstream social environment? For the typical child, early exposure to several languages may not present a problem. Children with language disorders exposed to two languages can develop both languages, but at a slower rate of acquisition. When one language is presented at home and another at school, there is an additional problem. The two separate language environments may limit children's exposure to both languages (Parke & Drury, 2001; Salameh, Hakansson, & Nettelbladt, 2004).

In José's case, due to his disability, the decision is made by his early childhood teachers and early intervention specialists that he should be exposed only to English. José, however, is neither a bilingual child nor a second-language learner. He was exposed to Spanish by his family for a relatively short period of time before he arrives in the United States. By the time he is evaluated, the primary language in the social environment is English, while Spanish continues to be spoken at home. José has not been provided with the same level of exposure to both languages as typical bilingual learners.

On the other hand, because he has not acquired Spanish in the first place, he cannot be considered a second-language learner when English is presented. A child's knowledge of both the sound and the structure of language plays a critical role in the development of preliteracy skills (Nelson, Benner, & Gonzalez, 2003, 2005). In the case of José, although Spanish was the "first" language, his exposure to English in the EI program has been more prescriptive and directed. English will be the language whose sound and structure will develop preliteracy skills.

Pragmatic Abilities

José as a preschool child shows pervasive pragmatic deficits because he still has not developed (1) a range of communicative functions, (2) gaze interaction skills, (3) prototypical behaviors such as protodeclaratives or protoimperatives, (4) attention and joint action schemes, (5) an awareness of agent, action, or object contingencies, (6) turn-taking or reciprocal interaction skills, and (7) gestural or imitative behaviors (Woods & Wetherby, 2003).

José is also echolalic. The transition from mute to verbal was abrupt. There is little understanding of the factors precipitating the change or why 50% of autistic children remain mute. Of those who acquire speech, over 75% show disordered speech features (Miranda-Linné & Melin, 1997; DeMyer et al., 1973; Kelly, Paul, Fein, & Naigles, 2006; Ornitz, 1973; Peppé, McCann, Gibbon, O'Hare, & Rutherford, 2006; Rutter, 2004; Wing, 2005).

The description of the child with autism as noncommunicative and noninteractive is not accurate (Calloway, Myles, & Earles, 1999). Even with a limited range of communicative behaviors, José responds differently to different interactional partners. So it is not that José cannot interact, but rather that his range of communicative options is limited. Another factor that interferes with a child's communicative effectiveness is his idiosyncratic behaviors (Blackwell & Niederhauser, 2003). Whereas a typical learner develops conventional behaviors to communicate personal needs, José utilizes nonstandard linguistic forms. The result is frequent misinterpretations and misunderstandings of his intentions by peers and adults.

The communication context is therefore more important for José than for a typical child because it provides a framework for adults and peers to disambiguate José's meaning. Whereas typical learners are beginning to use conventional linguistic structures to explain or clarify their intentions, José's intentions are often embedded within a social context. Adults and peers try to figure out what José is attempting to communicate by combining a number of components: vocalization + action + object (i.e., just as one would have to do with an infant or toddler). Adults are better at this skill than peers, so José tends to approach adults when he wants something.

Semantic Abilities

As a preschooler, José is echolalic, which means that he usually repeats a word or phrase spoken by another person. Echolalia may occur as either an immediate or delayed form to verbal stimuli within a social context. Immediate echolalia occurs when José repeats something that he has just heard. Delayed echolalia occurs when he repeats something that he heard in the past. Although José is echolalic, he does not imitate motor or physical behaviors, even if they involve the use of a familiar object (i.e., telephone, bell, or hat). His gaze behavior is still poor, but during echolalic exchanges that involve a request for food or a preferred object, José looks at the teacher and then at the item requested. This is the beginning of joint attention.

Communication and/or interactional exchanges that involve nonverbal turn-taking behaviors are maintained with direct physical guidance and prompting from the teacher. José's echolalic behavior consists of phrases and sentences derived from commercials, songs, and high-frequency social phrases (e.g., Teacher prompts: "José, say you have to go to the bathroom." "Don't do that José you'll get hurt."). These utterances (delayed echolalia) are the result of a loose association between a social event and a linguistic form that may be a commercial, phrase, or sentence. For instance, when José goes to the bathroom, he will say, "Jose, say you have to go to the bathroom." He consistently uses echolalic utterances with specific objects or actions. José says, "Juicy Juice has one hundred percent real juice and nothing artificial" when he wants something to drink. José does not initiate communicative exchanges to request information or clarification.

If he wants an adult's attention, he approaches, rocks back and forth on his feet, and flaps his hands. Over time, he may also produce verbal utterances that were produced by a specific adult, such as his teacher or mother (e.g., "Okay, children it is almost time to put things away." "Turn off the TV, José, it's time for bed."). At this stage, production and comprehension are still poor, and the expression of various pragmatic functions is highly restricted to physical needs (Light, Roberts, Dimarco, & Greiner, 1998).

If a child with autism becomes verbal, often his initial words or phrases are quite intelligible. There seems to be a quantum leap or change in José's performance that cannot be explained by means of the standard developmental model. José does not evidence the gradual developmental changes in pragmatics, phonology, semantics, and syntax during the first 36 months that are seen in the typically developing child. José's developmental history presents a dramatic and unexplainable change from one stage to another. When a child with autism starts to "speak," imitated utterances, although understandable, interfere with natural social interactions, particularly with typical peers (Dipipi, Jitendra, & Miller, 2001; Nientemp & Cole, 1992). Finally, by age 4, José is hyperverbal, with a sophisticated but highly restricted lexicon.

Language Processing Continuum

Children with autism have often been described as "language chunkers." Prizant (1983) suggests that the characteristics of ritualistic behavior and echolalia indicate a gestalt processing style that is at the opposite end of a continuum from analytic processing. The failure to move along the continuum toward analytic processing is due to cognitive limitations. The movement toward the analytic side of the processing continuum is required for the development of semantic–syntactic relations. As a result of José's gestalt preference, he produces whole phrases and sentences without understanding the individual linguistic elements. This means that the child with autism cannot manipulate the building blocks of language to combine and recombine linguistic structures (i.e., phonemes and words) creatively (Brownell & Walther-Thomas, 2001).

Although gestalt processing occurs as a part of typical language development, it is utilized with an analytic processing strategy. The interface between these two processing approaches provides language learners with a creativity and flexibility that José does not exhibit in his language productions. Without a working knowledge of the meaningful units of language, José forms only surface associations between long language chunks and contexts; as a result, the relationship between the memorized chunk and the context is often tangential. This discrepancy between form and function presents a serious strain on José's ability to communicate effectively; adults derive his communicative intent based on what they think he means.

Prizant and Wetherby (1987) describe how immediate echolalia functions for children interacting with familiar adults. *Immediate echolalia* is structurally similar to the speaker's production. For some children with autism, echolalic responses are produced more frequently with evidence of comprehension than without. Comprehension is based on the child's related and intentional actions immediately prior to, during, or after the production of the echolalic utterance. The *meaning* of José's echolalic utterance is determined by the function it serves for him within a context.

Echolalia represents an important transitional phase in José's development to more complex forms of language. His linguistic knowledge and comprehension can be determined by his ability to *change* syntactic structures and suprasegmental features. For example, consider the following exchanges:

MOTHER: Go open the door.

JOSÉ: Go open the door.

Nonverbal behavior: José looks at the door, and then gets up and opens it.

José indicates by means of his *behavior* that, although he echoes his mother's production, he understands the meaning of her message and its related action; José's nonverbal behavior (i.e., gaze, gestures, and actions) provides an indication of his understanding of the linguistic message.

MOTHER: José, where is your coat?

JOSÉ: José, coat.

Nonverbal behavior: José looks at his coat, and then gets it.

In this second exchange, José provides further information about his developing comprehension. First, the linguistic form of José's production is different from his mother's. Second, his intonation pattern, which is different from his mother's upward inflection, indicates his ability to make changes in supersegmental features. Third, his actions underscore that he comprehends his mother's message. These interchanges illustrate how the form and function of José's semantic abilities can be analyzed.

Prizant and Rydell (1984) investigate the functions of *delayed echolalia*, which refers to the use of echolalic utterances at a much later time. "Echolalic behaviors, both immediate and delayed, are best described as a continuum of behaviors in regard to exactness of repetition, degree of comprehension, and underlying communicative intent" (p. 183). Delayed echolalia has also been referred to as the use of old forms applied to new situations. José's ability to verbally reproduce sophisticated linguistic sentences and paragraphs (such as commercials) is not congruent with his actual spontaneous ability.

During the preschool years, typical children acquire a working lexicon at a rapid rate. The language problems presented by children with autism indicate ongoing deficits with the following: semantic functions, categorical skills, vocabulary development, word meaning, relational meaning, inferential skills, associations, narrative schemata, and nonliteral meaning. Deficits in word knowledge result in a limited vocabulary that cannot be used to further the ability to comprehend and produce spoken language (Nippold, 1993). In José's case:

- Semantic development is limited by his restricted use of functions.
- Lexical development is limited to objects and actions that meet his immediate physical needs.

José is slow to add new words to his lexical system because of pervasive information-processing difficulties (Tiegerman-Farber, 2002a). Most of his words are nouns, specifically food items, that relate directly to his physical needs. He has significant difficulty with information retrieval and categorical organization, so the integration of new information is as difficult as the retrieval of old information. Whether José's problem is information storage and/or retrieval, the severe word-finding difficulties affect his ability to function as a social communicator.

Syntactic Abilities

The development of a normal linguistic system, in which structure is related to meaning, requires an interfacing of linguistic and nonlinguistic congnitive development. In typical children, lexical and relational semantic abilities are linked to broader conceptual developments, but morphological and syntactic abilities are not. The language pattern in children with autism indicates that the structural development of language occurs independently from the pragmatic–semantic development. This separate developmental pattern highlights the devastating impact of two language subsystems that do not "communicate" with each other (Conti-Ramsden & Botting, 1999).

Initially, José utilizes language patterns characterized by repetitions of unanalyzed forms, indicating an inability to use generative rules for production purposes and to analyze the internal structure of another's production. José's echolalia constitutes a protracted period of developmental freeze. Echolalia represents a phase of development that signals severe limitations in information processing and linguistic comprehension. As José's spontaneous utterances increase, his echolalia decreases, which indicates more flexibility in the use of combinatorial rules.

With pervasive problems in broader conceptual areas, deficits in morphological and syntactic structures are not surprising; grammatical morphemes and function words are often omitted; speech is telegraphic, simplistic, and structurally restricted (Klinger & Renner, 2000). José also has difficulty with the developmental use of verb endings, such as past tense and present progressive, and with the acquisition of grammatical forms, such as auxiliaries, inflections, pronouns, and conjunctions. These language forms prove to be particularly difficult because they do not have a concrete referent. As a result, José's limited semantic–conceptual foundation does not provide a strong base for syntactic development. José does not understand conceptual ideas, such as past occurrence, that contribute to the formulation of language. José also has difficulties producing and comprehending various sentence types: complex, conjoined, conditional, question, and negative. He does not understand their underlying meanings, and he does not have the cognitive flexibility to change the order of linguistic units within sentences. Linguistic forms are acquired late in children with autism, if at all.

José's syntactic delays and limitations are related to conceptual delays in his understanding of language as a system of symbols that can be used for communicative purposes. Linguistic analyses by José's SLP indicate the emerging use of rule-governed behavior, despite José's limited production and comprehension of language. His productions at 48 months are presented within the framework of various contextual and interactional situations to highlight his limited linguistic processing abilities.

Consider José's use of the following morphemes: present progressive, past tense, personal pronouns, relative pronouns, copula, articles, and plurals.

CLINICIAN: What is Mommy doing?
JOSÉ: Mommy is opening juice.

Within the framework of an interaction with the adult, José is able to use the copula and present progressive morpheme within his own speech. He also responds to the question by altering the inflectional form of the adult's utterance (i.e., he does not imitate the question's inflectional pattern).

CLINICIAN: What did you do?
JOSÉ: José eat three cookie.

Within the framework of this interaction with the adult, José responds to the question by referring to himself as José; he does not use any personal pronouns. He is not able to code the past-tense form. When José is not able to code the morphemic structures presented by the adult, he reduces his own utterance or reverts to a string of content words. Plural forms are coded by the use of number without the plural –s. In these examples, there is a structural relationship between the linguistic input presented by the adult and the child's linguistic response; José's linguistic structure is a function of the adult's input. The following interaction shows what happens to José's linguistic structure when adult input is not provided:

CLINICIAN: (has just poured José some juice)
JOSÉ: Drink juice. (describing his own action)
JOSÉ: More. (requesting more juice)
JOSÉ: Pour juice. (directing clinician to perform an action)
JOSÉ: Give. (requesting cup from clinician)

In this interaction, the clinician responds nonverbally to all of José's requests and directions. José does not have the adult's linguistic structure to rely on to formulate his own utterances. The result is a reduction to the minimum use of a single word that effectively communicates his need. This reduction process is typical of José's spontaneous or self-initiated speech. To understand José's syntactic abilities, it is important to analyze if and how his structural form changes within various interactional situations. For José the adult's input provides a linguistic framework for his responses. Finally, José rarely provides gestural support for his verbal productions unless he is agitated; then he flaps his hands.

Phonological Abilities

José's phonological abilities and syntactic skills are more advanced than his pragmatic and semantic abilities. The suprasegmental features of rate, prosody, rhythm, and quality, however, represent disordered aspects of José's speech. Suprasegmental features such as stress and intonation are distinctive, with a monotonic voice quality. His stress and pitch patterns are often inappropriate to the meaning of his linguistic utterances and the context of the situation. In addition, José's lack of affect may be explained by his inability to process and use intonational features.

This explanation of José's speech behavior is more parsimonious than the suggestion of emotional impairment. The frequency of distribution of José's phonemes is similar to that found in children with mental retardation, with the highest percentage of errors involving phonemes that are generally acquired later by typical children. The order of his phonemic acquisitions seems to follow the typical developmental pattern, despite his delayed speech onset. José's phonological abilities contrast markedly with his developmental delays in other linguistic and communicative areas.

Cognitive Abilities

José's perceptual deficits severely limit his interactional experiences within the environment. "Researchers have hypothesized that abnormal amygdala function may account for some of the impairments seen in autism. One specific impairment is recognition of socially relevant information from faces" (Adolphs, Sears, & Piven, 2001). Children who see the world in a distorted manner interact with that world in a distorted manner. Because the roots of representational behavior are based on a child's interactional experiences within the environment, it is important to examine the interrelationship between cognitive and communicative functioning (Tager-Flusberg, 1999).

The relationships among perception, language, and cognition remain controversial. Current trends are influenced by cognitive theories that stress the importance of early social and interactional experiences with peers and caregivers. Harris, Handleman, Gordon, Kristoff, and Fuentes (1991) describe changes in intellectual and language functioning in children with and without autism over the course of a year. The results indicate that, relative to their typical peers, preschool children with autism show a greater increase in intellectual progress in a clinical program than anticipated. A 19-point increase in IQ provides support for the effectiveness of early intervention programming and the ability of children with autism to benefit from comprehensive programming. Approximately 75% of children with autism are reported to have IQs below 70, although intelligence is not uniformly impaired across all domains (Folstein, 1999; Siegel, Minshew, & Goldstein, 1996).

Differential diagnosis is complicated by the fact that children with severe or profound mental retardation may exhibit behaviors similar to children with autism. Children with mental retardation exhibit quantitative delays in social interaction, communication, and behavior that are commensurate with their developmental level. In contrast, children with autism present qualitative differences in functioning that are not typically exhibited by other children with language delays, as well as a wide variability of skills.

The uneven developmental pattern in children with autism is difficult to explain. José's abilities are often in contrast to extreme delays in other areas of skill acquisition; these extreme abilities are often referred to as savant skills (Freeman, Cronin, & Candela, 2002). José has an excellent memory and rote recall; however, these abilities should be viewed in terms of his use of these skills within a social context. His remarkable memory is often used for noncommunicative and self-stimulatory purposes. Information is frequently extracted as a whole chunk and not used for interactional purposes. José will sit in a corner of the classroom and recite verbatim the news report from the previous night including all the commercials. (One afternoon, José's dirty clothes were being changed and he produced a Tide commercial with a monotonic vocal quality.)

At 48 months, José exhibits hyperlectic skills. Sparks and Artzer (2000) describe hyperlexia as reading without comprehension and decoding skills beyond a child's linguistic abilities. José reads everything that comes into his line of vision, wherever he is, no matter what is going on contextually.

Children with autism also have difficulty in generalizing learned behaviors from one context to another. Because these children cannot identify the relevant information within the complexities of a situation, they cannot identify what is important and what is not, creating a further problem in establishing conceptual or perceptual relationships. The ability to establish categories depends on the ability to discriminate differences and to determine how stimuli are associated and related to one another. José's perceptual deficits contribute to his failure to generalize learning and to develop strategies for adapting to continually changing social contingencies. Social rigidity limits the ability to adjust to changing social contingencies, and perseverative responses interfere with the development of problem-solving skills (Prior & Hoffmann, 1990; Russell, Mauthner, Sharpe, & Tidswell, 1991).

Deficits in generalization indicate a cognitive impairment in children, a problem that seriously limits their ability to learn spontaneously and to benefit from more structured and formalized learning (Tager-Flusberg, 1999). The inability to develop conceptual relationships, to extract and use similarities across situations, and to learn from past experiences condemns children with autism to repeated learning experiences. Typical children search for rules by identifying relevant and related stimuli within conceptual categories. Generalization involves the ability to identify the relationship between situation A and situation B and then to apply the *rule* to situations A' and B'. Without rule-governed behavior, children such as José have difficulty processing, categorizing, and interpreting social events (Tiegerman-Farber, 2002a).

Theory-of-Mind

The ability to view a situation from another person's perspective represents a metacognitive skill that begins to develop in typical children during the preschool years (Baron-Cohen, 1997). The ability to understand the thoughts, feelings, and beliefs of others is referred to as *theory-of-mind* and represents an important adaptive mental ability (Ozonoff & Miller, 1995). Bretherton, McNew, and Beeghly-Smith (1981) indicate that children as young as 2 years of age acquire a mental terminology and use it in the context of everyday life.

Around the age of 4, children begin to recognize that the thoughts and knowledge of others are different from their own. Theory-of-mind, which develops over several years, provides the child with an ability to understand the social relativity of behavior. Cultural, religious, racial, and gender experiences help to explain why people behave as they do. Children's interpersonal relationships are based on their ability to read and understand the feelings and thoughts of others.

The inability to take into account the viewpoint or perspective of a peer in generating a response has been referred to as "mindblindness" (Baron-Cohen, 1997; Silliman et al., 2003). Even after José has learned a task, he is not able to share his knowledge with others or to talk about what he knows or what he feels. He is not able to acknowledge when another child is hurt, and he does not understand what the child is feeling based on his verbal and nonverbal behaviors. José does not notice a breakdown in the communicative process or a linguistic error produced by another speaker. Finally, even when a child with autism spectrum disorder acquires the ability to comprehend or produce a linguistic structure, it does not ensure that he is able to judge the appropriate use of that structure in another speaker's language (Tager-Flusberg, 2001).

Social and Emotional Abilities

During this preschool period, despite José's emerging language, his expression of personal feelings and emotions and/or his recognition of emotions in others does not develop. His vocal quality can be characterized as monotonic. Shriberg et al. (2001) describe the speech patterns of autistic children as having phrasing and stress that are flat and staccato, with nasal resonance. José's interpersonal interactions with peers and adults develop into ritualized routines involving dressing, washing, toileting, circle time, and reading.

Unanticipated changes in a child's rituals and/or routines can result in temper tantrums. Reese, Richman, Zarcone, and Zarcone (2003) have documented such behaviors. If free time, which involves looking through books, always follows circle time, change in the sequence of the two activities precipitates a catastrophic response from José. Within a social context, aggressive behaviors such as biting, kicking, thrashing, and screaming can disrupt classroom harmony, frighten the other children, and agitate an already overwhelmed teacher (Hall, DeBernardis, & Reiss, 2006; Carr & Blakeley-Smith, 2006). José's tantrums are getting worse because he is bigger, stronger, and more difficult to manage physically.

During a tantrum, typical peers need to be separated from the child with autism, which may require isolation and removal of the child from social situations (Simpson, de Boer-Ott, & Smith-Myles, 2003). Jose has an individual aide who works with him in the back of the room when his behaviors cannot be managed in a group. José's peers are anxious about playing with him because most of them have experienced a tantrum at close range and have been the object of José's aggressive behaviors.

José does not understand the emotions exhibited facially or behaviorally by others, so he is not aware of how his behavior affects his peers. Some of the girls refuse to sit near José. Peer reactions vary from fear to dislike, with the children being very expressive about their concerns.

The central concern for any teaching staff involves encouraging, but not coercing, peers to engage the child with autism spectrum disorder in an activity (Buschbacher & Fox, 2003). José does not initiate social interactions. He prefers to remain by himself in a corner, so a peer has to be prompted to approach José. Although many of José's self-stimulatory behaviors remain within his repertoire, they are now only exhibited when José becomes anxious or agitated. Many autistic children develop expanded behaviors, which include ritualized sequences and often contain long chains of learned behaviors (Myles, Cook, Miller, Rinner, & Robbins, 2000). José's echolalic tendencies result in ritualized sequences of verbal behavior. For children with autism, verbal rituals interfere with the creative spontaneity of reciprocal interactions and peers and teachers know better than to interrupt a ritual once it starts (Church, Alisanski, & Amanuallah, 2000). So, too, do Jose's peers realize that interactions with José are time intensive and behaviorally limited. Without direct teacher facilitation, they either play around him or ignore him. José does not engage in any group activity without an adult sitting behind or beside him, physically guiding, prompting, and/or reinforcing appropriate social behaviors.

Finally, self, parallel, and cooperative play skills remain severely limited in children with autism (Safran, 2002b). Objects are not interesting things to explore with peers, and they do not provide a creative framework for relational experimentation. Objects such as food are always of interest because they meet immediate physical needs. José does not play with toys or games or seek out peers with whom he can play; he usually isolates himself during social activities. During his preschool years, José does not refer to himself as "me" or "I." He never calls his mother "Mama," and he never tells his mother he is sick, happy, or angry. José does not refer to the rich internal world of feeling, thinking, dreaming, and imagining.

Although José evidences many language differences, let's consider his strengths.

SLP: A Strengths-Based Description

José is able to express his intentions by means of verbal imitation. He has developed meaningful associations between linguistic productions from television programs, commercials, news, radio, other speakers, and the like, and contextual events or objects. He has a vocabulary of nouns and verbs that he uses appropriately to express his needs and wants. Sometimes he is verbally spontaneous with adults and children. He has fewer temper tantrums because he is more responsive to the linguistic input of others. He engages in activities that involve food, water, lights, and motor actions. He sits and participates in circle and table-top activities with typical peers, given adult physical prompting. He is able to look at a communication partner when he wants something. He often remains near peers during unstructured play-group activities. José is developing an extensive vocabulary and can read anything that appears in printed form. José enjoys looking through books and carries books with him from activity to activity. In Box 6.1, Josés mother describes her feelings at this time.

Specific Language Impairment: Jeffrey

Children with specific language impairment (SLI) are described as late talkers with limited vocabularies who have difficulty acquiring novel words. When they have speech production deficits, there are phonological errors, morphological omissions, and a decrease in syntactic complexity (Weismer & Evans, 2002). Children may also have

BOX 6.1

It is painful to watch José in a classroom with children who sing and dance and play with each other. He doesn't know who they are even after all these months. I wonder if José knows who I am as his mother. There are times that I think it doesn't matter whether I'm present or not. I can't say that José loves me. I see José as alone in a group, but I don't know if he feels lonely. I was so relieved when he started to talk. I don't care that he repeats commercials, at least he has a voice. He just started to read and he likes to look at books. I carry his books when we have to leave the house along with his favorite treats. I'd like José to stay with normal children, but some of them are afraid of him. I know José has hit and bitten the other children. I know what their parents must be thinking. I would feel the same way. I don't want another child to hurt José. On the other hand, being disabled is not an excuse for hurting another child. I don't know what the answer is. If I took José back to my country, he would be in an institution for retarded children. José is a bright boy, he is not retarded. I don't want him to be in a class with retarded children and picking up bad behaviors.

Maria Martinez

 Use the Companion Website to help you answer the following questions:

1. Discuss the role of echolalia in children with autism, and describe José's language changes in terms of a linguistic processing continuum.

2. Explain the function of rituals in the development of chains of behavior.

3. Provide an explanation for José's uneven pattern of development.

4. The following problem is presented for classroom discussion. A research study by Coplan and Jawad (2005) reports that the prognosis for individuals with autism spectrum disorders (ASD) appears to be related to the relationship between the degree of atypicality and the level of overall intelligence. Only children with cognitive abilities in the average range showed a significant decrease in their atypical characteristics as measured by *The Childhood Autism Rating Scale* (CARS) (Schopler, Reichler, & Renner, 1988). The conclusion was that attributions of therapeutic effectiveness need to be reevaluated, given these results. The researchers indicate that intervention methods must show child improvement outcomes greater than those that would have occurred naturally. "This is vitally important, because many currently popular therapies may be capitalizing on the natural history of ASD and claiming such improvement on their own behalf" (Coplan & Jawad, 2005, p. 122).

   In this study, the level of intelligence is a significant predictor of long-term change in children with ASD. Language functioning was not measured or considered in this study. Consider that intelligence or IQ cannot be measured directly because it is based on language ability. Language ability can be measured directly and might provide a better measure of prognosis. Language ability as a measurable variable lends itself to direct outcomes based on clinical interventions. Finally, subjects ranged in age from 20 months to 13 years 11 months, which represents a large developmental range for child comparisons. The researchers conclude that there are two mutually exclusive subgroups of children based on two distinct clinical patterns. Discuss the following in class:

a. How might this study have been designed by an SLP?

b. Explain the results of such a study from the perspective that language is "a major predictor of outcome in children with ASD" (Coplan & Jawad, 2005, p. 117).

c. Describe some of the experimental limitations in studies of children with disabilities.

d. As an SLP, how would you respond to the final conclusion about two exclusive subgroups of children and two distinct clinical patterns?

e. Speech-language pathologists and psychologists may have different perspectives on child development and disorders. How might this affect their treatment approaches?

Children with speech-language impairments often communicate and socialize by means of gesture and nonverbal play.

Kriste Greco / Merrill

comprehension deficits that further impede the progressive acquisition and integration of linguistic and cognitive information. Weismer and Evans (2002) note that late-talking toddlers often evolve into cases of SLI when they enter school. Finally, a high percentage of preschool children with SLI become school-age children with metalinguistic deficits, academic learning difficulties, reading problems, and poor social–affective skills. Many children do not outgrow their language difficulties, although the qualitative aspects of the language impairment evolve (Gopnik, 1999; Johnston, 1999).

Pragmatic Abilities

The communicative process develops into a formalized structural exchange with rules that govern how speakers and listeners function in their respective roles. Jeffrey's phonological deficits influence the clarity of his productions. Because Jeffrey does not develop standard phonological forms, his peers do not understand what he is saying.

To the extent that phonological forms are independent of gesture and contextual information, the opportunity for misunderstanding and misinterpretation increases.

As a speaker, Jeffrey has a primary responsibility to effectively communicate his message to his listeners. This communicative responsibility requires that Jeffrey use strategies to change the structure of his language to meet the needs of his listener. He does not take the perspective of his listener and often refers to objects and events assuming that peers and adults know what he is talking about. Because he does not monitor his listeners to determine if they understand, he frequently misses critical verbal and nonverbal communication cues.

Often the child with SLI cannot modify his speech and/or language productions, and as the pressure to respond increases, the child's anxiety about the communication process increases (Brinton, Fujiki, & Higbee, 1998; Brinton, Fujiki, & McKee, 1998). Jeffrey withdraws from social activities and/or gets frustrated when his listener does not understand. Jeffrey experiences less pressure as a listener, so he tends to take on a more passive role in a group, listening and following rather than initiating and leading. He rarely speaks spontaneously to other children. When another child initiates a conversational exchange, the number of turns on a specific topic continues for one or two exchanges. Jeffrey does not elaborate on his productions, which are generally short and simple. Jeffrey's narrative skills generally consist of a broken string of words because his stories do not have a formalized structure with internal integration and cohesion of thematic content. Because narrative scripting requires that Jeffrey produce a monologue, he is most dysfluent when asked an open-ended question (e.g., What did you do over the weekend?) (Boscolo, Ratner, & Rescorla, 2002; Nippold, 2002).

Jeffrey does not perceive himself to be an effective speaker or communicator, so verbal interactions are avoided as much as possible. Jeffrey covers his mouth with his hand, shakes his head, and refuses to verbalize when his preschool teacher calls on him to answer in class. Although he needs the language practice, he avoids the very experiences that could facilitate his learning.

Semantic Abilities

The preschool period is one of rapid lexical development, with children's word definitions being concrete and requiring a referent's appearance and function. Jeffrey's phonological deficits inhibit the acquisition of novel words, with verbs being more negatively affected than nouns. Conti-Ramsden and Windfuhr (2002) indicate that limited verb development is a predictor of SLI. Given the delay in the acquisition of novel words, "new coded knowledge," Jeffrey falls further behind his peers in terms of the development of conceptual and abstract levels of language (i.e., nonliteral and inferential), which contributes to the development of metalinguistic and metacomprehension skills. The ability to revise, reflect on, and repair the rules of language is based on an internalized schema that children develop from repeated language experiences that highlight linguistic patterns. In contrast to typical peers, Jeffrey's linguistic descriptions and analyses are often simplistic and concrete. He compensates by focusing his attention on activities that do not require verbal skills or interactions: art, music, computer, and play.

Word-finding problems relate to the tenuous coding of linguistic forms that require "phono-logical" awareness (Felton & Pepper, 1995). Word finding may be related to either a storage or a retrieval problem. A storage deficit results when a child has not learned words sufficiently so that they can be recalled readily. A retrieval deficit occurs when words are adequately encoded, but the lexical form cannot be easily accessed. The reason for differentiating between word-finding problems involves the nature of the treatment to be provided. Word-finding problems may result in a high frequency of circumlocutions involving word substitutions and associations when a child cannot produce a specific word (McGregor, Newman, Reilly, & Capone, 2002). Jeffrey's word-finding problems interfere with the flow of a conversational exchange or a narration, because Jeffrey will start, stop, think, circumlocute, associate, and attempt to repair the communicative breakdown. A listener becomes confused when the child with SLI becomes distracted and produces a tangential statement (Perkins, 2001). As a result, word-finding problems can exacerbate a child's pragmatic difficulties when the organizational framework of the communication process is constantly disrupted (McGregor & Appel, 2002). Jeffrey appears to be dysfluent, and his early childhood teacher is concerned about stuttering.

Syntactic Abilities

By 48 months, most children's syntax is adultlike. Typical learners have acquired inflections and sentence types such as negation and questions that require the rearrangement of word elements (subject, verb, object) within a basic sentence (simple, active, declarative). Bishop, Price, Dale, and Plomin (2003) note that grammatical impairments are generally more evident in children with SLI.

Jeffrey's spontaneous speech is considerably shorter and less complex than his productions based on an adult's prior productions. This marked difference between spontaneous and modeled speech is also characteristic of José's speech production. Generally, the essential words (nouns, verbs, and adjectives) are present, but the morphological inflections (plurals, tenses, auxiliary verbs, and prepositions) are inconsistently used. Jeffrey's sentences do not have an internal cohesion that reflects the production of language by means of standard linguistic forms. When Jeffrey is asked a question, his response usually incorporates the syntactic forms from the adult, which are not present in his spontaneous productions. Just as with José, Jeffrey's level of syntactic functioning is deceiving unless a comparison is made between spontaneous and modeled speech productions.

Hick, Joseph, Conti-Ramsden, Serratrice, and Faragher (2002) note that differences between the child with SLI and his typically developing peers begin to emerge when multiword speech emerges, and there is generally persistent difficulty with verb use. Leonard et al. (2003) also note that children with SLI often have difficulty with verb morphology, separate from tense involvement.

As a child with SLI, Jeffrey's morphosyntactic productions are indicative of the productions of typically developing peers who are 2 years younger. From a different perspective, when communicative demands are increased because morphosyntactic structures have to be produced without the support of an earlier sentence, the child with SLI does more poorly than his typical peers (Leonard et al., 2002). Jeffrey's productions can also be explained by means of limitations in processing capacity. Jeffrey's linguistic productions are highly variable depending on the amount of cognitive pressure he perceives. The child with SLI may have an adequate lexicon for linguistic purposes despite his delays and be able to produce "short sequences of simple sentences," given low processing demands (Perkins, 2001).

Phonological Abilities

Children with SLI present phonological processing problems, which include a lack of phonological awareness, an inability to encode acoustic information into phonological forms, problems retrieving phonological units from memory, and deficits in decoding phonological information to derive meaning (Catts, 2001). Several of Jeffrey's problems are characteristic of children with phonological deficits:

1. Deficits in verbal memory
2. Deficits in naming (word finding)
3. Substitutions and/or circumlocutions for target words
4. Errors in the production of multisyllabic words

Phonological processing forms the basis for learning to read. Three phonological processes have been identified as most crucial to learning how to decode the printed word: (1) phonological awareness, (2) phonological coding in working memory, and (3) phonological coding in lexical access (rapid naming) (Felton & Pepper, 1995). Jeffrey's phonological processing problems result in the following:

1. Ongoing inability to express his needs, feelings, and thoughts in real time
2. Inability to acquire novel words and linguistic structures following a typical developmental sequence
3. Inability to identify and correct phonological errors in others
4. Inability to segment sentences into words
5. Difficulty with rhyming activities
6. Reduction of complex words and syllables into simpler forms

Several researchers note that children with SLI such as Jeffrey are at risk for literacy development (Bird, Bishop, & Freeman, 1995; Felton & Pepper, 1995; Major & Bernhardt, 1998). Like other children with SLI, Jeffrey has a limited phonetic inventory, a difficulty discriminating between phonemes, and a restricted syllabic pattern in words. The limited consonant repertoire especially, in word-medial and word-final positions, results in the persistent use of only a few consonants, which replace most others (Orsolini, Sechi, Maronato, Bonvino, & Corcelli, 2001). Jeffrey's speech is often unintelligible. He is frequently not able to get his needs met or get others to respond to his verbal initiations. Speaking is a difficult process for Jeffrey, which leads to frustration and confusion for adults and peers. So, when typical children are able to recite nursery rhymes, poems, and songs, Jeffrey cannot engage in word play.

Cognitive Abilities

The cognitive functions of perception, attention, and memory are related to each other and to the development of language. These functions interact to construct, organize, and internalize information that is verbally encoded. Jeffrey exhibits deficits in processing phonological information, organizing morphosyntactic structures, and categorizing verbal material. The interactive and facilitative relationship between language and cognition suggests that progressive growth in one area enhances the acquisition process in the other. So Jeffrey's deficits in phonological awareness and processing negatively affect both the encoding of linguistic information and his cognitive functioning. Although, the definition of SLI indicates that cognitive deficits are not part of the profile, the interdependent relationship between language and cognition suggests otherwise. Seidenberg (2002) notes that children with SLI often present with deficits in the use of higher-order cognitive strategies. They have difficulty with the simultaneous processing of perceptual information, the development of organizational structures that encode larger amounts of information, and the use of verbal strategies to facilitate storage and retrieval of information.

Dialect Use

Dialectal variations are a function of a cultural subgroup that maintains distinctive phonologic and syntactic structures (Labov, 1998). Structural linguistic differences are passed down from generation to generation and are enhanced by geographic and communicative separation. Regional and cultural differences are reinforced by linguistic differences between dialectal and mainstream speakers. Although language differences are not disorders, identifying a communication disorder in a linguistically diverse group of speakers is much more complicated than in a monolingual population.

Jeffrey has a specific language impairment, but he has also been raised in an African American community. Oetting and McDonald (2001) indicate that the study of SLI within nonmainstream communities has been nonexistent. Seymour, Bland-Stewart, and Green (1998) note that "some patterns of nonmainstream dialect, on the surface, can look very similar to those that characterize a language impairment" in children with SLI (p. 208). African American English (AAE) presents some distinctive characteristics, such as tense-based and question formation differences. Tense-related weaknesses in children with SLI need to be distinguished from dialect diversity differences in culturally diverse children. Although children with SLI are distinguishable from those developing language normally, the concern is that African American children such as Jeffrey may not be appropriately identified with SLI because of a nonmainstream pattern (Oetting & McDonald, 2001). In addition, African American children who are developing typically may be inappropriately identified as SLI because clinical practitioners are not familiar with the distinctive characteristics of the dialect (Craig & Washington, 2000). In Jeffrey's case, AAE was not a factor contributing to his phonological differences.

Social and Emotional Abilities

Jeffrey enjoys playing with peers. He observes their social and play behaviors to successfully imitate and follow his peers. He stays close to his peers and initiates social interactions that are generally successful when activities involve nonverbal interactions (e.g., blocks or puzzles). Peers may avoid a child with SLI when he is upset and reject him in situations in which outbursts have occurred in the past (Fujiki, Brinton, & Clarke, 2002). As typical children get older, they become more socially and emotionally competent. Children with SLI, however, continue to have difficulty managing their emotions, because they cannot effectively use language to express their needs in social interactions with peers (Fujiki, Spackman, Brinton, & Hall, 2004).

Gallagher (1999) notes that language is an important tool for developing self-reflection abilities, mediation, response inhibition, and behavioral direction. When a child with SLI is aware of his dysfluencies, he may react to his own speech, as well as to the reactions of others (Nippold, 2002). Jeffrey feels frustrated when he cannot control "his mouth," and he says so by slapping himself on the face. Jeffrey's teachers speak to Camille St. James about the possibility that he is a stutterer. His word-finding problems increase his dysfluencies, leading to further social and emotional conflicts. Jeffrey's aggressiveness is also related to his anxieties about his dysfluencies. He tries to avoid talking and compensates by using gestures when he is dysfluent. Peers perceive Jeffrey as aggressive, which only exacerbates the negative social cycle.

By 5 years of age, when other children exhibit school-readiness skills, Jeffrey's problems profoundly affect his self-esteem and self-concept. Although his preschool teachers and peers try to help him by answering for him or completing his sentences when he is dysfluent, it only adds to his sense of communicative failure and social anxiety. The difference between Jeffrey and his peers in terms of natural speaking abilities increases and becomes more distinctive, which further inhibits his intrapersonal growth. Whereas the development of friendships in children establishes the framework for emotional sharing and intimacy in later life, a child with SLI may remain isolated and alone (Fujiki, Brinton, Hart, & Fitzgerald, 1999). Finally, SLI increases the probability that a child will experience literacy and educational difficulties later in elementary school (Law & Durkin, 2000).

Having recognized Jeffrey's language differences, let's consider his strengths.

SLP: A Strengths-Based Description

Jeffrey has excellent nonverbal skills. He is able to play cooperatively with peers and respond to the social initiations of others. He listens, follows directions, and completes multistep activities. He has developed age-appropriate self-care skills so that he can dress, toilet, and feed himself. He has developed many prereadiness skills, such as match-to-sample; categorization; shape, color, and number identification; object–picture association; and picture (story) arrangement and completion. He has average intelligence, with strong abilities in visual sequential memory, spatial concepts, visual–motor integration, and fine-motor coordination. His arithmetic concepts and math skills are excellent for a preschooler. He has a precocious interest and ability in art and music. He is able to play the piano, paint, and sculpt at an advanced level. He enjoys athletic activities and tries to interact with his peers. He shares his toys and materials during structured classroom activities with peers and shows a sensitive awareness to another child who is emotionally upset. Jeffrey's mother explains her problems with him at this time in Box 6.2.

BOX 6.2

Jeffrey's not emotionally disturbed, but I have a problem managing his behavior at home. He gets frustrated very easily when I don't understand him. He refuses to repeat his words and at times he hits me and his cousins. Although there are a lot of children in our neighborhood, Jeffrey is not very popular. No one comes to play in our house, and Jeffrey doesn't have any friends. He's never been invited to anyone's birthday party and only my family comes to his. At times Jeffrey stands on the edge of the playground and watches the other children laughing and running. It's not that the other children are mean; they're not comfortable when he approaches them. They're never sure what he's going to do— scream, throw sand, or push someone. He wants to play, but he doesn't know how to talk to the other children. He needs to be with other children, but he can't control his frustration. The older children push him away and the younger children run away. I wouldn't like another child hitting Jeffrey, so I know how other parents feel. That doesn't help Jeffrey, who needs to learn how to make friends. If they don't teach him to behave in his child-care program, what's going to happen when he goes to kindergarten? I talk to Jeffrey, but there's no reasoning with him when he's screaming. I can't be around all day because I've got to work. It's so painful to watch him. He only manages to play with other children for a short time before something happens and he ends up alone.

Camille St. James

Use the Companion Website to help you answer the following questions:

1. Develop a phonological profile for Jeffrey and describe his speech pattern as a preschool child with a speech-language impairment.

2. Assume that Jeffrey uses African American English (AAE), rather than Standard American English (SAE); describe some of the characteristics of his speech.

3. Describe how cultural diversity might affect Jeffrey's pragmatic and social behavior as a child with an African American background.

4. Describe how an SLP might differentiate between developmental dysfluencies and stuttering.

Hearing Loss: Kaitlyn

Kaitlyn is now a cochlear implant user. Because she is exposed to sign language in her total communication environment, she is acquiring many important communicative skills. The sign system she uses is an invented system based on American Sign Language (ASL), but it uses English syntax and grammar. It is often referred to as Pidgin Sign English (PSE). ASL is a sign system with its own syntax and grammar and has evolved over time as a unique language, just as have German, English, or French. Children of parents who are deaf are exposed to ASL from birth and often develop a robust language. Kuntze (1998) makes an argument for using ASL rather than PSE. She states that ASL is an alternative route for English acquisition.

Once children acquire ASL as their primary language, the educational approach that would benefit them most is a bilingual approach. That is, children who are deaf would have a better chance of developing reading and written language if English is considered their second language, with ASL being their first language. Children who are deaf would then be taught using ASL and would be able to make adequate progress in all subject content matter. Wilbur (2000) indicates that early learning of ASL can contribute directly to developing the high-level cognitive skills that are needed for reading and writing. Nevertheless, most schools that utilize sign language use PSE, and there are documented success stories of children who acquire English through PSE and achieve solid literate and communicative abilities. Svaib (1994) documents a child who acquired literate abilities similar to her hearing peers after she was exposed to sign language. This child was studied for 18 months, and she could sign complex stories with a variety of linguistic structures. Unfortunately, not all children who are exposed to signs acquire English literacy skills.

Cochlear implants for young children have proved to be successful when certain factors are present. Children with pre-implant hearing experience typically show the most speech and language growth. Furthermore, implantation within 1 year of onset of deafness, enrollment in an intervention program, and high levels of family involvement also predict positive language outcomes. This is true for children from multicultural backgrounds as well (Spencer, 2004). Zwolan and Heavner (2005) state that children with profound hearing loss have the potential to develop normal speech and language skills when the following factors are in place: early identification of hearing loss; appropriate, immediate follow-up; early implantation; good medical, audiological, rehabilitative, and educational management; and consistent parent involvement. Moeller (2000) found that whether children use hearing aids or cochlear implants, the best language outcomes occur when there is consistent family involvement and early enrollment in an intervention program. Interestingly, it does not matter if the children are in an aural–oral intervention program (no signs) or in a total communication program. Once a child receives an implant, the rate of language growth matches that of hearing peers and, although a gap exists between chronological age and language age, this gap will not widen (Miyamoto, Svirsky, & Robbins, 1997). With appropriate postimplant management, the gap should decrease.

In an age-at-implantation analysis by Geers (2004) of 181 children born deaf who received implants by age 5 years, outcomes at age 5 for children implanted at ages 2 and 4 were compared. She found that those children who were implanted at age 2 (43%) achieved combined speech and language skills commensurate with their normal-hearing, age-matched peers. However, for those children implanted at 4 years, only 16% had speech and language skills commensurate with age-matched peers.

After implantation, the language approach chosen by parents many times is generally based on what is geographically available to the family. Often, when a child is evidencing other concomitant handicapping conditions, such as neurological problems or cognitive delays, a total communication approach is preferred. A typical trend for implanted children, regardless of educational approach, is that educational placements change as children have increased experience with their cochlear implants. Children generally move from special-education settings to public-school and mainstream programs (Geers & Brenner, 2003). This holds true for children with late (after age 3) implantation as well.

Pragmatic Abilities

Kaitlyn is becoming better and better at communicating. She is learning how to integrate syntactic and semantic elements and how to use these linguistic forms. Kaitlyn is exposed to communication partners who interact meaningfully with her. Katherine is learning sign language just for that reason. Kaitlyn knows how to initiate and how to terminate a conversation. When Kaitlyn is signing with Mom and wants to go outside to play, she signs "finish" and turns to leave and go outside.

Greenberg (1980) examined the communication intents of preschool children with hearing loss and found that their range of communication intent was similar to that of normal-hearing children. Day (1986) indicated that, even though children with hearing loss have limited syntactic production, the variety of communication intentions they communicate (through object manipulation, gestures, etc.) is similar to that of hearing children. However, Pien (1985) noted that children with hearing loss do not demonstrate extensive use of the heuristic function of language. Kaitlyn evidences many communicative intentions: she protests, calls attention to objects, and requests.

Syntactic Abilities

In the 1970s, extensive studies were conducted on the comprehension and production of syntactic structures of children and youth who were deaf (Power & Quigley, 1973; Quigley, Smith, & Wilbur, 1974). Their data reveal that the order of difficulty of syntactic structures is similar for both hearing and deaf children. Negation (easiest), conjunction, and question formation are the least difficult structures for children who are deaf. The same structures are least difficult for the hearing, but in a different progressive order of question formation (easiest), conjunction, and negation. The most difficult structures for children who are deaf are relativization (most difficult), complementation, the verb system, and pronominalization. The most difficult for normal-hearing children are verbs (most difficult), relativization, complementation, and pronominalization.

The only relatively well established syntactic rules for children who are deaf are negation, question formation, and conjunction; however, even these structures are often not mastered to any significant degree. Hearing students at a comparable age have mastered most of the difficult structures.

Syntactic structures progress through developmental stages. Children with severe hearing loss may reach these stages at a much delayed rate when compared with hearing children. Although children with hearing loss acquire the same syntactic rules as hearing children, certain syntactic structures may appear in the language system of children with hearing loss that do not exist in hearing children and are, in fact, not a part of English grammar. It appears that the children with hearing loss may generate syntactic rules peculiar to themselves. These idiosyncratic syntactic structures can be a combination of English grammar and attempted approximations of English grammar, and they are consistent in the written language of these children. Several implications can be applied to remediation techniques.

Kaitlyn is becoming better at putting words together. She can formulate sentences that are simple declaratives ("Mommy go car"; "bunny in yard"). Although her articulation is not always clear, she is using words in correct English syntax form. She is using adjectives now as well ("red car," "brown bunny"). Because Kaitlyn understands signs, stories are read and signed to her; then simple sentences are attached to each picture in her reading book ("Dog runs fast," "Baby fall," "Baby wants bottle"). She has learned to say these phrases and will "read" a story to her mother. Kaitlyn is making fine progress and it is expected that she will meet the linguistic challenges that hearing loss poses.

Kaitlyn's success can be attributed to her early exposure to a language system, early amplification (hearing aids), and early cochlear implantation.

Semantic Abilities

In children with normal hearing, new vocabulary is heard every day in naturally occurring conversations. For the child with a hearing loss, this natural context of vocabulary learning is reduced. Typically, developing children use a novel mapping strategy for acquiring new vocabulary (Lederberg, Prezbindowski, & Spencer, 2000). *Novel mapping strategy* refers to the fact that when children hear a conversation or experience an event, they map that new word to the object or experience without any explicit teaching of the word. This suggests that this strategy is the basis for true word learning and highlights the fact that meaning is more readily acquired in context.

Masur (1997) believes that this novel mapping strategy is a generalization that typically developing children make during their routine conversational interactions with their caregivers. Merriman, Marazita, and Jarvis (1995) show that the novel mapping strategy is demonstrated in typically developing children at ages $2\frac{1}{2}$ years and older.

For the child who is deaf, the process of acquiring vocabulary becomes more cumbersome if the parents utilize an aural–oral only approach. Early studies show that children who are deaf, but have hearing parents, do develop semantic abilities; however, this development occurs at a slower rate (Curtis, Prutting, & Lowell, 1979; Skarakis & Prutting, 1977). For children learning language through a total communication approach, sign words are more easily acquired because the sign is more salient than the spoken word. Futhermore, for the child using sign language, the ability to talk about the nonpresent and things that are not in the perceptual field develops more quickly. This ability is referred to as displaced reference and emerges in the typically developing child at approximately 20 to 24 months of age (Eisenberg, 1985; Sachs, 1988).

Only about 10% of children who are deaf learn language from deaf parents. Most have hearing parents, and even if the parents learn sign language, their skills are not commensurate with a native sign language user. Consequently, the parents' signing skills are in all likelihood insufficient to sign and label everything in the environment.

Phonological Abilities

The methodology for studying speech and language development in persons who are deaf parallels those used in studying normal language development. These methodologies chronologically trace important seminal research studies that examine the speech intelligibility of the deaf. In 1942, Hudgins and Numbers studied the speech production of children who were deaf between the ages of 8 and 20 years. This descriptive study concluded that 21% of all consonants and 12% of all vowels are misarticulated by subjects who are deaf. Specifically, errors include omission of initial and final consonants, errors in clustered consonants, voicing and nasality errors, numerous substitutions, and vowel distortions. In addition, the subjects who are deaf evidenced severe disturbances in the prosodic features of speech production that included errors of intonation, duration, and rhythm.

Later, other researchers (Jensema & Trybus, 1978; Markides, 1970; Nober, 1968) investigated speech articulation among persons who are deaf and found that a major portion of their speech production is unintelligible to inexperienced and experienced listeners alike. Smith (1975) examined the relationship of residual hearing and speech production in 40 children who were congenitally deaf. She found that speech intelligibility is related to hearing level for pure tones, but the measure most closely related to intelligibility is the test of phoneme recognition. The auditory recognition of speech features by children who are deaf is directly reflected in their ability to produce intelligible speech. She further stated that there is an interaction between prosodic errors and speech intelligibility and concluded that speech training of deaf children should emphasize improvement in the stress and intonation patterns of speech, rather than correct articulation.

During the 1970s, two other researchers examined the vocalizations of persons who are deaf, but they focused on the development of very early vocalization (Mavilya, 1978; Menyuk, 1974). They compared and described the vocalizations of infants who were deaf (birth through 6 months) to those of normal-hearing infants. They found that at the babbling stage (approximately 4 months) the vocalizations of the infants who were deaf differed significantly from those of hearing infants. This difference is one of quantity, not of quality. At the babbling stage, normal-hearing children engage in increasing vocalizations, whereas the vocalizations of infants who are deaf decrease.

In the 1970s, a phonological approach was employed to investigate the speech production of children with hearing loss. Several researchers (Oller, Jensen, & Lafayette, 1978; Oller & Kelly, 1974; West & Weber, 1973) studied the speech of young children who were hard of hearing with mild to moderate hearing losses to determine if their phonology is rule governed. All these researchers concluded that children who are hard of hearing demonstrate basically the same kind of phonological processes as those of younger, normal-hearing children. Knowing that specific phonological patterns are expected in children with hearing losses enables the SLP to plan effective speech-production intervention.

Suprasegmental patterns refer to the rhythm and voice-production characteristics of speech (Dunn & Newton, 1986). The suprasegmental characteristics of children with hearing loss vary; however, there are some constant characteristics. The rate of speech is often slower, caused by slow articulatory transitions. Stress patterns are also often atypical because the child does not always distinguish between stressed and unstressed syllables (Ling, 1976). The fundamental frequency of the child's voice may often be too high or too low, and intonation patterns can be restricted or routinized.

Several researchers have considered the relationship between perception of speech and production of speech. The better the perception of a speech sound is, the better the production. It has also been suggested that work on production facilitates perception of the same speech patterns and that perception and production develop together. With this in mind, speech training for the child with a hearing loss should emphasize the development of both production and perception simultaneously, with each skill contributing to the other (Calvert & Silverman, 1983; Ling, 1976; Osberger, 1983; Subtelny, 1983).

It has been shown that the central auditory pathways have plasticity and will develop with adequate sound stimulation provided through amplification (Kral et al., 2000; Ponton et al., 1996; Sharma, Dorman, & Spahr, 2002). If children with hearing loss do not receive early, adequate sensory stimulation through amplification, they will evidence delayed speech and language development. There has been recent interest in evaluating the benefit from intervention. The focus of this research is to determine a way to monitor the maturation of central auditory pathways after use of cochlear implant and/or hearing aids (Sharma & Dorman, 2005). If one can determine that the central auditory pathways are developing, one can determine if the intervention approach is appropriate.

Kaitlyn receives intensive speech and language therapy at the Mission School. She is putting words together to form short phrases, such as "Mommy up," "Bye-Bye," "Mommy more milk," "Baby bunny." Many of Kaitlyn's words are unintelligible to everyone except her parents and teachers at the Mission School. Her vocalizations are primarily vowel sounds, which are often neutralized vowels. Her vowel repertoire consists of /í/, /ʌ/, /Σ/, /e/, and /æ/. Vocal pitch is high and consonant sounds are often deleted. She can produce the / m/, /b/ and /p/, and /d/ sounds; however, she confuses /b/ for /p/. Her spoken words are not commensurate with her signed words, and she often vocalizes vowel sounds when signing. Kaitlyn is receiving intensive auditory and speech training. Her implant increases the range of her hearing, but now she must learn to attach meaning to what she hears. Auditory training objectives follow a hierarchy of development that matches the development of normal-hearing children. In therapy, Kaitlyn learns to consistently turn her head when her name is called. She also responds with a head turn when the dog barks, the phone rings, or a door slams. She can discriminate among these sounds, and signs the name of each when she hears it. Kaitlyn is learning that sounds have meaning. Because Kaitlyn has developed linguistic concepts through sign language, she is gradually mapping these concepts onto what she hears. Kaitlyn is now transitioning toward oral language. Her parents and teachers are requiring her to use vocalization and/or verbalization whenever she signs.

Cognitive Abilities

We know that children with hearing loss have the same cognitive abilities as hearing children. Research has focused on information processing models as they relate to reading and writing. Researchers are interested in how language and thought interact. The emphasis is on active learning. It is currently believed that there are multiple representations of knowledge, such as imagery, perceptual experiences, conceptual networks, and abstract propositions (Kretschmer, 1989). Long-term memory is also an integral part of information processing.

Adams (2001d) examined the cognitive styles in children with hearing loss and identified two fundamental styles: the wholistic–analytic style and the verbal imagery style (Riding, 1997; Riding & Chema, 1991; Riding & Rayner, 1998). Adams found that there is no correlation between degree of hearing loss and cognitive style and that no style is overtly dominant. Earlier researchers believed that cognitive styles develop as a result of either positive or negative interactional patterns with caregivers (Fuerstein, 1979). When these interactions positively assist the child in the learning process and enable her to comprehend and incorporate information into an organized schema, cognitive growth occurs. When these interactions are not appropriate or helpful, cognitive deficits occur (Kretschmer, 1989).

Kaitlyn's early exposure to sign language enables her mother and teachers to mediate learning through signs. She is passing through the Piagetian sensorimotor stages and is currently functioning at the preoperational stage. As her language develops, it becomes inextricably intertwined with cognition. Therefore, the key to Kaitlyn's cognitive development will be language.

Consider Kaitlyn's strengths from the perspective of the SLP.

SLP: A Strengths-Based Description

Kaitlyn has very good pragmatic skills, and she is developing a good sign language vocabulary at the Mission School. Some of her peers have deaf parents and consequently their signing skills are more developed than Kaitlyn's. Kaitlyn learns from these peers. Kaitlyn's cognitive skills are well developed, and she has no attentional issues. Her memory is strong, and she quickly makes associations between relevant linguistic–sign stimuli and environmental stimuli and stores that information for later retrieval. This is why her sign language vocabulary is developing so well. Other factors also support Kaitlyn's progress. Her mother has been very involved with Kaitlyn's education and learned sign language early on so that she could communicate with Kaitlyn. In addition, Mrs. Whiteside is well educated and pursuing a graduate-level degree. It has been shown that one strong predictor of positive language and academic development is parental communication skill (Calderon, 2000). Mrs. Whiteside has worked hard to develop her sign language skills and Kaitlyn will reap the benefits. Kaitlyn's mother describes her daughter's progress in Box 6.3.

BOX 6.3

Kaitlyn has several friends who are deaf at the Mission School for the Deaf. She engages in parallel play and cooperative play. When she's playing with her peers, she uses signs only, even though her teachers remind her to use voice by signing and speaking the words, "Kaitlyn, use your voice." She readily uses signs for "me," "I," "you"; she makes excellent eye contact and visually is very perceptive. Her vocabulary is extensive, and when she was 3 years old, a signed version of the Peabody Picture Vocabulary Test *was administered. Although not normed on children with hearing loss, she scored within the typical range. I'm so proud of Kaitlyn.*

I've worked very hard to develop my signing skills, and I make sure that I sign all my communications, not only to her but to my husband and other family members. I believe that this will provide a more natural environment for her. When people see me signing to Kaitlyn in public places like the supermarket, they usually stare, and some even come over to me to ask me about Kaitlyn. Most people are very interested in signs, and I show them how to make the sign for "I love you."

When Kaitlyn attempts to use her voice, most of what she says is not understood by people, except for me and her teachers. Kaitlyn doesn't get much opportunity to play with hearing children, except when we go to the playground. She's very friendly and outgoing and will walk over to them to play. Although they can't understand her when she signs, it's okay if she just plays next to them. Kaitlyn gets along well with her cousins, too, although they're older and generally do whatever she wants them to do. She'll use gestures with them and she definitely gets her point across.

Generally, Kaitlyn has a good disposition, although she'll tantrum out of frustration when she can't make me understand something. I have definitely noticed that her tantrums have decreased as her signing increased.

To me, Kaitlyn's just like any other little girl, except that she doesn't hear. I think a lot about Kaitlyn's future. I want her to have all the opportunities that hearing kids have. I know how important it is for me to have her in the best educational programs. When her special education committee meets to decide on a placement for her next year, I'll do everything I can to make sure it's the best setting to meet her needs.

Katherine Whiteside

Use the Companion Website to help you discuss the following questions:

1. Describe the speech characteristics you would expect in a 3- to 4-year-old child with a severe hearing loss.

2. Compare and contrast Kaitlyn's pragmatic development with that of José and Jeffrey.

3. Explain why children with hearing loss evidence the same communicative functions as hearing children, even though their speech and language lag far behind that of their hearing peers.

4. Do you think Katherine Whiteside's concerns about Kaitlyn being in the *best* educational programs are realistic, given IDEA?

5. What do you think the role of an interpreter is?

6. What can the SLP do to support a child who is deaf who is placed in a general-education classroom?

7. What do you think is the appropriate setting for Kaitlyn?

SUMMARY

This chapter has highlighted the language differences among José, Jeffrey, and Kaitlyn and typical children. Although their language development is different, these children need to be educated in an environment that will not only meet their learning differences, but will also prepare them to socialize and learn with typical peers. The learning environment must also focus on the development of self-esteem. It is important that each child learn how to communicate with peers and form friendships that develop a sense of competence and independence. Although this seems like a tall order for all our children, it is not an impossible one. Preschool experiences with other children lay the foundation for socializing with peers. Understanding language differences in children enables early childhood teachers to accommodate for these differences and enhance communicative exchanges among children.

The strengths-based description of each of our children is the springboard for developing peer-socialization opportunities. It is also the intermediary for learning language and preacademic skills. For example, we know that development of reading relies on phonological awareness. We also have learned that Jeffrey loves music. Using music activities as the vehicle for learning phonological awareness would be most beneficial for Jeffrey. He would more readily acquire these skills because they are presented through a learning channel that is strong for him and also enjoyable. It would give him opportunities to learn comfortably with peers and feel good about his accomplishments.

All our children have strengths. It is up to us to enhance learning through these strengths. We must keep in mind that the cup of learning is half full. It is our job to make sure that the children we work with continue to learn and meet their potential.

CHAPTER

7

Cultural and Linguistic Diversity

After studying this chapter, you should be able to answer the following questions:

1. What is naturalistic observation?

2. What are some nonstandardized assessments?

3. What diversity variables can affect assessment?

4. What is a dynamic assessment approach for identifying the disordered speaker of AAE?

5. What are the various kinds of modifications that need to be considered to meet the needs of diverse families?

T his chapter discusses assessment of the preschool child. This assessment process, like assessment of the child from birth to 3 years, requires a proficient knowledge of not only assessment instruments and child development, but also an understanding of diversity differences and expectations. Before embarking on the assessment process, issues of diversity must be considered.

Difference versus Disorder

Children with diverse backgrounds may develop at different rates. Cultural differences do not constitute disorders. For example, Western cultures place high priorities on language development, whereas many foreign cultures place priorities on silence. With these differences in mind, the professional team must approach the assessment process from an unbiased perspective.

During the last three decades, educators have been struggling with societal issues of difference versus disorder and monocultural versus pluralistic ideology. The fields of special education and bilingual education developed separately; children who are culturally and linguistically different may be identified as having a disability. When bilingual education programs developed, another equally disturbing outcome occurred. Many culturally diverse children with disabling conditions were not identified as such, but were placed in bilingual classrooms without the services that their conditions necessitated (Omark & Erickson, 1983).

Fortunately, educators have learned from their mistakes and now recognize the need to discriminate between cultural differences and actual language disorders. Diversity groups have unique cultural characteristics, so an understanding of salient cultural and linguistic factors is necessary for assessment of communication disorders.

By the year 2020, more than one third of the population will be people of color: African American, Asian American, Latino American, and Native American (U.S. Bureau of the Census, 1995). Educators must be prepared to identify exceptional children in their linguistic and cultural milieu (Bergin, 1980). The SLP must be sensitive to the characteristics of a child's ethnic community and be knowledgeable about acquisition and normative data of the child's first language.

African American English

African Americans are the largest minority population in the United States. An important cultural value of this community revolves around names and titles. Today, many African American children have names with unusual pronunciations or spellings that may be African names. It may be insulting to the family if an SLP uses a diminutive of the name. A good rule is to ask the family about their name preference. SLPs should also always address parents with their formal titles (Mr., Mrs., Doctor, or Ms.). Do not make the mistake of calling a parent by his or her first name in an effort to create informality and friendliness.

Several linguistic dialects are spoken among African Americans. The most predominant is African American English (AAE); however, others include Gullah (used by people living on islands near the coast of South Carolina and Georgia), Jamaican Creole, and dialects spoken by people from the Caribbean or African nations. African American English (AAE) is an American English dialect and consists of rule-governed, grammatical, phonological, syntactic, semantic, and pragmatic features. Not all African Americans speak African American English, and the factors that influence its degree of usage include age, geographic location, income, occupation, and education (Labov, 1966). Phonological rules include (1) silencing or substituting the consonants in a word (*day* for they, *brovah* for brother), (2) silencing unstressed initial phonemes and unstressed initial syllables (*bout* for about), and (3) silencing the final consonant in a consonant cluster (*mas* for mask).

Morphological and syntactical differences are extensive. Cole (1980), Dillard (1973), Labov (1966), and Taylor (1986) provide in-depth analyses of this subject. Cole (1980) documents normal acquisition of Black English patterns and suggests that, because of the difference in developmental patterns, it is difficult to identify language disorders utilizing conventional language tests. Goldstein (2000) and Haynes and Moran (1989) examine the phonological acquisition in AAE speakers. They find that by age 4, vowels and many consonants are mastered at the 90% accuracy level. However, instances of palatal fronting, fricative simplification, cluster simplification, final consonant deletion, gliding, cluster reduction, and velar fronting are evidenced occasionally (less than 10% occurrence) by these children.

When looking at morphosyntactic development in AAE children, there are multiple differences. Anderson and Battle (1993), Stockman (1986), Terrell and Terrell (1993), Roseberry-McKibben (1995), and Washington and Craig (1994) have identified some of these differences for children 3 to 5 years old (see Table 7.1).

Not all the mentioned differences are evidenced in all African American children who speak AAE, and the use of these dialect differences depends on socioeconomic status (Washington, Craig, & Kushmaul, 1998). Because of dialectical differences in children who speak AAE, some African American children may be misidentified as language impaired. To prevent misdiagnoses, Craig and Washington (2000) developed a dynamic assessment approach that distinguishes typically developing African

BOX 7.1

My son Jeffrey is being described as having behavioral problems. I think Jeffrey has problems talking. I also think that there is a general prejudice about African American boys.

Camille St. James

Use the Companion Website to help you answer the following questions:

1. What is the role of the SLP in assessing Jeffrey's cultural and language differences?

2. How would the SLP separate these two issues?

3. How would the SLP use the *Diagnostic Evaluation of Language Variation* (DELV) to separate Jeffrey's cultural differences from language differences?

TABLE 7.1 Typical Morphosyntactic Features of Standard English and AAE

3 Years		
Morphosyntactic Feature	**Standard English**	**AAE**
1. Present tense copula possessive	The dog is in the house.	The dog in the house
2. Regular past tense	She ate the sandwich.	She eat the sandwich
3. Third-person regular	She has some candy.	She have some candy
4 Years		
Morphosyntactic Feature	**Standard English**	**AAE**
1. Article "an" usage	an egg.	a egg
2. Negation	She doesn't want any.	She don't want none
5 Years		
Morphosyntactic Feature	**Standard English**	**AAE**
1. Possessive	It's John's bike.	It John bike
2. Plural	She ate two ice cream cones.	She ate two ice cream cone
3. Past tense	Joan danced last night.	Joan dance last night
4. Pronoun	My daughter, she is very nice.	My daughter she be nice
5. "To be" verb	He is my brother.	He be my brother
6. Past copula	They were sick.	They was sick

Source: Craig, H., & Washington, J., Dialect Forms During Discourse of Poor, Urban African American Preschoolers, 1994, *Journal of Speech and Hearing Research*, 37, 816–823.

American English (AAE) speakers from disordered speakers. This approach consists of measuring average length of communication units, frequencies of complex syntax, numbers of different words, and responses to "*wh*" questions and to probes of active and passive sentence construction as a low-structured assessment procedure. They compared these measures with the results of the *Peabody Picture Vocabulary Test*—III and the *Arizona Test of Articulation Proficiency, Second Edition*, which have been shown to effectively distinguish speech-impaired from non-speech-impaired AAE-speaking children (Craig & Washington, 1993).

They conclude that if the evaluator examines the syntactic forms that both speakers of AAE and speakers of Standard American English use, such as the use of articles, complex sentences, prepositions, present progressive (-ing), modals, conjunctions, verb particles, locatives and demonstratives, and does not consider dialectically different syntactic forms, such as third-person singular, auxiliary, copula, past tense (-ed), plural (s), and possessive (s), the assessment would be nonbiased and valid. It would successfully identify disordered speakers of AAE and those AAE speakers who were not disordered, but only speaking a dialect.

Eye contact, narrative style, and code switching are additional cultural differences that must be recognized as such and not considered disordered. For example, some African American children do not establish eye contact with an adult during a conversation because to do so would be disrespectful. Furthermore, children proficient only in AAE will use fewer words and less elaboration in school situations. However, in more familiar, informal settings these children are more talkative and elaborative.

Terrell and Terrell (1993) also identify a narrative-style difference among AAE children. Rather than adhering to a central topic during a discussion, African American children may utilize an associational discussion style. For instance, when a child is asked to talk about what he saw and did at the circus, mainstream expectation would be for the child to talk only about things seen or done at the circus. However, the African American child may make a statement that generates from what another child said previously about the circus. An example of this style would be as follows: first child states that she saw a clown at the circus; the second child says that he saw clowns on TV; the third child adds that he likes to watch cartoons on TV. This type of discussion narrative should not be considered off-topic or tangential, but rather a culturally different style of narration.

Latino Children

Within the Latino communities, there are different cultural backgrounds, socioeconomic levels, and educational levels. Because of the large numbers of Latino persons in the United States and the continuous arrival of new immigrants who maintain their primary language, Latino children often need to develop two languages. The Latino population is heterogeneous and varies in the ways adults socialize and interact with children. Although Spanish and English share many phonemes, there is not a one-to-one correspondence, and they differ in their phonological rules. For instance, final clusters do not occur in Spanish, and /s-/ blends do not occur in the initial position. Kayser (1993) delineates the morphosyntactic and semantic development of Spanish-speaking children. She states that these children use single words before 2 years of age, two-word constructions by age 2, and three-word constructions by age 3. By age $4\frac{1}{2}$, the child uses 38 Spanish syntactic structures (Garcia & Gonzalez, 1984).

An assessment of a bilingual Latino child should always include the status of both languages in the child's environment and consideration of the linguistic and cultural variables in that environment. Latino children often come from homes where only Spanish is spoken; because of this, assessing their communication abilities presents another set of issues for the SLP. If the SLP expects to assess Latino children in a nonbiased fashion, she or he needs to be aware of normal variations across and within Latino subgroups and be willing to implement the least biased assessment protocol.

Many Latino children use Spanish at home and learn English; consequently, they are either bilingual or second-language learners and exhibit different degrees of language proficiency, which is affected by social, emotional, educational, and demographic factors. Consequently, a perplexing issue arises when the SLP is asked to assess a bilingual Latino child. Interestingly, assessing a bilingual child in both English and Spanish does not necessarily address the problem, because developing two languages simultaneously is very different from the development of one language alone. The ideal situation would be to have test standards based on the development of two languages simultaneously, but these are not available.

Cummins (1984) identifies two groups of Latino children: those who predominately speak either English or Spanish and have very little proficiency in the second language and those children who have basic skills in both languages. In the second instance, assessments utilizing tests standardized on monolingual language users may overidentify Latino children as having a disorder. Furthermore, Latino children often code mix and use linguistic forms from both languages in their speaking. Testing in one or both languages does not tap into their full linguistic repertoire.

To further complicate the issue, several Spanish dialects are spoken, and these vary in terms of phonology, syntax semantics, and pragmatics. In addition, within the Latino community, there are different belief systems regarding the role of parents and how they interact with children. It is possible that, inherent in a family's social belief system, parents are very directive with children and do not spend much time playing with or expanding language (in terms of what the mainstream culture considers facilitative). This parenting style is very appropriate for parents and children, and it is not the role of the SLP to change the pattern because the family lives and socializes within that environment. Furthermore, some Latino children learn Spanish and English simultaneously, while some learn Spanish first and English second (sequentially). With this in mind, profiles of development will be different; presently, assessment instruments that are standardized on children in either group are not available.

How then does one assess and make a determination that a child has a disorder? Researchers suggest making modifications to assessment instruments. Modifications, such as rewording instructions, providing additional time, or even having a parent present test items, can decrease bias (Iglesias, 2001). However, other approaches are needed, and dynamic assessment provides an option.

Dynamic assessments examine the child, given an understanding of his social and linguistic environment, and they mediate learning experiences to teach children about the knowledge and strategies that are the underpinnings of standardized tests (Peña, 2002). The Latino child's speech-language abilities can be adequately assessed if consideration is given to the phonological skills, semantic knowledge, and morphosyntactic and narrative abilities in light of cultural differences. Care must be taken to use appropriate assessment strategies and make modifications to the assessment protocol when they are necessary.

Assessment

Phonological Assessment

Generally, the goals of phonological assessment are the same for the Latino child as they are for non-Latino English-speaking children. What sounds are in the child's phonological system? Is the sound system developing typically, considering dialectical variations? What are the dialectical variations? Many Latino children speak two languages, so the phonological skills in both languages need to be assessed.

Goldstein (2001) presents five questions that the SLP must address when assessing the child:

1. Does the child sound like other children of the same age?
2. What consonants does the child produce?
3. What vowels does the child produce?
4. How intelligible is the child?
5. How well do the child's family, teachers, and friends understand the child?

Because there is no formal phonological assessment instrument standardized on bilingual Spanish–English speakers, the SLP must use the assessment instruments that have been standardized on monolingual speakers of either Spanish or English, with the understanding that no normative data will be utilized to establish age, percentile, or standard score ranking. Instead, a profile of sound productions is assembled and then examined to determine the following:

- The sounds the child produces that are evident in both languages
- The sounds the child produces that are not found in both languages

Furthermore, the SLP should determine the syllable types used by the child (e.g., cv, cvc, ccv) and whether the child can produce two- and three-syllable words. Dialectical variations must also be considered because, depending on the country of origin, dialects will vary. For instance, Puerto Rican dialect has specific differences from Mexican Spanish. The SLP needs to gather information regarding these dialectical variations and incorporate this information for final analysis. However, phonological processes occur in both English and Spanish, such as final consonant deletion, cluster reduction, liquid simplification, fronting, stopping, assimilation, and final consonant deletion (Goldstein, 2001). Goldstein and Washington (2001) find that the most commonly occurring phonological processes in bilingual English–Spanish children under the age of 5 when tested in English are stopping and final-consonant deletion. When tested in Spanish, liquid simplification and cluster reduction are the most prevalent. Thus, once all the information is gathered and analyzed the SLP can appropriately diagnose a phonological disorder.

Semantic Assessment

Assessment of semantics in children from culturally and linguistically diverse backgrounds can also be challenging. Traditionally, semantics has been assessed using single-word receptive vocabulary tests, such as the Peabody Picture Vocabulary Test

(PPVT-R) or the Receptive One Word Vocabulary Test (ROWPVT), or expressive one-word vocabulary tests, such as the Expressive One Word Vocabulary Test (EOWPVT). Even though some of these assessments have been standardized on Spanish-speaking children, SLPs need to be cautious about using them as the sole measure of semantics, because multiple factors such as home language, individual experiences, word-retrieval skills, and concept knowledge are not factored into the standardization sample. Thus, single-word vocabulary tests are not an accurate measure of semantics.

Peña (2002) suggests using feedback and the clinical interview as two more authentic procedures for assessing semantics. Feedback consists of modifying the testing format; for example, when administering the EOWPVT, the child is provided with feedback after every response. The feedback can take the form of "Good," "That is a special name," or "Do you know another name?" With this feedback the child is given opportunities to change his response. It also gives the examiner information that indicates the child's conceptual understanding of a stimulus picture and his ability to retrieve the single-word name. When Peña compares results of feedback to no-feedback conditions of testing, she finds that the feedback condition gives more information regarding a child's conceptual knowledge of items. She cautions, however, that if the SLP utilizes the feedback condition, it must be reported in the testing results. Although the validity of testing is stable, there is no proven reliability for the clinical use of feedback. She suggests the following:

1. Script the feedback before testing and keep careful notes of the feedback.
2. Be consistent with the feedback techniques used.

It is Peña's belief that with feedback as a testing modification the SLP will gather a more accurate assessment of the child's vocabulary skills. Another technique proposed by Peña for use during the clinical interview involves probing the child for an understanding of the child's point of view regarding responses to test items. The clinical interview technique is not routinely applied when administering standardized assessments. Its purpose is to discover how children organize their semantic repertoire. So, for example, if a child is expected to recognize similarities and differences, the examiner might probe with the question, "What does different mean?" Probing gives the SLP insights into a child's thinking and ideas for mediated learning. It also allows the SLP to determine whether young children have well-developed categories in spite of exposure to two languages and possible vocabulary differences in both.

Morphology

Spanish morphology is different from English morphology. Spanish noun phrases demonstrate number and gender agreement. Articles, adjectives, and pronouns also are marked for gender and number, and this is accomplished through a rich repertoire of morphosyntactic forms (Bedore, 2001). Bedore describes the emergence of morphosyntax, noting that articles emerge at 18 months, and correct article–noun gender agreement for some nouns is produced by young children before 3 years. Noun-phrase agreement emerges around 4 to 5 years (Perez-Pereira, 1991). A variety of syntactic forms develop before the age of 5 years. These forms include subject pronouns, unstressed reflexive and object pronouns, and verb morphology,

TABLE 7.2 Spanish Language Assessments

Assessment Instrument	Source
Spanish Structured Photographic Expressive Language Test—Preschool	Werner E., & Resneck, J. Sandwich, IL: Janelle Publications, 1989
Spanish Test for Assessing Morphologic Production	Nugent T., & Shipley K. Provencio, CA: Academic Communication Associates, 1991
Preschool Language Scale-3, Spanish Edition	Zimmerman, I., Steiner, V., & Pond, R. T. San Antonio, TX: Psychological Corporation, 1992
Peabody Picture Vocabulary Test-R, Spanish Edition	Dunn, L., Jugo, D., & Padilla, E. Circle Pines, MN: American Guidance Services, 1986

such as third-person-singular present forms. Although an abundant body of normative data does not yet exist for typical development of Spanish in children who are bilingual, there are guidelines that can be applied. Bedore (2001) indicates that children with specific language impairment produce less accurate articles and direct object pronouns. In addition, their sentences have shorter MLUs. A few Spanish language assessments can be used for children who speak Spanish (see Table 7.2).

Language Sample

Besides using standardized instruments, the language sample is an integral part of the diagnostic process. When gathering a sample, it should be remembered that children produce representative samples of their productions when a task that is natural to the child is provided. Kayser and Restrepo (1995) suggest that the evaluator needs to provide structure and materials that are familiar when gathering a language sample. In addition, an MLU should be calculated based on words and not morphemes. When gathering the language sample, the SLP should speak Spanish and probe for specific grammatical forms to determine if the child's morphosyntactic development is commensurate with that of peers. Probes are used to gain specific information about children's morphosyntactic productions and, although not standardized, are valuable in determining whether a child evidences delays. It is important to use culturally familiar objects or toys to encourage verbalizations.

The *Parent Child Comparative Analysis* (PCCA) can be used to compare the child's communicative patterns to that of his family (Terrell, Arensberg, & Rosa, 1992). When the child's pattern does not match that of the caregiver and does not meet expectations for the child's chronological age, there is a possibility of a language disorder.

Sample size refers to the number of utterances gathered. Some investigators recommend a language sample of at least 100 communicative acts (Tyack & Gottsleben, 1975); others recommend between 200 and 300 (Muma, 1978). With a very young child (1 to 3 years), a sample of 100 utterances may be sufficient; with an older child (3 to 5 years), a 200-utterance sample is more representative.

Narrative Assessment

The development of narratives in monolingual English-speaking children is well documented (Applebee, 1978; Hedberg & Stoel-Gammon, 1986; Scott, 1988; Westby, 1984). Although the data compiled from this research do not provide the norm for the Latino child or other children from diverse backgrounds, they do provide a model for recognizing differences between children who speak Spanish and English. In English-speaking children between the ages of 2 and 5, narratives show a specific progression. Their earliest form is heaps, or collections of unrelated ideas that emerge at age 2. By age 3, narratives become sequences in which story elements are linked together loosely. By age 4, unfocused chains present an actual sequence of events that are logically linked and utilize cause and effect thinking. By age 5, focused chains appear in which a central character and sequenced events dominate the narrative (Hutson-Nechkash, 1990).

Another approach to examining narratives is qualitative. McFadden and Gillam (1996) and Reilly, Bates, and Marchman (1998) describe narrative assessments that establish rubrics for scoring the quality of narratives of children. This type of assessment has merit when evaluating Spanish-speaking bilingual children. However, it is only appropriate for children over the age of 5 years.

Sign Language and Bilingualism

Another culturally diverse group is the Deaf Community. It has long been recognized that persons who are deaf and use sign language share a culture, the culture of the Deaf Community. The language used by the Deaf Community is American Sign Language (ASL). This language has its own syntax, just as Spanish or French or any other language. In the past, persons who were deaf were deprived of equal opportunities for advancement and were considered deficient because of their deafness. This medical–pathological view of deafness is being replaced by a social–cultural view.

With the passage of IDEA and ADA, the mainstream hearing community recognizes that deafness is not a deficit. The Deaf Community considers deafness a difference and a heritage that is shared by persons who are deaf. From this culture has arisen philosophies of deaf pride and deaf power, and indeed persons who are deaf recognize the uniqueness, history, and importance of their cultural group. Medical research has examined the causes of deafness for many years. With the advance of genetic research, a recessive gene for deafness, connexion-26 has been identified. This gene has been found to be responsible for a significant percentage of deafness in children.

In the past, most children who were deaf were educated in residential schools that either embraced an aural–oral approach that utilized audition, oral language, and speech reading in their teaching or a total communication approach that utilized audition, oral language, speech reading, and sign language in its teaching approach.

In either context, the person who is deaf recognizes his inclusion in a society of persons with hearing loss that is different from the hearing society.

With the advance of technology, and specifically the cochlear implant, there is a controversy regarding the use of the implant and its impact on the Deaf Community. When children are implanted early, before the age of 2 years, they are often educated in an aural–oral program. Success in the development of speech and language has been impressive with the use of implants. Consequently, fewer children are being educated utilizing a total communication approach and thus are less likely to consider themselves members of the Deaf Community.

Researchers have suggested that children who are deaf and born to deaf parents who use ASL at home should be taught spoken and written English in a different manner from children who are deaf and born to parents with normal hearing (Cummins, 1981). The premise is that if children are exposed to spoken English initially in the educational setting, then English is their second language, and therefore the educational approach must be bilingual. In addition, since children who are deaf have also been exposed to Deaf Culture, with its traditions and customs, they are bicultural and this strengthens the position for teaching them with an ASL/ESL (English as a second language) approach. Cummins (1981) hypothesizes that using a bilingual approach would be more successful because the child already is proficient in ASL. If a child who is deaf is proficient with ASL, then she or he will more easily acquire English literacy skills, given the competency in the primary language. However, a bilingual approach to educating children who are deaf has not been implemented to any great extent.

There have been attempts to document and justify the use of a bilingual approach in education. An experimental curriculum described by Strong (1988) uses a storytelling format to introduce ASL into the classroom setting. English is then taught by ASL. This program is particularly interesting because it emphasizes metalinguistic awareness. Prinz and Strong (1998) note that there is a positive connection between ASL and reading and writing in English, as well as the need for more research and curriculum development in this area. The national Council on Education of the Deaf (CED) and the National Association of the Deaf (NAD) support the idea of a bilingual educational approach when educating students with a hearing loss.

Asian-Pacific American Children

Asian-Pacific Americans are a diverse group of people who have various ethnic backgrounds that include Chinese, Japanese, Indochinese, Pacific Islanders, Koreans, and Filipinos. Each cultural groups has its own set of values, norms, beliefs, attitudes, and behavioral styles. Cheng (1993, 1991) describes these groups as follows:

- In China over 80 languages and several hundred dialects are in use. These languages are noninflectional. In Mandarin Chinese, only two final consonants, /n/ and /n/, are present, and in Cantonese only seven. Consequently, Chinese speakers frequently omit final consonants when speaking English. The pragmatic rules of the Chinese language are also different from those of English, and it is not uncommon for a woman to break eye contact with a speaker and gaze down.

- The Japanese language is polysyllabic and has an elaborate inflectional system. There are 5 vowels and 18 consonants, and only the /*n*/ phoneme is used in the final position of words.
- The Korean language utilizes no word stress, and there are no labiodental, interdental, or palatal fricatives in the language. It contains 19 consonants. Pragmatically, silence is an important part of communication.
- Vietnamese is a six-tone language that is generally monosyllabic and has four consonants. The six tones are level, breathing rising, breathing falling, falling rising, creaky rising, and low falling.
- Laotian is a tonal language with a few final consonants. It contains 23 consonants.

For a more elaborate explanation of Asian languages, see Goldstein, 2000.

The various other languages of Asian-American people, such as Khmer, Hmong, and Filipino, utilize individual phonetic, semantic, syntactic, and pragmatic rules that differ from those of English. Because of these differences, Cheng (1993) suggests a communication assessment that considers the child in his or her unique naturalistic environment. This ethnographic assessment includes naturalistic contexts and behavioral descriptions. The clinician must address the following:

1. What are the child's purposes for communicating?
2. When does the child's communication break down?
3. How does the child communicate with family members?
4. Is the child successful in communicating his or her wants and needs?
5. Should other important environmental factors be considered?

Ethnographic Approach

In general, an ethnographic approach, which includes direct observation of the child interacting with caregivers in a familiar environment, is imperative in providing speech and language services to culturally diverse groups. An ethnographic approach considers factors such as how the child speaks with parents, siblings, other children, and adults. It also considers how the child listens and responds to others in the environment. Ethnographic information is gathered through observation, questionnaire, and ongoing discussions with family members.

Determining whether a communication disorder exists in a culturally different child requires a clear determination of whether the apparent communication difficulty is a product of language difference or language disorder. The SLP utilizes modified test procedures, adapts existing tests, and gathers a language sample that reflects the child's naturalistic communication pattern (Kayser, 1993). Some of these test modifications may include omitting items that you expect the child to miss because of language or culture, continuing testing beyond the ceiling, and rewording instructions. Taylor (1986) explains these modifications in detail. In some instances, especially when standardized tests are administered, an interpreter must be used; in these instances, Bernstein (1989) cautions that the interpreter must be involved with the assessment team throughout the assessment process and should have the freedom to ask questions.

When assessing the preschool child, the task is to assess communicative competence, which is determined by the norms of the child's community of speakers. The communicative norms of a mainstream society are not necessarily those of the culturally and linguistically different child being evaluated. A good rule of thumb is to gather a detailed family case history and identify the parents' concerns regarding the child's communication. Take into consideration how cultural differences affect testing, and expand your knowledge of the cultural group you are testing. Hanson, Lynch, and Wayman (1990) offer the following suggestions for professionals when gathering ethnographic information:

- When working with a child from a different culture, describe the ethnic group in terms of the family's country of origin, language, and number of people in the ethnic community.
- Be aware of the social organization of the ethnic community and resources in that community.
- Be aware of the belief system in the community, such as ceremonies, values, and symbols.
- Be aware of the attitudes in the ethnic community toward seeking help.

Dynamic Assessment

Peña, Iglesias, and Lidz (2001) utilize the dynamic assessment model as a nonbiased way to differentiate children from culturally diverse backgrounds into two groups: those at risk for a speech-language disorder and those who are not. It is theorized that, if a child from a diverse linguistic background is tested on a standardized measure such as the EOWPVT, given instruction in mediated learning, and then retested again,

It is important to determine whether a child evidences a language difference or a language disorder.

Krista Greco / Merrill

the typically developing child will evidence changes in his or her past test results, whereas the low-language-ability child will not. The results of their study indicate that, indeed, significant performance differences exist between two types of children, low-language-ability and typically developing children, when retests are given. Even though all the children start out with low test performances initially, only the typically developing child makes significant changes in retest performance after the mediated learning has occurred. Thus, dynamic assessment is a promising tool for allowing for the nonbiased assessment of culturally and linguistically diverse children.

Guiterrez-Clellen (2000) also uses a dynamic assessment model to assess children's language learning potential in children from culturally different backgrounds. She specifies the steps to be taken when trying to determine a child's potential for learning and thus to differentiate normal language differences from true language disorders.

Step 1 is to identify the process underlying successful task completion in an assessment. Does the child need to look at pictures on a given page to elaborate and give details in answering? Test the child and note incorrect answers and problem areas; then determine possible reasons for the errors. Are errors due to attention, task familiarity, or adult–child interaction?

In Step 2 the clinician designs a mediated learning experience. She utilizes activities that will facilitate the use of processes identified in pretesting, for example, teaching sequencing or interacting more regularly with the child. The SLP must explicitly show the child what the learning activity is about and why it is being taught. For instance, "I want you to learn to listen to a story and then line up the story pictures in the order that things happen in the story." Positive feedback needs to be given to the child during this mediated learning experience.

In Step 3, the SLP assesses the child's responsiveness to the mediated experiences. Does the child improve in his ability to interact with the examiner? Is he or she able to consistently scan four pictures on a page? Can he sequence pictures depicting a familiar activity like building a snowman?

Once the three steps are completed, reassess the child to see if language gains are seen on the assessment. This type of approach reduces the cultural bias of traditional assessment approaches and also the chance of misdiagnosing children from diverse backgrounds.

Ecological Validity

Ecological validity is another important issue when working with linguistically and culturally different children and families. We must ensure that our assessment instruments have ecological validity, are sensitive to cultural differences, and do not penalize a child for these differences. Culture and language are factors in national identity. If we want to understand people, we must understand their culture; if we want to assess children, we must understand their culture.

Bronfenbrenner (1992) expands and conceptualizes an ecological view to consider the child as a member of a family unit, which in turn is a member of a larger community (see Figure 7.1). The concentric circles highlight an ecological perspective that significantly changes the communicative and interactional relationship between professionals and families (Bronfenbrenner, 1992).

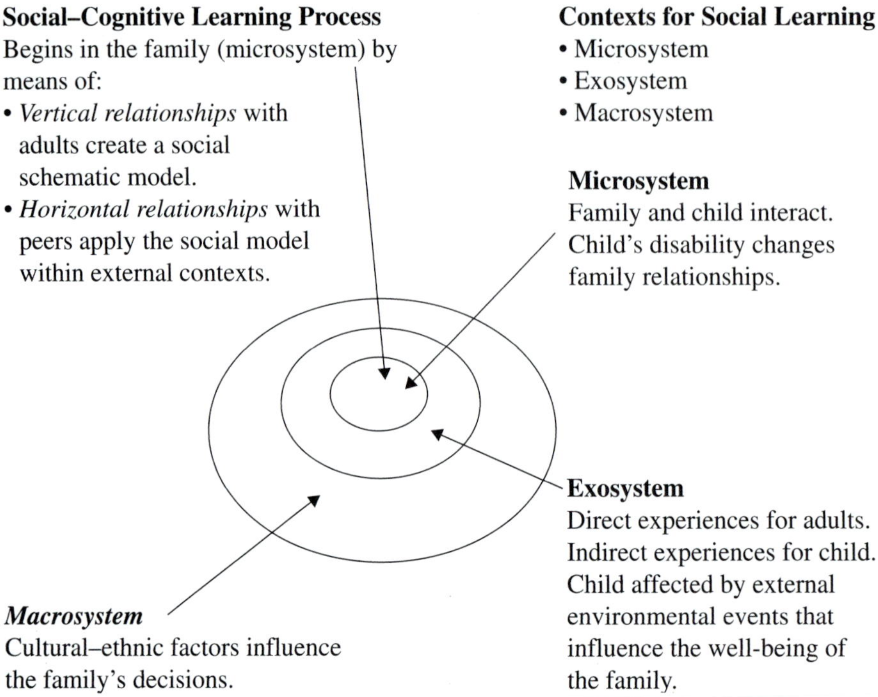

Social–Cognitive Learning Process

Begins in the family (microsystem) by means of:

- *Vertical relationships* with adults create a social schematic model.
- *Horizontal relationships* with peers apply the social model within external contexts.

Contexts for Social Learning

- Microsystem
- Exosystem
- Macrosystem

Microsystem

Family and child interact. Child's disability changes family relationships.

Exosystem

Direct experiences for adults. Indirect experiences for child. Child affected by external environmental events that influence the well-being of the family.

Macrosystem

Cultural–ethnic factors influence the family's decisions.

FIGURE 7.1

Ecological Systems Approach to Child Development

Source: Tiegerman-Farber, Ellenmorris; Radziewicz, Christine, *Collaborative Decision Making: The Pathway to Inclusion,* © 1998, p. 164. Adapted by permission of Pearson Education, Inc., Upper Saddle River, NJ.

Considering the distinct issues presented by linguistically and culturally diverse families, many teachers and therapists need to know how to apply an ecocultural approach to assessment and intervention (Weinrach & Thomas, 1998). Utilizing a family systems approach supplements the traditional approach of child-centered evaluation (Moes & Frea, 2002). The multidisciplinary team acknowledges the centrality of the family and conducts an assessment that is culturally sensitive.

A useful assessment technique that facilitates ecological validity for children who are culturally and linguistically different is naturalistic observation. This evaluation approach involves the recording of ongoing behavior without attempting to influence it (McBurney, 1991). Careful record keeping is of paramount importance. The evaluator keeps a record of the behavior of interest and under what circumstances it occurs. By using video cameras and tape recorders with slow-motion options and stop-action freeze, the evaluator is able to recognize critical behavior patterns.

The evaluation should focus on specific types of social, communicative, and cognitive behaviors. Note the language used by the caregiver and the language with which the child responds (Linares, 1983). At times the evaluator may wish to join the caregiver and child and conduct a participant–observer observation. When this occurs, it is important to continue to videotape the interactions and determine the changes that occur. Later analysis of the videotapes will give the evaluator insights into the cultural–social rules of the family.

When diverse SLPs are not available to evaluate a culturally and linguistically different child, it is necessary to utilize paraprofessionals in the identification and intervention process. In 1996, ASHA published *Guidelines for the Training, Credentialing, Use and Supervision of Speech Language Pathology Assistants*. It notes that paraprofessionals can assist and enhance the effectiveness of the SLP working with the culturally and linguistically different child. They can assist in recording, translating, and analyzing spontaneous speech samples. They can sensitize the SLP to cultural customs and social rules and help the SLP to understand the disorders of non-English- or limited-English-speaking children. Paraprofessionals can be recruited from the child's community and may include teaching aides, health-care workers, or other appropriate volunteers. They need to be specifically trained by the SLP to perform their assigned duties (Anderson, 1994). Of course, only the SLP can interpret the results of the speech-language findings.

From Assessment to Programming

The Role of the Speech-Language Pathologist

With increased emphasis on more naturalistic and inclusive programming, the SLP is being required to utilize interactive models to meet the needs of culturally and linguistically diverse children and families (Voltz, 1994, 1995; Welch, 1996). The SLP may provide direct services to children, function as a consultant to the classroom teacher, function as a co-teacher, provide direct therapeutic instruction to the parent within the home, and still maintain a clinical caseload of children.

In the preschool special-education system, the role of the SLP will be different because the service-delivery models (e.g., medical vs. educational) define different responsibilities. Collaborative teaming requires that SLPs, early childhood teachers, and parents, all of whom have different background experiences and training, work together to identify child-based learning problems to develop appropriate intervention strategies (Cohen, Thomas, Sattler, & Morsink, 1997; Tiegerman-Farber, 2002b). To facilitate successful collaboration, the SLP performs different professional responsibilities, resulting in different relationships with families:

- *The speech-language pathologist may be asked to provide parent training and education classes about development and disabilities.*
- *The speech-language pathologist may be required to work directly with a parent to facilitate parent–child interactions.*
- *The speech-language pathologist may counsel fathers, siblings, and extended family members at home or in groups about language and communication techniques to generalize appropriate behaviors to other settings and agents of change.*
- *The speech-language pathologist may be asked to develop a staff development program or seminar to educate and train other professionals on language-acquisition milestones and therapy techniques.*

CW 7.1

Use the Companion Website to help you answer the following questions:

1. How does the American Speech-Language-Hearing Association (ASHA) describe the collaborative and consultation models, given different developmental disabilities? Are there differences in responsibilities? Should there be?

2. ASHA indicates that the SLP may counsel parents about language-training techniques. The issue of counseling is also suggested in the statement that the SLP "can promote healthy lifestyle practices for the prevention of communication disorders. . . ." Are SLPs engaging in counseling activities similar to psychologists or mental health practitioners? Should the academic curriculum reflect the new responsibilities described by ASHA?

3. Do a literature search and find research articles on professional preparation. Is counseling described as a professional practice that needs to be part of the academic curriculum and requires clinical training experiences?

- *The speech language pathologist will work with families in many more settings and travel much greater distances: home, hospital, early child center, clinic, and anywhere parents can be reached.*
- *The speech language pathologist may assist parents to understand developmentally appropriate behaviors during evaluations and IEP team meetings.*
- *The speech language pathologist can train, supervise, and manage speech language pathology assistants and other support personnel.*
- *The speech language pathologist can advocate at the local, state, and national levels for access to and funding for services to address communication or other disorders.*
- *The speech language pathologist can foster public awareness of speech language disorders and their treatment.*
- *The speech language pathologist can promote healthy lifestyle practices for the prevention of communication disorders and their treatment.*
- *The speech language pathologist recognizes the special needs of culturally diverse populations by providing services that are free of potential biases, including selection and/or adaptation of materials to ensure ethnic and linguistic sensitivity.* (ASHA, 2001, Scope of Practice in Speech Language Pathology)

SUMMARY

Today, most early childhood programs within metropolitan environments have a culturally diverse population of children (Smrekar & Cohen-Vogel, 2001), and their differences already exist in many preschool classrooms because the major problem in community-based programs involves the inclusion of children with disabilities who are also linguistically and culturally diverse. Diversity is a pre-existing condition within early childhood classrooms.

Diversity can create stress in early childhood programs struggling to deal with the demands of parents and teachers who are clamoring for excellence, safety, and outcome-based instruction. Parents of typical children want quality programs just as much as parents of children with disabilities do. Parents are parents, and they often do not realize that their issues are similar. The program changes related to inclusion may infuse the early childhood system with new ideas, energy, and evaluative procedures. It is not going to be possible to include children with disabilities in early childhood classrooms without addressing resources, equipment, curriculum, instructional techniques, competency skills for teachers, attitudes, and individualized programming for all children (Kavale, 2002).

CHAPTER

8

Collaborative Language Assessment and Decision Making in Preschool

Chapter Objectives

After studying this chapter, you should be able to answer the following questions:

1. What is the interactive process that occurs in a match–mismatch model?

2. What is a classroom co-teaching model?

3. What are some drawbacks associated with a traditional model of providing services to children?

This chapter discusses professional collaboration among professionals working in preschool. Recall that the purpose of a collaborative model is to provide the interactive team with a ***representational structure*** that can be used to highlight why specific interactions do or do not operate effectively. Speech-language pathologists have been asked to collaborate (co-teach) and consult with both special-education and early childhood teachers (Harn, Bradshaw, & Ogletree, 1999). The result is the development of more diverse and cost-effective educational models.

Match–Mismatch

The description of a model of collaboration is helpful in understanding how the speech-language pathologist (SLP), early childhood teacher, and parent can work cooperatively to achieve the mission of child-centered educational programming. As agents of change, the collaborators must all share a common focus and commitment to change traditional roles and responsibilities (see Figure 8.1).

The *goodness-of-fit concept* can be used as a starting point because a collaborative team needs to make decisions about assessment, learning goals, instructional techniques, and program requirements for children, as well as resources for families (Chess, 1986). Tiegerman-Farber (2002b) and Tiegerman-Farber and Radziewicz (1998) describe collaboration as an interactional process that helps each member of the team understand the characteristics and behaviors of shared decision making. Although the operating principles for group decision making (i.e., co-equality, reciprocity, and consensus) may be the same across schools, professional barriers and educational constraints create significant problems to successful collaboration.

Professional Collaboration

Within the collaborative process, the role of each professional will be different from that in a consultation model. In addition, the legal and procedural requirements in preschool special education are different from those in early intervention. Although the process of collaboration *should* remain the same from early intervention to preschool special education to school-age special education, the family-centered

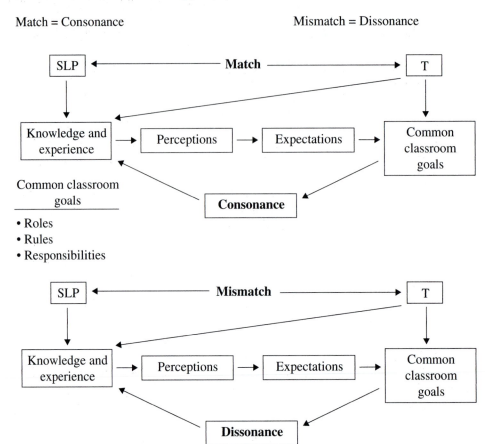

Match = Consonance

Mismatch = Dissonance

Note:

SLP, speech-language pathologist; T, teacher (SET or ECT)

FIGURE 8.1

Model of Collaboration

Source: Tiegerman-Farber, Ellenmorris; Radziewicz, Christine, *Collaborative Decision Making: The Pathway to Inclusion*, © 1998, p. 77. Adapted by permission of Pearson Education, Inc., Upper Saddle River, NJ.

approach in early intervention facilitates the collaborative process. The child-centered approach, which is the framework for decision making in preschool special education, encourages professional collaboration during the IEP process and even in the classroom, but there are significant barriers for parents (Tiegerman-Farber, 2002b).

Teaming is more difficult to accomplish in school settings since successful professional collaboration requires significant changes to the existing traditional preschool or child-care program (ASHA, 1996). Teams that attempt to work toward the development of a collaborative model indicate that there is a great deal of benefit to students, families, and professionals. It is important to keep this issue in mind as collaboration in preschool special education is compared to collaboration in early intervention; it is not the same. There are difficult communication problems among professionals and between professionals and families. How each professional functions in and outside the classroom will be changed by new inclusion requirements. The early childhood teacher, as a collaborator, needs to know about the social and behavioral needs of a child with a language disorder. The SLP needs to know about management strategies, that is, about the kinds of procedures and techniques that can be used to integrate the child with a language disorder into ongoing classroom and community-based settings.

The Co-Teaching Classroom Model

Co-teaching, or team teaching, is a collaborative relationship; it can be used in a self-contained classroom in which the special-education teacher and SLP work together and/or in an inclusion classroom in which the early childhood teacher and the special-education teacher or SLP share decision making. Early childhood programs and schools utilize different co-teaching models depending on fiscal and attitudinal factors.

Co-teaching requires a change in the interactional relationship between the SLP and the special-education or early childhood teacher. The fact that there are two professionals within a classroom presents instructional and interpersonal challenges for professionals who have been trained in separate discipline areas (Bruskewitz, 1998). The early childhood teacher, special-education teacher, and SLP have highly specialized foundations for knowledge; they approach the teaching situation from different perspectives because their academic training and work experiences have been different. Co-teachers need to acknowledge their academic and professional differences as they work side by side in the early childhood and/or preschool special-education classroom.

Krista Greco/Merrill

Team teaching is a collaborative relationship that requires shared decision making.

When there is a *mismatch* between professionals, collaborative decisions cannot be generated (Tiegerman-Farber & Radziewicz, 1998). Co-teachers need to analyze their interactional dialogue by evaluating perceptions and expectations that may interfere with shared decision making. If the two professionals do not clearly communicate, listen to each other, and/or maintain good rapport, it will be difficult to achieve shared perceptions and/or expectations concerning children in the classroom (see Figure 8.2 and 8.3).

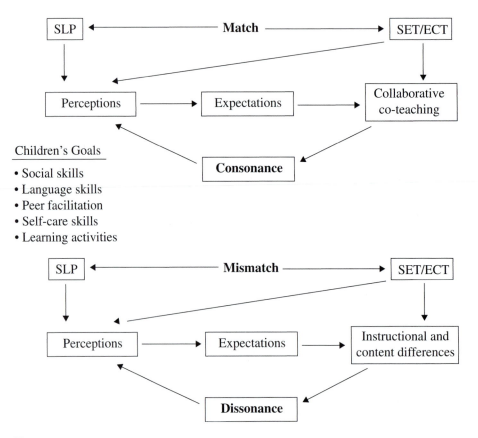

Note:

SLP, speech-language pathologist; SET, special-education teacher; ECT, early childhood teacher.

FIGURE 8.2

Co-Teaching Classroom Model I

Source: Tiegerman-Farber, Ellenmorris; Radziewicz, Christine, *Collaborative Decision Making: The Pathway to Inclusion,* © 1998, p. 80. Adapted by permission of Pearson Education, Inc., Upper Saddle River, NJ.

Match = Consonance   Mismatch = Dissonance

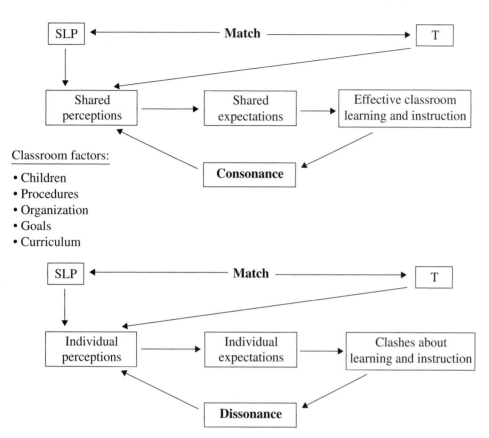

Classroom factors:
• Children
• Procedures
• Organization
• Goals
• Curriculum

Note:
SLP, speech-language pathologist; T, teacher (SET or ECT)

FIGURE 8.3
Co-Teaching Classroom Model II
Source: Tiegerman-Farber, Ellenmorris; Radziewicz, Christine, *Collaborative Decision Making: The Pathway to Inclusion*, © 1998, p. 72. Adapted by permission of Pearson Education, Inc., Upper Saddle River, NJ.

When professional differences cannot be resolved, the result is independent decision making rather than shared problem solving. When the collaborative process is operating correctly, expectations are based on clear communication, active listening and responding, effective brainstorming, and creative integration of ideas. Consequently, good decision making results in consonance between professionals (Gitlin, 1999).

Co-teaching or team teaching may also provide a mechanism for beginning the inclusion process in early childhood. Thus the roles of the SLP and the special-education teacher need to change from that of providing direct services to children with disabilities in a separate classroom to providing services to all children in the same classroom (Dinnebeil, Hale, & Rule, 1996). Team teaching allows the SLP or special-education teacher to work within the classroom as equal partners with the early childhood teacher. Classroom goals are developed by working to achieve a common educational concept—individual achievement for each child (Tiegerman-Farber, 2002b). Team teaching provides a means for each specialist to support and respect the unique contributions of other teaching professionals.

The special-education teacher can assist the early childhood teacher and the SLP to develop an understanding of the instructional and academic needs of children within the classroom. The special-education teacher has a set of specialty skills that includes management techniques, task-analysis skills, and instructional procedures that can facilitate programming for children within a group context. The special-education teacher can also assist in integrating interaction between the SLP and all the children, as well as between peer groups. The special-education teacher has an understanding of group learning techniques and a broad understanding of the learning needs of children with disabilities.

The early childhood teacher can contribute to the classroom by providing early childhood instructional activities. The early childhood teacher is uniquely skilled in identifying prereadiness developmentally appropriate activities that facilitate socialization opportunities for typical children.

Each teacher has something to share with colleagues. Each teacher has something to contribute to the development of a transdisciplinary curriculum and the integration of children within a classroom (O'Shea, Williams, & Sattler, 1999). Professional differences can create instructional strengths in an inclusion classroom.

Reciprocity

Collaborative instruction requires the SLP and special-education teacher or early childhood teacher to recognize their unique contributions to the classroom and their interdependence with the other professionals. To achieve effective collaboration, teams must play close attention to interactional variables, communication skills, problem-solving skills, and conflict-resolution strategies (Erchial, Covington, Hughes, & Meyers, 1995).

The formation and development of a collaborative team involves a learning process that includes a set of competencies. Members of the team should consider the following communicative competency skills (Crais, 1993):

- Willingness to listen to others
- Being supportive of someone else's ideas
- Being receptive to input
- Managing differences of opinion and conflict
- Accepting and integrating the suggestions of others
- Expressing opinions and ideas without criticism and/or judgment
- Acknowledging and using the ideas of others in an integrative manner
- Being flexible

In Figure 8.4 you can see that when the SLP and special-education teacher or early childhood teacher do not match in terms of providing personal support and

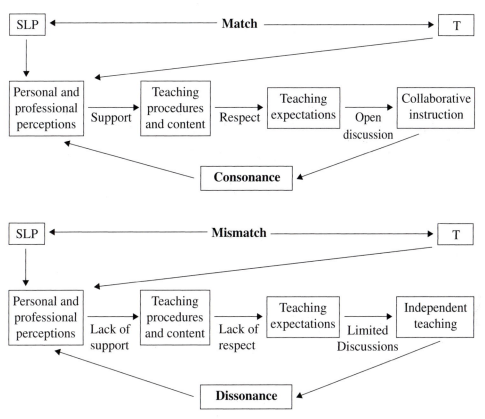

Match = Consonance   Mismatch = Dissonance

Note:
SLP, speech-language pathologist; T, teacher (SET or ECT)

FIGURE 8.4
The Collaborative Classroom: Consonance Versus Dissonance
Source: Tiegerman-Farber, Ellenmorris; Radziewicz, Christine, Collaborative Decision Making: The Pathway to Inclusion, © 1998, p. 78. Adapted by permission of Pearson Education, Inc., Upper Saddle River, NJ.

respect, they will work independently, creating an atmosphere of dissonance that results in unsuccessful collaboration. Reciprocal exchange between co-teachers suggests that the collaborative classroom is a bridge that spans across a professional divide; each professional from her side builds toward and reaches a meeting place in the middle.

Common Goals

Because special-education and early childhood teachers may be working with the SLP in classrooms, it may be of critical benefit to conceptualize the classroom as a working model (Denton & Foley, 1994). This conceptual approach allows co-teachers to design a new integrated classroom from the beginning. Co-teachers can approach the process pragmatically, given specific child dynamics and resource limitations. They can also approach the process creatively, given common goals and innovative curricula. The goal-setting task requires a considerable amount of time. When co-teachers are collaborating about goals, they should consider the following items:

- What are the desired outcomes of classroom instruction?
- How will these outcomes be measured?
- Are the parents in agreement with these outcomes?

The purpose of inclusion within an early childhood program is to diminish the isolation of children with disabilities from their typical peers and to provide socialization experiences for both groups of children. Figure 8.5 describes some of the theoretical, procedural, and programmatic complexities that must be addressed to successfully utilize a collaborative model.

The inclusion classroom requires that teachers, parents and SLPs think about developmental and educational learning in a different way. They must also be willing to change their roles and responsibilities to create a diverse instructional environment to meet the needs of all children (Friend & Cook, 1996). With this in mind, two common goals should appear on children's IEP:

Successful collaboration in the classroom requires that the speech-language pathologist, the special-education teacher, and early childhood teachers

- Identify effective communication strategies
- Create a partnership based on shared decision making
- Decide collaboratively about their new teaching responsibilities
- Collaboratively develop a profile of each child, as well as of the class as an interactive group
- Use their professional differences to identify learning techniques and strategies for each child and the children as a group
- Acknowledge that the classroom is diverse and heterogeneous rather than homogenous, (i.e., the classroom consists of diverse child learners at different levels of functioning)
- Learn to utilize a peer facilitation model in class that includes the following changes:

> How children interact with one another
> How children learn in the classroom
> How children contribute to their own learning and the learning of peers
> How children are taught to accept diversity and respect differences
> How children with disabilities are taught social skills so that they can function in small- and large-group learning contexts

---

FIGURE 8.5
Successful Use of the Collaborative Model

1. To provide services within the least restrictive environment
2. To provide maximum socialization experiences with nondisabled peers

In addition to these goals, the special-education or early childhood teacher and SLP must agree about the cognitive, linguistic, communicative, and social levels of functioning for all the children in the classroom. Once the professionals match their perceptions regarding these variables, they can then set common classroom goals (Jayanthi & Friend,1992; Tiegerman-Farber, 1995). Figure 8.6 describes how the perceptions and related beliefs of each professional can affect

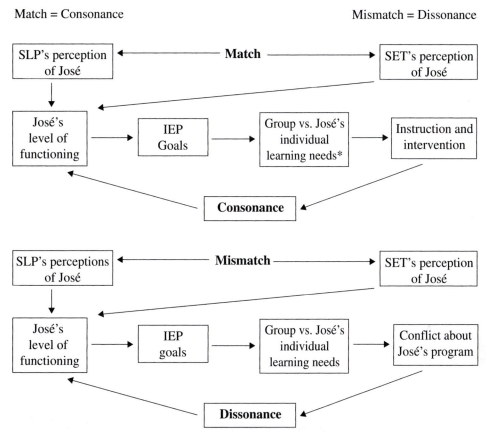

Note:
Classroom is an integrated setting.
* Group consists of preschool children with and without disabilities.
Typical children have more advanced social, communication, and language skills than the preschool children with autism.

FIGURE 8.6
Preschool Child with Autism in an Early Childhood Setting
Source: Tiegerman-Farber, Ellenmorris; Radziewicz, Christine, *Collaborative Decision Making: The Pathway to Inclusion,* © 1998, p. 82. Adapted by permission of Pearson Education, Inc., Upper Saddle River, NJ.

the development of a specific child in the classroom for example, José Martinez, a child with autism.

Each professional's belief system generates specific expectations in terms of (1) José's behavior, (2) his ability to learn, and (3) the instructional techniques that should be used to facilitate his learning. Each professional utilizes an individualized representational system that frames her decisions based on knowledge and past experience, which functions as an information-processing loop for her decision making. When perceptions and expectations match, there is a synchrony or confluence that flows from perceptions to expectations to environmental occurrences. Co-teachers must learn to translate their differences in educational training into learning themes that will establish a common classroom focus and facilitate the development of interdependent goals for children with and without disabilities in the classroom (Tiegerman-Farber, 2002). The child with a disability must receive programming, given his specific learning strengths, along with the other children. Professionals who are beginning the process of working together in an inclusion classroom need to spend time organizing the classroom and re-creating their roles and responsibilities; this requires a process of self-analysis, self-investigation, and self-inquiry.

The Consultation Model

Consultation within the preschool special-education or early childhood classroom provides a different interactive relationship between the SLP and the special-education teacher or early childhood teacher. The SLP provides related services either by means of a push-in model or of individual language therapy services outside the classroom. With teacher consultation, the SLP provides instructional advice about procedures and techniques that will facilitate the generalization of language goals for a specific child, from the individual therapeutic setting to the more natural setting of the early childhood classroom with peers (Bruskewitz, 1998).

In both collaboration and consultation, the SLP may have a caseload of children who require speech-language therapy services. One difference between the models is that, in collaboration, the decisions concerning children are shared. In the consultation model, the SLP assumes an advisory role with the early childhood and/or special-education teacher, while the teacher remains the primary decision maker about classroom functioning. Co-teaching and teacher consultation require mutual support and respect and an understanding that the professionals will work as interdependent partners (Winton, 1998).

Both co-teaching and consultation can also take place between an SLP and an occupational therapist or physical therapist concerning individual or group therapy services. In this case, the SLP and specialist work together to coordinate their therapy goals and strategies. Thus, collaboration and consultation teaming may take place between the SLP and the early childhood teacher, or the special-education teacher, or other specialists, or the parent.

Issues Related to Educational Models

Figure 8.7 presents three educational models: the traditional model, co-teaching/ collaboration model, and consultation model. In the traditional model, we find the following:

1. Children with severe language and communication disorders may require multiple services. The therapeutic process that provides services outside the classroom results in the child missing classroom instruction.
2. Collaboration and/or consultation between professionals requires creative scheduling, because they are not built into anyone's schedule. If consultation and/or collaboration are not specifically noted on a child's IEP, they will not be provided formally as a service and may result in informal and inconsistent meetings.
3. The therapeutic programs for related services remain outside the classroom. Generalization of learning into the classroom is always a problem for the child and the teacher.
4. Collaboration and/or consultation may not be considered important educational services, so instructional accommodations may not be requested or facilitated. Programs, schools, and agencies need to recognize indirect services, such as collaboration and consultation, that require changes in professional responsibilities. Meetings between special-education teachers and the SLPs can only be formalized when there is administrative support in schools.
5. Cost effectiveness becomes an issue for school administrators when it is expected that SLPs and other professionals will be paid to provide direct therapeutic hands-on services to children. It is not traditional that SLPs and other professionals have designated periods in their schedules to "talk to teachers."

In the co-teaching collaborative model, the following may occur:

1. Teachers and SLPs have not been academically or educationally trained to work together in a classroom.
2. The shift from individual language therapy to classroom-based instruction is a challenge, because the instructional techniques used by an SLP with an individual child need to be different in a classroom. The focus shifts to group language therapy in a special-education classroom because peers may be included. Children have different language needs in a classroom, and in an early childhood classroom most of the children are typical learners.
3. The classroom environment presents distractions and noise. Some children with language disorders may have difficulty learning in this kind of environment. In addition, the inclusion of other professionals into the classroom who may only spend part of the day in the classroom can be disruptive to the regular education teacher.

In the consultation model, the SLP faces the following:

1. This advisory model shifts the professional relationship between the classroom teacher and SLP and other professionals. Teachers note that

A. Traditional Model

Related services <u>outside</u> (pull-out) classroom:

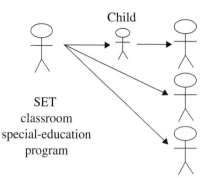

Child

SLP 3 × per week, 30 minutes

OT 2 × per week, 30 minutes

PT 2 × per week, 30 minutes

SET
classroom
special-education
program

B. Co-Teaching Collaboration Model

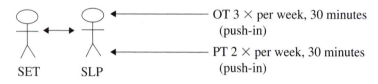

OT 3 × per week, 30 minutes (push-in)

PT 2 × per week, 30 minutes (push-in)

SET   SLP

C. Consultation Model

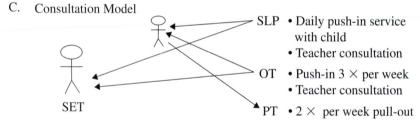

SET

SLP • Daily push-in service with child
• Teacher consultation

OT • Push-in 3 × per week
• Teacher consultation

PT • 2 × per week pull-out

Note:

SLP, speech-language pathologist; OT, occupational therapist; PT, physical therapist; SET, special education teacher.

FIGURE 8.7

Three Educational Models

psychologists who provide educational support on behavioral and management problems in the classroom are not always present when a specific child is tantruming. Teachers may feel at a disadvantage when the psychologist gives recommendations, but is not generally available during a crisis for direct intervention. The SLP faces similar interpersonal and professional complaints.

2. There may be several consultants to the classroom for a specific child, so professional teaming outside the classroom becomes critical.

3. The SLP needs to be trained to function as a teacher–classroom consultant.

CW 8.1

Use the Companion Website to help you answer these questions:

1. There are many professional associations for early childhood teachers and special-education teachers. What positions have they taken on inclusion, collaboration, consultation, and co-teaching?

2. Contact some local early childhood programs in your community and ask them to identify five barriers to collaboration.

3. How would you feel about completing your education and being in a classroom with a special-education teacher who has been teaching for 10 years?

4. How does the American Speech-Language and Hearing Association (ASHA) describe the collaborative and consultation models, given different developmental disabilities? Are there differences in responsibilities? Should there be?

Family Profiles

The Martinez Family

When José Martinez is 34 months old, he begins the transition process from early intervention to preschool special education. José is given a battery of tests, including the Childhood Autism Rating (CARS), Peabody Picture Vocabulary Test III (PPVT-III), which is administered in Spanish and English, and the Preschool Language Scale 3—Spanish Edition. Scores from these assessments show that José has a language delay in both English and Spanish, and language dominance is not present in either language. The evaluator does not formally assess José's phonology nor does she perform a formal language sample. Oral-motor skills appear adequate. The evaluator notes that eye contact is inconsistent and that José does not easily engage in play with her. Other evaluations are performed, specifically psychological, occupational therapy, physical therapy, and special-education evaluations. José is found to have significant delays in all areas. The occupational and physical therapy evaluations are performed by monolingual evaluators. The psychological and special-education evaluators are bilingual. The Committee on Preschool Special Education recommends that José be placed in an English-speaking child-care center with related services.

Because Mrs. Martinez's English has improved over the last year, no interpreter is present at the meeting nor are the evaluations translated into Spanish for her. The committee meeting lasts about 40 minutes, and Mrs. Martinez is told that José's IEP will be sent to her in the mail. At the meeting she is given copies of each evaluator's formal reports. Mrs. Martinez agrees to the recommendations and signs her approval for the formal IEP document. The educational program developed for José consists of the following services at the child-care program:

1. Consultation: The SLP will advise the special-education teacher and the early childhood teacher in the classroom about stimulating and facilitating language.

2. Direct services: Speech and language therapy (4× per week, individual; and 1×, group), occupational therapy (2× per week, individual), and music therapy (2× per week, group).

3. Consultation: The special-education teacher will work with the early childhood teacher to develop appropriate activities and management strategies for José in the classroom.

4. The school district will pay for the child-care program because integrated programming is not available in the local public school and can only be provided in a community-based program.

5. The school district will provide a paraprofessional to work with José in the child-care program.

6. The school district does not provide family support services, parent counseling, nutrition services, case management, and respite services that were available in early intervention, but it will provide parent training and applied behavioral analysis (ABA) programming. The long-term goals generated by the SLP for José include the following:

   a. Use of imitative interactional skills to develop the coding of agent + action + object combinations during ongoing events

   b. Expansion of object-manipulation skills

   c. Development of interactional behaviors that signal communicative intentions

   d. Generalization of communication behaviors to typical peers and to related social contexts

In Box 8.1, Maria Martinez describes her hopes and fears for José's education.

CW 8.2

Use the Companion Website to help you answer the following questions:

1. If the psychological evaluation was not administered in Spanish, would it be valid?

2. Because the teachers and some therapists do not speak Spanish, how can the parent be integrated into José's clinical program? What impact does this have on the process of generalization?

3. Should José be taught in English, Spanish, or both? Find research articles that discuss this issue.

4. Would you administer any other formal standardized tests?

5. Would you perform any other types of assessments?

6. What specific things would you look for in a child-care center that would meet José's needs?

BOX 8.1

I am concerned about José's lack of talking, playing, and socializing with other children. More than anything else, I want José to be with normal children. At the meeting the school psychologist explained to me that the least restrictive environment for José was a setting that had normal children. This would allow José to play with other children. I want to know if the other children will play with José. The psychologist said the children would learn to accept José. She was interested in the child-care program in my neighborhood. If the Little Tots Program would accept José, I could get a job. The school district's social worker agreed to contact the Little Tots Program to find if there was an opening for José. A paraprofessional, along with speech–language therapy, occupational therapy, and a special-education consulting teacher, were recommended for José. I am very happy about José's program. I want José to be with normal children. I don't want José to learn from other children with autism.

Maria Martinez

Use the companion Website to help you answer the following questions:

1. Do you think José will learn from other children, particularly his typical peers? What and how will he learn from them?

2. Is Maria's concern that José will acquire other atypical behaviors from children with autism a valid concern?

The Whiteside Family

Kaitlyn Whiteside is evaluated by the Committee on Preschool Special Education at the age of 31 months. She has a cochlear implant and is making satisfactory progress. The committee approves updated hearing tests and asks for progress reports from the Mission School for the Deaf, which has been providing speech-language therapy, auditory training, and audiological monitoring services to Kaitlyn. In addition, other assessments are performed, such as the Receptive Expressive Emergent Language Test 2 (REEL-2), the Preschool Language Scale—3, (PLS-3), the Expressive One-Word Picture Vocabulary Test (EOWPVT), the Carolina Picture Vocabulary Test, the Ling Phonologic Level Speech Inventory for Hearing Impaired Children, Ling Phonetic Speech Level Inventory for Hearing Impaired Children, Goldman–Fristoe Test of Articulation, Scales of Early Communication Skills for Hearing Impaired Children, Grammatical Analysis of Elicited Language, and a language sample.

Kaitlyn's meeting is held in her local school district with the SLP from the Mission School for the Deaf attending. The committee reviews the IFSP document from the Mission School and discusses Kaitlyn's eligibility to receive special-education services. The committee recommends that Kaitlyn be placed in a typical preschool with support services. The committee believes that, because Kaitlyn has a cochlear implant and her cognitive abilities are within the average range, she should be with typically developing peers. The latest audiological and psychological evaluations are also reviewed, and the following placements are considered:

- Full-day, special-education program for preschool children with hearing loss (the Preschool Program at the Mission School for the Deaf). This would require extended transportation because the program is available in a private preschool across town.
- Full-day, special-education program for preschool children with disabilities in the local school district. This is a noncategorical class for children having a variety of disabilities.
- Early childhood program with related services and a teacher of the deaf who would provide 1 hour of daily instruction in the classroom.

Katherine argues that "could" benefit is different than "would" benefit and that the members of the committee could not give her any guarantees that Kaitlyn would benefit. She feels that she knows what is best for Kaitlyn. Katherine says she does not understand the committee's explanation about Kaitlyn's cognitive abilities being higher than her language skills. Katherine argues that Kaitlyn misses too much if the hearing environment is not modified specifically to maximize her residual hearing and learning needs.

Katherine wants Kaitlyn to have a teacher of the deaf, not an early childhood teacher who is not trained to work with children who have a hearing loss. Katherine is upset; the support she received through the early intervention program has placed her in the position of primary decision maker. As a member of the preschool committee, Katherine is one vote on a five-member professional committee. She feels outnumbered and overwhelmed. Katherine is told that she is coming on too strong and she has to calm down because everyone has Kaitlyn's interest at heart. Katherine does not feel that way. The committee cannot agree, so Katherine is asked to visit all the programs, and the committee meeting is rescheduled.

CW 8.3

Use the Companion Website to help you answer the following questions:

1. Which of the tests administered to Kaitlyn are specifically for children with hearing loss?

2. Is it appropriate to use tests that have not been standardized on children with hearing loss?

3. Which assessments do you think are the most useful when evaluating Kaitlyn?

4. What does the word *benefit* mean in education?

5. Research the position taken by the Deaf Community about the least restrictive environment for children with deafness.

6. Who should make the final decision about the appropriate placement for Kaitlyn, the committee or the parent? What does IDEA tell us about this?

The St. James Family

Jeffrey St. James has not received early intervention services. Although he was evaluated, he did not meet the eligibility criteria to receive services. Jeffrey attends a child-care program while Camille works. He is referred to the Committee on Preschool Special Education by his early childhood teacher. Jeffrey has severe temper tantrums at home and in child care. The psychological evaluation indicates that Jeffrey has cognitive abilities in the average range, but the speech and language assessment presents a very different profile. Several assessment instruments are administered and include the Preschool Language Scale—3 (PLS-3), the Goldman–Fristoe Test of Articulation, the Expressive One-Word Picture Vocabulary Test (EOWPVT), and the Receptive One-Word Picture Vocabulary Test (ROWPVT). The SLP who evaluates Jeffrey recommends related services based on his assessment of Jeffrey. He finds that Jeffrey has a severe phonological disorder. But Camille is not satisfied because she is concerned about Jeffrey's behavior problems in child care. She insists that the school psychologist observe Jeffrey in his class.

Jeffrey's mother explains her reasoning in Box 8.2.

BOX 8.2

I am very worried that Jeffrey's behavior has gotten worse at home and in child care. Jeffrey doesn't have any friends at home or in the child-care program. No one in my family wants to take care of Jeffrey because he screams and has tantrums. Jeffrey is difficult to manage. Dr. Brenda Gucciani, the school psychologist, agreed to visit Jeffrey's program to do something called a functional behavioral assessment. Dr. Gucciani said that this would give her the chance to talk to Jeffrey's early childhood teacher and watch him in the classroom while he plays with other children. I think the evaluation is a good idea because Jeffrey must be in a child-care program since I have to work.

Camille St. James

Use the Companion Website to help you answer the following questions:

1. What is the role of a functional behavior assessment in improving Jeffrey's socialization with peers?

2. What behavior should be targeted to improve Jeffrey's ability to make friends?

The committee must meet again after Dr. Gucciani performs a functional behavioral assessment. Dr. Gucciani indicates that Jeffrey may have emotional problems and believes that a behavior management plan should be implemented by the early childhood teacher. Members of the committee realize that it will be difficult to explain to Camille that Jeffrey might have emotional problems. The evaluations and reports from the early childhood program are going to be critical to the committee's determination of disability. Before the committee reconvenes, Dr. Gucciani meets with Camille to discuss the results of the functional behavioral assessment. Camille is informed that Jeffrey is experiencing both social and emotional problems within the early childhood program, particularly during playtime and transitions.

Jeffrey's mother explains her reaction to this news in Box 8.3.

BOX 8.3

When Dr. Gucciani said that the preschool committee was considering classifying Jeffrey as emotionally disturbed and putting him in a special program for children with emotional and behavioral disorders, I cried. I am so upset. I wanted to see this program. After I saw the program, another committee meeting was scheduled. I told them Jeffrey was difficult and had behavior problems, but he is not emotionally disturbed. I also said I didn't want Jeffrey to go through school being labeled as emotionally disturbed. I want Jeffrey to be with normal children. The children in that program have bad behavior and some of them are really strange. Jeffrey will only get worse in a class with children like that. I don't want him imitating those children. The reason Jeffrey has problems is because he didn't get the early intervention he needed.

Camille St. James

 Use the Companion Website to help you answer the following questions:

1. Is Camille's concern that Jeffrey will acquire inappropriate behaviors from other children with emotional disturbance a valid concern?
2. How do you think Jeffrey's poor communication skills affect his behaviors?

In attempting to address Camille's concerns, Dr. Gucciani suggests that Jeffrey remain in the early childhood program with related services while he is in child care. The district agrees to send a consulting teacher who is trained in behavior management to work with the early childhood teacher. This provides the early childhood teacher with instructional support so that Jeffrey remains in his present setting with typical peers. Dr. Gucciani recommends that Jeffrey receive play therapy twice a week with a school psychologist. Finally, the district recommends speech–language therapy (2× per week) as a push-in service in Jeffrey's classroom. Camille is relieved and in agreement with the committee's recommendations.

Again, in Box 8.4, Camille explains her reasoning.

BOX 8.4

All this time Jeffrey's problem was not serious enough to do something about it. Now Jeffrey is emotionally disturbed? I don't think so. His behavior hasn't changed over the past 2 years. He's difficult to manage, but because his teachers can't manage him, he's considered emotionally disturbed? There's something wrong here. He's difficult at home, but we manage him a lot better than his teachers do. I think Jeffrey doesn't understand. He's not emotionally disturbed.

Camille St. James

Use the Companion Website to help you answer the following questions:

1. If you think Jeffrey is not an emotionally disturbed child, but a speech-language-impaired child, why do you think he was never diagnosed as such in the early intervention system?

2. If you think Jeffrey is an emotionally disturbed child, why do you think he was not diagnosed as such in the early intervention system?

CW 8.4

Use the Companion Website to help you answer the following questions:

1. What dialectical differences should have been taken into consideration when assessing Jeffrey's phonological skills and his syntactic skills?

2. Should the SLP have considered a dynamic assessment for Jeffrey?

3. Can we assume that Jeffrey is a child who uses African American English?

4. Jeffrey will be receiving counseling services and will have a behavior management plan. Do you think Camille should be involved in the use of behavior management techniques? Explain.

5. Do you think the various committees could be collaborating more effectively with each family?

SUMMARY

Moving away from the traditional educational model to a co-teaching–collaborative model or consultation model requires new skill development on the part of regular-education teachers, special-education teachers, and SLPs. Collaborative co-teaching models are effective when children with special needs are educated in the mainstream. The collaboration that takes place in each classroom and each school results in an individualized product. This product is the blueprint for successfully educating our children. The collaborative approach allows individual members to generate collectively holistic decisions about children. Each professional sees the child from a different perspective and a different context. These individual pieces provide a holistic mosaic—a more complete picture of the child's learning style and abilities. Professionals cannot generate appropriate decisions from an isolated vantage point. Collaborative decision making creates a profile of the whole child that facilitates a more accurate understanding of the child's individual needs.

Language Interventions and Professional Collaboration in Preschool

Chapter Objectives

After studying this chapter, you should be able to answer the following questions:

1. What modifications can be made within an early childhood classroom to accommodate a preschool child with a language and communication disorder?

2. What are the differences between individual and group (classroom) therapy?

3. What techniques can be used to facilitate social interaction between children?

4. What are the concerns of parents and teachers about peer facilitation?

5. What kinds of problems does José experience in an inclusive early childhood setting?

6. What are the arguments for and against a full-inclusion model?

7. What is the role of parents in determining what is appropriate for a child (i.e., choice of program, type and frequency of services, methodology used)?

8. How does the SLP collaborate with an early childhood teacher (ECT) to generalize language and social goals in the classroom?

9. Why is language so important to the development of early childhood readiness skills?

10. What are some differences between the ECT and the SLP?

In this chapter, an early childhood program is described to highlight the instructional, social, environmental, and curriculum changes that need to be made to successfully include preschool children with language disorders. The educational trend in many states involves the development of inclusive models and in some communities full inclusion. To understand the complexities of inclusive programming for children with autism, José's early childhood experiences are described. Children with different developmental needs, such as Kaitlyn and Jeffrey, require different accommodations and modifications. It is not possible to describe how every therapeutic intervention needs to be adapted to meet the needs of children with language and communication disorders because children with autism, mental retardation, hearing loss, and learning disability are both distinctive and varied.

However, if children are viewed in terms of their language characteristics and/or deficits and not their classification label, therapeutic interventions become more manageable for the SLP to understand (Tiegerman-Farber & Radziewicz, 1998). Therefore, a noncategorical approach is utilized in this text to provide a framework for describing some intervention techniques that can be used. Language techniques are described in terms of pragmatics, semantics, and syntax to present an overview of intervention goals that may be developed by SLPs in inclusive settings. José is profiled because, of the three children, his needs present the greatest challenge to early childhood teachers and typical peers. Because educational programming is not mandated for children below the age of 6, integrated experiences are often provided in child-care, nursery school, and early childhood settings for children with disabilities.

Naturalistic Facilitation

Although a co-teaching model with the early childhood teacher and the SLP is an option in schools and early childhood programs, it is not used frequently. The consultation model in which the SLP works with the early childhood teacher in an advisory capacity appears to be preferred in most inclusive settings (i.e., child-care programs, nursery schools, and integrated preschool special-education programs). Recall that the preschool special-education committee that placed José in an early childhood setting sent an SLP to consult with the teacher and to provide the following services:

1. Individual therapy services in a separate setting and/or in the classroom
2. Group therapy (dyad or triad) in a separate setting and/or in the classroom during daily activities

Because José attends a local child-care center, there is much discussion about accommodations and modifications that need to be made to include him, and the teachers will need to be trained to work with him. Faculty development and staff training are difficult to accomplish for many community child-care and nursery-school programs that serve children and families from various social service agencies. Also, many early childhood programs have difficulty hiring certified teachers because salaries are often low. In addition, these programs are often not regulated by state education departments, so the curriculum used may not be comparable to preschool special-education programs. In some communities, early childhood programs do not accept children with disabilities because they require a high degree of individualized care and educational expertise.

The chapter also highlights the role of the SLP in facilitating language behaviors in early childhood settings. Initiating communication, maintaining a topic, expressing relevant ideas, describing events, and narrating a story are skills that naturally develop in typical children in nursery school. Children with language and communication disorders have production and comprehension deficits in one or more of the language-component areas: pragmatics, semantics, syntax, morphology, and phonology. The early childhood classroom can be a context in which children apply the concepts and structures they learn in individual or prescriptive therapy to a setting in which typical peers can respond and provide feedback.

In the early childhood classroom, typical peers serve as role models for developmentally appropriate social and language behaviors (Clark & Smith, 1999). The SLP is able to use peer modeling as a technique to develop communicative behaviors (McCormick & Schielfelbusch, 1990). Understanding the social rules and roles that govern the interaction between communicators is important because José needs to learn how to interact with typical peers (Tiegerman-Farber & Radziewicz, 1998). The classroom context provides a learning-to-learn process; as José learns about the communication process, the better he functions with his peers.

The SLP functions as a consultant to help the early childhood teacher (ECT) create language opportunities that are highly structured, yet natural (Prelock, Miller, & Reed, 1995). Although activities are presented to the entire group, the SLP can show the ECT how to address the individual needs of children to facilitate successful interactions between peers, which we call *bridging*. Children with and without disabilities in an early childhood program can benefit from a developmentally appropriate curriculum that is language based (Tiegerman-Farber, 1995). For typical children, the language curriculum enhances their skills and the connection to literacy; language ability is the best predictor for reading and writing readiness (ASHA, 2001). Although the ECT and the SLP have a strong working relationship, there also needs to be flexibility in scheduling and programming, interpersonal trust, administrative and institutional resources, and a willingness among stakeholders to explore alternative, nontraditional instructional models (Gable & Manning, 1999).

Individualizing the Classroom Setting

How does the SLP provide individualized facilitation for José in an inclusive setting? Traditionally, the SLP works in a separate room. So the classroom and the therapy room appear to be two *places* that serve different learning functions. A simplistic explanation describes the classroom as a social setting and a natural setting for group interaction that utilizes facilitative, indirect techniques to generalize language behaviors from the therapy room. Individual or pull-out therapy, which occurs in a separate setting, offsets the traditional classroom description with terms such as prescriptive learning and targeted goals. Individual therapy utilizes adult-directed techniques targeting specific language behaviors. With the mandated emphasis on inclusion, the SLP has transitioned into the classroom with a push-in service to support the child with a disability within a less restrictive environment.

The SLP uses the same learning techniques (expansion, elicitation, extension, imitation, and semantic regulation) in both the classroom and the therapy room. To prepare José for the social complexities of the classroom, individual therapy (adult–child) needs to be balanced with push-in therapy with a small group of children (triad). With a full-inclusion model, José would not receive individual and small-group therapy in a separate room, but rather in a separate part of the classroom, where the SLP pushes-in. José's SLP sits behind or next to José during group activities to provide direct or targeted teaching. The SLP provides the transition from therapeutic intervention to language generalization. It is difficult for the SLP to work with José in the classroom because it is a complex environment and José is easily distracted. All José's language goals cannot be developed or facilitated in one environment. In addition, because children with disabilities learn differently, there needs to be a learning continuum with instructional and contextual options.

The purpose of individual language therapy is to target and facilitate the language skills that José needs to communicate successfully and effectively with his typical peers (Tiegerman-Farber, 2002a). Based on the goals generated by the preschool special-education committee, José's SLP generates short-term goals in each language component area. José's echolalia results in a marked discrepancy between his imitated utterances (MLU 3 to 5.0) and his spontaneous productions, which tend to be shorter and contextually routinized. When people, events, or objects change, José's limited verbal and/or gestural productions require maximum levels of prompting.

José's Language Goals

Pragmatic Goals

- To establish appropriate eye-gaze behaviors
- To increase the use of pragmatic functions in José's repertoire
- To increase the frequency of José's communicative responses to peers in structured and nonstructured (play) activities
- To increase the duration of José's interactions with peers first in structured and then in nonstructured activities
- To increase object-related interactions in naturally occurring activities with peers
- To decrease the levels of prompting provided in social activities
- To demonstrate verbal and nonverbal turn-taking skills in structured activities with peers as a precursor to conversation

Semantic Goals

- To increase object-related interactions with peers while coding semantic relations: action + object, agent + action, agent + action + object
- To improve José's ability to follow verbal directions
- To develop a functional vocabulary that is contextually appropriate and related
- To increase spontaneous verbal productions by means of a fading procedure
- To develop José's ability to respond to simple "wh" questions

Syntactic Goals

- To encode linguistically appropriate semantic–syntactic relations

Implementing Structural Changes

Classroom instruction can be individualized by altering the different kinds of structural aspects:

- **Environmental structure:** the organization of the actual physical setting
- **Learning structure:** the organization of activities or communicative responses expected from the child
- **Teaching structure:** the organization of the adult's language input

Environmental Structure

In viewing the organizational structure in the classroom, it is important to determine whether toys, materials, and activities are so accessible that there is no reason for children to use language to request or comment. Rearranging the environment so that toys and materials are out of reach provides a means of facilitating communicative initiation, even for typical peers. It is also important to determine if the objects and materials in the classroom are interesting, motivating, and desirable. Materials should be functional and authentic so that children can make the connection between school, home, and their community. The organization of the classroom enhances the learning opportunities for children with and without disabilities to interact with each other socially. The classroom should offer toys and activities that promote social interaction, such as blocks and building materials. Beckman and Kohl (1984) describe the kinds of objects and toys that can be used in a classroom with specific themes in mind.

Large objects and manipulatives provide a continual source of novelty and play. When typical peers are interested in toys and activities, they can be encouraged to interact with José as a play partner. Direct prompts and praise are provided to both the typical child who initiates interaction with José and to José, who responds. Children are encouraged to move from one play corner to another so that classroom activities are the primary means for facilitating social interaction.

The size of the social group also affects how children interact with one another during various activities. The larger the group, the more difficult it is for the teacher to individualize José's instruction. The SLP and the ECT develop a language profile for José that helps in the identification of his goals. Subgrouping and clustering the children in the early childhood classroom during play activities facilitate José's interactions with his peers. Presenting activities first in smaller groups and then in larger ones allows the SLP to monitor José's interactional abilities as a function of the number of children. It is difficult for José to sit, pay attention, and listen in a group of 15 to 18 peers. Spontaneous comments from José that are appropriately related to interactions with peers require a great deal of initial training in a smaller dyadic or triadic group. The smaller the class is, the greater the opportunity for interactions among peers and for José to receive individual instruction from the early childhood teachers. Communicative interactions are closely monitored and regulated by José's SLP.

Learning Structure

Making use of **milieu teaching** opportunities, such as circle time, snack time, play time, and even toileting, provide natural opportunities to facilitate language learning. These activities present José with daily social routines, not only in school but also at home, in restaurants, on playgrounds, and in other natural settings (Tiegerman-Farber, 2002a). Milieu teaching activities in which children are allowed to initiate and to interact based on their own decision making provide the teacher with an opportunity to act as a social director rather than a teacher director.

Language facilitations that take place during naturally occurring interactions are often referred to as **incidental teaching**. In incidental teaching the timing of interactions is critical. In a naturally occurring interaction, behaviors are child initiated, and the environment is arranged to create a mechanism for communication. The child's initiations represent a stimulus for the adult to request elaborated utterances, comments, models, and imitations. The teacher provides an action in a daily routine, such as pouring milk into pudding. José's communicative initiations can be reinforced socially by the SLP's or peer's responses to his specific requests. The SLP provides a prompt or a language model to José. The **prompt level** indicates how much information José needs to respond (see Table 9.1).

To facilitate José's response initially, the SLP provides the entire response: "José wants pudding." As José learns to request, the prompting is minimized so that less information or linguistic scaffolding is provided for José to respond. When José responds to the prompt, his approximation is **naturally reinforced** when he receives the requested object. The use of a sequence of prompts is an important feature in language-teaching strategies.

Prompt levels may be minimalized by various **fading techniques**. One fading strategy is for the SLP to provide the entire model: "José wants more pudding." Over successive presentations of this model, the SLP lowers the volume of her voice until it

TABLE 9.1 Prompts to Elicit Responses

Prompt	Example
Physical prompts	Hand over hand
	Touch cue
Verbal prompts	
Modeling	Performing an action and verbalization for imitation:
	Tell John, "It's my turn."
Questioning	"What do you need?"
Cloze questioning	"The dog has a bone or a cookie?"
Clarification/	Revising/regulating verbal input:
modification	"Give the ball to her."
	"Give the ball to Mary."
Associations	"It goes with a toothbrush."
Descriptions	"It's an animal with wings that can fly."
Negations	"It's not hot, it's _____."
Repetitions	Repeating verbal input: I said, "Put the crayons in the box."
Phonemic prompts	"You sleep in a b _____."
Gestures	Pointing
	Facial expressions
	Iconic movements (hand movements: big = hands wide apart)
	Pantomime: performing an action
Choices	Presentation of two choices … three choices … four choices … etc.
Visual prompts	Objects
	Pictures
	Photographs

becomes a whisper. Another fading technique is to successively present less of the model. The initial prompt is the entire sentence: "José wants more pudding." In the next training sequence, "José wants more ...;" in a third sequence, even less, "José wants ...." Eventually, the entire prompt is faded out, requiring José to spontaneously produce the appropriate response in relation to the contextual social routine.

Another teaching technique is referred to as a **time-delay** strategy. This technique is used during a familiar daily routine. When José is used to performing a routine in a specific order and sequence, he learns to expect specific objects to be presented and actions to occur. The time-delay strategy allows the SLP to create a natural break in the routine to give José an opportunity to initiate some communicative production. The facilitation begins when José becomes aware that the routine has stopped. The SLP may be poised to pour the milk, but she waits for José to comment. She provides a visual prompt, which is the associated action, she looks at José, and she holds out the object to José. If José provides the appropriate language response in a reasonable period of time, he is naturally reinforced by the continuation of the familiar routine. If José does not respond, the SLP provides a prompt that is progressively minimalized over time; José imitates the SLP's model, and the social routine continues.

Classroom **routines** are important because they create familiarity and a **semantic framework** that can be expanded, developed, and individualized (Tiegerman-Farber, 2002a). Changing the routine gives children the opportunity to repair the sequence and describe what has occurred (e.g., spilling the milk).

Teaching Structure

The relationship between the SLP and José is very different during a low-structured versus high-structured lesson. In a **high-structured** situation, the SLP often focuses on specific goals that are targeted for response. In a **low-structured** activity, the SLP follows the child's initiations and intervenes, facilitates, and comments, given the natural flow of the social activities (MacDonald & Carroll, 1992). There is a need for both high- and low-structured activities in the classroom to facilitate language development and to teach peers how to effectively interact with José. The SLP provides a language model that is carefully regulated to José's and the group's level of comprehension to increase the probability for reciprocal communication.

Figure 9.1 presents some general guidelines concerning therapeutic planning. Regulation strategies include modifying the length and complexity of input, utilizing gestured and visual cues, and providing a hierarchy of prompt levels by modeling, physical guidance, and verbal elicitations. The routine daily experiences that occur in an early childhood classroom provide a rich source for language facilitation.

1. The topic of conversation is the daily routine or activity in the classroom (Tiegerman-Farber, 2002a). The content of the interaction is determined by José's verbal and nonverbal behavior in the activity. When the SLP's input is directly related to what José is doing or saying during the activity, a semantic relationship enhances linguistic mapping. The SLP's input encodes what José is doing and/or saying, so he is in control of the topic and the content of the interaction. A mapping relationship between **linguistic structure** (i.e., what to say)

- Begin therapy at the child's level of functioning.
- Chart the child's pragmatic, semantic, syntactic, and social and play abilities on a developmental graph and share this with the classroom teacher.
- Regulate language input by presenting a model that is one linguistic level ahead of the child.
- Intervention procedures should be matched to the child's learning style and needs.
- Observe the child in the classroom before developing a treatment plan.
- Programming should focus on the process of learning, rather than specific content.
- Children with different developmental disabilities share some common characteristics. List these characteristics; this provides a therapeutic framework for the children on your caseload.
- Introduce new behaviors in individual therapy to a criterion level and then begin the facilitation process. Use old forms when teaching new functions. Use old functions when teaching new forms.
- Follow a developmental model when determining therapeutic content goals (i.e., what to teach) and the sequence of learning.
- If the child experiences difficulty at any developmental step, return to an earlier step.
- Collaborate with the teacher by working with all the children on your caseload in the classroom.

FIGURE 9.1
Guidelines for Intervention Planning

and contextual occurrences (i.e., what is happening) is developed and naturally reinforced by events and their consequences. For José, who has severe difficulties in language production and comprehension, facilitation is related to his interests and actions in daily activities.

2. Specific semantic functions are developed by utilizing expansion, extension, elicitation, imitation, and commenting techniques.
   a. In language **expansion,** grammatical aspects that have been omitted from José's production are filled in. If, for example, José says, "Boy run," language learning is facilitated by expanding his utterance with "The boy is running."
   b. In the case of an *extension* technique, the SLP provides new information based on José's language content. For example, if he says, "Boy run," the SLP provides additional information about contextual occurrences, such as, "The boy is running in the park." By using **elicitation**, additional information is elicited from José about the topic or activity. Here José might say, "Look, duck," and the SLP follows with, "Tell me more about it." Another type of elicitation is questioning used to obtain information from José, who does not initiate communicative interactions or include pertinent or significant content with regard to a topic. However, it is important not to rely on this technique. When José is questioned excessively, communicative responsibility for the interaction shifts to the questioner, which inhibits José's spontaneity and initiation.
   c. The goal of the **imitation** technique is to tie together the linguistic utterance with a nonlinguistic performance by using José's imitative (echolalic) tendency. In this particular case, it is getting José to "do and say" at the same

time—to perform an action and then linguistically code his own behavior. For example, as José opens his juice, the SLP provides a verbal stimulus by saying, "José is opening the juice." José might imitate all or part of the SLP's presentation, but the goal is to reinforce him for verbally coding what he is doing. Furthermore, the SLP can *comment* about contextual occurrences, such as, "José, your car fell."

Social Routines and Contingencies

Various activities lend themselves to becoming ***social routines*** in the classroom, such as making pudding, coloring, snack time, and storytelling, which are frequently repeated. These activities are usually highly motivating for children and communicatively enhancing within a group setting. Snack time provides a framework for José to learn to find his lunch box, eat, and share his food items. Because snack time is repeated on a daily basis, social routines, including patterns of behavior and natural contingencies, become stimuli for peer interaction. Behavioral consequences are emphasized, so José's socially appropriate behaviors are reinforced in a group setting. Initially, José needs to be reinforced by means of primary reinforcers, naturally occurring events, and/or verbal praise from the SLP, the teacher, and peers. Activities can be organized to develop social routines so that breaks in routines provide opportunities for communicative initiations: requests and/or comments (Yoder & Davies, 1992).

Classroom Themes

The assumption in an early childhood classroom is that children have the ability to talk about their actions during an activity. In addition, children are reinforced for helping, initiating, and maintaining an interaction with a peer because social behaviors are already present within their repertoires. This is *not* the case for José and other children with language and communication disorders. The SLP facilitates the development of the requisite social skills for José to function in a large-group setting by working on these skills in individual therapy and small groups.

Although certain activities are repeated over the course of several weeks so that the routines become more familiar each week, there is always a new *theme*: (a holiday or someone's birthday) around which daily activities are based. The theme provides a mechanism for relating information and knowledge to objects and actions that allow the SLP to develop José's vocabulary and semantic functions. Themes create a meaningful bridge between each child's specific language goals and the peer group's lessons that provide numerous opportunities for experiential learning. Themes are more meaningful when they are initiated by children.

Child-directed themes improve motivational and interest levels because the content is functionally related to children's personal lives. Activity sheets are sent home on a daily basis so that parents can duplicate experiences at home and talk to their children about activities that occurred during the day. When early childhood programs serve linguistically diverse families, activity sheets need to be translated on a daily basis. This becomes difficult when staff members do not speak a primary home language.

Peer Partners

The underlying theoretical premise of *peer facilitation* is that children can learn from one another (Fenrick, Pearson, & Pepelnjak, 1984; Guralnick, 1986). In the process of including children with disabilities into natural settings, educators consider how typical peers can serve as models (Owens, 1999). In the preschool population, children with and without disabilities, even at ages 3 and 4, can socialize and play together. Although the typical preschooler can be taught to function as a language facilitator and peer socializer for José, his early childhood teachers must be trained to use instructional methods that facilitate social integration. The pragmatic reality for the early childhood teacher and the SLP involves the modification of the natural setting to appropriately include José in ongoing activities.

Preschool children in early childhood settings might not deliberately exclude a child who looks different unless he acts differently—screaming, flapping his hands, biting, and hitting. Children clearly socialize along a hierarchy that involves a set of competencies and skills. The most socially competent children play together and function in a group together; children who are less socially competent form their own group (Craig & Washington, 1993).

Social skills are primarily acquired through learning, observation, modeling, and practice. Children learn early in the first 24 months of life that specific behaviors elicit social responses from others. Social skills are developed in steps of increasing difficulty. To teach José to interact, typical peers are encouraged to approach José (i.e., place José in the role of responder). José, however, does not respond to peer requests or directions appropriately, even after several attempts. As a result, the SLP facilitates these initial interactions so that neither José nor the child interacting with him become frustrated (Goldstein, English, Shafer, & Kaczmarek, 1997). To facilitate a successful

In order to ensure that peer facilitation is effective, typical children need to be taught how to interact with a child who has a disability.

Pearson Learning Photo Studio

communicative interaction between children, the SLP uses a procedure referred to as **bridging.** The typical child is reinforced for interacting with José, and José is reinforced for any gestural or verbal response to his peer. The bridging procedure is used because José does not have the social abilities to initiate a conversation, activity, or interaction. The initiation must therefore come from a typical peer.

A "special friends program" is developed so that José is paired with various peer partners. The SLP reinforces all interactional behaviors from peers who initiate and maintain play with José. The typical peer is told, "Here, take this toy over to José and give it to him." When typical peers participate as a special friend, their prosocial behaviors result in activity choices later in the day that are naturally reinforcing to them, such as extra computer, library, and play time.

By functioning as a social director, the SLP modifies the typical child's behaviors so that he more effectively influences José's responses. Once this goal is accomplished, maintenance of the interaction (i.e., increasing the number of turns or exchanges) between the two children becomes the goal. This working dyad sensitizes the typical child to José's communicative needs so that interaction occurs successfully between the children. The peer dyad also provides a form of socialization instruction that can be highly specialized for both children.

Learning to interact and communicate in a social dyad is a first step in the socialization process. Eventually, however, José learns to function communicatively in a larger-group context. José learns about play behaviors, peers, roles, and rules that govern the group experience. This presents a monumental problem when deficits in pragmatic, semantic, and syntactic areas limit his ability to learn to play, initiate interactions, maintain conversations, describe events, and share experiences (Weiss & Nakamura, 1992).

Even when presented with social opportunities, José does not benefit unless people accommodate and change their behaviors to meet his needs; this is instructionally time intensive. The classroom provides opportunities for the **generalization** of targeted behaviors to multiple communicators, activities, and contexts (Hadley & Schuele, 1998). The process begins in individual therapy, where social complexities and distractions can be limited to an adult–child interactional dyad.

Facilitating the Socialization Continuum

McEvoy, Shores, Westby, Johnson, and Fox (1990) suggest that the physical proximity of children in relation to one another cannot ensure that children with and without disabilities will interact. Specifically, providing a physical context only provides the opportunity for children to share the same space, but it does not ensure that children have the skill or the inclination to socialize with one another. Successful social integration only occurs with direct intervention from teachers and parents.

In addition, it is not clear what methodological procedures can be used to achieve successful socialization in diverse communities, given the cultural variations and characteristics related to children's disabilities. Several variables should be considered in order to begin the socialization process between children with and without disabilities; these include (1) peer training, (2) organization of the classroom, and (3) social contingencies. Perhaps one of the most important ideas is that the classroom represents an ecological environment that either facilitates or inhibits the social learning process. The variables that contribute to the ecology of the classroom need to be analyzed and appropriately factored into the placement of children with disabilities. To assume that the mere placement of a child with a disability into an early childhood classroom will successfully lead to social integration, acceptance, and friendship is rather naïve (Tiegerman-Farber, 2002a).

Bridging as a Facilitation Technique

The procedure used by the SLP to connect the special needs child's language to a peer so that the child–child interaction is successful is referred to as bridging. This requires the SLP to change each child's verbal and/or nonverbal behavior so that an interactional or communicative exchange successfully occurs. The change in the target child's behavior creates a more advanced production that more closely approximates the typical peer's production. Bridging is facilitative for the target child because it provides (1) a more complex linguistic model that (2) results in an interactional exchange between children.

For the peer, bridging creates a less complex linguistic model that more closely approximates the target child's level of comprehension. The bridging technique provides peer facilitation training to typical children, who can then actively participate in the socialization of children with disabilities. Often the typical peer needs to be encouraged to initiate communicative interactions with children who do not have the skills to socialize.

Bridging can also be used between two children with special needs. The bridging process is critical to child–child interaction since the typical child has neither the knowledge or the experience to facilitate the language of another child, especially a child with a disability. The bridging technique can be used with other teaching procedures:

1. **Modeling** Bridging by the SLP establishes a successful social and/or communicative interaction between peers. The SLP provides a model for each child so that their interaction is naturally reinforced by the contextual activities.
2. **Imitation** Bridging by the SLP involves each child's imitation of the SLP's language productions.
3. **Connective interaction** Bridging either establishes or continues the communicative and social interaction between children. The interaction would not take place or continue on a consistent basis, given each child's limited experience with the other child's language differences.
4. **Awareness** Given the spontaneous nature of children's interactions in social contexts, children who interact the most usually have the most sophisticated social skills. Play, social interaction, and communication are naturally facilitative and reinforcing for children. A learning-to-learn phenomenon occurs. The more they do it, the more they are inclined to do it. Within this dynamic exchange process is the implicit fact that children who are more socially skilled tend to socialize together and to attract peers who have similar skills. The result is that the child with a disability may not be *excluded* so much as not be actively included by typical peers.
5. **Inclusion** Social integration is based on the premise that children with and without disabilities are provided a social benefit. This requires an active process

that engages children with and without disabilities in communication exchanges. Physical proximity, sitting next to a typical child or sharing space, does not guarantee that children will interact with each other, particularly when the natural process suggests otherwise. Functions of inclusion include the following:

a. To teach typical children how to engage children with disabilities
b. To teach children with disabilities how to respond to their peer's initiations and how to initiate their own interactions

The SLP can directly engage children so that social interactions are communicative and reciprocal. Communication is a reinforcing experience for speaker and listener when it successfully connects them to engage in mutual exchange. The language discrepancy between the partners creates a barrier that cannot be removed by either child, given their language level or facilitative inexperience. Bridging by the SLP engages the two children so that some object or word is successfully exchanged. Each child's behavior is changed by the SLP to establish an interaction and to connect peers socially.

The following is a guideline for the SLP to facilitate social interaction in the early childhood classroom:

1. Identify contextual variables that affect the child's learning in:

    Individual therapy

    Small-group therapy

    Classroom setting

2. Identify the content of programming, given the following:

    Child's level of functioning

    Modifications to the early childhood curriculum to achieve special-education goals

    Language profile of the child compared to the profile of the class

    Child's language goals that are context specific

    Child's language skills to enhance social interaction and communication

3. Identify supportive strategies to:

    Review the general education curriculum with the teacher to understand what will be taught at each grade level

    Identify the general language requirements in specific academic or subject areas

    Prepare the child to understand the complexity of reading materials by facilitating the comprehension of core vocabulary, main ideas, and complex linguistic structures in specific subject areas

    Teach active listening (listening for words and ideas)

    Use activities that teach organizational planning and skills

    Teach the child to task analyze to ensure that classroom activities are manageable

    Practice newly acquired vocabulary and language skills in different learning contexts to facilitate generalization

Use a variety of presentation methods: visual representation, guided imagery, role playing, rehearsal strategies, verbal imitation, peer modeling, auditory cueing, and attention focusing

Identify computer-based materials that connect language skills and early literacy development

A guideline for the general-education teacher follows:

1. Use developmentally appropriate language for the child
2. Use clear, simple requests, questions, and directions
3. Check to determine that the child understands the task or activity; if not, repeat and/or rephrase and/or simplify instructions
4. Ask peers seated next to the child to check his work and to help him remain on task
5. Move closer to the child when speaking to him
6. Use small-group instruction in class to facilitate learning and child interaction
7. Allow the child to identify topics and subjects in curriculum areas that are of interest to him
8. Use activities that involve experiential hands-on learning (i.e., using the senses) and require teamwork to complete small-group or classroom activities
9. Teach to the child's learning strengths

Developing Learning Contexts in Individual Therapy and the Classroom

Learning contexts represent a means of generalizing communication experiences for José across different educational environments. The communication behaviors learned in these contexts are generalized across classroom activities and then to the home (Tiegerman-Farber, 2002a). The following operating principles are used to develop a learning context:

1. A learning context is defined as any activity that provides an interactional framework, that is, an opportunity for interchange between the adult and the child and the typical peer and the child. The activity is then described in terms of the type of (a) interactions to be developed, (b) communicative behaviors to be learned, and (c) semantic functions to be coded.
2. Each learning context establishes an activity routine to develop an anticipated sequence of events in a routine.
3. The learning context facilitates action and interaction; it allows for the development of reversible role relationships between the SLP and José and/or José and a peer.
4. A core lexicon is developed within each learning context to consistently and systematically focus communication and language training across all the adults working with José.
5. The core lexicon is based on the development of communicative behaviors that appear earliest in a child's language. These communicative behaviors are used across a variety of learning contexts to generalize language and communication behaviors.

6. Communicative interaction is stressed over production of stereotypic or routinized utterances.
7. Learning contexts developed are relevant and functional to José. To facilitate interaction and communication, the SLP focuses on activities that José prefers.
8. Input to José is limited in complexity and mean length of utterance. The SLP's input is functional and relevant to the immediate context and semantically related to José's vocal, verbal, and nonlinguistic behavior.
9. José is presented with a choice of learning contexts; at any time, he can maintain or terminate an activity. Verbal, vocal, and nonverbal behaviors are analyzed within learning contexts to determine his communicative intentions.
10. José is first trained to participate and interact within a context and then to produce behaviors that code the next occurrence in the routine.
11. The early childhood teacher working with José is given a copy of the communication or language description of each learning context and provides consistent input within and across activities (see Table 9.2).
12. Echolalic behavior is used to develop communicative interactions: José imitates and the adult codes, for instance, a nonlinguistic event:

Event: José opening the bubbles.

Adult: José open bubbles.

José: José open bubbles.

TABLE 9.2   Example of a Communication–Language Description of a Learning Context

Semantic Functions	Forms Trained–Adult Input
Object	Bubbles, fan
Action	Open, blow, give, turn on
Agent	Ellen, José, Mommy, Daddy
Agent + agent	José open, Ellen open
	José blow, Ellen blow
Action + object	Make bubbles, pour bubbles, open bubbles
Recurrence	Bubbles … bubbles … bubbles, more, more bubbles
Negation	No, no bubbles
Rejection	Stop, no more, no more bubbles
Cessation (action)	No pour, no blow
Agent + action + object	José open bubbles
	Ellen open bubbles
	Mommy open bubbles
	José pour bubbles
	Ellen pour bubbles
	José blow bubbles
	Ellen blow bubbles
	Mommy blow bubbles

Context: bubbles; materials: bottle of bubbles, bubble maker, fan.

CW 9.1

Use the Companion Website to help you answer the following questions:

1. Describe the advantages and disadvantages of inclusive programming for José, Kaitlyn, and Jeffrey.

   a. Explain how each child might benefit from an early childhood program and interactions with typical peers.

   b. Explain how typical peers might benefit from having José, Kaitlyn, and Jeffrey in their class.

   c. How would you explain to parents of typical children that José, Kaitlyn, and Jeffrey are going to be included in the early childhood classroom? Would you use the same explanation for each child, or would you vary your explanation as a function of his or her disability?

2. Discuss the advantages and disadvantages of using a collaboration versus consultation model in an early childhood program.

3. Kaitlyn is attending a school for the deaf. What information can you find about teaching techniques, curriculum, and equipment used in schools for the deaf?

4. Identify several preschool programs that serve children with disabilities and check their Websites. What kinds of children do they serve? What programs and services do they provide? Do they have parent-training programs? If they do, what do they teach parents, how often do classes meet, and when do they meet?

5. Identify several early childhood programs, child-care programs, and nursery schools from Internet Websites. Determine if they accept children:

   a. With autism

   b. With a physical disability (is the building handicapped accessible?)

   c. With emotional or behavioral disorders

   d. With hearing loss

The long-term clinical goals identified for José's training included:
   a. Development of imitative interaction skills
   b. Expansion of object manipulation skills (semantic knowledge)
   c. Development of sign and gesture forms
   d. Use of interactional behaviors that signal communicative intentions
   e. Generalization of communication behaviors

The Martinez Family

José's communication difficulties are offset by extraordinary abilities in memory and visual processing. He has developed many rituals about dressing, washing, and eating. José eats only Cheerios in a Snoopy dish and wears Elmo pajamas every night.

José's early childhood teacher indicates that he can read. The SLP describes José's reading ability as hyperlexia (i.e., advanced word recognition without language comprehension).

Because of José's social difficulties, the special-education teacher and the psychologist recommend that the early childhood teacher use behavioral techniques in the classroom. The psychologist stresses the need for the early childhood teacher to operationalize classroom procedures and training goals. Because the early childhood teacher does not know how to "operationalize" instruction, the psychologist provides teacher training and consultation services about applied behavioral analysis (ABA) techniques in the classroom.

José is placed on a reinforcement schedule, and the early childhood teacher tries to follow the schedule consistently. José's "discrete trial" training includes learning how to dress, eat, toilet, and manipulate toys and interact with peers. A contingency approach (McEachlin, Smith, & Lovaas, 1993) is used to manage José's inappropriate and self-injurious behaviors (e.g., biting his hand and banging his head) that are exhibited in the classroom. Generalization is a critical factor in the success of this program. The early childhood teacher and Maria Martinez meet once a week at 6 p.m. to go over José's program. Maria observes the teacher working with José and describes her feelings about his progress in Box 9.1.

BOX 9.1

José is making a lot of progress. The most wonderful thing is hearing him talk. Now he repeats things over and over again. He's able to remember all the commercials and he reads everything he sees. I think he's very smart for a little boy. I'd like to talk to other parents, but there's no parent program in child care. It's hard to take José to church on Sunday and visit with other people from El Salvador because José can have bad tantrums. I've asked my priest to help me find a baby sitter for José. I need to get out of the house on weekends to do things, but I can't leave José alone. I have steady work now. I've looked for a child-care program that's open on Saturday, but I can't find one. I'd like to send some money home to my relatives, but José's doctors are expensive. I don't have any money left over. I've moved to a house with relatives from El Salvador. I'm so happy José is talking.

Maria Martinez

 Use the Companion Website to help you answer the following questions:

1. The preschool special education system provides a full complement of direct services to children with disabilities. However, Maria has a set of needs that are not addressed in these services. How do parents such as Maria balance their needs with respect to the needs of their other children?

2. Is there a need for a service coordinator in the preschool special education system? Explain your answer.

The Whiteside Family

Kaitlyn is attending the Mission School's preschool special-education program. The Mission School uses a transdisciplinary curriculum and a collaborative approach to teaching. The SLP spends two periods everyday working in the classroom with the teacher of the deaf, since all the children are on her caseload. Time is set aside in her schedule to meet on a weekly basis with the education team and with Katherine. The Mission School provides parent-education classes, sign-language classes, parent support groups and counseling services for families of preschool children. The school has a wireless FM system in every classroom; the teacher wears a microphone – transmitter and Kaitlyn wears an FM receiver. The school audiologist monitors and troubleshoots the systems. The Mission School's preschool brochure indicates that "audiological management does not end with the fitting of a hearing aid or the use of an auditory trainer." Katherine is pleased and relieved that the placement process is over for now. She describes her experiences and feelings in Box 9.2.

BOX 9.2

A child who has a hearing loss needs to be monitored and followed throughout the educational year; that's one reason why I want Kaitlyn to remain in Mission. A child with a sensorineural hearing loss who is fitted with hearing aids needs to be seen by the audiologist at least every 6 months to be sure the ear molds are still secure and do not need to be remade. The tubing in the ear molds may need to be replaced or cleaned. I was trained in the use, care, and maintenance of Kaitlyn's aids when she was in the infant program.

Proper cochlear implant management is also important. The external components of the cochlear implant consist of a microphone, speech processor, transmitter, and cords. Someone who is knowledgeable about this kind of technology needs to be available in Kaitlyn's school.

The teachers in the Mission School preschool program are all trained to work specifically with children who are deaf. The school has a collaborative model, time to meet on every child, and time to meet with parents. The services are excellent and families are very involved with school and classroom activities. I go to every parent–teacher meeting, counseling service, parent-education class—everything. I want to know everything and the teachers are prepared to share everything. This is the most wonderful school. I have learned so much in the infant program that I knew I had to keep Kaitlyn in their preschool. These people are really devoted to the children. This school is exactly what I've been looking for. Kaitlyn's progress is fantastic. She is so happy. The stress of Kaitlyn's hearing loss is affecting our family. I feel that I have to take care of Kaitlyn first because she is a child and she has a disability.

My husband and I have separated for a while. Maybe I should have seen it coming, but I was so overwhelmed with guilt about Kaitlyn. It's true, we haven't spent much time together and I've been emotionally drained when we have. I'm there, but I'm not there. He's right when he complains that I've become obsessed with helping Kaitlyn.

> *The Mission School helps us deal with family issues. It's hard to be the parent of a child with a disability. This school understands that a child's health and welfare are based on the health and welfare of the child's parents. Even though these services are not on Kaitlyn's IEP, the counseling services are considered to be part of Mission's curriculum.*
>
> *If Kaitlyn had attended an early childhood program, the teachers wouldn't have had a clue about taking care of her implant or teaching her as a child who is deaf. There would be no parent-training classes or psychological counseling services. An early childhood program is for children who don't need Kaitlyn's specialized education. I know that there are parents who want their children to be in a normal environment because they think it's the least restrictive setting. The early childhood class is for normal children who don't need extra time and attention, not for children with disabilities. That's what disabled means, a child who is not a normal learner. I think the least restrictive environment is different for each child; it's the place that meets the individual needs of that particular child.*
>
> Katherine Whiteside

 Use the Companion Website to help you answer the following questions:

1. Describe various language therapy techniques that might be used to facilitate Kaitlyn's and José's language development.

2. Identify an activity that can be used with both children and describe how it might be organized differently to meet the language goals of each child.

3. What kinds of classroom modifications need to be made to meet Kaitlyn's and José's learning needs?

4. Describe how peer facilitation with José and Kaitlyn would require typical peers to interact with these children differently.

5. Describe the strengths and the weaknesses of the educational program provided to José and Kaitlyn.

6. What kinds of therapeutic techniques can be used by the SLP to support the teacher's classroom goals and educational instruction?

The St. James Family

Jeffrey is impulsive and highly distractible during structured activities. He is also disruptive in the early childhood classroom. He bites and hits his peers when he gets frustrated. He whines and cries when he does not get his way. He has difficulty sharing and waiting for his turn. Jeffrey does not sit still, and even during activities he enjoys, he moves around impulsively. He is constantly touching the other children; he has difficulty understanding physical boundaries.

Jeffrey's phonological problems are more evident as his language production skills develop. Jeffrey's "articulation problems" are now phonological deficits with related and emerging morphosyntactic difficulties. Morphosyntax is the interface between syntax and morphology. The possibility that Jeffrey's behavioral outbursts and frustrations might be related to his communicative difficulties is not acknowledged by his teachers. The ongoing perception that phonological deficits are just "articulation problems" remains the educational viewpoint in many school districts. In some schools, children with speech problems do not receive special-education services, so providing speech-language therapy as a related service is considered sufficient.

The SLP working with Jeffrey recognizes his phonological deficits early on and alerts the special-education consultant and the early childhood teacher (ECT). The SLP tries to help Jeffrey develop compensatory skills when his peers do not understand him. The special-education teacher works with the ECT to sensitize the other children and to minimize peer rejection. The ECT is shown management techniques to use when Jeffrey has a tantrum. The ECT is also asked to informally document the antecedent events to Jeffrey's tantrums. During the push-in sessions, the SLP shows the ECT how to redirect and bridge Jeffrey's speech so that his peers understand him. This also minimizes negative peer reactions and Jeffrey's frustration. The school district psychologist, Dr. Gucciani, feels that Jeffrey's behavioral problems exacerbate his communication difficulties. She believes if Jeffrey's behavior is managed his communication and social skills will improve.

Jeffrey's mother's thoughts on his behavior are given in Box 9.3.

BOX 9.3

Dr. Gucciani says that Jeffrey is going to need more than a functional behavioral assessment as he gets older. What's she talking about? I'm worried that Jeffrey is going to get kicked out of nursery school again. Why can't the teachers handle him? I'm not an expert, but they're supposed to be trained. Putting Jeffrey in a program with emotionally disturbed children will only make his behavior worse. He'll copy all the things they do and his behavior is bad enough now. I think it's Jeffrey's speech that's the problem. How would you feel if no one understood you? That's why Jeffrey is aggressive, he can't express himself.

Camille St. James

 Use the Companion Website to help you answer the following questions:

1. Consider therapeutic goals for Jeffrey, Kaitlyn, and José. Are there specific techniques that would be used for each child? Are there techniques that could be used for all three children?

2. Discuss what kinds of classroom modifications need to be made to accommodate Jeffrey's behavioral, social, and language needs in a typical setting.

3. Identify the prerequisite language behaviors that each child needs to interact and communicate with typical peers. What techniques would be used to facilitate the development of these behaviors?

Related Services

School districts across the United States provide different related services to preschool children with disabilities. Goals, activities, and interactions with children need to be coordinated among specialists. When a transdisciplinary model is used, educational programming is moved beyond the single-discipline approach to levels of commonality across specialty areas in terms of identification, assessment, and intervention to enhance a specific skill.

The integration of instruction across discipline areas facilitates learning (Bailey, Simeonsson, Yoder, & Huntington, 1990). Several disciplines, such as dance movement therapy, music therapy, and occupational therapy, can contribute to the language-learning experience. Each specialist highlights a different aspect of a particular skill through movement, music, and art. In this respect, the transdisciplinary approach is a multimodal approach; if the child is not able to learn a skill through one form of learning, there is opportunity to acquire that skill through another form of instruction. Learning is often context specific and context bound. The transdisciplinary approach allows the child to use the skill or apply the skill within another modality. This increases the opportunity for language generalization, which strengthens both the skill and the learning process.

Such facilitative services provide a means of enhancing the classroom language experience in a creative mode (Ploof & Feldman, 1992). Specialists can translate their educational areas into learning goals and activities that stimulate language development and communication interaction. This is consistent with the philosophy that language is a social experience and that children with language disorders require an integrated program. Related service specialists can be integrated into the classroom environment to provide additional opportunities to use language as a dynamic social process. Children with language disorders can be provided with group and individual therapeutic services, depending on their developmental needs. Children with severe deficits generally receive more intensive individualized programming. As progress is made, less intensive prescriptive services are required. The goal across all the specialty areas is to support children and develop behaviors to the point where the service can be provided in a group context.

Speech-Language Pathologist

The SLP usually does not function as the primary classroom teacher. The SLP facilitates generalization of each child's IEP goals in individual therapy and then generalizes these goals within the social context of the classroom. Thus, each child receives an application experience in the classroom; his language skills are generalized to a natural setting of typical peers. Pragmatic, semantic, and syntactic structures are facilitated in the classroom by getting children to communicate with each other, take turns, respond to questions, initiate topics, and participate in activities.

It is the responsibility of the SLP to interface directly with all the specialists. The SLP develops specific activities and lesson plans related to the child's IEP goals that facilitate language development, such as the following:

1. Maintaining appropriate eye gaze with an adult or a peer
2. Demonstrating appropriate nonverbal turn-taking behaviors
3. Requesting objects from an adult or peer through verbalization
4. Responding appropriately to one-step verbal directions
5. Encoding utterances utilizing a targeted mean length of utterance

The sections that follow explain how different therapists enhance language development.

Occupational Therapist

Occupational therapy involves the evaluation, diagnosis, and treatment of problems that interfere with functional performance in persons impaired by physical illness or injury, emotional disorder(s), congenital or developmental disability, or the aging process (Hanft & Humphrey, 1989). Specific occupational therapy services include, but are not limited to, activities of daily living (ADL); the design, fabrication, and application of splints; sensorimotor activities; the use of specifically designed crafts; guidance in the selection and use of adaptive equipment; therapeutic activities to enhance functional performance; prevocational evaluation and training; and consultation concerning the adaptation of physical environments for the disabled. These services are provided to individuals or groups through medical, health, educational, and social systems (American Occupational Therapy Association, April 18, 1977). Occupational therapy in an educational setting for children with language disorders may be provided on an individual or a classroom consultation basis. It is the intent of the occupational therapist to teach the whole child to perform essential preschool tasks (Hopkins, 1988).

Gross-motor skills involve the child's ability to move through space with regard to accomplishments and quality of movement. Skills, such as balance and equilibrium reactions, reflex integration, ball handling, ascending and descending stairs, and developmental motor milestones need to be within a child's ability to maintain an upright sitting position. Fine-motor skills take into account hand development: reciprocal, assistive, and bilateral usage. Sensory functioning requires the input of a stimulus for processing and output via an adaptive response. The sensory input may be auditory, visual, gustatory, tactile, proprioceptive, kinesthetic, or vestibular (Wilbarger, 1984).

Cognitive skills include age-level acquired knowledge in reference to color, shape, or size recognition; knowledge of the alphabet and numbers; and relatedness to toys or objects in the environment. Examples of perceptual skills involve nonmotor abilities to use figure ground, spatial relations, sequential memory, visual closure, form constancy, visual memory, and visual discrimination. Visual motor skills involve the ability of the hand to perform what the brain perceives, and the ability of the brain to perceive what the hand needs to perform.

Personal social skills include activities of daily living and the ability to perform developmentally appropriate self-care skills. These may include dressing activities and the ability to put on and take off outerwear and to manipulate buttons, zippers, fasteners, laces, and shoes. In a classroom, the child may be expected to manage his or her own lunch box, toilet independently, and assist in cleanup activities.

Treatment intervention typically follows a developmentally based sensorimotor approach (Anderson, 1986). A remedial approach may be utilized to teach a splinter skill to a child to meet expectations with peers (e.g., tying shoes). A sensory integrative approach is based on the premise that development occurs as the result of the organization of vestibular, tactile, and proprioceptive information. Development is enhanced in the areas of reflex maturation, body schema, postural control, balance and equilibrium reactions, and bilateral integration. Sensorimotor activities develop the perceptual skills for body coordination needed for skipping and descending stairs and for eye–hand coordination in lacing and printing.

The occupational therapist uses knowledge of physical, social, and emotional functions to determine the motor development needs of a specific child and group. The therapist then identifies a program of activity leading to the development of fine-motor skills (Williamson, 1988). The skills learned may be as basic as the daily living tasks of bathing, dressing, and eating, or they may be as sophisticated as the complex graphomotor skills of letter writing or figure drawing. The following occupational therapy goals, provided by Vera Gallagher, Occupational Therapist Registered, relate to the language goals and include appropriate activities that facilitate learning.

Drawing Design This activity involves visual, perceptual, motor, and sensory skills. The task uses different media, such as paper and pencil, brush and paint, shaving cream, or clay. Three-dimensional designs are made with Popsicle sticks or straws. The activity is graded by having the child imitate a design or, on a higher level, copy a design. In the first imitation, the child has a demonstration and visual cueing. The ability to copy means the item is presented and the child draws without demonstration. This activity follows a developmental sequence, beginning with random drawing and progressing to vertical, horizontal, circular, and intersecting lines and square and triangle shapes. Attention to boundaries is considered, as well as expansion of the activity by considering the combination of designs to make a picture, coloring within a designated space, and hand grasp.

When providing verbal directions, a child's eye gaze is maintained. Turn-taking during design construction is structured for sharing objects and nonverbal interaction with peers. If a specific item is needed, the child is prompted: "Want more?" or "Give me crayon." If the therapist wants to provide an opportunity for the child to respond appropriately to a one-step verbal direction, an array of choices is available: "Pick up pencil," "Draw here," "Make a circle." The child describes the picture, "That's a house" or "That's me," to utilize productive language skills.

Pinching To use our own "pinchers" or thumb and index finger, objects such as clothespins or blunt tweezers are used to manipulate clay, small beads, and coins. This activity is set up as a tabletop task or as the child sits straddled over a roll to facilitate midline crossing, trunk rotation, and visual tracking.

An array of cognitive skills are emphasized, including color, size, and shape discrimination. The pinching game facilitates hand development and proximal stability for distal motor control. The command to "Take peg" facilitates eye gaze with the adult and the child's ability to follow one-step verbal commands. Turn-taking is established by the child taking a peg, then the therapist taking a peg in sequence, establishing a routine. Pegs are positioned out of the child's reach or set up so as to require more pegs; thus requesting objects is facilitated.

The Swing The swing provides movement experiences. A child is placed on the platform in a prone position to encourage development of the extensor muscle groups. Trunk extension is required to maintain an upright sitting posture. The therapist asks the child to look at her face, take an object such as a beanbag from her hand, then throw the beanbag at a designated target. When the child completes the task, he is encouraged to verbalize "I do" or "I hit it."

Manipulatives (Legos or Tinkertoys) The child is presented with interlocking toys that require bilateral motor coordination; reciprocal, assistive hand usage; and visual motor and visual perceptual skills. The ability to interlock toys is used to encourage eye gaze by having the child seated opposite the therapist who holds a block and says, "I build." Turn-taking is facilitated by offering the block to the child to continue the activity.

Dance Movement Therapist

Dance therapy is defined as the psychotherapeutic use of movement as a process that furthers the emotional and physical integration of the individual. Social, emotional, cognitive, and physical problems are dealt with through intervention on a body movement level (Levy, 1992). Dance therapy is provided as part of a transdisciplinary approach, because it serves as a creative stimulus for expression and imaginative exploration of interaction with the environment. In addition to developing motor abilities, such as running, jumping, and leaping, dance therapy develops self-expression, authentic communication, and the pure joy of moving (Ekstein, 1983). The dance therapist is concerned with the quality of motor skills and the acquisition of those skills based on the integration of body awareness, body image, spatial awareness, rhythmic response, and coordination. The quality of interaction between the child and her or his classmates and the adults in the environment is also carefully monitored. Body movement, communication, and relatedness are interconnected; dance therapy addresses all three at once.

Movement is a basic and very important function of life. This is most apparent in the early years when children are naturally tuned into their bodies and when they learn by doing. During this period, they are also learning about the body and emotional responses to the environment. For example, a child's body receives a lot of attention during feeding, dressing, toileting, and other activities of daily living. The child is also learning about how his or her behavior is being accepted by parents and other significant adults.

Children view many activities in terms of how they feel. The excitement of an activity and the joy in performing it give children important positive reinforcement for their performances. Action is experienced on a body level and then becomes translated into self-esteem, self-confidence, and ultimately motivation to learn. It cannot be stressed enough how important positive self-regard and self-esteem are in the ability to communicate effectively.

The dance therapist can provide important experiences that will nurture healthy body attitude, develop a particular motor ability and, at the same time, be a lot of fun. Going up a climber and sliding down a slide to the cheering of teacher and classmates can be fulfilling to any child. Moving around in a circle, holding hands with classmates, and enjoying the rhythm of music can develop a sense of acceptance and belonging. Being given the opportunity to move freely or to improvise a dance can develop independence and creative expression.

The benefits of dance therapy are extraordinary because learning occurs on a body level. Prior to the development of formalized language, a child learns to express herself nonverbally. He communicates by crying, smiling, laughing, and eventually gesturing, all before she has the ability to speak. Young children are motivated by movement and receive instant physical gratification through the pleasure experienced during motor activity. The needs of the whole child are addressed in the natural, familiar context of movement games. As the child moves, he incorporates knowledge of himself, others, and his environment into his learning experiences.

Dance therapy is a viable tool to be used in an educational setting for children with language disorders. This multisensory approach helps to integrate nonverbal and verbal communication with physical coordination, motor planning and sequencing, body tension, spatial awareness, and rhythmic ability (Greenspan & Pollack, 1989). Speech and language aspects, such as pragmatic deficits, disfluency, apraxia, and syntactic errors, are frequently related to motor problems. Pragmatic deficits, such as interacting with one's environment, may be related to spatial awareness; disfluency, to upper body tension and limited rhythmic ability; and apraxia and syntax, to motor planning and sequencing. The interrelationship between symbolic language and motor aspects is undeniable; a motor-oriented intervention should be used to facilitate maximum success for young children. The dance movement therapist develops a program of prescriptive treatment to facilitate acquisition of motor skills in both individual and group sessions.

The following dance movement therapy activities, provided by Nancy Sheehan and Sarah Becker, Advanced Dance Therapists, Registered, relate to the language goals.

"Hello" Song The child sits facing the therapist as the group sings a "Hello" song. The child's and the therapist's names will be incorporated into the song.

Rhythmic Body-Part Tapping The child and therapist take turns as leader and follower during body-tapping exercises. The therapist elicits movement suggestions from the child.

Gross-Motor Obstacle Course Activity The child engages in an obstacle course activity, incorporating prepositional concepts, such as in, out, up, down, and under. The child also encodes actions such as "Go in" and "Go on."

Relaxation Activity The child requests hand lotion to rub on body periphery (hands, arms, and face) to promote relaxation and the development of body boundaries.

"Good-Bye" Song The child faces the therapist to sing good-bye in the same manner as the "Hello" song.

Music Therapist

The music therapist uses music as a primary modality in treating children with language disorders. She uses her expertise to facilitate auditory processing skills. Some aspects of speech are similar to aspects of music, such as rhythm, patterning, volume, pitch, and prosody. These aspects of music are used to facilitate verbal and social interaction among children (Alvin, 1975). According to Nordoff and Robbins (1971), music can be defined as experiences of rhythmic and tonal variety. These experiences relate to a child's view of the world, his body movement and dance, his emotional life, his communication, and his speech and language. Just as all human beings have an inborn capacity for learning language, they also have the innate capability of responding to music. It is no coincidence that the five basic elements of music, rhythm, pitch, dynamics, pulse, and form are intimately connected with the production of speech. Thus, music has a unique role to play in work with children with speech and language disorders (Bruscia, 1989).

Krista Greco/Merrill

Many special education programs do not provide music and dance therapies as related services. It is important for teachers and parents to understand how these services can stimulate language and socialization in children with disabilities.

Spoken language is both rhythmic and melodic. Each sentence has rhythmic forms, stress patterns, and variations in pitch and inflection that help to communicate its meaning. Through both singing and instrumental work, the child moves toward greater language proficiency. The music therapist is skilled at adapting conventional materials and finding new appropriate materials for use with children who have difficulty in the processing and production of language (Alvin, 1976). Singing is a natural musical activity for preschool children that aims to improve auditory perception, processing, memory, voice quality, production of speech sounds, learning and retention of language, and production of meaningful communication. Songs with actions, tempo, mood, and word phrasing can enhance the linguistic, perceptual, and cognitive goals set by the SLP.

An activity is introduced in several sensory modalities to make the experience more holistic and to reinforce learning on many different levels (Nordoff & Robbins, 1971). Eventually, visual and kinesthetic input is reduced to strengthen the child's auditory mode. For example, when exploring ranges of pitch, the child is asked to move his body up and down, corresponding to high and low pitches, while following a model or blackboard diagram. The music therapist utilizes the qualities of music and relates these qualities to language. She uses a wide variety of techniques and activities, including free singing, song singing, rhythmic work, instrumental work, and action songs, all aimed at teaching and reinforcing language development. Music therapy teaches basic vocabulary, as well as the difficult task of sequencing an event. It encourages creativity and vocal play, which helps the child to achieve vocal confidence to become an effective language initiator (Boxhill, 1985).

In music therapy, children use rhythm instruments, objects in the classroom, and their voices to create mood and action. In creating a thunderstorm, for example, the activity begins with the calm stillness before the storm. The excitement and activity of the storm is created by instruments that build a dramatic crescendo in the activity. When the storm subsides, the instruments are played more softly. The vocabulary emphasized includes *storm, cloud, start, stop, rain, lightning, thunder, loud,* and *soft.* At the conclusion of the music activity, children share the satisfaction of having made a personal contribution to a larger group experience.

Music therapy helps the child achieve health using musical experiences as dynamic forces of change (Bruscia, 1989). There are two separate and distinct aspects of a music therapy program:

1. Using music as a means to reinforce speech-language goals, based on the close connection between music and speech. For example:
   a. Repetitive singing and chanting aids fluency.
   b. Word substitution songs help build vocabulary and organize thinking in terms of categories and associations.
   c. Leaving out a word or phrase when singing a familiar song assists with word finding.
   d. Learning a song in its entirety promotes auditory memory and sequencing skills.
   e. Singing call-and-response songs gives children practice in the turn-taking skills needed for conversation.

2. Using music as an alternative mode of communication, because music is nonverbal communication. A basic principle of music therapy is the concept of the "music child," which includes the ability to respond to music (Nordoff & Robbins, 1971). Music reaches through a person's pathology or disability to the part of an individual that is healthy. By nurturing music in the child, the borders of the personality can be expanded and a new and richer self emerges through the following:
   a. Establishment or reestablishment of interpersonal relationships
   b. Development of self-esteem through self-actualization
   c. Utilization of the unique potential of rhythm to energize and establish order

The following music therapy activities, provided by Jackie Levin, Music Therapist Registered, relate to the language goals.

Greeting: Contact Song A greeting song that incorporates the child's name is improvised. This becomes the child's "contact song" and is repeated each week. The song helps the child become oriented to the situation and, through repetition, simple phrases are learned (e.g., "Hello, Jimmy, it's time for music"). The therapist seeks to establish eye contact and pauses to allow time for the child to respond both verbally and nonverbally.

Introducing a Simple Structure Using Movements to the Music The child follows song commands such as "Clap your hands to the music." The child verbally requests a movement when given a choice. For example, "Should we clap or stamp?" The child performs verbal closure when the therapist omits a word. For example, "Clap your _____ to the music."

Instrumental Improvisation The child selects an instrument he or she wishes to play; the therapist provides accompaniment. They take turns leading and following changes in tempo and volume.

"Five Little Fingers" (by Carol Robbins) In this song, the child counts his fingers and points to appropriate body parts. The child takes the initiative and chooses which body part to sing about next.

"Good-bye" Song Closure is provided by a "Good-bye" song, again using the child's name and stating, "It's time to say good-bye." The child and therapist take turns strumming a guitar and saying "Good-bye."

The School Psychologist

The overall task of the school psychologist is to identify specific needs of children through ongoing diagnostic evaluations and classroom consultations (Salvia & Ysseldyke, 1991). The psychologist uses a holistic approach and plays a major role in solving classroom-related problems. She works with the teacher in the classroom to help develop and implement behavior-management programs. In a program that serves children with severe language deficits, the school psychologist plays an integrative role. She participates in the daily functioning of the classroom and functions as a liaison between the school and the home setting. The school psychologist provides direct intervention to children and parents, provides individual and group play therapy, assists families in crisis intervention, and monitors the children's individual cognitive progress. The underlying policy concerning behavior(al) management is that as children learn language they more effectively and appropriately regulate their own behavior and the behavior of others.

Children with language disorders learn about social behaviors, language rules, and the communicative use of language in a social context. Language learning is a social process. The social basis of normal language development emphasizes the need to provide social experiences for language-disordered children. The social environment of the classroom provides a normalizing experience. Social learning provides children with the opportunity to use their language skills and behaviors to regulate the environment in more socially appropriate ways. The language-disordered child who tantrums, screams, and self-stimulates needs to be involved in an activity that will provide the opportunity to communicate his needs. When children learn that there is a contingency relationship between their behavior and the environment, inappropriate behaviors decrease.

A variety of social procedures is used to teach and to reinforce appropriate interactional behaviors. Modeling and imitation procedures, along with differential reinforcement of other behaviors (DRO), are utilized to systemically shape social behaviors. Primary reinforcers, tokens, and social reinforcers are used during daily activities to shape and to maintain appropriate classroom behaviors.

The most important aspect of social training is consistency and training across teachers, parents, and adults. Parents and teachers are trained to use behavioral procedures that are described during parent-training and staff-training sessions (Persampieri, Gortmaker, Daly III, Sheridan, & McCurdy, 2006; Reyno & McGrath, 2006; Lundahl, Risser, & Lovejoy, 2006). The variety of educational contexts provides a mechanism for generalization of behaviors. Finally, children and staff are closely monitored by the transdisciplinary team to determine the effectiveness of all teaching procedures; data recording and analyses validate child performance changes.

Dr. Helene Mermelstein, school psychologist, indicates that language goals generated by the curriculum team have direct correlation to the goals of the psychologist as a classroom consultant. The psychologist works closely with the classroom SLP to develop and implement management goals, interactional goals, developmental play goals, and self-concept goals (Sattler, 1988). For example, while helping the child demonstrate appropriate turn-taking behaviors, the psychologist, in conjunction with

CW 9.2

Use the Companion Website to help you answer the following questions:

1. What other related services are being provided to children with disabilities in your state? Explain how José, Kaitlyn, and Jeffrey might benefit from these services.

2. Some clinical treatments provided to children with disabilities are considered to be controversial. Identify several such treatments and discuss why they are controversial.

the teacher, develops a behavioral system that fosters self-regulation. The child is rewarded for successively approximated behavior through the use of a structured positive reinforcement program. Thus, appropriate modeling and teaching coupled with a behavioral approach lead to a child who communicates successfully and appropriately.

SUMMARY

This chapter describes how an early childhood classroom can provide a social context for language learning. As an instructional setting, the early childhood classroom allows the child with a disability, teachers, therapists, and the parents to come together with a common goal—language learning. The early childhood classroom represents a transitional setting for the child with a disability to learn to socialize in a natural environment.

For some preschool children with language disorders, the early childhood classroom may not be an appropriate setting. It is important, therefore, to understand José's, Kaitlyn's, and Jeffrey's language needs to determine the appropriateness of a program and therapeutic services. The early childhood classroom can be organized to provide many different learning opportunities for children with and without disabilities. The early childhood teacher, with the support of the SLP, can use facilitation techniques that will accommodate language learning; this is why collaboration is pivotal. Although an inclusion classroom may be the ultimate goal for José, Kaitlyn, and Jeffrey, they are at different points along the language continuum.

Finally, many early childhood and special-education programs provide a variety of related services, in addition to language therapy, that facilitate creative expression and language development and interaction among children.

PART 3

The Elementary School:
A Collaborative Approach

In this section, Maria Martinez, Katherine Whiteside, and Camille St. James realize the scope of their children's disabilities, given the requirements of an academic curriculum. Children with language disorders have lifelong learning problems that families learn to accept gradually. Elementary schools are large and diverse. There are greater expectations from teachers and peers that information will be processed and organized quickly. For children with language disorders, the general-education classroom can become a cyberspace if accommodations are not tailored to individual learning needs. The general-education classroom is not necessarily staffed with a special-education teacher. The traditional elementary school model defines speech therapy, special education, and occupational therapy as related services, with children leaving the classroom or specialists intervening within the classroom for two, three, or four periods a week. For a child with a disability, a classroom of 25 typical peers is at times overwhelming, complicated, and complex. Success for children with disabilities in general-education classrooms occurs for some, but not for all, children.

Maria Martinez, Katherine Whiteside, and Camille St. James are trying to understand what inclusion means and whether inclusion is appropriate for their child. Maria Martinez has always wanted José to be educated in an inclusive setting, but she now has some concerns. José has poor social skills and he is often the victim of bullying. At times he is encouraged to say and do inappropriate things. It is after such incidents that Maria realizes that a general-education setting that is not prepared to accommodate a child with José's problem can be a restrictive setting. José may need to be in an environment in which he is protected from the potential abuses of typical peers. Maria is frightened about the potential for other people either knowingly or unknowingly hurting her son. From an academic perspective, José can read, but his comprehension is limited. He acquires information with a great deal of specificity. Most people in her family and community are impressed with how much information José remembers. Maria is proud of José and how much knowledge he has. She does not understand what the future offers José as an adult. What will José become when he grows up? What kind of job will he have? Is her district prepared to meet José's educational needs? Will José graduate from high school?

Katherine Whiteside has made a critical decision about Kaitlyn's educational future. She wants Kaitlyn to be educated with other children who are deaf and wants her to become part of a community that will not label her as handicapped. Katherine is determined and persistent. She reads the law and talks to other families on the Internet. She searches for research studies and contacts legislators about educational problems facing children with hearing loss. Katherine is prepared to present her views to her special-education committee. She hopes that, as an informed parent and advocate, she can work effectively with her district. Although she is prepared to request an impartial hearing, she is aware that school districts have won 95% of impartial hearings. Katherine is not willing to accept the committee's arguments about the least restrictive environment for Kaitlyn. She is working with an advocacy group that helps parents who cannot afford private lawyers in the event of an impartial hearing. The stakes are high on both sides. For Katherine, it's Kaitlyn's future that is at risk. For the school district, it's setting a precedent concerning private-school placements.

Camille St. James feels a sense of relief that Jeffrey's real problem has finally been recognized by the school district. She always felt that there was an underlying explanation for Jeffrey's behavior problems. Jeffrey has not received the appropriate services, and now he is far behind the other children in terms of reading skills. This creates further embarrassment for Jeffrey with his peers. Camille is still puzzled as to why it has taken so long to determine what Jeffrey's problems really are. Now that Jeffrey is receiving the services he needs, Camille believes Jeffrey will catch up in school. Camille's life has changed. She recently married and has two stepchildren. She helps Jeffrey with his homework everyday. Jeffrey is having a very difficult time at home with his stepfather and stepsiblings. Camille is pregnant and thinks that a younger sibling will make a significant difference to Jeffrey. As an older brother, he will have someone to take care of. Camille is very positive about the future for Jeffrey and her new family.

At this point each child's disability has become a long-term reality. Each family's resiliency provides the strength and a belief system to face the challenges of an unknown future. Faith in each other and their supportive relationships create the connections to keep the family together as an organized system. At this time, many families describe a spiritual process that helps to explain the place of the child with a disability within the family. Parents realize that there is not going to be an explanation as to why they had a child with a disability.

CHAPTER

10

Understanding Elementary Schools

Chapter Objectives

After studying this chapter, you should be able to answer the following questions:

1. What are the political, social, and fiscal factors that resulted in the Regular Education Initiative (REI) and inclusive programming for children with disabilities in elementary school?

2. What is the difference between mainstreaming and inclusion?

3. How does inclusion change the general-education classroom in terms of learning dynamics, instructional techniques, and peer socialization?

4. How has inclusion changed the role and responsibilities of the speech-language pathologist?

5. What are some issues related to the overrepresentation of minorities in special education?

Since 1975, special education has expanded to include services to children from birth to 21 years. New programs, educational philosophies, professional practices, and funding mechanisms have been developed to meet the needs of individuals with disabilities across more comprehensive systems. During the past two decades, special-education programs (along with special educators) have been monitored, regulated, evaluated, and critiqued by public officials, parents, and researchers interested in educational policy as it applies to program efficacy. Over time, however, new issues have emerged. Limited resources and general dissatisfaction with U.S. education have focused attention on the escalating costs of special education. Clearly, public education serves more than just children with disabilities. As discussed in earlier chapters, programs for infants, toddlers, and preschoolers with a variety of developmental disabilities have developed since 1990. These populations and programs create a further demand and strain on an educational system that is already feeling the effects of decreased funding. In addition, growing social problems compete with educational problems to increase the public's demand for education reform (Cobb, Lehmann, Tochterman, & Bomotti, 2000). Vouchers, school violence, teenage pregnancy, HIV-AIDS, alcoholism, drug abuse, school dropouts, welfare reform, and managed health programs all require and compete for public funding.

Family Focus

In this chapter, Maria, Katherine, and Camille describe their concerns and experiences as they meet with school-district personnel to determine the children's needs for special-education programs and services in elementary school. Each mother reflects on her experiences in the preschool system as her child begins the transition process into elementary school. The families have learned a great deal about their role as advocates for their children. They are aware that José's, Kaitlyn's, and Jeffrey's language skills will affect their abilities to socialize and make friends. The peer relationships with typical children become more of a concern to the mothers as they familiarize themselves with classroom instruction, curriculum requirements, and academic performance expectations.

Diversity Focus

Public schools, particularly in urban communities, are faced with the growing diversity of their student population. The variety of languages and the children's cultural differences have made the communication process between home and school more complex. Although the only language barrier appears to relate to the Martinez family, the cultural backgrounds and values of Katherine Whiteside and Camille St. James present significant communication barriers as well. In addition, Katherine Whiteside's concern about Kaitlyn's social identification also relates to Kaitlyn's use of sign language as her primary mode of communication.

For all these families, parent and child must learn to acculturate within the larger school society. Following rules and regulations that are unfamiliar can be a challenge for parents. Maria, Katherine, and Camille must find an acceptable balance that allows them to integrate the children within their families, as well as in the school. Parents must feel comfortable and trust school personnel. If this is not in place, underlying suspicion will provide the foundation for future parent–teacher relationships. In this chapter, Maria, Katherine, and Camille reflect on their personal beliefs, providing insights about the upcoming choices that they must make.

School Focus

The elementary school system has been designed to meet the needs of typical children from an increasingly broader base of diverse children. Public schools are funded by means of levied taxes at the local level and targeted funds from state and federal governments. The increases in public-school education costs have not yielded commensurate increases in outcome-based measures, such as student performance.

Educational alliances have been created between advocacy groups representing parents and minorities. Research indicates that more diverse children are negatively affected by poorly performing schools. The growing frustration expressed by a cross section of parents, educators, education pundits, and public officials has resulted in growing demands for public-school reform. Two criticisms that underscore poorly performing community schools are the lack of collaboration and the top-down decision making, which further parental feelings of disenfranchisement. Elementary schools have not had a history of successfully involving families and community leaders in an evaluative process of change. It is within this climate that children with disabilities, who represent 10% of the student population, receive a disproportionate amount of the educational resources.

State Variations

As with early intervention and preschool special education, all the states vary in their service-delivery models, curricula, eligibility criteria, special-education programs, and intervention services within their public-school systems. The elementary school system also utilizes eligibility criteria and categories that differ from the early intervention and preschool special-education systems. Each state has discretion in defining what it means by mild, moderate, and severe language disorders. Some states utilize a categorical approach when classifying children with language disorders. Others use a noncategorical model in which language, social, and cognitive characteristics provide the parameters for grouping children with language disorders within programs or classrooms. For states that utilize a categorical model, there are differences in their definitions of language disorder and/or speech impairment and with the types of services provided to children. So, *within* any given state, differences in the following could exist across the early intervention, preschool, and elementary school systems:

- Categories, definitions, and eligibility criteria
- Service-delivery systems and therapeutic services

Numbers and Percentages

The single variable that remains constant within and across state systems is the difference in service delivery. Table 10.1 compares the percentage of children in preschool and school-age special-education programs across various states. There is a great deal of variability in the percentage of children served nationally in school-age programs (6 to 17 years). These percentages do not necessarily compare similar populations of children served, because the eligibility criteria vary across states.

CW 10.1

Use the Companion Website to help you identify information across states:

1. Contrast the elementary school programs and services provided in your state with those of another state.

2. Describe several program components that you might change in your state to enhance services to children.

TABLE 10.1 Percentage (Based on 2003 Population Estimates) of Children Served Under IDEA, Part B, by Age Group, in 2003, All Disabilities

State	3–5	6–17	3–17	State	3–5	6–17	3–17	State	3–5	6–17	3–17
Alabama	4.44	10.65	9.47	Maryland	5.67	10.37	9.50	South Dakota	8.34	10.78	10.32
Alaska	6.86	11.71	10.84	Massachusetts	6.37	13.50	12.17	Tennessee	4.97	11.27	10.05
Arizona	4.74	9.53	8.54	Michigan	6.93	11.56	10.52	Texas	3.96	10.78	9.41
Arkansas	9.70	11.60	11.23	Minnesota	6.69	11.23	10.39	Utah	5.13	10.33	9.19
California	4.20	9.22	8.28	Mississippi	6.56	10.96	10.12	Vermont	7.05	11.59	10.85
Colorado	5.16	9.01	8.25	Missouri	6.85	12.65	11.56	Virginia	5.72	12.22	10.98
Connecticut	6.24	10.71	9.89	Montana	5.62	11.08	10.13	Washington	5.49	10.23	9.34
Delaware	6.43	11.61	10.62	Nebraska	6.37	12.82	11.59	West Virginia	9.25	15.93	14.70
District of				Nevada	5.10	10.05	9.06	Wisconsin	7.53	11.41	10.71
Columbia	1.77	16.31	13.45	New Hampshire	5.78	12.53	11.38	Wyoming	12.05	12.68	12.56
Florida	5.73	12.91	11.57	New Jersery	5.48	14.64	12.91		.	.	.
Georgia	5.40	10.89	9.80	New Mexico	7.16	12.73	11.69		.	.	.
Hawaii	4.96	10.27	9.27	New York	7.90	11.82	11.09		.	.	.
Idaho	6.31	9.66	9.01	North Carolina	6.12	11.98	10.82		.	.	.
Illinois	6.34	12.48	11.30	North Dakota	6.76	11.54	10.68		.	.	.
Indiana	7.06	13.41	12.17	Ohio	4.44	11.39	10.09		.	.	.
Iowa	5.51	13.48	12.00	Oklahoma	5.46	13.71	12.10		.	.	.
Kansas	8.21	11.34	10.73	Oregon	5.48	11.28	10.17		.	.	.
Kentucky	12.58	11.99	12.10	Pennslvyania	5.74	11.87	10.78		.	.	.
Louisiana	6.09	10.77	9.87	Rhode Island	7.81	16.51	14.93		.	.	.
Maine	11.18	15.38	14.67	South Carolina	7.25	13.69	12.46	50 States and D.C.	5.78	11.46	10.38

Percentage is the number of children served under IDEA divided by the number of children in the population who are in that age group.
Estimates are for July 1, 2003, released October 2004.
Data based on the December 1, 2003, count, updated as of July 31, 2004.
Source: U.S. Department of Education, Office of Special Education Programs, Data Analysis System (DANS).

The percentage of children served increases not only from early intervention to preschool special education, but also from preschool to school-age special-education programs in *every* state in the United States. Table 10.2 shows that the number of children served in special education increases as children get older, except for children classified as speech-language impaired. Table 10.3 presents longitudinal data on the three programs: early intervention, preschool, and elementary school. The data show that the number of children served in all programs has increased between 1994 and 2003.

Given the variations in the systems within and across states, it is difficult to evaluate the efficacy of special-education programs on a national level. The fact that the number and percentage of children increase as children age may be related to a number of clinical issues:

TABLE 10.2 Number of Children Served Under IDEA, Part B, by Disability and Age (in years) 2003

Disability	3 Years Old	4 Years Old	5 Years Old	6 Years Old	7 Years Old	8 Years Old	9 Years Old
Specific learning disabilities	1,969	3,484	8,707	27,931	74,331	139,963	203,191
Speech or language impairments	57,699	107,676	165,948	222,063	214,960	190,224	155,292
Mental retardation	4,453	6,505	11,405	16,115	21,982	29,728	36,681
Emotional disturbance	819	1,539	3,455	7,269	12,914	19,495	27,003
Multiple disabilities	1,962	2,446	4,049	7,139	7,199	8,433	9,833
Hearing impairments	1,972	2,446	3,056	4,175	4,821	5,344	5,890
Orthopedic impairments	2,412	2,955	3,673	5,097	5,101	5,630	5,750
Other health impairments	3,332	4,295	7,190	15,321	21,338	29,951	38,257
Visual impairments	899	1,080	1,282	1,578	1,780	1,995	2,085
Autism	5,029	7,221	10,501	14,001	14,045	14,793	14,840
Deaf–Blindness	81	76	94	106	105	106	121
Traumatic brain injury	198	301	448	659	941	1,225	1,518
Developmental delay	68,726	114,808	55,951	29,216	22,492	11,948	2,611
All disabilities	149,551	254,832	275,759	350,670	402,009	458,835	503,072

Data based on the December 1, 2003, count updated as of July 31, 2004.

Source: U.S. Department of Education, Office of Special Education Programs, Data Analysis System (DANS).

TABLE 10.3 Number of Children Served Under IDEA, Part B, by Disability and Age Group, 1994 Through 2003

Age Group	1994	1995	1996	1997	1998	1999	2000	2001	2002	2003
0–2	165,351	177,281	186,527	196,337	187,355	206,108	232,810	245,775	268,735	272,454
3–5	522,699	548,588	557,063	570,312	573,640	589,122	600,573	619,751	647,984	680,142
3–21	5,430,068	5,627,426	5,787,726	5,967,199	6,113,328	6,267,005	6,374,436	6,481,121	6,607,107	6,726,193

States had the option of reporting children ages 3 to 9 under developmental delay beginning in 1997–1998.
Data based on the December 1, 2003 count, updated as of July 31, 2004.
Source: U.S. Department of Education, Office of Special Education Programs, Data Analysis System (DANS).

- The characteristics of developmental disabilities become more apparent as children get older, unless infants and toddlers or preschoolers present with physical deficits.
- Evaluative measures to appropriately assess developmental differences and disabilities in younger children have a greater degree of error.
- The elementary school special-education system has existed for the longest period of time, so more standardized tests are available.
- More experienced teachers and clinical specialists are working with elementary schoolchildren who have disabilities.
- The definition of disability expands in elementary school to include additional learning areas, such as literacy and writing.

Minority Overrepresentation

Zhang and Katsiyannis (2002) report significant regional variations in the identification of linguistically diverse students in school-age special-education programs that do not coincide with poverty rates in these regions. When the school-age special-education system is analyzed by race and ethnicity, diverse children appear to be overrepresented. The researchers propose that "misclassification or inappropriate placement may result in significant consequences for students, especially when they are removed from the general education classroom" (p. 6). A number of significant issues are raised by this report:

- There are regional variations in minority representation in school-age special-education programs.
- Culturally and linguistically diverse children (CLD) are overrepresented in higher-incidence disabilities.
- Variations in representation may not correlate with state poverty rates (i.e., CLD representation may be higher).
- The systemic variations in the definitions of disability categories appear to affect diverse children negatively and may result in overrepresentation in special education.
- Denying services to minority students when they require them presents as much of a problem as the overrepresentation of minorities in special education.

The fact that CLD children are overrepresented in special education is disturbing for several reasons (McLeskey & Skiba, 1990; Tiegerman-Farber & Radziewicz, 1998; Vaughn, Bos, & Schumm, 2003). First, the variations in eligibility criteria and categorical definitions across and within states may result in the misclassification of children. Second, overrepresentation suggests that CLD children are being removed from general-education programs and inappropriately placed in special education. Finally, overrepresentation also raises the issue that there are either professional negligence and/or discriminatory practices that place diverse children at a serious disadvantage when they are being evaluated by their special-education committees.

The possibility that linguistic and cultural variations may be perceived as *disabilities*, rather than as *differences*, should be underscored. From the data presented by Zhang and Katsiyannis (2002), it is difficult to refute the fact that CLD children are overrepresented in some communities. Salend (Salend, Garrick, & Montgomery, 2002; Salend & Taylor, 2002) notes that some CLD children are also underrepresented in other communities and educational settings, such as charter schools. Attributions of error that emphasize discriminatory practices by professionals are difficult to defend. What can be substantiated is that there are systemic variations that require new policies to effectively monitor special-education systems within and across states.

Before special-education services are reduced, the following questions should be answered:

1. What percentage of CLD children receiving special-education services are poor and/or from homeless families?
2. Given the relationship among poverty, single-parent family structure, and disability factors, should the appropriate number or percentage of CLD children in special education be based on a cluster of variables, rather than on any one variable?
3. What is the appropriate percentage of children and/or CLD children in special education?
4. Is there an appropriate percentage of children in special education?
5. Given the at-risk factors for CLD families, should service provision be linked only with a single variable such as poverty rate?
6. Homelessness, which also has a racial profile, presents a case of minority overrepresentation. Should homelessness be considered a factor that contributes to the overrepresentation of diverse children in special education? Perhaps the more fundamental question is whether services to CLD children should ever be limited when need is substantiated (Benner, 1998). States should investigate the overrepresentation of CLD children across a cluster of variables before services are reduced in special education.

Early childhood studies generally support the importance of early identification of and intervention for at-risk problems; the earlier identification occurs, the better the prognosis (Birnbrauer & Leach, 1993; Calderon & Naidu, 1999; Dunst, 2000; Guaralnick, 1998; Innocenti & Karl, 1993; Lennon & Slesinski, 1999; Mahoney & Bella, 1998; Mahoney, Boyce, Fewell, Spiher, & Wheeden, 1998; Sack, 2000; Sexton, Snyder, Wadsworth, Jardine, & Ernest, 1998). Children receiving therapeutic and medical services later will develop more severe deficits as they get older.

When considering the issue of overrepresentation of CLD children, it becomes important to determine if linguistically and culturally diverse families are being identified later, which in effect results in their receiving fewer services. This may explain why their representation may not correlate with residency poverty rates and appear to be higher. States should be required to collect and analyze data with a focus on at-risk families because they often function on the periphery of the health-care system. Intervention studies on culturally and linguistically diverse families report that the education system nationally has not developed effective outreach programs.

The collection and analysis of uniform data for children from birth to 21 years in special education on a national level are limited. The Federal Interagency Coordinating Council (FICC) should require states to standardize their data collection from system to system (both intrastate and interstate) so that issues such as under- versus overrepresentation can be investigated in a less emotional and more scientific manner. At this point, it is impossible to determine whether the overrepresentation of CLD children is due to system or human failures. If CLD children are underrepresented in early intervention and overrepresented in elementary school, new eligibility limitations in elementary school would penalize CLD children by denying them services at all levels of special education (Jenkins, 2005). Because there is no mechanism to track children by race and ethnicity *across* systems, there is no way to determine the following:

1. Which school-age children received early intervention and/or preschool services?
2. If they did, how many years of special-education services did they receive?
3. If they did, what types of services did they receive?
4. If they did not, when did they enter the special-education system?
5. It is critical to determine which children are:
   a. Entering special education at the three points of entry (early intervention, preschool, and school age)
   b. Exiting special education at these same points (Zhang & Katsiyannis, 2002)

A statistical measure that might be used to compare the efficacy of programs involves the percentage of children leaving special education. For example, if the percentages of children leaving the three systems were as follows, what explanations might you provide?

1. Early intervention, 35%
2. Preschool, 30%
3. School age, 5%

These numbers support the importance of early intervention and preschool special-education programming. In this scenario, the probability that a child with a disability is going to be declassified once he enters elementary school is very small. Children with disabilities benefit the most when intervention is provided during the formative language years (Gallagher, Swigert, & Baum, 1998). The criticism that special education does not work because there are adolescents who are still in special education is shortsighted. It does work, but it is also time sensitive. Program effectiveness needs to be assessed by many performance indicators, including exit data.

The elementary school population is not a single group of children, although they are aggregated. Early intervention was implemented approximately 10 to 12 years ago. As a result, only some of the younger children in the present 6 to 21 years group had access to and received early intervention services; these children have not been separated from the older children who did not receive services.

Children are not placed in special-education programs without having received a comprehensive multidisciplinary evaluation. That is, a developmental disability has been substantiated by a team of clinical professionals. If there are CLD children in special education who should be in general-education classrooms with typical peers, there is a more parsimonious explanation to the present concern about overrepresentation. The evaluation process, along with the team's decision-making process, may provide some insight. Before the special-education services are reduced, the process by which children are determined to have a disability should be investigated. What does it mean for a child to have a substantiated disability?

Families of linguistically and culturally diverse children may be at a serious disadvantage in elementary school. Professional caseloads and classes are larger in elementary school, and there is significantly less time for team meetings and parent meetings either during or after school. Children with emotional and behavioral deficits who are disruptive often receive the most attention in elementary school. It is important to remember that a medical disability may not affect educational functioning, so some children with medical disabilities may not be eligible to receive special-education services. Although emotional disturbance is recognized as an educational disability, a behavioral disorder is not (Kauffman, 2004). Within behavioral disorders are children with covert and overt conduct disorders, obsessive–compulsive disorders, and the like. These children are not considered to have an educational disability under IDEA, so they are not entitled to services.

The trend is to remove these children and place them in separate programs or to suspend them and let their parents find community-based services (Furney, Hasazi, Clark-Keefe, & Hartnett, 2003). A disproportionate number of CLD children presenting management problems are expelled and drop out of school. These children do not always receive the counseling or academic support services they need in the school system, despite research findings that many children with emotional and behavioral disorders are underachievers (Trout, Nordness, Pierce, & Epstein, 2003). These children are at-risk for delinquency.

The number of individuals in prison who have learning disabilities and have never received special-education services is staggering. Given the general-school problems of truancy, teen pregnancy, violence, academic failure, and teacher turnover and burnout, special-education children, who represent 10% of the student population, may not be priorities (Furney, Hasazi, Clark-Keefe, & Hartnett, 2003; Greene, 2000; Rist, 2000; Stone, 2002; Yanow, 2000).

Elementary School Requirements

A school district's board of education (BOE) is responsible for the education of all children residing in the district. The board of education must identify and register children, appoint a special-education committee (SEC), establish policy for the provision of special-education programs and services, and approve recommendations from its special-education committee. The SEC is responsible for the following:

1. Evaluation of all children suspected of having a disability
2. Classification of children with disabilities

CW 10.2

Use the Companion Website to help you compare information across states:

1. Find statistics related to child poverty rates and homelessness for your state by race and ethnicity. Describe how your state compares to the national averages on these variables.

2. Can you answer the following questions from the data available in your state?

   a. What percentages of CLD children receive early intervention, preschool, and elementary school special-education services?

   b. What percentages of children in the early intervention, preschool, and elementary school special-education systems are CLD?

   c. Why is it difficult to determine what percentage of CLD children receiving early intervention, preschool, and elementary school special-education services are poor and/or from homeless families?

3. Find the following information about children with disabilities for your state's educational system and compare it to data reported from another state:

   a. Percentage of children passing national examinations

   b. Percentage of CLD children passing state and national examinations

   c. Dropout rates for children by cultural group

   d. Graduation rates by cultural group

   e. Percentage of children with disabilities graduating from high school by cultural group

   f. Percentage of children exiting special education from the early intervention, preschool, and school-age systems

4. What position has your state education department taken on inclusion?

5. Identify several Websites that present special-education data and statistics.

3. Development of an individualized educational plan (IEP)
4. Identification of appropriate types and levels of services to meet a child's educational needs
5. Satisfaction of the least restrictive environment (LRE) requirements
6. Identification of an appropriate educational program
7. Review of the child's placement and services

Family Concerns

A special-education committee should consider all evaluative information on a child to make an appropriate decision about his or her label, placement, and educational needs. Notice that the elementary school procedure is similar to the preschool committee process. As parents transition from preschool to elementary school, their relationship with the special-education committee changes (Prendeville & Ross-Allen, 2002). The role of parents in committee decision making is different because (1) the elementary school system is compulsory; (2) special-education costs are paid by school districts (rather than counties, states, and the federal government, which pay for early intervention and preschool special education); (3) many more children in the elementary school system must be evaluated and placed; (4) there may be interpersonal differences between teachers and parents; (5) there may be tensions between parents of children with and without disabilities; (6) the language of IDEA is ambiguous concerning parent participation; and (7) it is less time consuming and contentious for school districts when parents accept the decisions of professionals concerning labels and placements.

Educational Labels

States have a great deal of discretion in determining an appropriate placement for a child with a disability. For the elementary school system, the categorical approach promulgated by the Federal Department of Education (Office of Special Education Programs, OSEP) requires that states use specific disability labels. As noted earlier, there is a great deal of variability from state to state in the percentages of children served in different disability categories.

Table 10.4 presents the number and percentage of elementary school children served by race or ethnicity and disability in 2003. The Individuals with Disabilities Education Act (IDEA) requires that special-education committees classify children and that special-education services be provided. School districts across the United States must utilize these educational labels. The use of labels such as mental retardation and emotional disturbance often creates an adversarial tension within the committee's decision-making process. Some parents are not willing to accept specific labels for their children (Fitch, 2002). If parents can negotiate with their special-education committees to change emotional disturbance to learning disability or attention deficit hyperactivity disorder, they do. Parents request impartial hearings on two issues primarily: placements and labels.

Continuum of Services

Special education can be provided in various types of settings or placements. The special-education committee must consider the issue of least restrictive environment and an appropriate placement that meets a child's individual needs. A child may be educated in any of the following placements depending on her or his educational needs:

- General classroom
- General classroom with a consulting special-education teacher
- Special-education classroom in the school district

TABLE 10.4 Percentage of Children Ages 6 to 21 Served Under IDEA, Part B, by Disability, 2003

State	All Disabilities	Specific Learning Disabilities	Speech or Language Impairments	Mental Retardation	Emotional Disturbance	Multiple Disabilities	Hearing Impairments	Orthopedic Impairments	Other Health Impairments	Visual Impairments	Autism	Deaf-Blindness	Traumatic Brain Injury	Developmental Delay
Alabama	8.46	4.03	1.62	1.26	0.30	0.13	0.09	0.06	0.55	0.04	0.13	0.00	0.03	0.22
Alaska	9.09	4.75	2.05	0.44	0.43	0.25	0.08	0.04	0.45	0.02	0.17	0.01	0.04	0.35
Arizona	7.66	4.31	1.33	0.62	0.57	0.16	0.12	0.05	0.27	0.04	0.16	0.01	0.03	0.00
Arkansas	9.10	3.65	1.75	1.86	0.11	0.20	0.10	0.03	1.18	0.04	0.17	0.00	0.03	0.00
California	7.30	3.97	1.59	0.46	0.32	0.06	0.12	0.14	0.34	0.04	0.23	0.00	0.02	0.00
Colorado	7.15	3.16	1.42	0.35	0.90	0.30	0.12	0.73	0.00	0.03	0.09	0.01	0.04	0.00
Connecticut	8.67	3.55	1.72	0.44	0.95	0.28	0.10	0.02	1.28	0.04	0.27	0.01	0.01	0.00
Delaware	9.14	5.06	0.92	1.23	0.48	0.00	0.14	1.04	0.00	0.03	0.22	0.02	0.00	0.00
District of Columbia	13.43	6.48	1.36	1.63	2.37	0.79	0.11	0.06	0.30	0.03	0.22	0.01	0.02	0.06
Florida	10.28	5.09	2.17	1.11	1.04	0.00	0.10	0.12	0.43	0.03	0.17	0.00	0.02	0.00
Georgia	8.49	2.60	1.82	1.40	1.20	0.00	0.08	0.05	1.01	0.03	0.20	0.00	0.02	0.08
Hawaii	7.74	3.74	0.45	0.73	1.05	0.12	0.14	0.04	0.79	0.02	0.23	0.00	0.03	0.40
Idaho	7.42	3.76	1.37	0.51	0.34	0.14	0.08	0.03	0.49	0.03	0.17	0.00	0.05	0.45
Illinois	9.89	4.90	1.93	0.96	1.04	0.02	0.12	0.09	0.56	0.04	0.21	0.00	0.03	0.00
Indiana	10.67	4.39	2.54	1.53	0.97	0.11	0.13	0.10	0.47	0.06	0.33	0.00	0.04	0.00
Iowa	10.37	5.70	1.09	1.80	1.13	0.06	0.12	0.13	0.07	0.02	0.19	0.00	0.04	0.00
Kansas	8.77	3.79	1.57	0.78	0.60	0.34	0.08	0.06	1.02	0.03	0.16	0.00	0.03	0.32
Kentucky	9.28	1.99	2.02	1.98	0.63	0.40	0.06	0.05	1.17	0.04	0.15	0.00	0.02	0.75
Louisiana	8.39	3.26	1.85	1.02	0.44	0.09	0.12	0.12	0.88	0.04	0.15	0.00	0.03	0.38
Maine	11.89	4.54	2.71	0.34	1.19	1.16	0.09	0.02	1.48	0.03	0.29	0.00	0.03	0.05
Maryland	8.19	3.27	1.78	0.54	0.78	0.42	0.10	0.03	0.87	0.04	0.28	0.00	0.03	0.05
Massachusetts	10.76	5.35	1.26	0.93	1.00	0.37	0.08	0.08	0.42	0.03	0.30	0.03	0.30	0.62
Michigan	9.23	4.18	1.82	1.08	0.85	0.12	0.13	0.37	0.33	0.04	0.27	0.00	0.01	0.03
Minnesota	8.71	3.17	1.40	0.82	1.47	0.03	0.17	0.13	0.89	0.03	0.44	0.00	0.04	0.12
Mississippi	8.52	4.35	2.25	0.72	0.16	0.08	0.09	0.08	0.37	0.04	0.09	0.00	0.02	0.27
Missouri	9.94	4.62	2.33	0.93	0.64	0.08	0.10	0.05	0.90	0.04	0.21	0.00	0.03	0.02
Montana	8.43	4.49	1.66	0.53	0.48	0.25	0.09	0.03	0.71	0.03	0.12	0.00	0.03	0.00
Nebraska	9.89	3.77	2.53	1.34	0.58	0.09	0.15	0.11	0.92	0.05	0.14	0.00	0.05	0.16
Nevada	8.08	4.95	1.26	0.39	0.45	0.16	0.10	0.07	0.46	0.03	0.18	0.00	0.04	0.00

(continued)

TABLE 10.4 *(continued)*

State	All Disabilities	Specific Learning Disabilities	Speech or Language Impairments	Mental Retardation	Emotional Disturbance	Multiple Disabilities	Hearing Impairments	Orthopedic Impairments	Other Health Impairments	Visual Impairments	Autism	Deaf–Blindness	Traumatic Brain Injury	Developmental Delay
New Hampshire	9.98	4.65	1.69	0.34	0.93	0.13	0.09	0.04	1.51	0.04	0.20	0.00	0.02	0.33
New Jersey	11.82	5.74	2.33	0.34	0.70	1.33	0.09	0.03	0.88	0.02	0.26	0.00	0.10	0.00
New Mexico	10.01	5.58	1.82	0.37	0.60	0.22	0.11	0.05	0.60	0.04	0.08	0.00	0.05	0.49
New York	9.41	4.45	1.67	0.36	1.01	0.53	0.13	0.06	0.90	0.04	0.23	0.00	0.03	0.00
North Carolina	9.44	3.80	1.56	1.51	0.55	0.09	0.11	0.06	1.18	0.03	0.22	0.00	0.03	0.28
North Dakota	8.67	3.49	2.30	0.78	0.82	0.00	0.09	0.08	0.72	0.03	0.15	0.00	0.03	0.18
Ohio	9.12	3.67	1.38	1.86	0.70	0.52	0.10	0.09	0.53	0.04	0.20	0.00	0.03	0.00
Oklahoma	10.60	5.79	1.40	0.89	0.60	0.18	0.10	0.05	0.69	0.05	0.12	0.00	0.03	0.69
Oregon	8.82	4.08	2.01	0.56	0.59	0.00	0.10	0.10	0.82	0.04	0.48	0.00	0.04	0.00
Pennsylvania	9.37	5.22	1.43	1.01	0.91	0.10	0.10	0.04	0.25	0.04	0.22	0.00	0.04	0.00
Puerto Rico														
Rhode Island	12.79	6.22	2.47	0.54	1.34	0.13	0.09	0.05	1.66	0.03	0.25	0.00	0.03	0.00
South Carolina	10.69	5.07	2.33	1.58	0.64	0.02	0.13	0.08	0.64	0.04	0.14	0.00	0.02	0.00
South Dakota	8.29	3.93	1.81	0.69	0.47	0.42	0.07	0.05	0.62	0.02	0.18	0.00	0.03	0.00
Tennessee	8.88	3.97	1.93	1.08	0.30	0.13	0.10	0.07	0.82	0.05	0.13	0.00	0.02	0.26
Texas	8.57	4.62	1.32	0.49	0.67	0.15	0.10	0.09	0.87	0.05	0.19	0.00	0.02	0.00
Utah	7.95	4.41	1.49	0.48	0.46	0.21	0.08	0.03	0.35	0.04	0.16	0.01	0.05	0.17
Vermont	9.03	3.20	1.33	0.90	1.50	0.06	0.09	0.06	1.23	0.02	0.21	0.00	0.03	0.39
Virginia	9.58	4.29	1.43	0.85	0.80	0.16	0.08	0.05	1.32	0.03	0.22	0.00	0.02	0.34
Washington	7.98	3.55	1.18	0.41	0.36	0.18	0.09	0.05	1.38	0.02	0.20	0.00	0.03	0.51
West Virginia	12.34	4.89	2.98	2.47	0.61	0.00	0.11	0.05	0.99	0.06	0.14	0.01	0.03	0.00
Wisconsin	8.99	3.90	1.50	0.96	1.29	0.00	0.12	0.09	0.80	0.03	0.26	0.00	0.03	0.01
Wyoming	9.56	4.35	2.25	0.51	0.87	0.08	0.12	0.11	1.03	0.04	0.14	0.00	0.06	0.00
50 States and DC	9.05	4.28	1.70	0.87	0.73	0.20	0.11	0.10	0.68	0.04	0.21	0.00	0.03	0.10

Data based on the December 1, 2003, count, updated as of July 31, 2004.

Source: U.S. Department of Education, Office of Special Education Programs, Data Analysis Systems (DANS).

- Special-education classroom in a neighboring school district
- Private special school
- At home or in a hospital
- State-operated residential care facility

These educational programs provide a range of services along a learning continuum for children with progressive levels of severity. The first placement considered by the committee is a general classroom. If the child requires (1) more intensive individualized instruction and/or (2) rehabilitative services and/or (3) highly structured classroom instruction, other placement options are considered. Although a general classroom is considered to be the least restrictive setting on this continuum, any one of the other settings can be the LRE for a specific child with a disability, given the uniqueness of her or his needs.

Legal Support for Inclusion

The Individuals with Disabilities Education Act (IDEA) and the Americans with Disabilities Act (ADA) both facilitate the inclusion of children with disabilities into educational environments, such as nursery schools, preschools, and child-care programs. Several federal court cases established the framework for school districts to educate children in general education using supplementary aides and services. These cases are particularly interesting, given the diversity and differences among the children and the degree of severity of their disabilities. Because IDEA does not use the term *inclusion*, the Department of Education does not directly define the term. Before the enactment of IDEA, the children in these cases would have received services within special-education classrooms.

Successful inclusion requires major changes in classroom instruction as well as educational reforms.

Tom Watson/Merrill

Full Inclusion

Full inclusionists argue that special education as a parallel but separate system is discriminatory. Children with disabilities are legally and morally entitled to placement within general classrooms (Fitch, 2003). Mainstreaming is based on the concept of learning readiness for a child to benefit from general education. Inclusion is based on social benefit, given the premise that children with and without disabilities benefit socially from their interactions with one another. Many inclusionists argue that the moral principle underlying integration, which is based on civil rights legislation, applies to education. Teachers and peers must accommodate the needs of all children with language, social, emotional, and behavioral disabilities. With the inclusion model, academic readiness or benefit is not a prerequisite to placement in general education. Schools and/or parents can argue for an inclusive placement based on the child's social benefit with typical peers (McLeskey & Waldron, 1996). The definition of social benefit was never formalized by the Department of Education, so it varies from community to community. Figure 10.1 describes the relationship between the child's level of functioning and the need for individualized instruction.

The child with a severe disability needs to be provided with a prescriptive individualized program. The child with severe disabilities and/or complex health-care needs also requires a curriculum that includes intensive therapeutic programming and management instruction (Nolan, Young, Herbert, & Wilding, 2005). This kind of curriculum often focuses on developing prereadiness and basic language, communication, and social skills in a small, self-contained classroom. If the committee places

Child's Level of Functioning	
Severe	Type 1: Physical Mainstreaming Children with disabilities share the same physical environment. This does not ensure that there will be any social interaction between typical children and children with disabilities.
Moderate	Type 2: Physical Social Mainstreaming The contextual setting is structured to facilitate the interactions between children with disabilities and those without. The educational staff provides opportunities for children to interact as peer partners.
Mild	Type 3: Physical Instructional Mainstreaming Typical students and students with disabilities are educated in the same contextual setting. The regular classroom provides an inclusive opportunity for typical children and children with disabilities.

FIGURE 10.1
Relationship Between the Child's Level of Functioning and the Need for Individual Instruction

a child with pervasive learning needs in a general classroom, the teacher and typical peers will have to accommodate by making significant instructional changes. This child's academic and social programming will require strong collaboration between general and special educators, as well as support from typical peers. Full inclusion is not appropriate for all children with disabilities.

At the other end of the developmental continuum is a child with a mild disability (McLeskey & Waldron, 1996; Zigmond, 2001; Zigmond & Baker, 1995). This child can function more independently because his basic developmental skills in language and communication are emerging. The child with a mild disability can socialize and interact within a larger group setting and can readily benefit from interactions with typical peers. He requires less individualized attention and adult-directed instruction. He responds more readily to incidental cues and clues within the social context. He has also acquired an awareness of his own behavior within the social context; he can manage his play interactions with peers. This child presents with emerging self-regulatory behaviors, social judgment, and social awareness. His prereadiness skills may not be as strong as his social skills, but it appears that he can benefit from a more challenging social context with typical peers.

The purpose of special education is to develop programming that meets the individualized needs of each child. It is just as inappropriate to place all children with disabilities in a self-contained class as it is to place all children in an inclusion class. One program cannot fit all children. A full-inclusion model eliminates educational options for children with disabilities and undermines the choices of parents (Tiegerman & Radziewicz, 1998).

The Association for Supervision and Curriculum Development (ASCD) and the National Association of State Boards of Education (NASBE) have advocated in favor of full inclusion. Many educational groups have advocated for dramatic reforms in education that would result in the dismantling of the special-education system that presently exists (Jenkins, 2005). The result would be a single inclusive system of education, providing services to all children within general education (Behrmann, 1993).

When determining the appropriateness of inclusion as an option, it is important to consider not only the general philosophy of inclusion, but also the pragmatic realities and limitations of a general-education classroom: teacher, peers, space, instructional techniques, staff development, and financial resources. In so doing, it becomes critical to focus on the profiles of the children who are being considered for inclusion and not just the issue of social benefit (Tiegerman-Farber & Radziewicz, 1998).

Mainstreaming versus Inclusion

Salend (1994) indicates that the philosophy of mainstreaming is based on the principle of *normalization*. Normalization for the child with disabilities involves the identification of activities, educational experiences, and social interactions that simulate realistic and natural events. This normalization process attempts to provide real-world challenges for children with disabilities. Through these realistic experiences, children can more readily make the transition from institutional and/or self-contained settings to natural, less structured environments (Bogdan & Kugelmass, 1984;

Madden & Slavin, 1983). *Mainstreaming* is a process that incorporates a continuum of learning steps or programming changes that progressively approximate the general-education experience in preparation for placement (see Figure 10.2). Mainstreaming includes a series of inclusion steps that takes time and can be achieved over months or even years. Successful mainstreaming can involve either academic or nonacademic experiences. The basic assumption is that the child must be prepared and ready for the next step, which is more challenging.

Special Education Committees (SECs) consider placement options from the most specialized (self-contained) to the least specialized (general-education) settings. As the child moves along the placement continuum from year to year, the programmatic curriculum and instruction change to prepare the child socially and academically for a general classroom with typical peers. The last step on the special-education continuum is full mainstreaming, or inclusion. Here the child spends a majority of his instructional day in the general classroom learning alongside typical peers. Ongoing monitoring from

---

Step 1: Self-Contained Only
- Small class with 6 children with disabilities
- Paraprofessional teacher
- Special-education teacher
- High degree of structure and individualized attention
- Multiple individual and related services

Step 2: Self-Contained: Mainstream for Lunch (nonacademic instructional area)
- Larger class with 15 children with disabilities
- Special-education teacher
- Consulting regular education teacher
- Less structure, more group work, and more socialization
- Limited related services provided in classroom (push-in service)
- General-education experience (lunchroom with typical peers)

Step 3: Partial Mainstream
- Larger class with 18 children with disabilities
- Special-education teacher in the morning only
- Afternoon mainstream in general education with typical children for nonacademic subjects: lunch, gym, music, assembly, art, and the like

Step 4: Full Mainstream
- Special-education class first period with special-education teacher
- General-education classes in most academic areas and all nonacademic areas
- Special-education resource room in academic areas
- Self-contained instruction in subjects where individualized small-group learning is critical (e.g., math)
- Special-education class last period of day with special-education teacher to ensure children have appropriate homework assignments and classmates

---

FIGURE 10.2
Mainstream Continuum

educational specialists will determine if the child is ready to be declassified or still needs supplementary aides and services.

Note that when the child with a disability is mainstreamed for lunch, physical education, music, art, and the like, the inclusion process actually begins. Inclusion takes several forms and also increases along the placement continuum. Mainstreaming strives for the instructional readiness of children with disabilities before they enter the general education classroom. At each step, there is an inherent responsibility to provide more challenging learning experiences that require that classroom organization, curricula, and instructional techniques be adapted to benefit the child. Inclusion does not require academic readiness for placement in a general-education classroom. The purpose of inclusion is to provide the child with a disability the opportunity to be educated along with typical peers (Freeman & Alkin, 2000).

Least Restrictive Environment

The *least restrictive environment* (LRE) is related to, but is not the same as, mainstreaming. Briefly, LRE is the *mechanism* by which the child's individual needs are matched with an educational placement, whereas mainstreaming consists of a *series* of placement steps. Because LRE has major implications for child placement and educational decision making, the term *least restrictive environment* is often open for interpretation (Taylor, 1988). School districts use the *meaning* of LRE to determine a child's appropriate placement. Changes in educational needs should be reflected in what constitutes the LRE for a specific child with a disability. Figure 10.3 describes some factors that may influence the special-education committee's decision about appropriate placement.

Factors such as social problems, pervasive language disorders, and management needs present significant challenges to a general-education classroom. However, if a child has high-level communication and socialization skills and mild behavioral needs, the child can be more readily included in a general class with typical peers (Smoot, 2004). The special-education committee tries to link a child's characteristics with his or her educational needs to identify a placement that will appropriately address these needs. In making its decision, the committee attempts to construct a "learning environment on paper" that will benefit the child and then identify a program that meets these educational criteria.

Maria Martinez

Maria Martinez is notified by a psychologist from her local school district that José needs to be evaluated by the school district's Special Education Committee (SEC). José is evaluated by a school psychologist, a speech-language pathologist, a special-education teacher, and an occupational therapist prior to the formal meeting. Maria is fortunate because the school district provides both a bilingual psychologist and SLP. At the committee meeting, the school psychologist translates the reports into

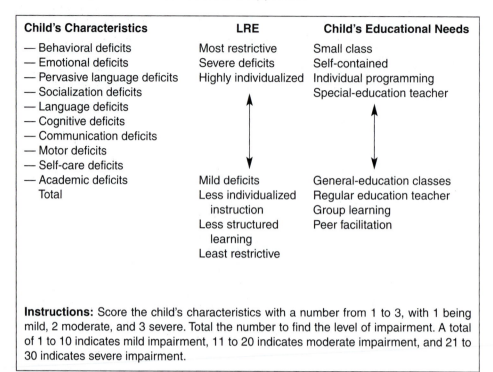

Child's Characteristics	LRE	Child's Educational Needs
— Behavioral deficits	Most restrictive	Small class
— Emotional deficits	Severe deficits	Self-contained
— Pervasive language deficits	Highly individualized	Individual programming
— Socialization deficits		Special-education teacher
— Language deficits		
— Cognitive deficits		
— Communication deficits		
— Motor deficits		
— Self-care deficits		
— Academic deficits	Mild deficits	General-education classes
Total	Less individualized instruction	Regular education teacher
	Less structured learning	Group learning
	Least restrictive	Peer facilitation

Instructions: Score the child's characteristics with a number from 1 to 3, with 1 being mild, 2 moderate, and 3 severe. Total the number to find the level of impairment. A total of 1 to 10 indicates mild impairment, 11 to 20 indicates moderate impairment, and 21 to 30 indicates severe impairment.

FIGURE 10.3
Characteristics and Educational Needs of Children with Special Needs

Spanish for Maria Martinez. The translation of the clinical and technical information is complicated and time consuming, resulting in a meeting that lasts over 2 hours.

After the evaluations are presented, Maria is asked if she wants to ask any questions about them. Because Maria feels very uncomfortable about her understanding of the technical information, she does not ask many questions. The committee then discusses various placements and educational options. Maria is not clear about the various school placements and services that are being discussed. The committee indicates that José is being classified multiply disabled and is going to be placed in an inclusion class with typical peers. This class will consist of 18 children, 12 without and 6 with developmental disabilities (mental retardation, learning disabilities, and autism). There will be two teachers (general and special education) and a paraprofessional.

Maria feels that this program is similar to José's preschool program. She does not understand why José has to be labeled and wants to know if the label will appear on all of José's records? She also wants to know who else will see José's evaluation reports. The committee chairperson, Dr. Joseph Smith, gives Maria a copy of the State Education Department's guidebook for parents printed in Spanish, which describes the special-education procedures and her parental rights. Maria asks if she can speak to someone after she reads the guidebook. The committee agrees that the school psychologist, Dr. Carmen Sanchez, will meet with Maria to answer her questions. There are many new professionals at the meeting and Maria is feeling overwhelmed. José's mother describes her feelings and concerns in Box 10.1.

BOX 10.1

*I didn't say anything at this meeting because I didn't know anything. I wish the profession-
als spoke to me after their evaluations to give me some time to think about José's problems. It wasn't helpful to get a parent guidebook after the meeting; I should've gotten it
before the meeting. I'm not a teacher. I'm concerned about his label and what it's going to
mean when other people see it. If teachers think José is autistic, they're going to treat him
that way. I want José to be treated like a normal boy. I would like to see his new classroom.
How can I put José someplace without seeing the other children?*

Maria Martinez

Use the Companion Website to help you answer the following questions:

1. How are Maria's reflections on her CSE experience relevant to systemic problems
   within special education?

2. What role should the SLP have in discussing educational labels with parents in terms
   of explaining what they mean?

Katherine Whiteside

Katherine Whiteside has several meetings with her committee. In this particular
school district, some members of the preschool education committee also serve as
members of the school-age committee. Katherine wants Kaitlyn to receive special-
education services at the Mission School with other children who are deaf. When
Kaitlyn was in preschool and the preschool committee recommended an early
childhood program with related services, Katherine requested an impartial hearing. Fortunately, Katherine and the preschool committee finally agreed on the Mission School for preschool and Katherine withdrew her request. Now appearing at
the Special Education Committee meeting are some of the preschool committee
people who were originally opposed to placement in the Mission School for
the Deaf.

Should Kaitlyn continue in a program with children who are deaf? Is this the
least restrictive environment? Because the school district does not provide separate programming for children with hearing loss, the school district proposes a
half-day special-education program with partial mainstreaming. In the morning,
Kaitlyn would be placed in a noncategorical special-education class with children
having a variety of disabilities, many of them considered learning disabled. In the
afternoon, Kaitlyn would be mainstreamed with typical peers. The Special Education Committee does not recommend a continuation at the Mission School.
Katherine reiterates her concerns that Kaitlyn's hearing loss is severe enough that
she needs to receive educational services in a school for the deaf. She also argues
that Kaitlyn has become proficient in sign language and that she needs to

BOX 10.2

Well, here we go, again, the same people, the same issues, the same agenda. If I hadn't argued so adamantly about Kaitlyn's preschool placement, I wouldn't have a precedent for Kaitlyn's placement in a school for the deaf. Kaitlyn is deaf. She should be a member of the Deaf Community. She needs to have friends who are deaf and feel like other children who are deaf. They think Kaitlyn is handicapped. I don't think Kaitlyn is handicapped, I think Kaitlyn can't hear. In the Deaf Community, Kaitlyn will be normal. She'll have a language. She'll be accepted and have lifelong friends who are deaf. It doesn't matter to me if they think that they're right. She's my daughter and I know what's best for her. They don't live with her. At the end of the day, if they make a mistake, they go home at night to their families. Kaitlyn is going to the school for the deaf even if I have to go to court.

Katherine Whiteside

 Use the Companion Website to help you answer the following questions:

1. How has the role of the parent changed from the preschool system to the school-age system?

2. How far should the school-age system go to accommodate the viewpoints of parents in deciding placement issues?

communicate, socialize, and make friends with other children who are deaf and use sign language. In Box 10.2, Kaitlyn explains her opposition to the committee's decisions.

Camille St. James

Camille St. James is notified by her special-education committee that Jeffrey needs to be evaluated to determine his eligibility for special-education services in public school. Jeffrey is attending a local early childhood program and receiving speech and language therapy services along with play therapy. Camille meets with a psychologist on a monthly basis to evaluate Jeffrey's behavior and to modify the behavioral management goals on his preschool IEP.

The results of the psychological evaluation indicate that Jeffrey's cognitive abilities are in the average range, with a discrepancy between verbal and nonverbal functioning. Dr. Gina Brown, the school's speech-language pathologist, informs the committee that Jeffrey has speech and language delays, particularly in the areas of phonological processing, morphosyntactic development, and auditory processing. Dr. Brown agrees with the school psychologist that Jeffrey is at-risk for having a learning disability. The committee recommends a general-education kindergarten program with individual speech and language therapy as a related service two times per week. The school

BOX 10.3

I have really been through a lot with Jeffrey and I'm still concerned that he has a problem. I don't think it's my imagination; I see Jeffrey with other children. He has a lot of problems in the early childhood program with his letters and sounds. At times, Jeffrey gets very frustrated and throws everything on the floor. He also knows that he sounds funny and that his speech is different. At times he doesn't answer even when he knows the answer. When he doesn't answer, they think he doesn't know. I don't want them to think he's retarded. I'm not happy with the "wait and see" attitude. I don't want to wait until it's a problem. I want them to do something now so that he doesn't have to fail later.

Camille St. James

Use the Companion Website to help you answer the following questions:

1. When a mistake is made in placement decisions or recommended services, will compensatory services moving forward be sufficient? Support your answer with relevant research.

2. What could the SLP as a member of the CSE say to Camille?

psychologist indicates that Jeffrey's behavior has improved dramatically and that he has benefited from his interactions with typical peers in the early childhood program.

Camille indicates that she is very pleased with Jeffrey's progress, but expresses her concern that Jeffrey's poor speech negatively affects his social relationships. She tells the committee that other children are teasing Jeffrey about his speech. Camille is worried that his speech problems will interfere with the development of literacy skills.

Dr. Michael Jones, the chairperson of the committee, indicates that the district will monitor both Jeffrey's reading development and his social development. He stresses that, if and when Jeffrey's speech becomes a social or a learning problem in school, the committee will discuss additional services. Jeffrey's mother expresses her concerns with the latest evaluation in Box 10.3.

SUMMARY

The school-age system is the largest of the three educational systems and provides services for the most children and for the longest period of time (from 6 to 21 years). The primary focus of public elementary and secondary schools is not special education—it is general education. Children with developmental disabilities represent anywhere from 8% to 12% of the student population. Many state education departments provide evaluations on performance indicators, such as the percentage of third-, fifth-, and eighth-grade children in general education who pass state or national examinations for reading, mathematics, world history, and science. The quality of a community public school is based on the percentage of students passing competitive academic examinations, graduating from high school, and attending colleges and/or universities.

A "good" school district is *not* defined by the number of children with disabilities either exiting special-education programs or graduating with diplomas to attend college. The public school system focuses on general-education programming for typical children; special education remains a parallel program within general education.

We want to highlight this point because of a growing concern. Special education represents a disproportionate part of every public school and state education budget. Some stakeholders argue that public schools should make accommodations in instruction, teaching schedules, and classroom organization by committing additional resources to include children with a wide range of disabilities (Furney, Hasazi, Clark-Keefe, & Hartnett, 2003). However, there is no consensus among the stakeholders, the parents of children with disabilities, parents of typical children, regular and special-education teachers, administrators, community boards of education, and politicians, about where the additional funds should come from (McLeskey & Waldron, 2000; Shanker, 1995).

The issue of the individual needs of children with disabilities may become relativized by typical students' needs, limited fiscal resources, unions, teachers' attitudes or preferences, parents' attitudes or preferences, and school programs such as band, athletics, and foreign languages. What is appropriate for children with disabilities? This is answered differently by the various stakeholders. There has been very little dissension from parents of typical children. Some schools are experimenting with different inclusion models in elementary school, (e.g., eight typical children and eight children with developmental disabilities in a general classroom). The question arises as to whether this is still a general-education classroom? When the dynamics of general-education instruction change and the number of children with disabilities increases, parents of typical children may become more vocal.

What are the instructional implications for academic classes in middle and high schools when children with different types of disabilities are included? How should teachers and parents be involved in the decision to place children with disabilities in general-education classrooms? The educational reform movement advocates the reorganization of public-school education with parental choice as a key component (Vassallo, 2000). Keep the issue of reform in mind as you read the next chapters. What does reform mean for teachers, families, and children?

Language Disorders in Elementary School

Chapter Objectives

After studying this chapter, you should be able to answer the following questions:

1. What are the language characteristics presented by the three children? What are their language differences?

2. What are the advantages of being in an inclusive setting for each child? Are there disadvantages?

3. How does each child's language disorder affect the development of conversational and narrative skills, and how does this in turn influence social–emotional relationships?

4. What kinds of modifications might be made to accommodate a child with a disability?

5. What are some reasons why children with Asperger syndrome may be diagnosed late or misdiagnosed?

This is the third chapter on language disorders, and it describes each of the children now in elementary school. The issue for our children in this part involves how each child's evolving language characteristics affect the development of early literacy skills and their ability to function within a general-education classroom.

The No Child Left Behind Act (NCLB), enacted in 2001, challenges school districts across the United States to ensure that student achievement improves. It underscores the importance of standards and the delineation of state content standards. Across the nation, individual states are measuring individual student progress through mandated testing in specific grades. Just like typical learners, children with special needs are expected to take these tests and demonstrate academic proficiency. It is necessary that teachers of special-needs children not only be aware of their state's academic content standards, but also be able to modify their teaching techniques, strategies, and materials to accommodate the individual learning styles of all the children within their classroom.

Including children with special needs can be a goal and a challenge. The school reform movement that began more than 20 years ago heralded the cry for ambitious school improvement goals. With this in mind, consider our three children, José, Jeffrey, and Kaitlyn, and how they fare in this era of school achievement accountability. Will they be able to achieve within their educational settings? Will they develop the literacy skills necessary for future academic learning? Will they meet the skill and knowledge standards mandated by their school district and state? Will teachers be able to implement their IEP goals and meet federal benchmarks for adequate yearly progress?

Autism Spectrum Disorders: José

Maria Martinez

When José starts elementary school, Maria is working as a nanny to help other members of her family come to the United States. Maria's employer is sponsoring her so that she can apply for a resident alien card to begin the long application process for citizenship. Eventually, several members of her family rent a house near the church she attends in a culturally diverse community. José's father, Raul, is working as a gardener in a landscaping business that was started by an Italian-American family who came to the United States two decades earlier. Raul talks to the owner of the business, Carmine Mariano, about starting his own business. The two men are good friends, and both express their hopes and expectations for their children to go to school—their daughters to become teachers and their sons to take over the business. Raul Martinez and Carmine Mariano acknowledge that their families have many more material conveniences and their children are growing up with very different values and expectations. The children speak English rather than the "old language," and are not very interested in their parents' cultural heritages. There is not only a generation gap, but also a social-value difference between parents and children.

Maria would like José to go to parochial school, but St. Christopher's does not accept children with disabilities. Maria travels by bus everyday to her employer's home in the city, so someone in the family picks up José from school at 3 p.m. because the afterschool program cannot accommodate a child with autism spectrum disorders. Work is hard and life is difficult, but the Martinez family feels safe from war and poverty. Everyone is working and family members help one another emotionally, spiritually, and financially.

Maria is grateful for all that she has accomplished over the past 5 years. She now understands that José has autism, but she sees a difference, not a disability. The success of the Martinez family can be explained by individual and family resilience, the ability to bounce back after defeat and face life stressors with a positive, adaptive perspective. The Martinez family has a strong value system that includes a belief in self, a strong work ethic, the motivation to achieve, religious beliefs, the commitment to and cooperation with family, and a strong cultural identification with the Latino community (Hacker, 1992). José's mother describes José's problem behavior in school in Box 11.1.

Definition

Despite the diagnosis of autism, by the time José reaches kindergarten, his language develops so significantly that the school district's special-education committee changes his classification to multiply disabled (language impaired–autistic). The issue discussed by professionals at the SEC meeting involves José's educational classification. Current conceptions of the spectrum of autistic disorders propose that there is a continuum of severity in children, from severe mental retardation and absence of speech to average intelligence and typical structural (but not pragmatic) language at the higher end of the ASD continuum. Asperger syndrome (AS), which is at the higher end of the ASD continuum, includes children who have normal intelligence

BOX 11.1

I always knew that José was a bright boy, but he doesn't have any friends to play with at home or at school. There have been several incidents in which José has done some bad things because other children have told him to do these things. José gets frustrated and anxious when other children approach him. He has had tantrums in school and sometimes has hit children. Once José was suspended for 3 days because the principal was concerned about the other children's safety. Why should José be suspended for acting like a disabled child? He wasn't making fun of other children. José was teased and he overreacted. I don't think any normal person would react calmly to being teased. How long could anyone stay calm and not get angry? I get angry thinking about this. He got angry—he's supposed to get angry—that's an appropriate reaction. His inability to control his anger is part of his disability. The other children weren't suspended because they did not hit, and they said they wouldn't bother José anymore. This isn't fair treatment. I don't want José to be victimized anymore.

Maria Martinez

Use the Companion Website to help you discuss the following questions:

1. What do you think about Maria Martinez's feelings? Is she being realistic about her expectations of teachers and typical children?

2. What would you say to Maria about how José is doing in class if you were a speech-language pathologist working for the school district?

and whose speech developed at the age-expected times (Folstein, 1999). Wiig (1997) defines the *autism spectrum* as "a group of disorders of development with life-long effects that have in common a triad of impairments in: social interaction, communication, imagination and behavior. It can be found together with any level of ability, from profound general learning disability to average or even superior cognitive skill." Similar to autism, Asperger syndrome (AS) is characterized by significant deficits in peer relationships, social reciprocity, nonverbal behavior, and emotional relatedness. The child with Asperger's syndrome can verbally describe detailed information on a limited set of topics (e.g., dinosaurs, geography, or cartoons), but cannot have a conversation, tell a story, or talk about his feelings (Safran, 2002b).

Approximately 72% of children with Asperger syndrome do not receive a formal diagnosis until after the age of 5 because their sometimes subtle differences are attributed to shyness and/or immaturity. As a result, some children with autism spectrum disorders may go undiagnosed or misdiagnosed during the formative period of early development (Cohen, Davine, Horodezsky, Lipsett, & Isaacson, 1993). Many children with AS are not diagnosed initially with AS; instead, 92% carry other diagnoses or educational labels. Many times the diagnosis or educational label was attention-deficit-hyperactivity disorder (20%), other health impaired (15%), learning disabilities (12%), and emotional disturbance (10%) (Church, Alisanski, & Amanullah, 2000).

Prevalence

The prevalences for children with autism spectrum disorders is cited as 4.0 cases per 1000 and 2.7 cases per 1000 for children with Asperger syndrome (Bertrand et al., 2001). The cited prevalences appear to be higher in some communities (e.g., Brick Township, New Jersey) than in others.

Pragmatic Abilities

José's echolalia now occurs only in situations in which there is a communication breakdown. This behavior indicates that he does not understand the interactional exchange, so he does the best he can—he repeats the speaker's input. José can be hyperverbal to the point of being intrusive. Often he talks when other children are speaking, and he continues to talk even when other children are not listening. He cannot modulate his vocal intensity, so his voice is either too loud or too soft. He frequently needs to be reminded to use "his inside voice." José manifests a number of autistic characteristics that have been noted in the literature (Freeman, Cronin, & Candela, 2002; Tiegerman-Farber, 2002a). José does not use appropriate inflections, so his voice can sound unemotional, robotic, and flat. He does not use gestural behaviors either appropriately or effectively. At times José misses ongoing social cues that require an integration and interpretation of contextual events. He is not always able to anticipate what is going to happen, and he rarely understands the consequences of his behaviors in relation to his peers.

José's movements are clumsy; his body orientation is asymmetrical; his posture is stiff and his eye contact is variable. He does not understand the proxemic rules related to communication, so he is either too close to or too far from his listener. At times José is not engaged with peers and activities because he sings, engages in self-talk, makes noises, and comments during classroom lessons. José is socially inappropriate, not just socially immature. He does not pay attention and follow the social rules and routines within the class. The other children were initially frightened by José's unusual behaviors, but eventually accepted his "weird" differences.

CW 11.1

Use the Companion Website to help you discuss the following:

1. What formalized tests can be used to evaluate higher-functioning children along the autism spectrum continuum? Try to identify formalized tests that can be used to evaluate higher-ordered *pragmatic* functioning in children. If you cannot find any, what informal methodologies can be used in natural contexts to describe pragmatic functioning?

2. Develop a social context in which José might interact with a peer, and describe his pragmatic functioning within this interactional exchange.

3. In the early intervention and preschool sections, José was described by means of a strengths-based approach. Develop a description of José's pragmatic abilities using a strengths-based approach.

Semantic Abilities

Ogletree and Fischer (1995) note that the focus of research has shifted from the structural aspects of language (i.e., phonology, morphology, and syntax) to the development of meaning within social contexts. Brook and Bowler (1992) list some of the semantic–pragmatic deficits that autism spectrum disorders present:

- Confusion specific to the intent of communicative acts
- Problems encoding meaning relevant to conversation
- Difficulty with verbal and nonverbal cues of partners
- Problems initiating or responding to questions
- Impaired language comprehension
- Literal interpretations of verbal messages
- Poor turn-taking and topic maintenance
- Inappropriate speech volume and intonational patterns
- Semantic confusion specific to temporal sequencing
- Poor sense of semantic relationships
- Low rates of conversational repairs
- Providing too little or too much information to conversational partners

José's knowledge of a limited number of topics is both extensive and impressive. José can describe minute details, facts, and information about dinosaurs, cars, and plants, but his knowledge is not shared to engage others in reciprocal interaction. José cannot modify his language to the requirements of a conversation or to the needs of a listener. He reproduces entire chunks of information from documentaries and books without analyzing or understanding what they mean. Children comment that "José is a talking book."

José's monologues are often disruptive to ongoing discussions occurring naturally in the general-education classroom. The group learning process in class requires moment-to-moment communicative modifications between children and teachers. The teacher and the other children are distracted by José's inability to control himself as their attention shifts from the lesson to José. Dynamically, the teacher and children find it difficult to resume their lesson, often forgetting what was said and who was speaking.

Because José cannot modify his behaviors to the communicative needs of the group, the learning process in class needs to be modified by his teachers and peers to keep José appropriately engaged in academic activities. José's verbal monologues represent one form of his many rituals. These monologues can be inappropriately interpreted as advanced knowledge and vocabulary (Frith & Happe, 1999). There is an unfortunate assumption that sophisticated knowledge reflects a commensurate social ability, which results in the conclusion that a child with autism is being deliberately annoying (Safran, 2002b).

Cognitive Abilities

With autism, a deficit in cognitive functioning often results in an associated diagnosis of mental retardation. With Asperger syndrome, cognitive functioning is usually within the average range when intelligence is measured by traditional IQ assessments.

CW 11.2

Use the Companion Website to help you discuss the following:

1. What informal methodologies can be used in natural contexts to describe semantic functioning?

2. Develop a semantic profile for José; develop a description of José's semantic skills by means of a strengths-based approach.

3. Contrast the use of the two approaches (deficit vs. strengths-based) in profiling José's semantic development as a school-age child.

Although some children with ASD appear to develop an interpersonal mental representation between the ages of 9 and 14, it is only developed after repeated learning (Frith & Happe, 1999). Deficits in theory-of-mind, referred to as *mindblindness* by Baron-Cohen (1995, 1997), provide an explanation for many of the difficulties presented by children with autism spectrum disorders in elementary school (Myles & Southwick, 1999). This mindblindness is characterized by the following:

- Inability to understand the intentions of others: misinterpretation of another person's social behavior and/or linguistic meaning
- Inability to appropriately code personal and interpersonal emotions: inappropriate emotional reactions
- Lack of self-awareness as a social communicator: lack of self-insight, self-reflection, and self-concept as "I am"
- Inability to express empathetic and sympathetic feelings toward others
- Lack of understanding concerning how personal behaviors affect the feelings and social functioning of others
- Inability to internalize higher-order rules critical to defining cultural boundaries or parameters of appropriate group social behaviors
- Inability to understand verbal and nonverbal social cues: poor social judgment often results in the child appearing as awkward, clumsy, immature, and boorish
- Inability to understand the nonliteral aspects of semantic meaning: deriving concrete and literal interpretations
- Inability to anticipate what other people would do based on past experience, personal knowledge, and environmental or contextual factors

Social and Emotional Abilities

Children with autism spectrum disorders have difficulty relating to and interacting with other communicators, peers, and adults in social environments (Buschbacher & Fox, 2003). Because communication and social learning involve verbal and nonverbal reciprocal exchanges, José's behavior sometimes negatively affects the emotions of his parents and peers (Tiegerman-Farber & Radziewicz, 1998). Socialization implies reciprocity,

CW 11.3

Use the Companion Website to help you discuss the following:

1. What informal methodologies can be used in natural contexts to describe José's ability to take the perspective of another person?

2. Contrast the use of the two approaches (deficit vs. strengths-based) in profiling José's cognitive development as a school-age child.

3. How might typical peers react to and interact with José in class, given his cognitive problems?

Laura Bolesta / Merrill

"Mindblindness" presents a significant barrier to the social awareness of children with autism as they interact with their peers. So inappropriate behaviors may not really reflect oppositional behaviors.

so there is expectation of a reaction or response from José. When he does not respond to his mother or peers, they may experience feelings of rejection and frustration.

Lainhart (1999) indicates that children with autism spectrum disorders may have problems of mood and thought. Parents and siblings of children with ASD may also experience affective difficulties because of the stress and anxiety related to caring for the child with ASD (Forest, Horner, Lewis-Palmer, & Todd, 2004). José's inability to share his feelings with his family and peers deprives José of a basic intimacy with and connection to other human beings.

The relationship between language and behavior has recently received a great deal of attention, given the increasing demand for behavioral intervention programs and treatments (Lovass & Buch, 1997). Some behavioral programs emphasize the primacy of behavior. Behavioral intervention programs are developed, given the underlying premise that children exhibiting noncompliant behaviors are oppositional. However, Gallagher (1997) believes that some children's noncompliance could be due to their inability to understand instructions or directions or to use language to appropriately seek clarifications.

Intrapersonal and interpersonal functioning are interrelated and language dependent. José's limited emotional vocabulary negatively affects his ability to control his emotions and regulate his own behaviors in the classroom, lunchroom, and gym. His emotional and behavioral responses need to be viewed by his teachers as a function of his pragmatic and semantic language deficits. Current studies emphasize the critical role language serves in facilitating emotional and behavioral functioning (Gallagher, 1996; Prizant et al., 1990).

Because José cannot talk about his thoughts, he either over- or underreacts to classroom changes and transitions. His difficulty in interpreting verbal and/or nonverbal behaviors makes him appear to be unsympathetic and uninterested when a peer is hurt. He does not respond appropriately when other children tease him or make him the target of their jokes. Sometimes children encourage José to do and/or say inappropriate things, which they think is funny and he does not understand.

José, like other children on the autism spectrum, is easily overwhelmed by sensory stimulation and often becomes anxious, hyperactive, and emotionally reactive when unanticipated outcomes occur or routines are changed (Olney, 2000). Emotional meltdowns are usually preceded by increased hand-flapping, humming, and self-talk. Children with autism require careful instructional preparations for transitions and changes to avoid emotional outbursts (Tonge, Brereton, Gray, & Einfield, 1999). José's social anxieties result in an avoidance of new experiences, creating a vicious cycle that does not allow for adaptive learning. The relationship between anxiety and negative peer relationships can be explained by social deficits in children with ASD (Bellini, 2004; Ginsburg, LaGreca, & Silverman, 1998).

To protect José from becoming a target, his teachers prepare the typical students for his idiosyncratic and inappropriate behaviors, as well as for *their* responsibilities as supportive models for José. Connor (2000) suggests developing a peer-training program that can be implemented by school staff for the child with autism and his peer group to teach social behaviors and to avert possible abuse problems.

CW 11.4

Use the Companion Website to help you discuss the following:

1. What informal methodologies can be used by the SLP in natural contexts to assess social and emotional functioning?

2. Contrast the use of the two approaches (deficit vs. strengths-based) in profiling José's social–emotional development as a school-age child.

Academic Abilities

Within the classroom, José has difficulty paying attention, listening, and comprehending information that the teacher presents in front of the room. He does significantly better when he works individually with teachers and therapists. In a group learning situation, which requires self-regulation, monitoring, and control, José loses focus and begins to sing or recite memorized information. José exhibits compulsive tendencies when he organizes his food, objects of interest, clothes, and school materials; this rigid but self-imposed structure provides recognition, emotional control, and security for José. José does not "know" what to do to reorganize his social behavior, language, and emotional reactions during transitions. He does not have the conceptual skills to understand what is happening around him or the executive functions to organize his behavior in the classroom.

Despite José's intellectual abilities, he exhibits learning disabilities that limit his comprehension of oral and written language. José does not understand idiomatic expressions or jokes. He cannot problem solve by adapting his behavior to manage his escalating emotional anxiety. Although José is hyperverbal, he has difficulty interpreting oral language and using his verbal skills to think critically.

José is hyperlectic with an advanced reading decoding level. Hyperlexia occurs along a continuum and is described as a precocious reading ability in children with developmental disabilities that exceeds both abilities in other areas and expectations for children of their age (Kupperman, 1997). This reading ability often occurs without comprehension and is referred to as a *splinter skill*, which appears to be related to a gestalt processing style (Tiegerman-Farber, 2002a).

José is hyperlectic and reads without comprehension. His visual recognition of words does not enable him to recognize the same word when it is presented auditorily. José has difficulty with the development of narrative skills, so it is not surprising that, although he can memorize and repeat a story, he cannot answer inferential questions about what he has read. He cannot creatively "tell" or "make up" a story about fictional characters, nor can he generalize his textbook knowledge to solve daily social problems.

By the time José is in third grade, he still does not understand his role as a communicator, so he does not use language as a tool to expand his social knowledge. José is still unaware of social rules, as well as the subtle, polite requirements of social behavior. José does not function well in a traditional classroom that is structured to provide teacher-directed lectures to children who are seated either in rows or small groups. The traditional classroom configuration is based on the assumption that children have internalized the specific regulatory skills that allow them to sit, attend, and listen in a classroom (Jewett et al., 1998).

José's fact-based knowledge is further enhanced by his memory skills and further impaired by his conceptual deficits. As typical children get older, there is an assumption that factual knowledge will serve to develop abstract abilities. So, as children progress through elementary school, there is a shift from (1) literal to inferential, (2) knowledge acquisition to information application, and (3) specific to generalized abilities (Kemp & Carter, 2005). In elementary school, which emphasizes academic knowledge, children learn the rules to read and then read to learn. José's typical peers are learning to read in order to use reading as a tool for further learning in academic subjects such as history and science.

José does not understand that reading is an extension of language and a conceptual tool that facilitates further acquisition of knowledge. José needs intensive teacher-directed instructions to remain on-task. Whereas reading is an analytical and interpretive process for typical children, José continues to memorize large chunks of information. While discussing historical events, José's teachers often encourage the children to relate their experiences to historical figures and fictional characters (i.e., extrapolate from a personal frame of reference to a global, conceptual perspective). José's deficits in theory-of-mind affect his ability to *conceptualize* information that limits his thinking to a concrete level of understanding.

Because José does not have an internal locus of control, his learning problems are heightened by children's discussions, movements around the room, and transitions. At these times he may be removed from the group and placed in the back of the classroom with an individual aide. Educational appropriateness *requires* that instructional and contextual variables be modified for José to maintain him in a general setting with typical peers. However, instructional changes can only be tailored to the needs of children with autism when teachers understand their unique learning requirements (Bullard, 2004). José requires the support of an individual paraprofessional who travels with him from class to class and acts as a scribe in each class by taking notes for him. At the end of the day, José goes to a resource room class, and his special-education teacher reviews the notes with him and helps him organize his homework assignments for the next day. Because José is anxious in a large-group situation, he is sometimes given the choice of going to the computer lab instead of to a general assembly or other schoolwide activity. José is taught to "use his words" to signal his emotional distress, rather than deteriorating to the point of a tantrum and an emotional meltdown.

CW 11.5

Use the Companion Website to help you discuss the following:

1. Describe tests that have been specifically designed to evaluate reading and writing skills in children with autism spectrum disorders.

2. Develop a profile describing José's reading and writing deficits as a third-grader.

3. Contrast the use of the two approaches (deficit vs. strengths-based) in profiling José's academic development as a third-grade child.

4. Identify several studies that describe instructional accommodations for children with autism spectrum disorders, and describe what else can be done to maintain José in a general-education class.

Specific Language Impairment (SLI): Jeffrey

Camille St. James

Camille is happy in her new marriage to Kaneer and is willing to be an involved mother for his children. She has finished her educational training and is a medical technician. Kaneer's relationship with Jeffrey is more complicated, because Jeffrey has not been raised with a father in the house. Jeffrey has never competed with anyone for his mother's attention, and now his mother has a husband and two other children, Chantel and Christian. Camille and Kaneer move to their own home. The new household is more organized, and the strict rules present some significant problems for Jeffrey. The transition to a new family life is difficult for all the children, but especially Jeffrey. He refuses to listen to Kaneer, and his behavior and academic work deteriorate in school. He is oppositional with his teachers and aggressive toward his peers. Camille and Kaneer argue about how to manage Jeffrey's behavior and finally agree to consult a school psychologist.

Camille and Kaneer's new family requires a great adjustment, since Kaneer has a different parenting style and much less tolerance for Jeffrey's oppositional behavior. The couple cannot expect Chantel and Christian to respect house rules, but allow Jeffrey to follow a different set of rules. Camille and Kaneer agree that this is not fair to any of the children, especially Jeffrey. Jeffrey's mother describes her feelings at this time in Box 11.2.

Pragmatic Abilities

Initially, Jeffrey's language deficits are viewed as behavioral difficulties, with management problems originating at home. Over time, Jeffrey internalizes the peer rejection

Laura Bolesta / Merrill

Children with specific language impairment often miss classroom information in a traditional instructional setting. Classroom procedures should be changed to accommodate their learning needs.

BOX 11.2

I always knew that there was something wrong with Jeffrey. There were so many things he did not understand. I knew Jeffrey was not a bad boy, but everyone said he would grow out of it. If Jeffrey had gotten early intervention services years ago, he would not have these problems now. So what can I do about that mistake now? Jeffrey can't read because he doesn't understand what he hears. He's like a child with hearing problems, but because he could talk his problems were ignored. How can he read if he doesn't hear the sounds in words? It might have been better if Jeffrey had been deaf, because then his problem would have been identified early and he would've gotten the appropriate services. I bet children with hearing problems do better than children like Jeffrey.

Camille St. James

Use the Companion Website to help you discuss the following question:

What would you say to Camille about Jeffrey's academic and social functioning in class if you were a speech-language pathologist working for the school district?

he experiences in preschool and early elementary school to exhibit a great deal of frustration about his inability to make others understand his needs. Jeffrey's low frustration tolerance results in temper tantrums similar to José's, which are often related to environmental transitions.

Jeffrey's pragmatic deficits however are *not* in the area of social interaction that is a characteristic of children with autism (Bishop, 2000). This is a critical difference between the two children. Jeffrey, unlike José, uses gestures to support his speech productions when he is communicatively unsuccessful. On the whole, Jeffrey's conversational interactions with peers are poor because he cannot remember, integrate, and organize information as it is shared in longer turn-taking exchanges.

The language demands of an elementary school classroom require a level of social communicative competence that heightens Jeffrey's frustration and impulsive behaviors. In a classroom with 25 typical peers, Jeffrey cannot follow the complex instructional process. Group learning requires a level of linguistic comprehension and production that Jeffrey does not possess. Children with SLI are likely to have language difficulties through their high school years for several reasons (Crosbie, Dodd, & Howard, 2002):

- Only seven states in the United States have early intervention programs for at-risk children. So children with SLI may not receive early intervention or preschool services because they come from poor or CLD families.
- Children with SLI present language difficulties that become progressively worse over time, although they may not have reached the threshold of disability to receive services in either the early intervention and/or preschool programs.
- The early symptoms are subtle because children with SLI are interactive and communicative, often using compensatory strategies that mask their language difficulties in a social context.

CW 11.6

Use the Companion Website to help you discuss the following:

1. Develop a pragmatic profile for Jeffrey.
2. Develop a description of Jeffrey's pragmatic skills as an 8-year-old child by means of a strengths-based approach.

- The standardized assessments utilized by evaluators and special-education teams "are more restrictive and less sensitive to language disorders than clinical judgment" (Dunn, Flax, Sliwinski, & Aram, 1996).
- Although the natural social context provides a more authentic assessment of children's language abilities, it may *not* be part of the evaluative process for a multidisciplinary protocol.
- The social – pragmatic and conversational – narrative aspects indicative of the quality of children's language abilities are generally not assessed because they are not part of a standardized test.

Semantic Abilities

Jeffrey's phonological deficits inhibit the acquisition of novel words that would increase the complexity of his language production and comprehension skills. Jeffrey's word-finding difficulties result in an inability to access appropriate labels for referents. Such difficulties limit his vocabulary development and his narrative skills to structure a sequence of ideas into connected discourse (Adams, 2001a). Jeffrey's oral narrative descriptions are often disorganized and poorly sequenced in terms of content and structural cohesion. In comparison to his peers' stories, which increase in length and syntactic and ideational complexity, Jeffrey's are shorter, less complex, and less creatively coherent.

Jeffrey's semantic deficits inhibit his use of language as a tool for further learning—learning to talk versus talking to learn. Jeffrey was expected to learn third-grade academic content and subjects along with his peers. However, he does not have an expanding vocabulary that provides him with the language abilities to keep up with the ideas and concepts expressed by his typical peers. The vocabulary gap between Jeffrey and his peers isolates him further, because he cannot engage in conversational exchanges with peers and discussions during class activities. When the teacher asks the class a question, Jeffrey is still processing the question while the other children are answering the question. His word-finding deficits and vocabulary delays increase the time he needs for comprehension processing. Jeffrey cannot keep up with the learning pace within the classroom as information is shared both rapidly and spontaneously in verbal and written forms.

Comprehension processing becomes more laborious as learning expectations increase and written language substitutes for oral language (Kemp & Carter, 2005). Jeffrey needs extra time to process the teacher's question and someone to simplify the information presented. He also needs his peers and teachers to slow down and wait

CW 11.7

Use the Companion Website to help you discuss the following:

1. Identify several informal methodologies that can be used by the SLP to determine a child's semantic functioning in the general-education classroom.

2. How might typical peers react to and interact with Jeffrey in class, given his word-finding problems and vocabulary limitations?

3. Compare Jeffrey and José in terms of their semantic abilities and disabilities.

for him to interpret the meaning before the discussion progresses. This is not always possible in a general-education classroom, so Jeffrey misses a great deal of the curriculum content.

Syntactic Abilities

Jeffrey is functioning several years below his chronological age in the production and comprehension of semantic and syntactic structures, which negatively affects his ability to develop literacy skills. Jeffrey's spontaneous productions present morphological errors (i.e., omissions or incorrect use of prepositions, pronouns, and tense). Testing indicates that he is having difficulty acquiring and using verb forms. Assessment of Jeffrey's discourse skills reveals word-finding difficulties and simplification of syntactic complexity when he attempts to clarify or elaborate his responses. Jeffrey still relies heavily on the use of gestures and objects or pictures that are present within the classroom to answer his teacher's questions. When he is required to respond in class or feels communicatively pressured, Jeffrey reduces the syntactic complexity of his utterances, becomes dysfluent, repeats his answers without variation, and uses deictic forms rather than appropriate lexical terms to clarify his answer.

Jeffrey's language production difficulties are related to a processing simplification that occurs when linguistic complexity is reduced by processing demands (Masterson & Kamhi, 1992). Jeffrey does not have an understanding of word order as a syntactic cue to help him derive the meaning of spoken language. In addition, he has phonological deficits, and when language development and speech production are negatively affected by phonological features, the following syntactic problems are evident (Conti-Ramsden & Windfuhr, 2002):

- Verb-related morphosyntactic errors
- Fewer developed novel nouns
- Grammatical difficulties that relate not only to verbs
- Uneven development of word classes (e.g., noun vs. verbs) and within noun and verb categories [e.g., morphology, verbal inflection (-ing) is acquired before -ed/third person singular (-s) inflection]
- A *greater* number of required learning examples (e.g., nouns and verbs) to develop a conceptual framework (Conti-Ramsden & Windfuhr, 2002; Hansson, Nettelbladt, & Nilholm, 2000).

CW 11.8

Use the Companion Website to help you discuss the following:

1. Develop a morphosyntactic profile for Jeffrey and compare it to what typical peers have acquired by 8 years of age.

2. How might typical peers react to and interact with Jeffrey in class, given his morphosyntactic problems?

3. Compare Jeffrey and José in terms of their morphosyntactic functioning. Would their morphosyntactic differences facilitate the process of differential diagnosis? Explain.

In some children with SLI, the semantic and syntactic difficulties are secondary to deficits in phonological processing (Evans, Viele, Kass, & Tang, 2002).

Phonological Abilities

SLI may be an impairment in "phonological processing and the consequent disruption of the mapping process through which the words and sentence structure of a language are established," (Chiat, 2001, p.113). The *mapping theory* of language challenges the more traditional grammatical theories that would explain Jeffrey's problems as a deficit in specific linguistic structures. Given the mapping theory of SLI, Jeffrey must learn the following:

- To identify linguistic form from the acoustic stream (speech input)
- To connect the linguistic form (consistent structures) to the social context within which it is embedded (Snow, 1995)
- To conceptualize a symbolic relationship between linguistic form and semantic meaning

Phonological difficulties create deficits in lexical and syntactic development, ultimately leading to reading and writing problems (Constable, Stackhouse, & Wells, 1997; Tomasello & Brooks, 1999). In third grade, Jeffrey is still functioning 2 years below his chronological age in language production and comprehension skills; Jeffrey's language skills are described as *"poor"* by his SLP.

The phonological theory of SLI can also explain Jeffrey's syntactic and morphological deficits. Because of poor phonological processing and perception, he cannot store and retrieve sounds and sound syllables. As a result, Jeffrey performs poorly on word discrimination tasks as compared to his age-matched peers. Jeffrey presents evidence of auditory discrimination and lexical deficits. He does not develop conceptual representations *for* and identify phonological patterns *from* the acoustic speech signal. The productive language of children with SLI may indicate omissions of syntactic and morphological inflections (Bishop, 1997). Jeffrey is similar to a typical 4-year-old in his morphological skills and a typical 5-year-old in his lexical abilities. Phonological deficits negatively affect the development of semantic–syntactic relations and contribute to semantic, morphological, and syntactic difficulties throughout elementary school, ultimately resulting in a reading deficit (Catts, 2001).

CW 11.9

Use the Companion Website to help you discuss the following:

1. How might typical peers react to and interact with Jeffrey, given his phonological problems in school?

2. Compare Jeffrey and José in terms of their phonological skills as 8-year-old children. How would you describe their speech? Would phonological differences highlight critical differences, leading to a differential diagnosis between children with autism spectrum disorders and specific language impairment?

Cognitive Abilities

Often Jeffrey forgets what he said earlier and uses stereotypical and/or linguistically reduced phrases. As he attempts to describe or clarify his productions, Jeffrey becomes anxious. During such exchanges, he assumes that the listener has the same contextual knowledge of an event, which causes listener confusion. In addition, he does not modify his linguistic form or content to take his listener's perspective into consideration. When his listener does not understand, Jeffrey repeats what he has just said. Jeffrey uses deictic forms such as "it," "he," and "there," which places further strain on the listener's ability to follow and to understand conversational exchanges or narrative descriptions. Even when peers try to assist the child with SLI with the communicative process by asking questions, offering clarifications, and providing directions, the organizational pressure results in the use of compensatory strategies that confuse, both the child and his listener (Perkins, 2001).

Finally, Jeffrey does not acquire the skills to engage in the progressively complex conversational exchanges that provide the means for the expansion of knowledge and the development of interpersonal relationships. Typical children learn many things about their environment and the physical world through direct experience; however, it is not possible, or even practical for that matter, to learn everything from personal experience. To avoid unfortunate consequences, it becomes important for children to learn from others by observing their behaviors and their mistakes. The learning process is further facilitated by asking questions and listening to the narrative experiences and stories of others. For a child such as Jeffrey, who has difficulty comprehending and formulating questions, his ability to acquire new knowledge and to expand his ideas about the world is compromised. Johnson (1992) believes that children with SLI show cognitive delays and deficits across a considerable range of tasks due to their weaknesses in language. So Jeffrey's *thinking* is affected by his phonological and syntactic deficits.

Social and Emotional Abilities

Children use language to learn about the social rules that govern appropriate or polite group behaviors. Clearly, what a speaker says is modified by variables related to the listener, the context, and the speaker's communicative intentions. So language also provides the means for children to expand their social contacts and develop friendships (Gallagher, 1999). In every culture, learning about social rules is of critical importance by the time children enter elementary school. Like José, Jeffrey has already had negative social experiences with peers. The SLI child perceives himself more negatively in academic ability, peer acceptance, and behavioral appropriateness than children with typical language skills (Jerome, Fujiki, Brinton, & James, 2002).

Both José and Jeffrey need to be in social settings to learn appropriate social behaviors; neither, however, has the skills to maintain interactions with the peers who can facilitate the learning process. Neither child has the ability to explain what he needs to know or to learn; José and Jeffrey cannot help others to help them socially. Jeffrey's teacher indicates that she cannot make other children play with him in class or set up play dates for him outside school.

The development of language as a symbolic system creates an internal personal world that includes feelings and thoughts. Jeffrey's language deficits limit his ability to express his feelings and to share his thoughts. Because the semantic terms referencing his feelings and thoughts are difficult to acquire, Jeffrey is often socially and emotionally isolated.

CW 11.10

Use the Companion Website to help you discuss the following:

1. Contrast the use of a deficit and strengths-based approach in profiling Jeffrey's cognitive development as a third-grader.

2. Compare Jeffrey and José in terms of their cognitive abilities. Would cognitive differences highlight critical differences between children with autism spectrum disorders and specific language impairment? Explain.

Academic Abilities

Jeffrey is often reinforced for his disruptive outbursts despite his teacher's attempts to integrate Jeffrey into the ongoing learning activities with the other children. When the teacher attends to Jeffrey's behavior, she shifts her focus from the general lesson and the other children to him. His needs are so great that Jeffrey requires more attention than any other child. The teacher gives Jeffrey about 20% of her time and the remaining 80% is distributed across the other children.

The teacher and the other parents complain about Jeffrey's disruptions to school administrators, because the other children receive much less individualized attention when he is in class. Jeffrey's peers perceive him to be a distraction and comment that classroom lessons flow better and they learn more when he is out of the room. Initially, a paraprofessional is assigned to sit with Jeffrey. However, there are instances when Jeffrey and the paraprofessional move to a separate corner for more

CW 11.11

Use the Companion Website to help you discuss the following:

1. What informal methodologies can be used by the SLP in a natural setting to assess Jeffrey's social and emotional functioning?

2. Develop a social–emotional profile for Jeffrey and compare him to his typical peers.

3. Describe how typical peers might react to and interact with Jeffrey in class, given his social–emotional problems.

4. Reflect critically on whether SLPs are qualified to "work on" social–emotional behaviors in children. Explain.

individualized work when his behavior becomes too disruptive to the group learning process.

Reading

Reading acquisition requires an awareness of redundancies in language that allows for the prediction of words and their meaning. Jeffrey's reading deficits are a reflection of his language deficits. To learn to read, Jeffrey has to conceptualize a linkage between the auditory phoneme and its visual representation in print or text form. Just as speech has meaning that must be decoded, text or written language must also be decoded to derive meaning. Jeffrey lacks the ability to phonologically segment the acoustic speech signal to derive linguistic sound patterns and develop phoneme – grapheme correspondences. His reading problems also highlight metalinguistic and metacognitive deficits involving judgments about the properties of language as an organized system of rules:

- Jeffrey cannot sound out words that he does not recognize.
- He is not able to predict word usage based on textual or linguistic information.
- The more linguistically complex and embedded the text material is, the greater Jeffrey's comprehension difficulties.
- Jeffrey has poor comprehension, monitoring, and repair strategies when he fails to understand print material.
- Because Jeffrey's language is literal, he will have difficulty understanding written analogies, figurative language, and idioms.
- He is not able to extract information from a written text to draw conclusions or inferences.

Jeffrey's learning problems are *underestimated* until his reading deficits interfere with his academic achievements. Jeffrey has not done well on state-mandated language arts testing administered in the third grade. Consequently, his CSE will need to reevaluate whether he is receiving the appropriate support services needed to make progress in school.

CW 11.12

Use the Companion Website to help you discuss the following:

1. Identify several research studies that investigate long-term educational outcomes for children with SLI.

2. Discuss how and why Jeffrey's academic problems further exacerbate his negative self-esteem and school failure.

Hearing Loss

Katherine Whiteside

Katherine decides to move closer to the city, closer to the Mission School. While Kaitlyn is in school, she enrolls at St. Joseph's College to complete a master's degree in social work. Katherine's husband, Connor, sees her on weekends and eventually gets a job in the city so that they can live together as a family. Katherine and Connor are also in a marital counseling program so that they can strengthen their relationship and stay together.

Katherine starts an advocacy agency for parents of children with disabilities, which includes counseling, parent training, and advocacy support services. She is a successful and effective advocate for parents and is eventually appointed by the governor of her state to the Early Intervention Coordinating Council. She serves as chairperson for the statewide Parent Action Committee, which provides her with access to state legislators who make policy decisions about programs and services for children with disabilities.

Kaitlyn's mother describes her daughter's characteristics and feelings in Box 11.3.

Pragmatic Abilities

Children with hearing loss need to develop communication repair strategies when their understanding of a communication exchange breaks down. Their role of listener is much more fragile than that of their typical hearing peers. If the child with a hearing loss is utilizing a sign-language system, there is less likelihood of communication breakdown than if the child is utilizing an aural–oral approach. In either situation, the child who is deaf needs to develop an array of communication repair strategies that facilitate clear communication when acting as speaker or listener.

Can the child recognize when he does not understand? If so, does he request clarification? When functioning as speaker, does he provide additional information to ensure that his listener understands? Does he ask the listener to repeat the communicative intent when he thinks there is a possibility of misunderstanding? These repair devices are an integral part of adequate communication, and many children who are deaf who do not develop them become isolated from their peers. These devices must be specifically taught.

BOX 11.3

I always considered Kaitlyn to be a bright, independent girl. She learns sign language quickly and her sign vocabulary is almost equal to that of hearing children her age. My school district tells me that the regular classroom is the LRE (least restrictive environment) and that she should attend public school. In the public school she would work with a teacher of the deaf for one period a day. However, I am concerned as to whether she will be able to keep up with the academics as she progresses to upper elementary grades. Kaitlyn is a very social child. She loves interacting with other children and wants to do all the things other kids do. She is a leader when she is with other deaf kids, but when she is with hearing kids, she just stands by the side and watches. I learned sign language so that Kaitlyn would always understand what is being talked about at home. I believe this is one of the reasons that she became independent, happy, and secure in herself. I still am not sure that Kaitlyn will reach her potential in a general-education classroom with hearing children. She still has to work so hard to learn the academics. At night I always spend a few hours with her doing her homework. She can't understand everything "spoken" to her, and I know that she misses a great deal of spoken language even with the cochlear implant. She loves sports and plays basketball with the children from the Mission School for the Deaf. I love to see her signing animatedly with her friends on the team. She often has play dates on the weekends with these girls. I know how important it is for girls to have friends. The girls in the neighborhood treat Kaitlyn well, but there is a difference. Kaitlyn feels different.

Katherine Whiteside

Use the Companion Website to help you discuss the following questions:

1. What would you say to Katherine about Kaitlyn's academic and social functioning in a general-education class if you were a speech-language pathologist working for the school district?

2. What would you say to Katherine about Kaitlyn's long-term academic and social problems in the "hearing world" versus the "deaf world"?

Now that Kaitlyn is in school, it is important for her to refine her communication skills. She needs to adjust her message according to the needs of her listener. She has learned that she must use politeness markers such as "please" and "thank you" with all adults. She carefully watches people's faces and body movements to derive an understanding of their feelings and intentions. When she is with more than one person, she cannot always follow a conversation. She will often speak when someone else is still speaking. Although she easily negotiates communication with others who use sign language, the task is much harder when no signs are used. Her hearing does not allow her to fully participate in the ebb and flow of oral communication.

Kaitlyn has the same interests as hearing peers, but she cannot share her ideas or experiences as easily with hearing peers. When Kaitlyn is with signing peers, they

CW 11.13

Use the Companion Website to help you discuss the following:

1. Can standardized instruments be used to evaluate pragmatic functioning in children with hearing loss? Are there instruments for normal-hearing children?
2. Compare Kaitlyn's pragmatic skills to those of Jeffrey and José.
3. Kaitlyn has good pragmatic skills when using sign language. Does she still have good pragmatic skills when communicating orally? Explain your answers.

exchange information freely; communication flows. Although Kaitlyn has a cochlear implant, she still does not have the capability to understand all verbal communications. She still misses a good deal of what is being said, even with her good speech-reading ability. When she is with hearing persons who do not sign, the communication cycle becomes lopsided: Kaitlyn will spend more and more time listening and trying to comprehend with little opportunity to reflect and comment.

Semantic Abilities

When children, who are deaf are educated using an aural–oral approach, limited information is available regarding the rate or sequence of acquisition of linguistic comprehension (McConkey, 1986). In typical hearing children, there are three stages of comprehension development (McLean & Snyder-McLean, 1978). Stage 1 is from birth to 12 months. During this period, normal-hearing children respond to phonemic and paralinguistic features of speech, rather than linguistic features. In stage 2, 13 months to approximately 30 months, the child begins to focus on linguistic stimuli, but does not process syntactic information. In stage 3, above 30 months, the child is more aware of and comprehends syntactic information. For the child with a hearing loss, longer time is spent in the first stage (Moeller & McConkey, 1984). For the child exposed to a sign-language system early in life, linguistic and syntactic knowledge develops more quickly and approximates that of the normal-hearing child.

Kaitlyn has a solid sign-language vocabulary. If she were a typical normal-hearing child, she would have an understanding of approximately 20,000 words when she was in first grade (McLaughlin, 1998). Although Kailtyn has good vocabulary development, she is unable to produce speech that reflects this. Learning how to say the words she already has internalized is arduous work. She has grown in her understanding of vocabulary conceptualization both vertically and horizontally. *Horizontal development* refers to the process of adding features to a word. For example, the word "dog" may refer to only one specific, brown-haired, small dog; eventually, this word will embrace Chihuahuas to Great Danes. Meaning has expanded in a horizontal fashion.

Vertical development refers to the use of individual, multiple meanings of words. The word "block" at first refers to square, three-dimensional toys used for building. However, this word can also be used in other ways. Kaitlyn now understands and uses the sign for "block head," knowing that it has a very different meaning from the toy. This vertical development will reflect the enriched language understanding that is so critical for reading comprehension (McLaughlin, 1998).

Syntactic Abilities

The relationship between comprehension and production is complex. At one time it was believed that comprehension preceded production. However, today we realize that this relationship probably varies at different stages of linguistic development and that, at the semantic–lexical stage of verbal learning, a child may acquire under-standing of a word by using it (Bloom, 1974). Several comprehension strategies are used by children who are deaf: key-word comprehension strategy, order of mention strategy, probable-event strategy, and novel mapping. In the key-word comprehen-sion strategy, the child infers the meaning of an utterance based on the understand-ing of one key word. For example, if the child is told, "Make the dolly kiss the dog," the child might press the doll close to the dog, not because she understood all the words, but because she may understand the word "kiss" and the action associated with it. The key-word strategy is used by children with hearing loss much longer than by normal-hearing peers. It will still be used even when normal peers are capable of syntactic comprehension (Moeller, Osberger, McConkey, & Ecarius, 1981).

The order of mention strategy is a later developing strategy whereby the child in-terprets occurrence of actions based on the order of words in a sentence. For exam-ple "Before the dog barked, the door slammed." This would be comprehended as the dog barking first and the door slamming. This strategy does not take into account the meaning of the word "before." Typical hearing children use this strategy at 4 and 5 years of age. The child with a hearing loss will first use this strategy long beyond that.

The probable-event strategy is used more frequently by children who are deaf than by normal-hearing children (Quinn & Tomblin, 1985). This strategy is based on the child's past experiences with events. The child will suspend or ignore word knowl-edge and relationships and interpret sentences based on previous experiences of similar sentences. This strategy is often used by children who communicate by sign language. These three comprehension strategies highlight the deaf child's weakness in using and integrating specific syntactic, semantic, and grammatical markers to indicate semantic meaning.

Novel mapping is a more recently identified comprehension strategy for vocabulary acquisition. Typically developing children and adults use a word-learning strategy that infers that a novel word will refer to a novel object. In a study by Lederberg, Prezbindowski, and Spencer (2000), children 3 to 6 years old who were deaf were given a trial period of word learning during which a novel word was introduced with three familiar words. Specifically, the child was asked to give the examiner an object that cor-responded to the word (e.g., shoe, shoe, where the shoe? dax dax, where the dax?) The child would then give the examiner the shoe upon request and then, when asked for the "dax," would hand the examiner an object that was unfamiliar, such as a corkscrew. This consistent behavior demonstrated that, when trying to teach children who are deaf new vocabulary words, it is appropriate to embed the new word or object with a familiar object, and the child will quickly learn to associate the new or novel word with the appropriate object and retain that word in his or her lexicon.

CW 11.14

Use the Companion Website to help you answer the following questions:

1. What formal tests would you use to assess Kaitlyn's semantic development?
2. How do you think Kaitlyn's semantic development affects her syntactic development?
3. How has Kaitlyn's sign language helped ready her for reading?
4. Do you think Kaitlyn should continue to be exposed to sign language? Why or why not?

For the cochlear-implanted child who utilizes an aural–oral approach, the expectation is that appropriate habilitation procedures will focus on developing integrated understanding of syntax, morphology, and grammar to develop language comprehension. The linking of meaning to connected speech is highly correlated with the child's ability to perceive speech. This is where the cochlear-implanted child will often have an advantage, because the implant provides a wider range of perceptual stimuli.

Phonological Abilities

It is imperative that Kaitlyn develop clear articulation so that she can communicate with persons who do not sign. Kaitlyn evidences numerous phonological errors in her speech production. In normal-hearing children, these errors are classified in terms of phonological processes. A phonological process is a simplification on the part of the child to alter natural classes of sounds in a systematic way (Ingram, 1981). In children with hearing loss there is also a tendency to simplify sounds; however, the impact of reduced range of hearing complicates and interferes with the type of phonological errors found in these children.

A study done by Huttunen (2001) found that in children 4 to 6 years old the number of phonological simplifying processes of children with severe hearing loss exceeded that of younger, normal-hearing children. In addition, these children evidenced distortions, frequent additions, vowel substitutions, and prolongations. Thus, the children were seen as not only delayed in their development of phonology, but also as having many deviant processes that needed special intervention.

Phonetic errors (articulation errors) were frequent in the speech of children with hearing loss, with consonant place errors occurring more often than manner errors. Furthermore, children with hearing loss had more voicing and final consonant omissions, more vowel substitutions (front vowels substituted by back vowels), and more substitutions of a vowel by the neutral vowel /ʌ/. The amount of both articulation errors and phonological processes was strongly related to the degree of hearing loss of the child.

Two recent studies have examined the factors affecting speech development in children with cochlear implants. The first study, by Connor, Heiber, Arts, and Zwolan (2000), looked at consonant production and vocabulary development of children with cochlear implants who were being educated using either sign language or speech (no sign language). They found no difference between these two groups of children.

The second study (Geers and Brennen, 2003) had a very different outcome. They found that the primary factor responsible for desirable performance outcome for the children with cochlear implants was an educational environment that emphasized an aural–oral approach. These two disparate conclusions, which appear to contradict each other, only highlight the need for additional studies regarding educational environments and approaches.

However, we can surmise that there are a number of variables and considerations other than communication strategy (aural–oral communication or total communication) that go into the mix of outcome predictions for children with hearing loss, such as age at which children receive implants and the consistency and integrity of educational programs. Zwolan & Heavner (2005) suggest that the success of children with cochlear implants is greatly influenced by the expectations of the parents, early identification of hearing loss, appropriate and immediate follow-up, early implantation, and good medical, audiological, and educational management. With all this in place, the child has the potential to develop normal speech and language.

Spencer, Barker, and Tomblin (2003) examined the relationship between language and literacy skills in pediatric cochlear implant users. They found that the performance of cochlear implant users compares favorably with that of their age-matched hearing peers, with the exception of conjunction and correct verb form usage in written language. More research such as this will elucidate our understanding of appropriate intervention for children with cochlear implants.

Kaitlyn's speech production is still delayed. She speaks in sentences; however, it is difficult for the listener to understand her. She can produce multisyllabic words of two to three syllables, but needs to be reminded to do so. Her intonation patterns have also improved in that she employs a rising pitch at the end of interrogative sentences. Kaitlyn still has some inappropriate pitch rising for the tense vowel /i/, and this is perceived as pitch breaks. She can modulate the loudness of her voice now and, although it is somewhat loud, it is appropriate for the classroom. Kaitlyn's narrative skills are better when she signs as opposed to using just speech. When she signs, stories and narratives are elaborate and well sequenced. When she speaks, her narratives are short and consist of simple sentences only, with few descriptive adjectives or adverbs.

CW 11.15

Use the Companion Website to help you discuss the following questions:

1. What would you expect to find in Kaitlyn's phonological assessment that might not be so prevalent in Jeffrey's?

2. What articulatory skills would you expect a child with normal hearing to develop by the time she is in kindergarten?

3. What articulatory skills would you expect a child with a severe to profound hearing loss to develop by the time she is in kindergarten?

Cognitive Abilities

Kaitlyn's sign-language skills have allowed her linguistic proficiency to parallel her cognitive abilities. Kaitlyn has acquired basic concepts, and she has paired these concepts with signed words. Signs have enabled her to comprehend a great deal of language and explore and cognitively grow through questions and answers. Mrs. Whiteside continued to use signs with Kaitlyn even after her implantation. Kaitlyn's cognitive abilities are well developed, and she is developing theory-of-mind, which can be illustrated in the following scenario. The three bears come home from their walk and find clues that someone has been in the house, but they do not know who. The reader knows that it is Goldilocks, but the bears do not know this until they find her in Baby Bear's bed. For the child with adequate theory-of-mind development, the perspective of the bears' is assumed; that is, even though the child knows about Goldilocks, the bears don't.

Children who are deaf have delays in their understanding of theory-of-mind. This is most likely due to the limited access they have to information that is constantly being discussed around them in their environment. However, unlike the child with autism, the child who is deaf does not have fundamental cognitive differences, and theory-of-mind differences between the child who is deaf and a typical child are not as great nor as readily apparent as these differences are when the child with autism is compared to the typical child. Interestingly, children who are deaf and exposed to sign language do not exhibit delays in the development of theory-of-mind. In fact, the better the sign-language skills of the child who is deaf, the better developed is his theory-of-mind. In the normal-hearing child, theory-of-mind skills are developed around 4 years of age. For children who are deaf it may not develop until they are 7 or 8 years of age, depending on their level of language development. Vocabulary skills and the ability to comprehend syntactic complements are predictors of theory-of-mind development (de Villiers, de Villiers, Schick, & Hoffmeister, 2000).

When Kaitlyn was 5 years old, she was primarily in the first stage of comprehension development, with some emerging use of comprehension of linguistic units when communicating with speech only. When she communicated using sign language, her comprehension level spanned into level 3, whereby she was beginning to integrate syntactic and grammatical information into her comprehension of communicative contexts. After implantation of the cochlear implant, her understanding of spoken (oral) speech improved. Eventually, she was able to recognize and comprehend spoken linguistic units and use the key-word understanding strategy. Context was always critical to understanding, and Kaitlyn did best when communication was transparent, that is, when meaning could be derived easily through environmental cues. For example, if Kaitlyn is in the school cafeteria and her teacher does not use signs but verbally asks her, "Do you want milk or juice?" Kaitlyn may understand the communication only because she sees other children selecting milk or juice from the teacher's cart.

As Kaitlyn matures in her language comprehension, she will attend more to the linguistic elements in communications in which meaning is not so transparent. For instance, Kaitlyn is at home and her mother asks her, "Do you want one cookie or two cookies?" She has not used signs and Kaitlyn sees the tray of cookies, but must respond to the quantity issue. In this instance, although the communication is somewhat transparent, the linguistic units of one or two must be comprehended by Kaitlyn for her to receive what she desires.

Kaitlyn is on her way to higher levels of comprehension. She does not always need transparent communication environments to support her in her integration of linguistic semantic comprehension and syntactic grammatical comprehension. Kaitlyn's understanding and perception of critical linguistic markers such as plurals or negatives allows her to respond to questions, such as "Where should we eat dinner tomorrow?" If Kaitlyn responds "I am hungry," it can be concluded that she did not perceptually process the word "where." If she responds, "I want to eat at McDonald's," it can be assumed that she attended to the linguistic unit "where." If the question was asked mid-morning, it can further be assumed that Kaitlyn was able to comprehend language that was distanced from the environmental situation (Blank, Rose, & Berlin, 1978).

Academic Abilities

Learning how to read presents a challenge for children with severe to profound hearing losses. Many children who are deaf leave school with reading competencies between the second and fourth grade, although 1 out of 5 has a reading level below second grade (Dew, 1999). Paul (1998) finds that the typical high school graduate with a profound hearing loss reads at the fourth-grade level. Reading requires that the child have an understanding of a language and of the relationship between that language and the printed word (Goldin-Meadow & Mayberry, 2001). Persons with profound hearing losses who have poor reading skills are also found to have both verbal and visuospatial short-term memory deficits. Interestingly, this also appears to be true for normal-hearing persons who evidence a reading disability (Tractenberg, 2002).

Kaitlyn develops some phonological skills such as rhyming, and she can discriminate the number of beats or syllables in a word (a maximum of three syllables). She has good visuospatial memory. In school great emphasis has been placed on the development of phonological skills; however, because of her hearing loss, Kaitlyn's development in this area is limited. She does retain sight words in her memory. This is a strength for her. She learns her letters and the phoneme–grapheme connections quickly.

The basis for future learning ability lies in early language experiences. Language is the foundation, and before children learn to read they need to experience a rich linguistic environment. For Kaitlyn, this occurred at home and the Mission School. The focus of the curriculum is to develop language.

At the Mission School the teachers use a technique called *embedding* to teach Kaitlyn language. Basically, embedding occurs when the child is engaged in an engrossing activity and the teacher uses the child's interest to teach the language surrounding that activity (Dunst, Herter, Shields, & Bennis, 2001). For instance, when Kaitlyn's class makes gingerbread men cookies after reading a story about the gingerbread man and the fox, new vocabulary words, such as "oven," "temperature," and "dough," are introduced and used repeatedly. By hooking these words to an activity, the words and concepts are internalized.

Later, during early elementary school years, embedding can be used in many curriculum areas, such as science, social studies, and language arts. This hands-on technique is invaluable when teaching children.

Other appropriate techniques for learning language are elaboration, self-talk, and parallel talk (Bowe, 2002). In elaboration, the teacher gives directions to the child, but explains why. For instance, instead of just telling Kaitlyn to move the plant away from the heating vent, she explains that the heat causes the leaves to droop and the dirt to dry out. In self-talk, the teacher narrates an action. For example, "I am moving the plant away from the heating vent because it dries out the soil and causes the leaves to droop."

In parallel talk, the teacher narrates words that accompany an action of the child. "You built a good terrarium today. What kind of soil did you put in, sandy soil? What plants are in the terrarium, succulents or nonsucculents?"

Besides these techniques, Kaitlyn's SLP always does a miscue analysis at the beginning of the school year. This technique can be used through all the grades. A language sample is gathered and from that sample the SLP gathers information about what syntactic forms, morphological markers, and types of utterances were spontaneously formed by Kaitlyn. This sample was videotaped when Kaitlyn signed and spoke. This technique is very helpful in targeting appropriate language goals. Goodman, Goodman, and Hood (1998) use miscue analysis to analyze what children do while reading aloud. Sometimes, they make spontaneous corrections of misread words. If no corrections are made, it suggests that the child is not comprehending while reading.

Miscue analysis is also useful in informal assessment. Does the child make reasonable predictions about what will happen based on what has been read? If the child uses signs, does the child fingerspell a word rather than sign it. If so, this suggests that the child may not understand the word read and has not attached it to the sign that represents the concept or meaning of the word.

Because children who are deaf have imperfect knowledge of language, they have more difficulty understanding language when it is in written form than the normal-hearing child. If other phonological awareness skills are generally less developed than hearing children's, they must rely on other avenues to learn how to decode print. Research has not clearly shown what it is that enables some children who are deaf to become good decoders of the printed word. However, we do know that children who are deaf read by using a code that is not based on sound. We also know that steady growth in language acquisition throughout early childhood and elementary school leads to the development of reading (Goldin-Meadow & Mayberry, 2001).

However, just knowing a language does not guarantee that a child will learn to read. We know this because there are thousands of normal-hearing, cognitively intact children who have great difficulty learning to read and are diagnosed as dyslexic. Goldin-Meadow and Mayberry (2001) describe several factors that contribute to reading achievement in children who are deaf, use sign language, and have deaf parents versus those who have hearing parents. Deaf children between the ages of 7 and 9 and then again later at ages 13 to 15 were evaluated for reading ability. It was found that at ages 7 to 9 there was little difference in reading ability between the two groups of children, but by the ages of 13 to 15 the children of parents who were deaf made steady and good progress in reading printed English, while the children of hearing parents did not. The critical factor appeared to be that the children of parents who were deaf were exposed to a rich language from their parents who used sign language, and this enabled them to develop their reading comprehension skills.

Chamberlain, Morford, & Mayberry (2000) believe that children who are deaf who experience limited exposure to language early in life are less likely to learn to read adequately. Furthermore, one of the best predictors of reading skill for children who are deaf and sign is whether a child's parents are hearing or deaf. If the parents are deaf and use sign language, the prognosis is better for later reading acquisition (Hoffmeister, 2000; Padden & Ramsey, 2000; Strong & Prinz, 2000).

Considering all this, how does Kaitlyn learn to read? She develops a language, sign language, that she uses at home and at school. She also develops some phonological awareness skills. In addition, she has good visual memory and is cognitively within normal limits. She receives early intervention and benefits from skilled teachers who are familiar with the challenges that deafness brings. She has consistent amplification, first with hearing aids and then with a cochlear implant. She has parents who are an integral part of her habilitation and education. Kaitlyn has come far, and her success is due not only to her own hard work, the love and support of her family, and the commitment of her educational teams, but also to the legislation that mandates her right to an appropriate education and the research that delineates how to educate children who are deaf.

CW 11.16

Use the Companion Website to help you discuss the following:

1. Identify several research studies that investigate long-term educational outcomes for children who are deaf and educated in general-education programs and in schools for the deaf.

2. Discuss the importance of friendship in early childhood development.

SUMMARY

Our three children have come a long way with their families. Although the intent of inclusion was to provide children with disabilities an extraordinary opportunity to access the general-education curriculum and to interact with typical peers, the practical realities present complex learning problems for parents, teachers, and children. It is possible that the three children would not have had the same educational opportunities if their families were not so involved. The families grew along with their children and became effective advocates over time. Programs and teachers may change, but parents and caregivers remain as more consistent forces in the lives of children. For each of the children, inclusive programming is considered as an educational option.

Although this textbook provides a longitudinal description of how language disorders change during the early years of development, children eventually move on to middle and high school programs. Educational requirements become focused on academic content areas, with higher expectations about job training and career development. Where will these children be at the end of their high school careers? Two of the children have been placed in general-education settings. Although Kaitlyn remains in a school for the deaf now, at some time, consideration will again be given regarding an inclusive education for her and preparing her for a life in the hearing world.

The promise of inclusion presents not only opportunities for children with disabilities, but complex realities for teachers and families of children with and without disabilities. The growing diversity within public schools presents significant problems in successfully educating typical students as the range of students' needs has increased. The legal requirement to meet the individual needs of children with disabilities in general-education classrooms has added an educational stressor.

To accomplish the mission of inclusion, typical peers need to be prepared to receive, accept, and interact with children who have disabilities. Preparation should include the implementation of a formal program developed by major school stakeholders. Preparation should also include talking to peers about social and behavioral differences that can be expected during class, recess, and conversational exchanges. Young children in particular may be surprised or frightened by unusual and unexpected behavioral reactions to daily classroom activities. Teachers' discussions with children should also include explanations that children with disabilities are not deliberately being disruptive or hurtful.

Given the importance of typical children in the inclusion process, preparation needs to occur prior to the arrival of the child with the disability in the classroom. Just as there will be an adjustment period for the child with a disability into classroom routines, typical peers will also require time to adjust to the changes created by the child with a disability. Important to the success of this process are the collaborative discussions that should take place between teachers and parents. Such discussions provide a framework for the development of a peer acceptance program that should be culturally and ethnically sensitive.

As children get older, family relationships shift to peer relationships. The quality of childhood and adolescence is enriched by peer friendships. The importance of friends cannot be overstated, because adolescent development is in fact defined by peer relationships and experiences. Studies indicate that children become part of a social hierarchy that establishes their popularity within the peer group (Lindsay, 2003). Children who are chosen by peers as desirable partners and friends have high competency skills. Children often choose to be with peers who have been identified as socially popular. During adolescence, emotional self-esteem is enhanced and impaired by peer-group experiences.

There is no way for lawmakers and educators to mandate friendship inside or outside school. Although children with disabilities may be included within the parameters of classroom activities, social relationships usually do not generalize to extracurricular activities outside school. The child with a disability may find himself or herself outside the social mainstream. When friendships are based on social competence, how do children with disabilities establish social relationships? (Jerome, Fujiki, Brinton, & James, 2002). The child with a disability may need to socialize with other children who have disabilities.

General education provides a social opportunity for children with disabilities. Often, when typical children move to a new grade, they maintain their friendships with other children, which may not always be the case for the child with a disability. Even children with learning disabilities who have more advanced language skills than children with autism may not feel equal to or the same as their typical peers. During adolescence, children with disabilities may feel more comfortable with other children who have disabilities and may in fact prefer to learn in an environment in which their differences and deficits are not so obvious. It may be embarrassing for an adolescent to receive services, knowing that his peers are aware of his disability. In addition, there is no assurance that children with disabilities will not be bullied or ridiculed by typical children.

Finally, although educational instruction can be measured by standardized assessments, the social aspects of the school experience are difficult to measure. Specifically, assuming that schools have developed peer acceptance programs, how are these programs evaluated? The educational and legal incentives for inclusion have not systematically followed children's experiences longitudinally. How do children with disabilities feel about themselves and their peers as they are included? For children with a level of language who can answer probing questions about their sense of personal identity, this may be an important area of investigation. It would be both revealing and relevant to discuss these issues with Jeffrey and Kaitlyn when they get older. For children such as José who have autism, the evaluative tasks have to be approached from a life-skills perspective. As children complete middle school, their perceptions and concerns need to be included into the decision-making factor.

Collaborative Language Assessment and Decision Making in Elementary School

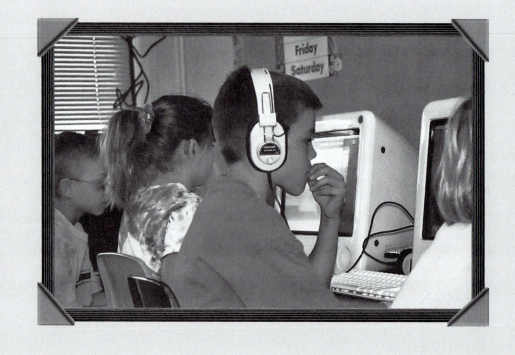

Chapter Objectives

After studying this chapter, you should be able to answer the following questions:

1. What are alternative assessments?

2. How does the assessment connect to school achievement?

3. What are nonstandardized assessments?

4. What is auditory processing?

5. What are the differences between the educational responsibilities of the speech-language pathologist and the classroom teacher?

Assessing the speech and language abilities of the school-age child 5 to 8 years old is a challenging task. Language is a complex, dynamic system that needs to be assessed in elementary school, given the additional requirement of literacy-based skills. Generally, the SLP is asked to assess language for the purpose of determining whether a language deficit exists and, if so, in what areas and how severe is the deficit. Is there a deficit in syntactic, semantic, phonological, or pragmatic development? Does the child have difficulty processing spoken language or is the difficulty in formulating language? How severe is the problem? Does the child's performance differ significantly from his peers and, if so, by how much?

IDEA has set guidelines for determining which children are eligible to receive support services in school. Specific categories of disability are listed, such as learning disability, speech impairment, mental retardation, and autism. For children to receive special-education support services in school, they must be classified and labeled as having a specific categorical diagnosis.

Consequently, when the SLP evaluates a child, he or she is part of a team that determines if a disability exists, the nature and severity of the disability, and the impact it has on educational performance. The SLP must carefully consider the assessment instruments to be used and how useful they are for determining the severity of the language impairment and planning an intervention model.

Assessments generally used by the SLP in elementary school are norm referenced or standardized and give information regarding how a child performs when compared to peers of the same age. Performance is translated into standardized scores and percentiles. If a child's performance is outside the range of typical, that is, more than 1 standard deviation (SD) below the mean, the child's performance is considered to be delayed. The problem for the multidisciplinary team is to determine if and how the child's disability affects her or his educational functioning.

Figure 12.1 shows the normal curve with percentiles and standard scores. For a child's performance to be outside the range of typical, the child must receive a score that is more than 1 SD below the mean of 100. Therefore, a standard score of 85 or less and a percentile of 16 or less would identify a child as having a significant delay.

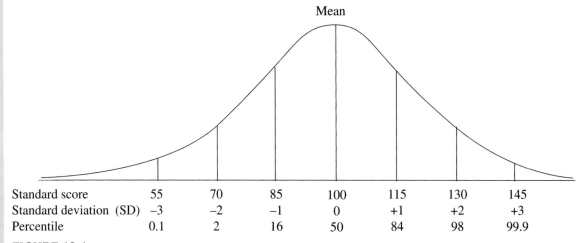

Standard score	55	70	85	100	115	130	145
Standard deviation (SD)	−3	−2	−1	0	+1	+2	+3
Percentile	0.1	2	16	50	84	98	99.9

FIGURE 12.1

Normal Curve with Standard Scores and Percentiles

Many researchers consider language scores between 1 and 1.5 SD below the mean on one or more tests as the cutoff.

The disability categories, such as learning disabled, autistic, mentally retarded, multiply handicapped, and other health impaired, involve language-learning difficulties as well. Consequently, the SLP will be asked to assess many children whose primary classification may not be speech-language impaired. However, the speech-language assessment will be a cornerstone of future program planning. The purpose of assessment is not only to classify, but also to determine the intervention approach to be used.

What Do We Assess?

Federal legislation has greatly influenced speech-language services in the schools. Legislation such as IDEA (2004), the Educate America Act (2000), and more recently the No Child Left Behind Act (NCLB) all shape how children are educated. Under NCLB of 2001, all students are to participate in the general-education curriculum. The emphasis on educating all children, regular and special education, in the LRE is a cornerstone of educational philosophy today. All children deserve an education that promotes achievement and the ability to function in the world by exercising their rights and responsibilities as citizens. With this in mind, there is greater emphasis on the integration of oral communication skills and literacy development. Because language underlies all learning, the SLP has become an integral member of the educational team that assesses children who are not making academic gains.

States are reemphasizing standards and competencies for all grade levels. Some states have adopted the goal that all children will be able to read independently by the end of third grade. Many of these competencies integrate speech, language, and communication skills, such as phonological and phonemic awareness, listening, understanding and following directions, speaking with age-appropriate vocabulary and grammar, taking conversational turns, participating in group discussions, and giving feedback to others during discussion.

When Do We Assess?

In most instances the request for assessment comes from the teacher; however, many times families will request an assessment as well. Once the process of formal assessment begins, standardized assessments are generally utilized because they can provide quantitative standardized measures that delineate the child's abilities in relation to peers. Special-education committees use these standardized measures to decide how the child's disability contributes to academic difficulties. Assessment of phonological, morphological, semantic, and syntactic skills can be readily assessed using standardized assessment instruments. Most of these instruments have been standardized on English-speaking children. Some have been standardized on Spanish-speaking children. Tables 12.1 and 12.2 list a variety of the instruments used in educational settings.

Most recently, great attention has been given to the concept of dialect-free assessment principles and the need to assess phonology, syntax, and discourse across widely varying dialect communities in the United States. Dialect refers to a form or variety of spoken language peculiar to a region, community, social group, or occupational group (Webster, 1983). Making the distinction between development, dialect, and disorder is the job of the SLP.

Most standardized assessments are normed on children who speak Mainstream American English (MAE) (Seymour, 2004). When these assessments are used to

TABLE 12.1 Standardized Tests for Spanish-Speaking Children

Test	Ages (yr:mo)
Expressive One Word Picture Vocabulary Test, Spanish Edition (EOWPVT-Spanish Edition) (M. Gardner, Academic Therapy Publications)	2–18:11
Receptive One Word Picture Vocabulary Test, Spanish Edition (ROWPVT-Spanish Edition) (M. Gardner, Academic Therapy Publications)	2–18:11
Clinical Evaluation of Language Fundamentals Fourth Edition, Spanish Edition (E. Wiig, W. Secord, and E. Semel, 2006, Psychological Corporation)	5–21
Spanish Test for Assessing Morphologic Production (STAMP). (T. Nugent, K. Shipley, and D. Provencio, 1991, Academic Communication Associates)	5–11
Assessment of Phonological Processes, Spanish Edition (B. Hodson, 1986, Los Amigos Research Associates, San Diego, CA)	3–12
Test—de Vocabulario en Imagenes Peabody (L. Dunn, D. Lugo, E. Padilla, & L. Dunn, 1986, American Guidance Service, Circle Pines, MN)	2.6–90.11

TABLE 12.2 Standardized Tests for School-Age Children

Test	Ages (yr:mo)
Clinical Evaluation of Language Fundamentals, Fourth Edition (CELF-4)(E. Wiig, W. Secord, and E. Semel, 2003, Psychological Corp.)	5–21
Comprehensive Assessment of Spoken Language (CASL)(Carrow-Woolfolk, 1999, American Guidance Service)	3–21
Diagnostic Evaluation of Language Variation (DELV) (Seymour, Roeper, and de Villiers, 2003, Psychological Corp.)	4–12
Expressive One-Word Picture Vocabulary Test (EOWPVT), 2000 Edition (Gardner, 2000, Linguisystems)	2–18.11
Receptive One-Word Picture Vocabulary Test (ROWPTV), 2000 Edition (Gardner, 2000, Linguisystems)	2–18.11
Peabody Picture Vocabulary Test III (PPVT-III) (Dunn & Dunn, 1997, American Guidance Service)	2.6–90.11
Test for Auditory Comprehension of Language—3 (TALC-3) (Carrow-Woolfolk, 1999, Psychological Corp.)	3–9.11
Oral, Written Language Scales (OWLS) (Carrow-Woolfolk, 1995, American Guidance Services)	3–21
Phonological Awareness Test (PAT) (Robertson & Salter, 1997, Linguisystems)	5–9
Test of Language Competence—Expanded Edition (Wiig & Secord, 1989, Psychological Corp.)	5–18
Test of Language Development P:3 (TOLD P:3) Primary (Hammill & Newcomer, 1997, Psychological Corp.)	4.8–8
Comprehensive Test of Phonological Processing (CTOPP) (R. Wagner, J. Torgensen, C. Rashotte, 1999, Pro-Ed.)	5–24.11
Test of Auditory Processing Skills Revised (TAPS-R) (M. Gardner, 1996, Psychological and Educational Pub.)	4–12
Test of Pragmatic Language (TOPL) (Phelps-Terasaki, D., Gunn T., Psychological and Educational Publications)	5–13:11
Test of Word Finding Second Edition (TWF-2) (D. German, 2000, Psychological and Educational Publications)	4–12:11
Test of Early Language Development, Third Edition (TELD-3) (W. Hresko, K. Reid, D. Hamill, 1999, Psychological and Educational Publications)	2–7
Bracken Basic Concept Scale—Revised (B. Bracken, 1998, The Psychological Corp.)	2.6–8
Carolina Picture Vocabulary Test for Deaf and Hearing Impaired Children (T. Layton & D. Holmes, 1985, Super Duper Publications)	4–11.6

TABLE 12.2 *(continued)*

Test	Ages (yr:mo)
Rhode Island Test of Language Structuring for Deaf or Hard of Hearing Children (E. Engen & T. Engen, 1983, Pro. Ed.)	3–20
Test of Early Reading Ability—Deaf or Hard of Hearing (TERA-D/HH) (D. Reid, W. Hresko, D. Hammil, S. Wiltshire, 1991, Super Duper Publications.)	3–13.11
Test of Word Knowledge (E. Wiig & W. Secord, 1992, The Psychological Corp.)	5–18
Test of Written Language—Third Edition (D. Hammil, S. Larsen, 1995, The Psychological Corp.)	7.6–17.11
Test of Narrative Language (R. Gilliam & N. Pearson, 2005, Academic Communication Associates)	5.0–11.11

evaluate African American children who speak African American English (AAE), it is likely that their performance scores will be penalized. Assessments that focus not on differences among dialect communities, but on commonalities, are the appropriate wave of the future for assessments of culturally different children (Bernstein-Ratner, 2004).

Seymour, Roeper, and de Villiers (2003) developed an assessment instrument specifically designed for both AAE and MAE speakers ages 4 to 12 that assesses phonology, syntax, semantics, and pragmatics. This assessment, *Diagnostic Evaluation of Language Variation* (DELV), looks for the presence or absence of typical developmental patterns that show a child's growth toward adult phonology, syntax, semantics, and pragmatics. This culturally dialect-neutral assessment readily discriminates dialect and difference from disorder.

Of equal importance and challenge is the issue of identifying a language disorder in a bilingual child. For the truly bilingual child, both languages can be used in one conversation. When this occurs, the term *code switching* is applied, alternation between two languages within or across sentences. When children of immigrants learn to speak, they often speak in a vernacular of the bilingual community that is neither the ethnic language nor the language of the society. This vernacular may often be the child's dominant language (Backus, 1999).

Often, testing by a bilingual SLP will indicate that neither language is dominant. In this instance the child will be educated in the language of the society (English). Determining if the child requires ESL (English as a second language) services or speech-language services or both is a task that cannot be accomplished without good collaboration among professionals. Assessment requires a linguistically nonbiased approach that recognizes the cultural rules of an ethnic group and does not penalize a child for adherence to these rules, even though they may be different from the dominant culture.

We live in a society enriched by its cultural diversity. According to Cheng (1996), we need to "go beyond bilingualism to the essence of human communication." What this means is that we cannot view only the linguistic codes of those children with whom we work. It is necessary to consider cross-cultural communicative competence. Within the United States we traditionally consider the bilingual child to be the child whose home language is different from the school language, English. What often occurs is that the first language influences the form of the second language. When this occurs, one must determine if the form or structure of English as spoken by the child represents merely a difference or is a disorder.

A multitude of languages are spoken in the United States, and it is unreasonable to expect that this diversity can be matched exactly with speech-language clinicians who also speak specific languages. However, there are guidelines that every SLP must adhere to when working with children from multicultural backgrounds:

- SLPs need to be aware of the sociolinguistic factors that are operating within the culture of children with whom they work.
- SLPs must be aware of which assessment instruments are suitable for the children with whom they work.
- SLPs must continually focus on the issue of differentiating language difference from language disorders.
- SLPs must be acquainted with and understand the phonological, grammatical, and prosodic variations utilized in the different home languages of the children with whom they work.

Child Diversity

African American Students

Many users of AAE code switch; that is, they may use AAE at home, but use Standard American English (SAE) in other situations outside the home. However, this depends on the age of the speaker. Some features that contrast AAE from SAE are phonological features that do not develop until after the age of 5 years. Therefore, it would be expected that a child using AAE might utilize the /f/ phoneme in place of the /th/ phoneme in the final position of words ("bof" for "both") or use the /d/ phoneme for /th/ ("dey" for "they"). (For more extensive descriptions see Terrel and Terrel, 1993). To distinguish a true language disorder from AAE it is necessary to focus on the non-contrastive features between AAE and SAE. These features are shared in SAE and AAE and include the use of conjunctions, articles, prepositions, and demonstrative pronouns (Battle, 1996).

Unfortunately, children who speak a nonstandard variety of SAE are potentially at-risk academically because curriculum and academic instruction are based on SAE (Thompson, Craig, & Washington, 2004). A significant number of African American students evidence lower academic achievement than do their majority peers (Jencks & Phillips, 1998). Fishback and Baskin (1991) call this the "Black–White Achievement Gap." Many variables may contribute to this gap, such as low socioeconomic status and all its related risk factors and schools that lack resources for effective teaching

(Snow, Burns, & Griffin, 1998). It has been shown that many African American students are dialect shifters; that is, they can shift from AAE to SAE. These children may outperform African American students who cannot shift their dialect (Craig & Washington, 2000). This positive outcome for dialect shift has been studied further, resulting in the following findings:

- Most third-grade African American students produce variable amounts of AAE during spoken discourse.
- AAE feature use decreases from the oral to literacy contexts.
- Third-grade African American students demonstrate distinct AAE feature profiles within oral and literacy contexts. (Thompson, Craig, & Washington, 2004)

Important academic and clinical information is obtained from these results. Because AAE decreases to a usage level of one third in written contexts when compared to spoken contexts, enabling children to dialect shift will support them in accessing information from textbooks written in SAE and learning from teachers who teach using SAE.

Spanish Speakers

Many children from Spanish backgrounds have no command of English or speak it to a limited degree (Chapa & Valencia, 1993). These children often are met with conflicting and confusing contexts for learning English. Some children go to schools where very few children speak Spanish and academic instruction is in English only; bilingual tutoring is done in English, and school staff believe dual-language instruction is confusing and unproductive (Langdon, 1996). To be successful when assessing Spanish-speaking American children, it is important that the SLP recognize that an evaluation must be performed by a bilingual professional when the child's home language is Spanish (Langdon, 1996).

Establishing the language status of the child, administering a battery of tests, and documenting the linguistic and cultural differences of the child are all part of the assessment process for the Latino child (Kayser, 1993). Language samples need to be gathered in both languages, and information about where, when, and to whom the child speaks English and Spanish is also necessary. Standardized testing may not reveal enough information. If a child is unfamiliar with the testing situation, he or she may not perform optimally, even when the test has been standardized on Spanish-speaking children. It may be necessary to modify test procedures, recognizing that scores cannot be reported as standardized, but rather using the information to gain a better understanding of the child's functioning level within the language tested. Finally, it is up to the SLP to consider the linguistic and cultural differences of the socioeconomic status of the child's family. All this requires dedicated time for data collection and analysis. In addition, Kayser (1993) suggests the following:

1. Observe sequencing, memory, and attention span. If a child is language disordered, these processes will be affected in both languages.
2. Determine if the parent feels there is a language problem. Parents are good informants in recognizing problems in their native language.

3. Determine if a disorder, such as voice, fluency, or articulation, exists in both languages.
4. Consider the possibility that when children are exposed to English they may lose their linguistic abilities in Spanish.

In addition to standardized tests for Spanish speakers, there are also criterion-referenced assessments, such as the Spanish Language Assessment Procedures (SLAP) (L. Mattes, 1995) and the Spanish Articulation Measure (SAM) (L. Mattes, 1995).

In sum, Spanish-speaking American children in the United States are a heterogeneous group who are changing, given their contact with the English language in schools and society. Bilingualism is complex and includes biculturalism. Assessment is a challenge.

Children with Hearing Loss

Testing children who have a hearing loss presents a different kind of challenge to the SLP. Many assessment instruments used with these children are inventories or checklists and do not provide standardized measures. Often children with hearing loss are administered tests that have been standardized on hearing children, and the test results or scores provide information regarding the language-area strengths and weaknesses. For instance, the EOWPVT-R could be used to provide a measure of how many words can be named by the child. Keep in mind though that the standardized scores that have been determined cannot be used.

However, a few tests are standardized on the child with hearing loss, such as the Carolina Picture Vocabulary Test (1985), The Rhode Island Test of Language Structure, and The Test of Early Reading Ability Deaf or Hard of Hearing (1991). In addition, there are checklists and inventories such as the Ling Phonetic Speech Level Evaluation (1976), Schedules of Development in Audition, Speech, Language Communication for Hearing Impaired Infants and Their Parents (Ling, 1976), and the Craig Lipreading Inventory (1977). The SLP needs to look at all the assessments available and select those that will give the best information regarding phonology, syntax, semantics, and pragmatics.

Another pertinent issue is whether sign language is used in the home or the educational environment. Factoring in this variable is critical. Assessment of the personal amplification system of the child (hearing aids, cochlear implant, or both) can only be done by an audiologist, so this professional's input is necessary during the assessment process and throughout the course of educational programming. If a child is newly implanted or a new recipient of hearing aids, the auditory learning needs are of utmost importance and are identified by the audiologist. Later, after implantation and during the child's progress through the educational system, the assessment of the child's changing auditory needs as they relate to the educational environment requires continual monitoring.

Auditory Processing

Within the last 10 to 15 years, traditional standardized testing areas have been expanded to include testing of auditory processing. Children's ability to process the auditory signal in an efficient manner is being investigated vigorously by audiologists. It is believed that much of what is considered to be within the realm of central auditory processing (CAP) is not performed at a conscious level. Auditory processing testing includes the following:

1. Sound localization
2. Auditory pattern discrimination
3. Auditory pattern recognition
4. Temporal aspects of audition, such as temporal resolution masking, integration, and ordering
5. Auditory performance deterioration in the presence of competing acoustic signals
6. Auditory performance deterioration in the presence of degraded signals

Interest in auditory processing disorders has increased because of the many children who exhibit significant academic difficulties due to a learning disability or language disability. From this population, Bellis (2003) believes that a large number of school-age children will have a central auditory processing disorder and that it is necessary to screen for this disorder. The screening requires a team approach whereby educational, psychological, social, speech-language, and medical information is gathered. The audiologist will perform an audiological evaluation to rule out a hearing loss. Based on this information, a referral for a complete CAP battery is made. Several audiological assessments are administered and include the SCAN-C Test for Auditory Processing Disorders in Children—Revised (Keith, 2000), the Dichotic Digits Test (Musiek, 1983), and the Gap Detection Test (Keith, 2000).

Once a screening identifies a child likely to have an auditory processing disorder, a full CAP battery of tests is administered by an audiologist and includes dichotic speech tests, tests that examine temporal processing abilities, tests that evaluate the ability to discriminate degraded speech, and tests that assess binaural interaction (for more complete explanation, see Bellis, 2003). Children can be tested as young as 3 years of age, although reliability of testing increases considerably for children over 7 years old (Bellis, 1998). Several characteristics of children who evidence auditory processing disorders can be found in Figure 12.2 (Richards, 2001).

Narrative Development

Narrative development is another area of interest. Narratives are not assessed utilizing standardized tests. Instead, narrative structure and narrative thought and comprehension can be assessed informally using guidelines developed by Westby, Van Dongen, and Maggart (1989) and Applebee (1978). Generally, the assessment is performed when

Majority are male
Normal hearing
Difficulty following oral directions
Short auditory attention
Poor short- and long-term memory
Difficulty listening in the presence of background noise
Difficulty localizing sound
Academic difficulties with phonics, reading, or spelling
History of otitis media
Frequent requests for verbal repetition
Disruptive behaviors: distracted, impulsive, frustrated

FIGURE 12.2

Characteristics of Auditory Processing Disorders
Source: Richards, 2001.

children retell stories or create their own stories. Recently, a standardized measure has become available, The Test of Narrative Language (Gillam & Pearson, 2005).

Applebee's (1978) six basic types of narrative structure delineate the emergence of true narratives by the time a child is 6 to 7 years old. By 7 to 11 years, children begin to summarize and categorize stories. True narratives consistently include a plot, sequence of events, and some character development. Hutson-Nechkash (1990) uses story grammar assessments to determine a child's level of narrative development. Children's stories are assessed to see if they include setting, character, events and causal relationships, consequences, and goals. Based on this assessment, the SLP determines to what stage a child's narrative adheres and if it is age appropriate.

Westby (1989), however, goes beyond narrative structure. She examines not only narrative structure, but also narrative thought and comprehension. She believes that how a child thinks shapes the organization of the child's physical and social knowledge, which is reflected in the child's narrative. There are multiple ways to obtain a narrative from a child. A child can be asked to retell stories, reorder scrambled stories, and even complete stories (Coggins & Carpenter, 1981). When evaluating the thought and comprehension skills behind narration, the SLP assesses the child's ability to develop cause–effect relationships and interpret the feelings of characters in a story.

Tough (1981) suggests the use of wordless picture books. By having the child narrate a story based on the picture book, the SLP gains information about the child's ability to report what is happening; project what he or she thinks a character is saying, thinking, or feeling; reason why certain actions are occurring; and predict further actions.

Using narrative assessments as part of an overall assessment of children's language competence is useful in diagnosing language disabilities in young children. Children who tell shorter narratives than do their peers, leave out major narrative components, use unclear pronominal reference, and basically only "heap" a series of unrelated sentences together with no central theme or sequence have an expressive language deficit (Westby, 1989).

McFadden and Gillam (1996) examine the narratives of students with language disorders using a holistic scoring procedure. This scoring analyzes narratives according to quantifiable elements, such as grammar, vocabulary, and episodic organization, as well as less quantifiable elements, like charm, interest, and clarity. Holistic scoring is achieved by grouping a collection of stories into quality-based categories, selecting the stories that best exemplify the identified categories (called *anchors*), collaborating with other professionals on descriptions of the commonalities among anchors (called *rubrics*), and assigning a single score to the stories collected based on a comparison with the anchors and rubrics (Kirby, Liner, and Vinz, 1988).

From using this type of analysis, it appears that students with language disorders are more likely to have their narratives, both written and spoken, judged as weak. Furthermore, judgments of the overall quality of narratives are linked to textual-level measures of form and content, whereas sentential-level measures, such as longer, syntactically complex utterances, are not associated with positive quality judgments. This finding is useful for the SLP and suggests that the quality of a student's stories can be improved by improving textual-level elements, such as story length and episodic organization, as well as qualitative elements, such as charm, interest, and clarity. It seems that teaching children to use longer, syntactically more complex utterances will not necessarily improve overall quality.

Western societies consider the term *narrative* to be synonymous with story. However, in some sociocultural groups, fictional narratives may be rare. Consequently, when assessing children from culturally different backgrounds, the SLP needs to take this fact into consideration. There are four universal types of narrative: recounts, event casts, accounts, and stories (Heath, 1986). The account is the earliest type of narrative that children produce independently. Accounts vary widely among speakers and come from children's personal experiences. Different cultural groups provide different experiences and situations for children. In some cultural groups, children may be encouraged to give accounts of their personal experiences; in other groups they may not. Because of this, SLPs need to be cautioned that when analyzing children's narratives; an ethnographic approach needs to be taken. That is, the SLP needs to take into consideration the ethnography of each child's community and what, when, and how narratives are developed within the community.

Alternative Assessments: Curriculum-Based Language Assessments

Alternative assessments are frequently used in educational settings to measure and quantify the progress a child is making in academic learning. Alternative assessments are curriculum based, are criterion referenced, and do not use standardized data for scoring. Curriculum-based language assessments assess a student's language strengths and needs using curricular content for the purpose of developing intervention goals (Nelson & Van Meter, 2002). Curriculum-based language assessments facilitate access to and progress in the general-education curriculum for children with special learning needs. This type of assessment is timely and necessary when one considers that the 1997 Reauthorization of IDEA requires that children with special learning needs have access to the general-education curriculum.

Curriculum-based assessments are not generally utilized for determining eligibility for special-education services. Instead they are used to find out if a student has the language skills to learn the curriculum and to measure a student's progress within the general-education curriculum. Nelson (1989, 1998, 2002) recommends that curriculum-based language assessments begin with interviews of students, teachers, and parents to determine the curriculum areas of the greatest concern. Specifically, what language skills are required? What does the student currently do? What does the student need to do differently? Does the curricular task need to be modified and, if so, how?

Many times these questions relate to the reading and writing curricula. Consequently, the role of the SLP has expanded to include these two curricular areas. ASHA has defined the SLP's responsibility and role in literacy development and states the following:

> Individuals with reading and writing problems also may experience difficulties in using language strategically to communicate, think, and learn. These fundamental connections necessitate that intervention for language disorders target written as well as spoken language needs.

> (ASHA, 2001)

Therefore, the SLP has the responsibility of analyzing the reading and writing skills of children in elementary school. Nelson (1998) developed a model that examines the three linguistic knowledge systems of phonological–orthographic, syntactic, and semantic, and the related systems of pragmatics, discourse, and world knowledge. In this model the phonological–orthographic system includes words and syllables and morphemes, and sound–symbol associations. The syntactic system includes sentence relations, sentence combining, sentence structures, and grammatic morphemes. The semantic system includes figurative meaning, lexical referents, and event and case relations. Pragmatics includes speaker's intention, listener information, topic management, and contextual variation. Discourse includes scripts and genre, story grammar, text cohesion, and formats. World knowledge includes schemata, categories, and inferences.

The model is inclusive, and it can be used to analyze samples of a student's writing. Interestingly, written-language disabilities can remain long after spoken language and reading skills have shown improvement (Johnson, 1987). If the clinician wants to utilize a formal assessment of writing, The Test of Written Language (TOWL Third Edition) (Hammil and Larsen, 1995) is useful for children 7.6 to 17.11 years old.

Technological Applications in Assessment

In this age of technology, any chapter about assessment would be lacking if information regarding the use of technology for assessment of speech-language disorders was not addressed. The numbers of software programs available designed specifically for assessment have grown. These nonstandardized assessment tools are time saving and worthy of attention. They have numerous applications for adult and child populations. They can be utilized to assist in the computation and analysis of data gathered from standardized assessments. For example, scoring software is available for the Woodcook Language Proficiency Battery—Revised, the Clinical Evaluation of Language Fundamentals—4, SCAN-C, and the Peabody Picture Vocabulary Test III. To date, computerized test administration has not been standardized, and therefore technology use is limited to data analysis; however, it lends itself well to being an invaluable tool for informal assessment.

Long (1999) reviews two excellent software programs that can be used for language assessment. They are Systematic Analysis of Language Transcripts (SALT) (Miller & Chapman, 1998) and Child Language Analysis (CLAN) (MacWhinney, 1995). These programs assist the SLP to analyze MLU, types of utterance, conversational assertiveness and responsiveness, word finding difficulty, syntax, grammar, semantic relations, lexicon, phonological processes, and narratives.

Masterson & Oller (1999) examine two other computer programs that are useful for phonological assessment, the Interactive System for Phonological Analysis (ISPA) (Masterson & Pagan, 1993) and Logical International Phonetic Programs (LIPP) (*Oller*, 1991). They are described as useful not only for diagnosis, but also for targeting intervention procedures.

The Computerized Speech Lab (CSL from Kay Elemetrics), the Computerized Speech Research Environment (CSRE, from AVAAZ Innovations), Speech Viewer II (IBM), and Soundscape are software programs that give visual feedback about the child's speech using spectrographic display. These programs are useful for older children, and some have been used successfully for children with hearing loss.

Story Weaver Deluxe (MECC) and KidWorks (Davidson & Associates) are good software programs for treatment and home practice activities for articulation training. A software program that is beneficial for phonemic identification and remediation is Speech Assessment and Interactive Learning System (SAILS, AVAAZ, Innovations, Inc.). The CD-ROM Articulation by Loco Tour Multimedia is also a good tool for articulation training. (For more information, see Masterson & Rvachew, 1999.)

In sum, computer technology will continue to develop and become a valuable tool for assessment and intervention. To take advantage of its usefulness, clinicians must continually increase their knowledge and expertise in computer use.

Collaborative and Inclusive Education

Assessing the child and identifying issues that negatively affect the educational programming of a child is only the beginning. Once the child is identified as requiring educational supports, an equally challenging process begins: providing an inclusive education for the elementary school child. The benefits of the collaborative process appear in educational journals crossing many professional fields. Gitlin (1999), however, cautions that there are many forms of collaboration with limited understanding of the specific aspects that result in good practice. Professional configurations that are described as collaboration in schools vary, along with the resulting teaching goals. The researcher indicates that

Robust forms of collaboration can achieve broadly defined progressive ends when the effects of collaboration on the intensification of teachers' work are limited, when teachers play a significant role in setting the agenda for the collaborative process, and when the issues raised as part of the collaborative process emerge from the contextual realities of a particular school. (p.630)

The Role of the Speech-Language Pathologist

The SLP may provide direct services to children within special- and general-education classes, function as a consultant to the classroom teacher, and still maintain a clinical caseload of children. Consequently, there is not much time left for collaboration with teachers, specialists, and parents in elementary school. Although the SLP has become an integral member of the special-education committee's evaluation and decision-making process, she or he may not work directly with the child being evaluated.

The demand for speech-and-language therapy services has increased over the years as the relationship between language and academic learning, particularly reading and writing, has been emphasized (ASHA, 2001). In addition, with the development of the early intervention and preschool special-education systems, language development has become the most important indicator for a developmental disability. Because *only* SLPs can assess and remediate language functioning, their numbers have increased in all areas of education. The SLP is being encouraged to work with other professionals in diverse settings outside the traditional therapy room; as a consequence, professional relationships and responsibilities are changing.

The SLP and the Teacher Connection

In elementary school, there is an important connection between language, literacy, and writing. Observing a child with a disability in the classroom provides the SLP with important information about her metalinguistic, metapragmatic, metacognitive, and metacomprehension skills. Is the child able to keep up with the method and pace of instruction? Does she understand the information or material presented well enough to respond appropriately and follow directions? When she becomes distracted is she disruptive? Can she ask the teacher or a peer for help? So, how does the SLP work with a child in a general-education classroom?

The traditional approach limited the SLP's practice to a separate area or room. With the recognition of integrated therapy models as an educational option in schools, the focus has shifted to classroom-based interventions. Wilcox, Kouri, and Caswell (1991) compare the efficacy of classroom intervention to pull-out individual therapy sessions and find that the integrated approach facilitates an increase in the generalization of targeted goals. Kaufman, Prelock, Weiler, Creaghead, and Donnelly (1994) compare the effectiveness of instructional methodologies and note that collaboratively taught lessons improve children's understanding of what constitutes an adequate explanation, whereas the control-class peers did not. Ellis, Schlaudecker, and Regimbal (1995) show that, when the teacher and the SLP collaborate on concepts that are taught in class, children in an experimental group achieve a higher level of performance than children in a control group.

Earlier we indicated that both the classroom teacher and the typical children in the classroom will benefit from a language approach to academic learning. The teacher and the SLP can teach the same activity by using instructional methods that emphasize different goals. In special and general education, the focus of learning is on the acquisition of knowledge, and children's competencies are evaluated based on the accumulation of information. The focus of language learning in school includes the use of knowledge for communication purposes. Developing and expanding a child's vocabulary is important, but explaining, questioning, narrating, and elaborating are more important because they represent skills that facilitate further learning. The collaboration of the teacher and the SLP introduces a learning dynamic that will enhance and enrich the general-education curriculum for all children.

There is not a subject area in elementary or secondary education that does not require language competencies; math, science, and history all require language skills. The degree to which language is impaired is the degree to which these academic areas will also be delayed. Ehren (2000) believes the role of the SLP is to assist children in acquiring the underpinnings of the academic curriculum. She suggests that, although the SLP should share responsibility for curriculum learning, she or he needs to maintain a therapeutic focus. The SLP's goals and activities should be different from the teacher's curriculum goals and activities. She or he can aid the teacher in the following ways:

1. Help a child understand the language on a math test.
2. Help the teacher generate test questions that are less complex linguistically so that the test reflects the child's skills in that area (math, science, etc.) and not his inability to understand that question or task.
3. Teach the teacher to rephrase her question to a child with language disorders so that he experiences success in functioning as a contributor to the academic activity.
4. Teach peers to verbally assist and nonverbally guide the child with language disorders so that he can remain engaged in an activity and function as a member of a group.
5. Help teachers present their lessons without asking too many questions. Show teachers how to facilitate learning by teaching children to ask questions and elaborate their answers for peers.
6. Support reading and writing activities by teaching vocabulary, semantic mapping, and multiple meanings. This also enhances curriculum content because it develops the language skills necessary to access the general curriculum through reading.

A partnership between the SLP and the teacher will ensure that the child with language disabilities will be able to keep up with the academic curriculum. An important area of collaboration is reading comprehension. Children spend their early years in school learning how to read, but must eventually read to learn. When reading comprehension is intact, children will be able to keep up academically. Reading comprehension is affected by different types of text. Textbooks can be poorly written or poorly organized. Children with language impairments do not know how to comprehend complex academic language. They need to learn specific strategies; they need systematic instruction; they need responsive instruction (individualized to match learning style); and they need intensive instruction (Ehren, 2006). It is the responsibility of the SLP and the classroom teacher to provide these.

Collaborative Teaming: Community Based

Collaboration also extends to the community. Just as professional teams dialogue during assessment to determine if a disability exists and then identify the supports needed to appropriately educate children, so too is collaboration necessary between the community and school. When districts institute inclusion classrooms, they need to dialogue with the community so that there is clear understanding that inclusion programming does not dilute education, but rather enriches it.

The community-based team should have a broad representation, consisting of parents, administrators, school board representatives, community residents, and teachers. This team holds public hearings to engage members of the neighborhood to share their ideas about educational reforms (Tiegerman-Farber, 2002b). The response from the public should be analyzed and presented to educators along with the team's recommendations. Schools are supported and funded by taxpayers; schools need to work within communities to reflect their issues. Schools are embedded within diverse multicultural environments, and the community as a whole needs to understand the educational mission and the changes that are evolving in response to educational legislation (Smrekar & Cohen-Vogel, 2001).

The community-based team also identifies community issues, such as cultural diversity and barriers that are likely to occur as educational reform continues (Buysse & Wesley, 1999). If the community does not support the mission and goals of school initiatives such as inclusion programming, the school will have a difficult time achieving physical, social, and instructional interactions between children with and without disabilities (Tiegerman-Farber, 2002b; Tiegerman-Farber & Radziewicz, 1998).

Collaborative Teaming: School Based

The collaborative team within a school incorporates the concerns and issues of the community to implement a school-based inclusion program (Small, 2002). Will the community support the school's mission? School-based teams need to discuss what might happen if community leaders object to the new program. How will teachers and administrators deal with the community's dissension to facilitate a better understanding of the legal requirements and educational benefits of inclusion? This team should consist of representatives from the school: an administrator, a special-education teacher, a speech-language pathologist, a regular teacher, and parents of children with and without disabilities (Tiegerman-Farber, 2002b). This team needs to accomplish the following:

1. Ensure supportive networking between the school and community before, during, and after inclusive programming has been developed.
2. Provide a timeline for programmatic changes that includes community updates on progress.

3. List the strategies to achieve classroom inclusion.
4. List the school modifications and possible classroom problems related to implementing an inclusion program:
   - Financial costs and underlying programming changes
   - Need for new staff
   - Number of children with and without disabilities in the inclusion classroom
   - Organizational and instructional issues to meet the needs of all children
   - Classroom resources, such as additional supplies and materials
   - Fears and concerns of parents, teachers, and children
   - Need for teacher training and other types of teacher supports

Collaborative Teaming: Classroom Based

The classroom-based collaborative team consists of a teacher, a speech-language pathologist, a psychologist, and parents of children with and without disabilities. This team has the most complicated responsibility, because short- and long-term problems require discussion, negotiation, and resolution as classroom problems occur and changes need to be implemented (Tiegerman-Farber, 2002b). The team needs to discuss ways to achieve physical, social, and instructional integration between children with and without disabilities in the classroom. Changes in instructional methodologies, curriculum, educational goals, and outcome goals that are linguistically and culturally relevant to children must also be addressed at this level. It may also be important to consider discussions with children as classroom programs and procedures begin to change (Tiegerman-Farber & Radziewicz, 1998).

Figure 12.3 provides a checklist for achieving success in the inclusive classroom.

Are parents collaborating at the district level to generate school mission and policy?
Are parents collaborating at the school level to generate decisions about inclusion in specific classrooms?
Are there collaborative teams for each inclusion classroom? Parents and teachers need to be directly involved.
Did the collaborative team decide about:
1. Classroom community goals?
2. Classroom organization?
3. Profile for children in the classroom?
4. Adaptations in curriculum?
5. Individual goals for each child?
6. Special equipment needs?
7. Additional staff–instructional supports?
8. Staffing ratios?
9. Learning profiles of children with special needs?
Are parents of general education students committed to the goals of inclusion in this classroom? If not, what strategies can be used to change the negative attitudes expressed by parents?
Are parents of children with disabilities committed?

FIGURE 12.3
Checklist for Inclusion Success

The Martinez Family

José Martinez is ready to enter kindergarten. The elementary school psychologist performed several assessments that included both standardized and nonstandardized instruments. The Test of Nonverbal Intelligence (TONI—3) was administered because it did not require a verbal response. The CARS (Childhood Autism Rating Scales) indicated that José has moderate autism. José did not perform many of the tasks required on the standardized assessments. He does not sit for more than 5 to 10 minutes, and he does not respond to most questions. José has a lexicon of about 250 words, but because he does not consistently point to pictures, the Peabody Picture Vocabulary Test—Revised cannot be administered. Maria Martinez is interviewed and answers questions from the Autism Diagnostic Interview Revised (ADIR).

Psychological testing indicates that José is functioning below the average range of intelligence. This is a terrible shock for Maria; she believed that once José learned to talk he would be fine. The special-education committee recommends that José be seen by a neurologist. The committee recommends that José enter their 18–2–1 kindergarten program (18 children, 2 teachers, 1 teacher assistant) in a local elementary school. Because of his intense individual needs, it is felt that this classroom with 12 typical children, 6 children with special needs, 2 teachers, and 1 teacher assistant is appropriate. José is not yet toilet trained so that is a goal on his IEP.

Maria has concerns about José's fine-motor control; he still does not hold a crayon or a pencil very well and prefers to eat food with his hands. The committee recommends the continuation of occupational therapy services, but now it is provided in a group. His speech services are also decreased to individual speech one time a week and group speech two times a week.

Maria has concerns about transportation to and from school. The psychologist tells her that a minibus will be provided for José and that other children with special needs will also be on the bus. Although there will be a matron on the bus, Maria wonders if one person will be able to handle the children.

CW 12.1

Use the Companion Website to help you answer the following questions:

1. Do you feel that José was evaluated properly? Why or why not?
2. If you were evaluating José, what other assessments would you perform?
3. José has deficits in most language areas. What do you think most negatively affects his ability to socialize with peers?
4. What goals would you target for José?

The St. James Family

Jeffrey has been receiving services in his child-care program. The committee reviews his progress reports before conducting a complete evaluation. He still has tantrums; he is also very impulsive and occasionally hits other children in child care. He does not seem to be able to regulate his emotional responses to peers without negative behaviors.

Jeffrey is administered several assessments: Test for Auditory Comprehension of Language—3 (TACL-3), Peabody Picture Vocabulary Test III, the Expressive One Word Picture Vocabulary Test, and the Goldman–Fristoe Test of Articulation. His performance places him within the typical range of functioning, although his articulation is still compromised by immature phonological processes. The psychological testing also shows Jeffrey to be in the average to high-average range. The committee discusses placement in a program for emotionally and behaviorally disordered children.

Camille objects to the label and the placement. Jeffrey is placed in a general-education classroom with 22 children and 1 teacher. In addition, for 2 hours each day a teacher assistant will be in the classroom. Camille is very concerned about Jeffrey's behavior. Punishing Jeffrey for inappropriate behaviors does not seem to work at home. Jeffrey hits other children when he becomes angry and then denies that he did so. Camille is concerned about this and considers his denials to be lying. She is also worried that he does not have any friends, and she hopes that when he starts kindergarten things will be different.

CW 12.2

Use the Companion Website to help you answer the following questions:

1. Do you think Jeffrey will have an easy transition into kindergarten? Why or why not?

2. Jeffrey receives standardized assessments. Do you think any nonstandardized assessments should have been performed and, if so, which ones? What information could have been provided?

3. Do you think Jeffrey is a child at-risk? If so, for what kinds of difficulties?

The Whiteside Family

Kaitlyn Whiteside has responded well to her cochlear implant and her preschool program at the Mission School. Sign language facilitates good language understanding and Kaitlyn develops most kindergarten readiness skills. Because she receives intense speech therapy at school and her teachers use both signing and speaking, Kaitlyn's speech improves. In preparation for the committee meeting, several standardized assessments are administered, such as the Carolina Picture Vocabulary Test, the Expressive One Word Picture Vocabulary Test (Kaitlyn is allowed to respond with speech and sign), and the Test of Auditory Comprehension of Language—TACL (the test is administered using sign and speech). The Craig Lipreading Inventory for Children is also administered, and Kaitlyn is found to have good speech-reading skills. The Test of Non Verbal Intelligence (TONI-3) is administered by the psychologist and Kaitlyn is found to have high-average intelligence.

The special-education committee considers all the test data and recommends that Kaitlyn attend their general-education kindergarten. An SLP will see Kaitlyn for individual therapy two times a week. However, Kaitlyn will not be provided with a sign-language interpreter in the classroom. Instead, a teacher of the deaf will consult with the classroom teacher and work for one period a day with Kaitlyn.

Katherine Whiteside is pleased to see how much progress Kaitlyn has made at the Mission School. The kindergarten teacher in the public school has only 1 year of teaching experience and has never worked with a child who has a hearing loss. Furthermore, although Kaitlyn's speech has improved, she is still unintelligible about 50% of the time when she speaks in sentences. Kaitlyn has made good friends at the Mission School and is often invited to play dates with her friends. Kaitlyn never seems to be overly concerned about her deafness because her family and school friends communicate well with her. Katherine takes great pride in Kaitlyn's good social skills, but the school district's kindergarten class would have 26 children.

In preschool Kaitlyn is able to follow the instruction because of sign language and technological supports. How will Kaitlyn make friends if her speech is not always intelligible? Katherine fears that in the public school Kaitlyn may become isolated from her peers and become keenly aware of her deafness and her difference from other children. Katherine also wonders about how much knowledge the kindergarten teacher has about deafness and cochlear implants? Who will train the kindergarten teacher to utilize appropriate teaching strategies and when will this training take place? Is the special-education committee putting Kaitlyn into a setting that she is not ready for? Will Kaitlyn experience failure in this setting and, if so, what will the effect be on her self-esteem? Katherine Whiteside cannot decide what to do and is considering an impartial hearing.

CW 12.3

Use the Companion Website to help you to answer the following questions:

1. Do you agree with the special-education committee's recommendation to place Kaitlyn in a regular kindergarten? Why or why not?

2. Educating Kaitlyn in the mainstream will present challenges for her and the professionals working with Kaitlyn. What challenges do you see for Kaitlyn? Who are appropriate collaborative team members and what is the role of each?

3. How can social interactions for Kaitlyn be facilitated in a general-education setting?

Determining Child Benefit: Kaitlyn's Case*

It is time for you to *apply* your knowledge. We want you to comment on Katherine's arguments about Kaitlyn's inability to *benefit* from a general setting with typical peers. The school district's committee recommends a general-education classroom in the local public school, but Katherine is not certain that Kaitlyn is ready for this placement. The committee argues that the least restrictive environment for Kaitlyn is the general classroom with hearing children. The committee also stresses that it is required to provide what is "appropriate," and not what is "better or best for Kaitlyn." The school district is not obligated to provide a sign interpreter nor a private school. Keep in mind that Katherine Whiteside is an exceptionally determined parent. Many issues within Katherine Whiteside's argument lead her to a final conclusion: Kaitlyn will not *benefit* from the general-education program.

Kaitlyn's Least Restrictive Environment

It is up to the CSE to determine the LRE for Kaitlyn. Since the reauthorization of IDEA (2004) and NCLB (2001), the focus of education is to provide improved instructional activities so that all children with and without special-learning needs can function appropriately in the mainstream classroom. Consider Mrs. Whiteside's perspective in Box 12.1 on what the LRE for Kaitlyn is.

Mrs. Whiteside believes that Kaitlyn needs to be in an educational program with other children who are deaf. The Deaf Community argues that the LRE is not the general classroom, and normalization for the deaf cannot be achieved in a hearing environment. The potential of the child who is deaf must be understood, given the backdrop of deaf education, specialized training, and deaf models and peers. Members of the Deaf Community object to the notion of normalcy, which is based on the

*Tiegerman-Farber, Ellenmorris; Radziewicz, Christine, *Collaborative Decision Making: The Pathway to Inclusion*, © 1998, pp. 138–142. Adapted by permission of Pearson Education, Inc., Upper Saddle River, NJ.

BOX 12.1

Kaitlyn has very little residual hearing and has very poor speech intelligibility, even at 5 years of age. The committee wants to place her in an inclusion classroom. The principle of normalization suggests that all children who are deaf could be educated in an environment with hearing peers. Many members of the Deaf Community object to a definition of culturally normal for deaf children. The issue of normalization suggests that there is a formal definition of normal, which provides an educational reference standard. Within this normalized environment, a child with a disability should have access to a cultural experience, a common language, a social process, and an opportunity to achieve her potential. The inclusion classroom does not provide Kaitlyn with access to any of these.

Katherine Whiteside

hearing environment, because they do not perceive themselves as being abnormal. The deaf have a commitment to their community and a sense of self-respect and self-esteem, and they do not strive to be like hearing peers because they share a Deaf Culture. The Deaf Community feels that social justice involves the process of personal decision making and that they have a right to decide what is best for their children and for themselves. Their accomplishments and achievements are closely tied to a separate cultural community and self-determinism. The Deaf Community has historically established a separate school system that utilizes a distinctive language, curricula, teachers, models, and goals. Many educators of the deaf do not see inclusion as the only mechanism to achieve educational equity, personal opportunity, or academic development. The American Deaf Association has taken a strong position against inclusion for all students; decisions must be made based on the individual needs of the child and family. Education for children who are deaf must include a continuum of placements, with separate schools as an option.

Most deaf parents of children who are deaf argue that their unique human experience relates to their identification with their own cultural community. Inclusion for the deaf involves an identification with the Deaf Community; a full-inclusion model would be anything but inclusive for the child who is deaf. To include this child in a general classroom would in fact deny the child a basic cultural identification and the human experience of social communicative development.

Kaitlyn's Language Development

Mrs. Whiteside believes that Kaitlyn should be a member of the Deaf Community. If Kaitlyn is to be considered a member of the Deaf Community, she must be able to communicate effectively with other members of the Deaf Community. It is important for her to develop facility with sign language, because this is the preferred mode of communication. Sign language is used by the deaf and provides Kaitlyn with access to a world of communication and socialization. This issue arises: If Kaitlyn is denied continued development of a formalized system of language, will it isolate her from other deaf communicators? Sign language is the mechanism for Kaitlyn to "talk" to other members of her community.

The key question for public schools is whether public schools must provide Kaitlyn with the same degree of proficient–efficient instruction in sign language as a school for the deaf? Many research studies indicate that there are not enough teachers of the deaf or sign interpreters to teach in schools for the deaf, let alone in public schools. Polowe-Aldersley (1994) states, "inclusion settings are particularly hostile to teachers of the deaf who are themselves deaf. Policies of inclusion have all but wiped out the field's modest gains in hiring teachers who are deaf role models for minority deaf students" (p. 162).

To place Kaitlyn in a general classroom with hearing children involves a complex process, with an intermediary between Kaitlyn and her hearing peers. Most hearing children do not know sign language. General-education teachers do not have the facility to mediate between Kaitlyn and her hearing peers. Certainly, the general-education teacher is not going to become a teacher of the deaf. For normal development to occur, a child must acquire a standardized language. Where can the child who is deaf best acquire language? It is important to consider the problems related to bilingual instruction because they are similar to Kaitlyn's situation. Kaitlyn can only acquire sign language, her language, in a setting in which there is a teacher of the deaf, who is teaching language to other children who are deaf.

Education should not be impeded by the communication process. Language and communication must be utilized to facilitate education and instructional learning. Language cannot be learned in a vacuum; it is a social process. A community of peers becomes pivotal to language development and communicative interaction. What does inclusion provide for the child who is deaf when there are no means or mode to facilitate the language exchange between teacher and child and between Kaitlyn and her hearing peers?

Kaitlyn's Social Development

Because the peer experience is so critical to the inclusion process, it becomes important to consider how Kaitlyn will socialize with her hearing peers. Basic to the inclusion philosophy is the principle that children will be better off in a class with hearing peers. Members of the Deaf Community object to this claim because they do not see an inequity within their own community and schools. For some children who are deaf, socialization may be enhanced and facilitated by interaction with hearing peers. The child's level of hearing loss, type of hearing loss, language ability, mode of communication, and social–emotional needs should be taken into consideration in determining the individual placement of the child who is deaf. Many parents believe the needs of their child who is deaf can be appropriately met only within a specialized program provided within a school for the deaf. Another problem within the general classroom is that Kaitlyn will be the only child with a hearing loss. Can Kaitlyn and a hearing child socialize without a shared fluent language system? If they do socialize, can the interaction simulate what educators refer to as "normal" social and emotional interaction? Can Kaitlyn be included in an environment in which no one understands her language? How can Kaitlyn develop peer relationships, play games, attend parties, and make TTY telephone calls?

Innes (1994) notes that placing any child in an environment where basic social activities require constant intervention may actually obstruct normal development. In placing Kaitlyn within an inclusive environment, accommodations must be made to bridge the language barrier to integrate her into the hearing classroom. Providing a sign interpreter or teacher of the deaf is a necessary prerequisite accommodation. Will the school district make a commitment to the accommodations and resources Kaitlyn needs to be included? This question remains: How can Kaitlyn tell a hearing peer a secret that is shared only between the two of them?

Kaitlyn's Identity

To appropriately meet Kaitlyn's long-term social and emotional needs, it is critical to acknowledge that her self-respect and self-esteem will come from her sense of identification within the culture of the Deaf Community. Cultural identification is important to all of us; it establishes a framework for who we are and who we aspire to be. We all need to have social models and people we look up to and identify with. As a child who is deaf in a hearing world, Kaitlyn will always define herself as disabled and different. Can an inclusion class with hearing children provide Kaitlyn with an identification that is not based on disability?

Most deaf educators argue that the Deaf Community provides appropriate peers and models to facilitate peer interaction, self-identification, and positive role models for children who are deaf. They propose that Deaf Culture cannot be taught in a hearing environment by hearing teachers with hearing peers. Social identification and dynamics must be presented by the community itself. The values, social ideas, and aspirations of any cultural community must be presented by representative leaders of that community. For Kaitlyn to learn to be a member of the Deaf Community, she needs to network with deaf role models and be instructed by means of a process that uniquely reflects the values of the Deaf Community. Can a hearing teacher or hearing peers appropriately teach Kaitlyn about who she is as a child who is deaf?

CW 12.4

Read the Supreme Court Rowley case (*Board of Education of the Hendrik Hudson General School Dist.* v *Roarley*, 458 US 176, 102 S Ct. 3034, 73 L. Ed. 2d 690 [U.S. 1982]) and use the Companion Website to help you answer the following questions:

1. Can Kaitlyn function adequately in a typical classroom without a sign interpreter? Should the school district attempt to maximize a child's learning? Why or why not?

2. Who should make the final decision about Kaitlyn's education, the parent or the school district? Why?

3. Notice that Katherine refers to *hearing* peers and not typical peers. Comment.

4. What do you think about Katherine's arguments concerning Deaf Culture and the Deaf Community? Can this concept of culture–community be applied to other groups? Why or why not?

5. In the section on language development, Katherine Whiteside argues that general-education teachers do not have the knowledge or training to mediate between Kaitlyn and her hearing peers. Can this problem be generalized to other disabilities?

6. The Rowley case specifically says that special education does not require schools to provide services for children to "reach their potential." Explain the court's reasoning about educational opportunities for children with and without disabilities. Are they treated differently by the law? How does disparate treatment create educational difficulties for children with disabilities?

7. You are now the impartial hearing officer. What would be your determination concerning placement for Kaitlyn? Explain the basis for your decision.

8. What kinds of accommodations must be made within a classroom to meet the needs of a child who is deaf?

9. What are the possible responses to people who advocate for a full-inclusion model?

SUMMARY

Making appropriate placement decisions for children with special learning needs is a process and a place. The goal of an appropriate placement is that a child will be educated in a classroom that, whenever possible, exposes the child to the typical curriculum and provides the necessary supports to access this curriculum; and this is accomplished in an environment that is not too restrictive. The SLP plays an integral role in both the process and placement. The SLP uses appropriate assessment materials, integrates the results with the assessments performed by her colleagues, counsels parents about her test findings, sits on the CSE, suggests intervention goals, collaborates with classroom teachers to enable them to use language-facilitating techniques in the classroom, and monitors the progress of the child. Many times the SLP is the one professional who is consistently involved as the child progresses through the grades. Consequently, she or he becomes invaluable in the role of educational historian. The SLP weaves together the strands of techniques, strategies, and approaches and creates a cohesive pattern or blueprint for learning that will be shared with the child's next teacher.

Language Intervention Strategies for 5- to 8-Year-Olds

Chapter Objectives

After studying this chapter, you should be able to answer the following questions:

1. What various modifications within a general classroom can be used to accommodate a child with a language and communication disorder?

2. What techniques are used by the SLP to facilitate language learning in a general classroom?

3. What kinds of problems will José, Kaitlyn, and Jeffrey have in general education?

4. How can the SLP collaborate with the general-education teacher to generalize language goals for the children on her caseload to the classroom setting?

5. What are several facilitation techniques that can be used by the general-education teacher?

6. How does the SLP support academic learning in the general-education classroom?

In this chapter, a general-education inclusion classroom is discussed to highlight some of the language, reading, and writing problems presented by children with language disorders. Several studies of preschool children with language delays indicate that they still experience learning difficulties many years after their initial diagnosis (Aram, Ekelman, & Nation, 1984; Rescorla & Schwartz, 1990; Scarborough & Debrich, 1990). These longitudinal studies suggest that many of these children are reclassified in elementary school as learning disabled, given their academic difficulties, and/or as emotionally disturbed, given their behavioral difficulties.

The process of including children with disabilities in the general-education classroom requires a curriculum that must be adapted to the diverse instructional and academic learning needs of children with and without disabilities. The conceptual model of an inclusion classroom must be based on a curriculum that can be modified to meet these diverse needs.

Instructional teams should work collaboratively to develop a profile of the language, social, and educational needs of children within the inclusion classroom. The class profile will vary from class to class, given the number of children in the class, the number of children with disabilities, the types of disabilities and children's levels of functioning, the range of functioning within the class, the linguistic and cultural differences presented by children, the student to staff ratio, and the resources available to the teacher, including supplies, equipment, and personnel.

In addition, it might be important to identify children's social and academic needs. Social goals should reflect the interpersonal aspects of classroom interaction. Goals such as self-esteem, friendship, communication, personal achievement, leadership, and peer facilitation create a classroom community for children that can be either positive or negative. These are goals that all the children, those with and without disabilities, can strive to achieve as individuals and as group members. Complex discussions among the stakeholders, the general- and special-education teachers, and parents of children with and without disabilities, require negotiated solutions to possible conflicts. Only clear, honest, and respectful communication will resolve these issues.

Guidelines for Intervention Planning

Role of the SLP in Intervention Planning

- The SLP teaches language skills that enhance the child's ability to access the general curriculum; she or he does not teach academic subjects.
- The SLP should work in the classroom with the children who are assigned to her caseload. In the process, she may need to involve peers both with and without disabilities.
- The SLP is not the teacher's assistant or aide.
- The SLP and the teacher may develop different learning goals for the child and use different instructional techniques to meet these goals.
- The SLP and the teacher may develop the same learning goals for the child and use different instructional techniques to meet these goals.
- Language learning is a continuum of abilities. The SLP can work with a child who has autism and with a child with learning disabilities who has reading and/or writing problems.
- The SLP needs to understand the language skills and competencies underlying the development of reading and writing skills.
- The SLP develops metalinguistic knowledge of phonotactic and semantic structures.
- The SLP works with all children who have disabilities to improve comprehension monitoring by teaching strategies for predicting, questioning, clarification, summarization, narration, and conversation.

In this era of the Individual with Disabilities Act (IDEA, 2004) and the No Child Left Behind Act (NCLB, 2001), the SLP shifts her focus of practice from a traditional medical model to a curriculum-relevant model. In the traditional medical model, it was expected that the SLP provided a classroom pull-out service for 30 minutes twice a week. The curriculum-relevant model means that the SLP assesses, plans, and carries out intervention that is relevant to facilitate the child's ability to learn and progress within the general curriculum. Now the SLP identifies students with speech and language disorders and helps them to manage better in curricular contexts, identifies any mismatch between the student's language needs and the language expectations of the curriculum, and provides intervention utilizing curriculum-relevant content and contexts (Staskowski & Rivera, 2005).

Intervention Axioms

For the SLP to be effective when working with elementary schoolchildren, she must adhere to certain rules. She must focus on academic success, emphasize student strengths rather than weaknesses, and deliver intervention that is student centered. Curriculum-related language intervention is primary, and the communication strategies that are taught need to be age appropriate.

There are developmental prerequisites for strategy use. For children between the ages of 5 and 7, it is appropriate to transition from impulsive responding to reflective responding. Also, the ability to consider more than one facet of a problem emerges at this time, as does the ability to formulate hypotheses to solve problems. Taking another's perspective does not occur until age 8 (Wiig, 1992). When the SLP is aware of these developmentally appropriate behaviors, she or he will know when to introduce them into a child's intervention program.

How then does the SLP support curriculum-relevant therapy and at the same time develop specific language areas? Key to making therapy curriculum relevant is to use academic materials in the therapy situation. For the elementary-age student, working on answering questions that include key words such as "who," "why," "how," "name," "when," "which," "find," "match," "label," "select," and "show" is very useful. Practice answering questions prepares the student to participate more fully in classroom activities and discussions. Learning how to ask questions is also important; it enables the language-impaired student to independently seek and clarify information. Pragmatics can be addressed using academic materials when teaching students to express attitudes and opinions about academic content or formulate reasons why they prefer one subject over another. Teaching students to give examples, answer why questions, and learn how to change affect and intonation patterns when speaking to peers and teachers are all useful. In addition, children should have practice scripting questions, explanations, or narratives related to academic material. Dialogue scripts for common classroom interactions or lunchroom interactions can also be rehearsed.

Word knowledge is primary when learning new academic information. By age 6, it is expected that the child have approximately 14,000 words. The SLP can collaboratively work with the classroom teacher to identify new vocabulary words that the child will encounter in the classroom. Using these words, the SLP develops lessons to enrich vocabulary understanding, modify meaning, develop semantic links to other vocabulary words, and generalize those words to new contexts. The SLP will consider vocabulary words in terms of how necessary they are to a topic. Are they unusual words or familiar words used in an unusual way? Does the word contain many syllables?

The SLP can also work with the classroom teacher so that the student keeps a word box of new, important vocabulary. Syntax is addressed when complex syntactic constructions are explained and, if necessary, modified. SLPs can also analyze text and preteach words, concepts, and expressions that will be challenging for the student. Collaborating with the classroom teacher and informing her of a student's learning needs enable the teacher to incorporate supports throughout the academic day, such as using illustrations, color coding, and redundancy to achieve concept understanding (Wiig, 1992).

Academic Goals

Academic goals reflect traditional domain areas, such as math, social studies, reading, and science. Although the academic areas may not be unique to the inclusion classroom, consider the concept of giving each child (special education *and* regular education) an IEP as an innovative component. Preparing an IEP for the general-education student is unusual, given the history of IEP programming and individualized instruction, specifically for children with disabilities. The inclusion classroom will become more diversified as children with disabilities and at-risk needs share the general classroom with second-language learners and gifted or talented students.

Language-intervention strategies could be based on each child's profile along a developmental continuum. For children with intact production and comprehension skills, the SLP focuses on enhancing the child's abilities to access the curriculum. The connections between oral language and reading, oral language and writing, and reading and writing require direct work with the child and consultation with the teacher.

The inclusion classroom should provide individualized instruction for all children. Academic areas can be facilitated by peers and individualized by level (see Table 13.1). The child with a disability is provided with an extraordinary opportunity for peer instruction that is much more complex and advanced. He has the opportunity to receive instruction at his level and exposure to a learning environment that may facilitate his academic and social learning.

Curriculum Modification

Levels of Development

Diversity already exists within the general-education classroom, which incorporates a population of heterogeneous learners. So it is important to start with the concept of general diversity and work to modify instruction for each child. Typical children have multilevel abilities, and these abilities will vary across the academic curriculum. Group activities will provide a mechanism to understand each child's individual potential, given the academic curriculum. Child diversity provides a framework for understanding stylistic differences in all children in the classroom. Developing a curriculum beginning with the basic concept of child difference allows parents and teachers to develop program content that has built-in levels of academic complexity.

Just as the development of the curriculum requires a prerequistic assumption of child diversity, the programming created by teacher teams assumes that each child will be at different levels of the academic curriculum. The SLP works with the classroom teacher to recognize the diverse linguistic levels of the children in the classroom. When necessary, the SLP also assists in the development of the curriculum differentiation that is an integral component of every inclusion classroom.

Differentiated Instruction

Differentiated instruction is an inclusion practice that can be successfully applied in inclusive classrooms. Several types of curriculum differentiation are appropriate for children with language-learning disabilities (Switlick, 1997). They include accommodations, adaptations, parallel instruction, and overlapping instruction.

An *accommodation* is a change in the delivery of instruction or expected type of student performance that does not change the content or concept difficulty of the curriculum. For example, a child has to answer only 5 questions for homework instead of 10. The SLP collaborates with the classroom teacher to identify the type of questions and the inherent language abilities required to answer different types of questions.

TABLE 13.1 José Martinez: Individual Education Plan

Classroom Cultural Goals	Academic Long-Term Goals
Long-term goal 1. José will develop appropriate social behaviors.	*Math* José will develop number-recognition skills from 1 to 100.
Short-term goals 1a. José will be included in all academic and nonacademic activities.	José will develop primary computation skills.
1b. José will develop participatory skills in all activities.	José will hand out materials to classmates and count all the materials.
1c. José's negative and aggressive behaviors will decrease as a function of a behavior-modification program.	José will be assigned an aide and a peer tutor: Bryan Smith.
1d. José will learn to sit and attend during . . .	*Social Studies* José will assist the other children during their cultural presentation.
1e. José will learn to transition . . .	José will be assigned a peer tutor: Susan Pierponte.
	Science José will participate in the laboratory projects by handing out materials and following directions.
	José will be assigned a peer tutor: Mary Brown.
	Reading José will listen to narratives and follow directions after each story.
	José will appropriately identify words and phrases.
	José will be assigned a peer tutor: Carl Adams.

An *adaptation* changes the content and concept difficulty of the curriculum. For example, a child has to identify only the parts of a plant, while the rest of the class must discuss the reproduction of plants. Again the SLP collaborates with the classroom teacher to identify the language-loaded concept with which a special-needs child will have difficulty learning.

Parallel instruction does not change the content area, but does change the conceptual difficulty of the curriculum. For example, the class is working on telling time to the quarter hour, while the student with special needs is working on telling time to the hour. *Overlapping instruction* changes both content and conceptual difficulty and modifies student performance during a shared activity with typical peers.

Children with severe physical and cognitive disabilities often require this type of curriculum modification. An example is when typical peers and an inclusion student are creating a dialogue between two historical figures in a social studies class. The typical peers may write and act out the dialogues, while the inclusion student is responsible for handing out props (Switlick, 1997).

Curriculum Development

How can a transdisciplinary curriculum be created by the teaching staff? Teacher teams, consisting of multidisciplinary professionals including the SLP, can work collaboratively to translate their domain areas into inclusion goals that reflect the diversity of the learning experience for children with and without disabilities (Salisbury, et al., 1994). The SLP considers the complexity of the language of each curriculum area and advises the teacher how to best modify language when explaining or teaching specific curricular areas. For instance, can the child understand key words, such as "select," "define," "label," "compare," "contrast"? If not, it is up to the SLP to develop understanding of these terms and to enable the child to process information and answer questions that use these terms.

Within each goal area, the team takes into consideration the developmental steps that must occur to achieve the goal. Consideration is given to the heterogeneity of classroom instruction, rather than the homogeneity of the group. A transdisciplinary curriculum provides for the diversity of group instruction. Each child is seen as a multilevel learner. For instance, a student may be better at math and therefore functioning at a higher level than she is in reading or social studies or science.

The transdisciplinary team should approach the development of a curriculum with the viewpoint of capturing and reinforcing multilevel instruction and conceptual programming as a cornerstone of the curriculum (Ellis, Schlaudecker, & Regimbal, 1995). Rather than comparing the child to the group or to some concept of the group standard, the IEP allows the instructional staff to compare each child to himself or herself over time. Each child serves as his or her own learning assessment and provides his or her own baseline for instructional learning. Academic success can be evaluated by comparing individual child achievement from one time period to another.

Educational Plans: José, Jeffrey, and Kaitlyn

Figure 13.1 presents the academic integrated curriculum plan for social studies for José, Jeffrey, and Kaitlyn. An integrated curriculum is a thematic learning approach that meets academic goals by presenting a topic that spans content areas. The social studies curriculum in Jose's class includes a unit on immigration. The idea of immigration can be approached not only in social studies, but in science, English, and math.

Figure 13.1 can be utilized not only for José, but also for Jeffrey, Kaitlyn, and all the typical learners in class. However, because of the individual learning styles and

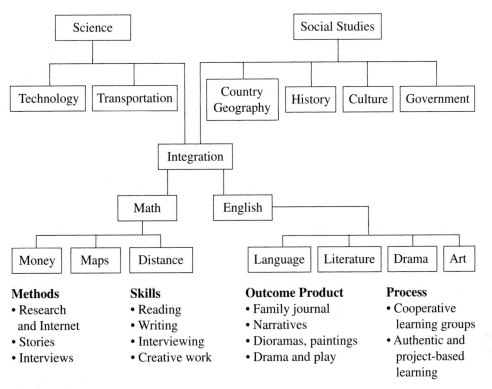

Methods
- Research
  and Internet
- Stories
- Interviews

Skills
- Reading
- Writing
- Interviewing
- Creative work

Outcome Product
- Family journal
- Narratives
- Dioramas, paintings
- Drama and play

Process
- Cooperative
  learning groups
- Authentic and
  project-based
  learning

FIGURE 13.1
Integrated Curriculum Plan

skills of each child, specific activities and outcome products will have to be carefully considered so that outcome products can be targeted.

The Speech-Language Pathologist and José

The SLP must analyze a targeted activity and identify the prerequisite skills necessary to complete an activity. He or she must list the sequential steps José needs to follow to produce an outcome product. The outcome product in this case is developing a journal about José's family's experience with immigration, specifically, how his family came to the United States.

Jose's Individual Strengths

The SLP must identify José's individual strengths:

- José is hyperlectic; he can read fluently.
- José can perform an activity if it is task analyzed.
- With individual guidance, José can follow a checklist that outlines with words, pictures, and visual prompts the steps to follow to complete an activity.

The SLP must work with the classroom teacher to make modifications to the interview process so that José can interview his mother, Maria Martinez. Some of these modifications follow:

- Provide José with a checklist of the items he needs to acquire to organize the activity.
- Review the questions José needs to ask his mother about his family, and show him how to use a cassette recorder.
- Send home instructions written in Spanish and English so that Maria Martinez can help José with the interview and the audiotaping.

In addition to working on some of the assignment modifications for José, the SLP must also incorporate specific intervention strategies to prepare José for understanding and development of the immigration theme. It is important to increase José's understanding of specific vocabulary related to immigration. Use of semantic mapping, scaffolding, graphic organizers, the Know–Want–Learn Strategy, and Think Alouds are all useful in helping José connect what he hears and reads to meaning.

In Box 13.1 José's mother describes the difficulties she and her family faced in coming to America, her family's strengths, and her hopes for José's future.

CW 13.1

Use the Companion Website to complete the following:

1. Develop a semantic map for José that will help him with the theme on immigration.
2. Identify vocabulary words that will be useful in developing an understanding of immigration.

The Speech-Language Pathologist and Jeffrey

The integrated curriculum in Figure 13.1 applies to Jeffrey as well. In the case of Jeffrey, the SLP again needs to analyze and identify the targeted activity and determine what skills Jeffrey has and what modifications are necessary so that Jeffrey can complete his assignment, a journal describing some of the experiences of his great-aunt, a West Indian immigrant.

Jeffrey's Individual Strengths

Jeffrey's individual strengths are these:

- Jeffrey can read at a first-grade level.
- He can visualize and verbally describe the family journal he would like to produce and the family member he wants to interview.
- Jeffrey can select the questions he would like to ask his great-aunt from a spoken list presented to him by the SLP.
- With individual guidance, he can write some of his questions. And with individual guidance he can read some of the questions generated by him and his peers that he will ask his great-aunt.

BOX 13.1

I've been in the United States since José was 2 years old and we've all struggled as a family to make a new life. At first, it was a shock to me and my husband that José had autism. I didn't know anything about autism or children with disabilities when I was back in my country. The programs in special education that many Americans take for granted don't exist in most countries in Central and South America. It was hard leaving my home and coming to America, but I'm glad to be here because José wouldn't receive these services in my country. My family's been poor for generations, and we couldn't afford to send any of our children to private school or to therapeutic programs like in the United States. As hard as it was for my family to relocate, learn a new language, and create a new home, the thought of living with José in a country that didn't have extensive special services was more difficult.

For José's sake, I'm glad to be here. I feel we've been very fortunate, and I'm grateful for all the support my family's received from the government. I know that José has a serious problem, but I see that he's made a lot of progress in the last several years. I've always wanted José to be in programs with normal children so that he'd learn from them. Now that he's in third grade, I can see how different he is from other children and the other children in my family. When we take José to church, to parties, to the store, and to the playground, people stare at him because his behavior is so different.

My family's very religious and I believe that God has given José to me for a reason. I don't know what José will do when he grows up, but I do know that God'll provide for him.

In the United States, children who have problems like José are given many services. In my country, people with disabilities don't get such services, but they're treated with a great deal of dignity. Right now, José doesn't have any friends in school or in our neighborhood. I hope that someday he will have friends. I'd like José to grow up like other people and get married and have his own family. If this does not happen, I know my other children will always take care of José. He has his own special talents and special abilities. I've learned a lot about autism from José. I'm not sorry that I have a child with a disability.

Maria Martinez

 Use the Companion Website to help you answer the following questions:

1. Do you think that Maria has realistic expectations for José?

2. Depending on your answer, explain how the three systems (early intervention, preschool, and school age) have either facilitated or not facilitated realistic expectations for José.

The SLP must consult with the classroom teacher to make some assignment modifications:

- Simplify the questions Jeffrey needs to ask his great-aunt.
- Show Jeffrey how to use a cassette recorder.

- Listen to the audiotape with Jeffrey and write his great-aunt's answers to the questions.
- Use the computer and a word-processing program to assist with the journal narrative.

In Box 13.2 Jeffrey's mother expresses her concerns about Jeffrey's correct treatment and her hopes for his future.

CW 13.2

Use the Companion Website to complete the following:

1. Identify some word-processing programs that might be useful for Jeffrey.

2. Identify some books that the SLP can read with Jeffrey to help prepare him for the kinds of questions he will ask his great-aunt.

The Speech-Language Pathologist and Kaitlyn

Kaitlyn will also be doing a project in class for social studies, but her project will be a group project with some of her classmates at the Mission School for the Deaf. She and her peers have decided that they would like to act out a particular event that is related to immigration. Specifically, they will dramatize an incident when immigrants entered the United States on ships and had to pass immigration inspection at Ellis Island in New York.

Kaitlyn's Individual Strengths

Here are Kaitlyn's individual strengths:

- Kaitlyn can sign well. Her signing skills are typical for a third-grade student being educated in an educational environment that uses signs.
- Kaitlyn learns new signs quickly.
- Kaitlyn can sign short narratives.
- Kaitlyn enjoys acting out stories and using her body movements and facial expressions to communicate more completely.

The SLP must consult with the classroom teacher to become familiar with the particular immigration concept that Kaitlyn and her peers will be dramatizing. The SLP will not have to modify the assignment for Kaitlyn or her peers. She will assist Kaitlyn as follows:

- In writing the script for her character in the immigration drama
- In matching her signs to her spoken sentences of the script
- In writing her character's description for a separate playbill that will be distributed at the class drama presentation. The use of a computer writing program will be used to help organize Kaitlyn's written descriptive narrative.

BOX 13.2

Jeffrey's in third grade and he's struggling with reading and writing. He's done so poorly that he doesn't want to do his homework and practice. Jeffrey's being taught to read in a resource room by means of a phonetic approach. He hates being pulled out of class to go to the resource room. The other children know he's going to a special class. There've been several episodes of children making fun of Jeffrey's reading problems and classroom work. He's slow in answering the teacher when she asks him a question. He'd rather say he doesn't know than give the wrong answer. Jeffrey's audiology report says that he has a central auditory processing problem. Some recommendations of the audiologist include an auditory trainer and preferential seating in class. I hope these things help him. I will need to speak to the SLP and the resource room teacher about it. My niece, who is 2 years younger than Jeffrey, reads and writes better than he does. Jeffrey receives speech therapy two times a week. I think that the school district believes that children who are classified as speech impaired don't have severe learning difficulties like autistic or retarded children. Right now, Jeffrey doesn't receive any counseling or therapy from a school psychologist.

I am concerned about keeping Jeffrey in school. I want him to graduate from high school, but the graduation rates for African American children and disabled children are very low. Jeffrey's now getting special tutoring after school, but he's still very negative about going to school. My husband feels that Jeffrey will need to learn a trade. But if you can't read, how can you learn a trade. Even car mechanics have to read technical manuals. Jeffrey's very artistic and creative. I'd like him to develop his art skills. I'm not saying that school professionals discriminate against African American children, but I think some have low expectations and negative perceptions for their future.

Jeffrey says that he's never going to learn like the other children. He's given up on himself and he's only 8 years old. I want Jeffrey to go to college and be whatever he wants to be. The other problem is that Jeffrey doesn't have any friends in his class. He doesn't play after school with any of his classmates. No one invites him to play dates or birthday parties. I've enrolled Jeffrey in a church youth group that meets twice a week. The children participate in sports activities, arts and crafts, as well as Boy Scouts. Jeffrey has made friends with several boys in the church group. This is the first time that Jeffrey has friends. His sports skills are good and he feels a sense of accomplishment and pride. In the youth group, his disability is not apparent. Jeffrey has flourished outside school, not in school.

Camille St. James

Use the Companion Website to help you answer the following questions:

1. Camille St. James is concerned about Jeffrey dropping out of school in the future because of his lack of success within school. He does not have self-esteem in terms of his abilities as a learner. Why do you think Jeffrey has poor self-esteem, and what programming needs to be provided by school systems to prevent students from dropping out?

2. Where would development of self-esteem fit in the general-education system, and how would you measure it?

CW 13.3

Use the Companion Website to complete the following:

1. Identify some books on immigration that would be appropriate for Kaitlyn to read in preparation for her class project.

2. Identify any videotapes of signed stories or plays that would be useful for Kaitlyn to view in preparation for her class project.

In Box 13.3, Kaitlyn's mother explains why she wishes to continue her daughter's education in the deaf community and her hopes for Kaitlyn's future.

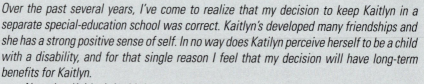

BOX 13.3

Over the past several years, I've come to realize that my decision to keep Kaitlyn in a separate special-education school was correct. Kaitlyn's developed many friendships and she has a strong positive sense of self. In no way does Katlyn perceive herself to be a child with a disability, and for that single reason I feel that my decision will have long-term benefits for Kaitlyn.

Now that Kaitlyn's in third grade, I'm beginning to see that some of her learning differences will always be magnified in hearing environments. Kaitlyn's speech has a distinct quality that identifies her as a person who is deaf when she communicates with hearing people. Kaitlyn socializes and interacts with friends using sign language. In a hearing environment she misses many incidental cues around her. When children are standing behind her and talking, she may not hear them in a noisy context. Kaitlyn speechreads, but this skill can't be used by itself. There's a time delay for Kaitlyn as she processes information in a hearing environment. She needs to focus on verbal and nonverbal behaviors of hearing communicators. Sometimes people talk louder and slower when they recognize that she's deaf. Her interactions with hearing people are not as spontaneous and relaxed as they are with other communicators who are deaf.

Kaitlyn's fingers seem to fly when she's signing to her friends and her physical expressiveness is beautiful. Kaitlyn's teachers have told me that because of her strong language skills she'll achieve reading levels that are comparable to peer typical learners. However, the more sophisticated language interpretations in complex written texts will be very difficult for Kaitlyn to understand. In addition, Kaitlyn's writing skills will also be limited by any spoken narrative language limitations.

The educational instruction she receives at the Mission School is specifically designed for children with hearing loss. If Kaitlyn had been placed in a general-education classroom, I don't think she would be able to handle the academic curriculum, because teaching instruction would not be provided by a teacher of the deaf. Inclusion is described as an opportunity in the federal law, but it has become a mandate that may limit educational options in many school districts. Kaitlyn's not a hearing child and I don't want her to be educated as a hearing child. The general-education classroom, because it is geared to general learners, is not specifically designed for Kaitlyn. Kaitlyn's a child with very special needs.

As a parent of a child with a disability, I believe that the formative period for learning in school is very short. Learning becomes significantly harder as children get older. When they can't fit in with their peers and feel good about themselves as learners, they drop out. I have thought a lot about cochlear implants and I am glad that Kaitlyn has one. It is important for Kaitlyn to hear speech and other sounds within her environment; it makes it easier for her to learn. However, I also feel that as cochlear implants improve, the Deaf Community, its language and its culture, will begin to disappear.

Inclusion proposes that all children should have the opportunity to be educated together. But in the process I fear that children's individual differences will be ignored. Many CLD groups, such as African Americans, Latinos, and Asians, want to maintain their distinctiveness through their cultures, dialects, and languages. Will the use of the cochlear implant eventually erode the Deaf Community and culture as fewer children are exposed to sign language? I know that Kaitlyn will find her place as an independent young woman with job skills and career goals; this is what every parent wants. Many parents of children with disabilities don't feel as optimistic about their children's future.

Katherine Whiteside

Use the Companion Website to help you answer the following questions:

1. Katherine had made the decision to have Kaitlyn educated within the Deaf Community with other children who are deaf. Because of this decision, Kaitlyn has good self-esteem and a very rewarding social life. However, there is the risk that Kaitlyn will not achieve as much academically as she would if she were in an inclusion classroom in a typical school. What decision would you make in terms of long-term placement if you were Kaitlyn's parent? Explain your answer.

2. Katherine feels that it is important for Kaitlyn to identify with the Deaf Community. How important do you feel it is to consider this issue as it relates to educational placement of a child who is deaf?

Elementary School Years

Working with children in the elementary school years is exciting because the role of the SLP expands to include work on literacy and writing. In the kindergarten years, the development of phonological-awareness skills in conjunction with printed letters is essential in learning to read. Explicit linking between letters and sounds promotes literacy development. The SLP working with children with phonological impairments must incorporate a phonological-awareness approach into the phonological intervention program. Smith, Downs, and Mogford-Bevan (1998) show that combining phonological-awareness training with a more traditional articulatory approach is useful and beneficial to children who have phonological difficulties.

More recently it has been shown that children who receive phonological-awareness training for rhyme awareness and nonword spelling perform better on these literacy tasks than children who do not (Nancollis, Lawrie, & Dodd, 2005). Training children to become proficient in syllable–phoneme deletion, another phonological-awareness task, is also useful for the development of later literacy. In fact, the level of kindergarten children's ability to perform syllable–phoneme deletion is more predictive of second-grade word reading than proficiency in letter identification (Hogan, Catts, & Little, 2005).

The primary focus of the early elementary school years is learning to read. For children who fail to learn to read despite conventional instruction, adequate intelligence, and sociocultural opportunity, the term dyslexic is used to explain their disability (Critchley, 1970). The SLP will most definitely be working with children who fit into this category and needs to be aware of the large body of evidence that indicates that dyslexia is a language-based disability.

Phonology and Reading

When talking about the school-age child, one cannot consider phonology without considering reading. The structural-lag hypothesis suggests that a lag in phonological awareness explains difficulties encountered when learning to decode phonemes. This is just one theory about why children have difficulty learning to read, but it does not explain what causes the lag. Other researchers tackle this question with their own hypotheses:

1. Difficulty forming accurate representation in long-term memory (Vellutino, Harding, Phillips, & Steger, 1975)
2. Difficulty accessing verbal information stored in long-term memory (Miles & Ellis, 1981)
3. Perceptual deficits (Tallal, 1980)
4. Poor regulation of information in working memory (Shankweiler & Crain, 1987)
5. Difficulty developing narrative and discourse schemata (Perfetti, 1985)

Kamhi (1991) believes that hypotheses 1 and 2 are the primary factors involved. With this in mind, we will examine the relationship between phonological processing and reading disabilities.

Adults have four types of phonological knowledge: perceptual knowledge, articulatory knowledge, higher-level phonological knowledge, and social–indexical knowledge (Munson, Edwards, & Beckman, 2005). Figure 13.2 explains each type.

Each phonological knowledge type has a protracted development pattern (Hazan & Barrett, 2000; Lee, Potamianos, & Naryanan, 1999; Nittrouer, 2002). As children grow, they develop skills in each area. Interestingly, children with atypical speech sound development do not appear to have a specific deficit in higher-level phonological knowledge (Munson et al., 2005).

Phonological processing refers to the way the linguistic mechanism manages the sounds of language. It appears to be relatively independent of cognitive abilities. When children are exposed to spoken language, they learn the speech sounds associated with words, and these phonological units are stored in long-term memory. It is possible that some children have difficulty developing phonological memory codes

Perceptual knowledge	Refers to the perception of speech sounds
Articulatory knowledge	Knowledge of the articulatory characteristics of speech sounds
Higher-level phonological knowledge	Knowledge of how to divide words into sounds and how to combine sounds into words
Social–indexical knowledge	Knowledge of how differences in pronunciation convey social identity

FIGURE 13.2

Phonological Knowledge

Source: Munson, Edwards, & Beckman, 2005.

that are necessary for storing words. Many researchers have explored this theory (Done & Miles, 1978; Snowling, Goulandris, Bowlby, & Howell, 1985; Vellutino et al., 1975) and have found that children identified with reading disabilities do perform more poorly than typical peers on tasks that require paired associate learning of verbal and nonverbal stimuli (learning to associate spoken nonsense words with visual stimuli).

Word-finding difficulties are also frequently evident in children with reading disabilities. The existence of this difficulty supports the notion of hypothesis 2 that dyslexic children have difficulty accessing the verbal information stored in long-term memory. This difficulty could be related to both semantic and phonological factors. The semantic factor may be caused by a slowness in learning the semantic features that characterize a word, and thus words are not fully represented or elaborated in their conceptual schema. The phonological factor may be due to having problems in merely establishing phonological representations of the word. In either event, the dyslexic child has difficulty retrieving this information during the process of reading.

Other word-finding research (Messer, Dockrell, & Murphy, 2004; Blachman, 1984; Denckla, 1972) shows that dyslexic children have difficulty rapidly naming colors, objects, and letters, even though these are common objects and well known by the children. Therefore, the idea of slowed-down retrieval of stored information in long-term memory is supported.

Another area of interest regarding phonological processing and reading is the use of phonologic codes in memory. One way a mature reader decodes words is by sight, that is, by connecting the word's orthographic structure and phonologic structure in long-term memory. The mature reader does not attempt to sound out or convert letters or letter strings into corresponding sounds and then reassemble these sounds to pronounce the word (Torgensen et al., 2001). If the child cannot develop, store, and easily access phonological codes in memory, he will not be a fluent decoder.

Verbal short-term memory is another documented area of weakness in children who are poor readers or at risk for reading disabilities (Mann & Liberman, 1984;

Torgesen, 1985). Sometimes children with phonological processing difficulties will have adequate short-term memory for digits, but poor memory for sentences and words. These children may also have great difficulty repeating complex multisyllabic words (Catts, 1989). When short-term memory is weak for words and sentences, the child cannot hold decoded words or sentences in short-term memory long enough to manipulate and extract meaningful understanding of what has been decoded or read.

Intervention for children with phonological processing weaknesses can take many forms. Catts (1991) suggests several phonological-awareness procedures for preschool children. For the child with speech-language impairments, these activities would be appropriate in early elementary school (kindergarten):

1. Teach nursery rhymes, songs, and finger-play-activities for developing speech sound awareness.
2. Teach sound-play activities for creating sequences of rhyming words.
3. Teach rhyme and alliteration.
4. Teach sound-segmentation tasks and blending tasks.
5. Teach sound-manipulation tasks.

Rhyming games and nursery rhymes highlight the fact that words are composed of sounds (MacLean, Bryant, & Bradley, 1987). Once children master the concept of rhyme, determining what doesn't rhyme or belong can be introduced. Teaching children initial sound sets is another effective activity. When the children recognize that words such as "hat," "hen," and "hop" all begin with the same sound, the written letter representation is introduced. Teaching segmentation skills is another component of early phonological-awareness skill. Many activities can be used to teach this skill. Blackman (1991) describes several activities that teach phoneme awareness, phoneme segmentation, and sound–letter correspondences. Many commercial programs that systematically train phonological-awareness skills are also available.

As children master phonological-awareness skills, the natural progression is to then introduce the alphabetic principle (letters stand for sounds). Children need to recognize that letters are connected to sounds. This code emphasis approach incorporates drill to develop explicit and systematic relationships between symbols (letters) and sounds.

Quick and ready word recognition is imperative to the development of a good reader. It goes beyond sounding out words. Roth and Troia (2005) identify four critical instruction characteristics to develop word recognition:

1. Instruction must address alphabetic and orthographic reading.
2. Instruction must be intense and explicit.
3. Instruction must begin early.
4. Instruction must be coordinated between classroom teachers and SLPs.

The SLP is an integral part of the educational collaboration team. The SLP can determine some basic reading skill components. For the child in kindergarten, the SLP can assess for skills such as rhyming, blending, and sound manipulation. For the child in first grade, using graded word lists to determine the ability to read high-frequency words, assessing the ability to decode phonetically regular words, and assessing comprehension of oral and silent reading, as well as comprehension of teacher-read stories, are all important tasks that the SLP needs to include in her intervention (Blackman, 1991). The information gained will target areas that need strengthening. The SLP can use multiple formal assessments. Three that have proved useful are the Phonological Awareness Test (Robertson & Salter, 1997), the Decoding Skills Test (Richardson & DiBenedetto, 1985), and the Woodcock–Johnson III Tests of Reading Achievement (Woodcock, McGrew, & Mather, 2001).

Language Processing

Processing of information presented orally in the classroom is also problematic for children with speech-language disorders. The following classroom modifications benefit all children in a classroom.

- Reduce background noises.
- Keep doors and windows closed to reduce external noise.
- Buffer chair leg bottoms.
- Reduce noise using sound-absorbing acoustic tiles.

Teacher modifications should also be implemented to support language processing in the classroom.

- Speak slowly and clearly.
- Provide cues to gain attention, such as tapping the blackboard.
- Repeat, rephrase, and offer examples.
- Take breaks between tasks.
- Alternate activities that require intense listening with ones that are less demanding.
- Provide many visual supports when presenting information: pictures, charts, graphs, drawings, and videos.
- Allow wait time to students who are answering questions.
- Ask short, specific questions.
- Highlight important vocabulary words on the blackboard. (Banbury & Miller, 1993)

Recently, a great deal of attention has been centered on auditory processing and auditory processing disorders (see chapter 12). Children with auditory processing problems may evidence auditory memory problems as well. There are several interventions for this weakness.

- Make sure the children have sufficient and repeated practice at learning a new concept.
- Aim for overlearning.
- Teach memorization supports such as chunking, visualization, and mnemonics.
- When learning new vocabulary words, encourage children to keep a vocabulary word box.
- Use visual aids, such as overheads, models, charts, and handouts.
- Provide for many hands-on projects.

Literacy

Childrens reading problems can be manifested in several ways:

- Sound–letter identification
- Blending sounds
- Confusing similar letters and words
- Reading aloud fluently, without hesitations
- Reading syllabic patterns
- Developing a sight-word vocabulary
- Attending to punctuation in oral reading
- Answering content questions
- Paraphrasing
- Retelling
- Drawing conclusions (Banbury & Miller, 1993)

Reading researchers agree that most reading and spelling disabilities are rooted in language-processing impairments, rather than visual perceptual deficits or inability to construct meaning from context (Adams, 1990; Goswami & Bryant, 1990; Gough, Ehri, & Treiman, 1992; Stanovich & Siegel, 1994; Vellutino, Scanlon, & Tanzman, 1994). If the reading difficulty is due to a decoding weakness, Fox (2000) recommends teaching children several decoding strategies. (See Table 13.2)

Generally, emergent literacy interventions take either a top-down or bottom-up approach. The top-down approach emphasizes whole-language principles whereby literacy is enhanced through child-directed, informal, naturalistic interactions with oral and written language (Clay, 1998; Katims & Pierce, 1995; Watkins & Bunce, 1996). In the bottom-up approach, specific literacy targets are directly taught utilizing adult modeling, elicitation, and repetition. Targets are selected based on their direct correlation to reading skill development. The order and content of the targets are carefully planned

TABLE 13.2 Decoding Strategies

Strategy	Explanation
Analogy decoding	Children use familiar words to identify an unknown word. For example, child knows the word "boot" sees the word "toot" and utilizes the rime segment to decode the word "toot."
Letter–sound decoding	Children need a good deal of experience developing letter–sound correspondences to sound out words.
Letter neighborhoods	Children develop automatic consonant–vowel recognition skills for six syllable neighborhoods: VC, CV, VV, Vr, Vce, Cle.
Multiletter chunking	Children learn to decode and blend larger segments of words, such as words within compounds, base words, prefixes, and suffixes.

Source: Fox, B., *Word Identification Stategies: Phonics from a New Perspective* (2nd ed.), 2000. Upper Saddle River, NJ: Merrill/ Prentice Hall.

and organized, with an emphasis on part-to-whole learning. That is, targeted goals include frequent exposure and practice in manipulating and analyzing words, syllables, rimes, and phonemes. Several computer software programs enhance this approach (Earobics, Sound Solutions, Fast ForWord). O'Connor, Notari-Syverson, and Vadasy (1996), VanKleeck, Gillam, and McFadden (1998), and Brady, Fowler, Stone, and Winbury (1994) support explicit approach programs that they believe are effective for developing phonological awareness and early reading. Russo (2000) demonstrates that a combination of computerized instruction and intense, explicit teacher lessons produces the best outcomes for developing literacy skills.

Justice and Kaderavek (2004) describe a program that utilizes a combined embedded–explicit model of emergent literacy intervention that is beneficial for children with language impairments. They characterize the model as an integrated approach that includes daily naturalistic contextualized interactions with oral and written language, as well as focused, therapeutic, clinician-directed interventions. It incorporates both top-down and bottom-up techniques. The specific literacy domains targeted are phonological awareness, print concepts, alphabet knowledge and writing, and narrative and literate language. Table 13.3 lists the domains and specific targets as implemented in an embedded–explicit emergent literacy program (Justice and Kaderavek, 2004).

Once children learn to decode, reading comprehension develops. Reading comprehension includes understanding of individual vocabulary words, as well as sentences and paragraphs. To develop understanding of vocabulary words, semantic mapping and contextual redefinition are useful. In semantic mapping children are taught the new word in the context of words that have similar meaning. They are taught to make associations between the new word and associated words that are already in their vocabulary. In contextual redefinition, which is appropriate for older children, the teacher or SLP follows a five-step model that includes identifying an unfamiliar word, writing the word in a sentence, presenting the word in isolation, presenting the word in context, and using a dictionary for supplementary explanation (Readence, Bean, & Baldwin, 1995).

To develop reading comprehension of extended-text, children need to use thinking to develop an interaction between themselves and the text they are reading. The Directed Reading–Teaching Activity (Blachowicz, 1994) is very useful for upper-elementary-level children. In this activity, children are taught to engage in preview activities, such as prereading the title, subtitles, and introduction and looking at pictures. Then students are asked to predict what the book or chapter will be about and discuss what clues in the title or pictures led to this prediction. Next, students read the chapter or passage to determine if their predictions are accurate. Finally, the students reflect back on their predictions and analyze the reasons why their predictions were correct or not.

For older children, Vaughn and Klingner (1999) suggest the Collaborative Strategic Reading Strategy. In this method, students are taught to preview or brainstorm a topic before reading it. They then identify the "clicks," those parts of the reading that they understand, and the "clunks," those parts of the reading passage that they do not understand. Another useful strategy is the K–W–L strategy (Know–Want–Learn) (Ogle, 2005). This strategy's purpose is to enable students to connect knowledge that they already have about a subject to new information that they will be reading. This strategy should be used when reading expository texts.

TABLE 13.3

Domains and Specific Targets as Implemented in an Emergent Literacy Program

Domain	Activities to Promote:
Phonological awareness	Identification of word and syllable boundaries Production of rhymes
	Comprehension and production of words in a syllable-by-syllable manner and phoneme-by-phoneme manner
	Identification of sounds in initial and final position of words
Print concepts	Book-reading conventions
	Metalinguistic knowledge regarding acts of writing and reading (familiarize child with terms such as word, title, etc.)
	Recognition of local environmental print (building signs, street signs)
Alphabet knowledge and writing	Recognition of sight words (words are printed on cards and sorted according to long words, such as "bicycle" and short words such as "boy" (Rozin, Bressman, & Taft, 1974)
	Singing of the alphabet song
	Recognition of letters in the children's names
	Independent sorting of uppercase letters
	Recognition of the first letter in environment print (W for Wendy's)
	Learning how to independently print children's names
Narrative and literate language	Narrative development stories (reading *Little Red Riding Hood*, acting it out, dressing up, felt-board activities, puppets)
	Comprehension of cause and effect (model asking "why" questions and then answering the "why" questions; encourage children to ask "why" questions)
	Descriptions of actions (sequence card stories, felt board stories).

Source: Justice & Kaderavek, 2004.

Linguistic Processing and Reading

Catts and Kamhi (1986) propose three levels of information processing (processing the spoken and written word): (1) perceptual analyses, (2) word recognition, (3) and higher-order processing (processing sentences and extended texts). The first level involves the phonological decoding of words. The second level involves word recognition, that is, recognizing the word and matching it to a stored representation in memory. If the child cannot recognize words quickly and automatically as visual wholes, this will negatively affect the third level of processing, higher-order processing of text.

Assessing children's reading fluency is a good measure of how well children automatically recognize words. The more attention and energy expended on word identification, the less ability there is to comprehend text. Comprehension of text requires the following:

- Understanding relations between words signaled by morphological endings
- Understanding relations between sentences signaled by cohesive devices
- Identifying words based on familiarity with content or context
- Understanding both literal and inferential meaning
- Understanding the author's communicative intent
- Recognizing relevant versus irrelevant information
- Utilizing knowledge of narrative structure (Roth & Spekman, 1991)

Semantics, syntax, and discourse need to be integrated flawlessly during reading. If one of these language components is weak, it will affect the reading process.

Written Language

Children with language-learning difficulties have written-language difficulties that often persist into adulthood (Johnson, 1987). Several researchers propose theories regarding written-language development (Bereiter, 1980; Kroll, 1981; Perera, 1984). Kroll's (1981) model of written-language development consists of four phases: preparational phase, consolidation phase, differentiation phase, and systematic integration of oral and written language. Bereiter (1980) bases his stages of development on the development of cognitive processes. On the other hand, Perera (1984) does not believe that writing develops through a series of stages; rather, he believes it develops within a two-dimensional continuum. Let us examine each theory and consider the implications for intervention.

According to Kroll (1981), writing is part of the language system. It begins in the preparation phase when children learn about graphemes (written letters) and the technical aspects of writing. Most of the child's energies are consumed by the mechanics of writing. This phase occurs during the late preschool and kindergarten years (Singer, 1995). In the consolidation phase, which is some time around age 6 or 7, written language is really oral language written down.

In the differentiation stage, children become aware of the differences between spoken and written language and can write texts that are not generally spoken. This emerges at around 9 or 10 years (Scott, 1989, 1994). In the systematic integration stage, children can integrate and apply their knowledge of both oral and written language. They adjust their style of writing to meet the needs of their readers and the purpose of communicating. This stage is reached by mature writers beyond the elementary school years. It is expected in the high-school-age child.

Bereiter (1980) divides the development of writing into five different stages: associative writing, performative writing, communicative writing, unified writing, and epistemic writing. Bereiter believes that, when a child has mastered one stage or has attained automaticity, an easy progression to the next stage will take place. In associative writing, the child writes to suit himself rather than the reader. Any thought that comes to mind is age appropriate. This stage occurs in the early school years. In the performative stage the child's energies are concerned with spelling, punctuation, capitalization, and the use of specific language forms provided by teachers. This stage occurs in the middle school years.

In the communicative writing stage, social cognition is integrated into writing. Now the child attempts to take the reader's perspective and write for a particular audience. This occurs at the high school level. Unified writing occurs when the writer moves beyond just communicating to a particular audience. In this stage the writer "crafts his skill." Writing is more precise and well crafted. This stage is achieved during late high school or college years. Finally, in the epistemic writing stage, writing moves beyond merely communication or reflecting. It becomes the vehicle for exploration into the discovery and development of new ideas (Singer, 1995).

Perera (1984) views writing as a process in which the writer moves from one dimension that focuses merely on the text organization to the dimension that focuses on the relationship between the text and the reader. As the writer develops, the written text becomes independent and self-sufficient, not needing shared experiential events with the reader. Wallach and Miller (1988) call this the oral-to-literate shift.

Besides problems related to the content of written language, children with special needs may have problems with the form of writing, that is, handwriting. It is not unusual for the writing of special-needs children to have the following:

- Irregular or illegible letters
- Letters written with too light or too strong a stroke
- Letters that are too small or too large
- Letters written above or below the line
- Spacing that is too wide or close or irregular within a word or irregular between words (Banbury & Miller, 1993)

These issues are generally managed by the occupational therapist. However, the classroom teacher can help as follows:

- Allow the student to write single-word answers
- Allow the student to write word webs, diagrams, draw pictures, or use photographs when completing assignments
- Reduce written-work assignments (Banbury & Miller, 1993)

Regardless of the model of written-language development that one embraces, it becomes clear that the language-impaired youngster will not move easily through the stages of written-language development. The SLP can help in this development in various ways. Englert (1992) and Scardamalia and Bereiter (1986) suggest that SLPs focus on developing metacognitive awareness. The language-learning disabled child needs to be taught how to plan for, draft, and edit written work. Specific strategies such as modeling and Think-Alouds (Wilhelm, 2001) will enable the students to learn the process of writing text.

Think-Alouds is a strategy that involves having children read their written passage silently and then asking them to identify trouble spots in their writing. Previous to writing, the teacher scaffolds their thinking with questions, such as "When you write the title, what do you think it says about what you wrote?" "What did you write that doesn't seem to make sense to you?" "Do you think the reader will understand what you wrote?"

Discussions about the difference between oral language and literate language will also enable the later-elementary-age child to begin to acquire a more mature writing stage. Recognizing the stage a child's written language is in and then utilizing activities to facilitate ease and automaticity in writing at this stage will ensure progression to a higher level. The SLP who works on increasing oral language inherently works on increasing written language. When the SLP teaches a child how to orally answer "how" questions, she can easily progress into having the child write the answer to a "how" question. For example, the question "How do you make a jack-o-lantern?" can be answered orally by teaching the child to use temporal words such as "first," "next," "then," and "last." Next, the SLP works on written language by framing out a written expository text that matches the oral text.

Ehren (1994) states that at all times the SLP is using curriculum as the "reference point for teaching the language skills and strategies needed to deal with the content." Curriculum-relevant therapy means that the SLP teaches the language underpinnings that are prerequisite to understanding and managing the academic curriculum. Ehren and Jackson (2003) list specific ways the SLP can implement curriculum-relevant therapy:

1. Be familiar with the standards required of the curriculum.
2. Analyze the curriculum for linguistic, related cognitive, metalinguistic, and metacognitive underpinnings.
3. Use specific content as the raw material for teaching language-related skills.

Narratives

By the time the typical child is in kindergarten, he or she is able to generate extended accounts, descriptions, and stories. These narratives are often mapped onto knowledge that comes from experience (Schank & Abelson, 1977). These experiences form the basis for scripts that are integrated and organized mental representations of experienced events. These scripts prepare the child for anticipating what will occur when experiencing a new instance of a past event. For example, the preschool experience serves as a script for what a child will encounter in kindergarten.

Besides this, scripts are frames on which children can organize verbal accounts. Thus, listening to a story about a child's first day of school is easily understood by a child who has already had a school experience. If the child is asked to retell the story, the organization for that retelling is the script that the child has already experienced.

Interestingly, the child's attention to the internal response of the main character in the story is the critical element in differentiating the typical child from the child with a language disorder (Scott, 1988). Children older than age 6 are expected to be able to retell stories giving more attention to feelings, motives, inner responses, and intentions. Their retellings include less recalled information and fewer important aspects of the story (Garnett, 1986).

Kintsch and others hypothesize that long-term memory is critical to the development of strong narrative frameworks on which children can comprehend narratives and formulate them (Ericsson & Kintsch, 1991; Kintsch, 1988, 1992, 1994; Van Dijk & Kintsch, 1983). Retelling a story, recounting an experienced event, or comprehending a written passage all require accessing scripts automatically from the child's long-term memory (Naremore, 1997). Key elements in this process are adequate storage of scripts and ready access to them. For the child with structural deficits, such as syntax and morphologic deficits, there is no ready access to the stored script. Westby (1984) states that language impairments result in insufficient automaticity. She gives the analogy of an adult who has studied a foreign language for 4 years. When the adult attempts to speak with a native speaker of the language, it is a slow, painstaking event. Although the vocabulary and syntax of the language are stored in long-term memory, ready, easy access, or automaticity, is not. If a child has not developed scripts in long-term memory, no easy access is possible.

It is the role of the SLP to expose the child to varied stories based on school-relevant scripts (Naremore, 1997) or to inform teachers about the linguistic and metacognitive aspects of narrative comprehension and formation. But what if we assume that scripts are stored in the long-term memory, yet the child still cannot retrieve them? Perhaps it is because the child has not recognized the retrieval cue. For example, if the child is asked how to make a jack-o-lantern after the child has experienced making jack-o-lanterns, and the child is unable to do so, using pictures and modeling descriptions of what is happening in each picture are useful. Or what if a child has word-finding difficulties or a limited vocabulary? These will negatively affect easy access of scripts and organization and formulation of narratives. Singing songs, finger plays, and repeated story telling about Halloween and jack-o-lanterns will not only expose the child to pertinent vocabulary, but will also facilitate retrieval of these vocabulary words.

The elementary-school-age child must manage more and more decontextualized language. Cook-Gumperz (1977) calls communication events that are high in contextual support as "situated meaning." These communication events are familiar, involve routines, and rely on nonverbal contexts. School and written contexts are "lexicalized." They rely less on routines and familiar contexts and are challenging for the language-impaired child. Now the child must apply linguistic processing strategies to extract meaning from spoken language and use language to talk about language (Tomasello, 2002).

If the child's processing breaks down at the sound, syllable, word, sentence, complex sentence, or text level, impaired understanding and production of language will result. Typical breakdowns, such as transforming syntactic structures to perform reciprocal defining and labeling, recognizing that two surface language structures can share the same deep structure, or recognizing synonymy in two different texts, are some of the difficulties the language-impaired child's experiences (Nelson, 1986). The SLP can work with the regular education teacher in recognizing that language challenges can be managed by providing supports in the general-education classroom. Utilizing a slower rate of speaking, supplementing new information with experiential activities, and visual supports are all helpful. Providing word banks and extended time and clarifying written directions on tests are all IEP items that support the language-impaired child.

SUMMARY

The SLP is the language specialist who facilitates the development of language skills either directly or indirectly. When working directly with the elementary-school-age child, she or he focuses on the development of language skills that are required for academic learning; this is done by building language competences, such as understanding verbal and written directions, increasing vocabulary, seeking assistance or information, listening when the teacher or peers speak, and asking questions. The SLP functions as a bridge by not only increasing language skills in the child, but also by training teachers and peers to be facilitative in their communicative interactions with the language-impaired student. She or he works on phonological development, literacy skills, language comprehension, expressive language, and written language. The SLP helps the teacher recognize the language challenges embedded in the curriculum and develops classroom supports to diminish the effect of these challenges on learning. She works with parents to help them understand the specific nature of their children's language disorders. She is a teacher, a mentor, a collaborator. Her role is constantly changing, yet her goal is always the same, to ensure that the student who has a language disability will receive an education that is supportive, enriched, and effective—an education that prepares the child for a future in higher learning.

References

Adams, D. (2001). Cognitive styles in hearing impaired students. *Educational Psychology*, 21, 351–366.

Adams, M. (1990). *Beginning to read: Thinking and learning about print.* Cambridge, MA: MIT Press.

Adolphs, R., Sears, L., & Piven, J. (2001). Abnormal processing of social information from faces in autism. *Journal of Cognitive Neuroscience*, 13(2), 232–240.

Als, H., Lester, B., Tronick, E. Z., & Brazelton, B. (1982). Manual for the assessment of preterm infants' behavior (APIB). In H. E. Fitzgerald, B. M. Lester, & M.W. Youngman (Eds.), *Theory and research in behavioral pediatrics*, Vol. 1 (pp. 35–53). New York: Plenum Press.

Alvin, J. (1975). *Music therapy.* London: John Clare Books.

American Speech-Language-Hearing Association. (1990). The roles of speech–language pathologists in service delivery to infants, toddlers, and their families. ASHA, *Supplement* 2 (32),4.

American Speech-Language-Hearing Association. (1995). *Central auditory processing; current status of research and implication for clinical practice. A report from the task force on central auditory processing.* Rockville, MD: Author.

American Speech-Language-Hearing Association. (1996). Guidelines for the training, credentialing, use and supervision of speech language pathology assistants. ASHA, *Supplement* 16 (38),2.

American Speech-Language-Hearing Association. (1997). *Preferred practice patterns for the profession of speech-language pathology.* Rockville, MD: Author.

American Speech-Language-Hearing Association. (2001). Roles and responsibilities of speech-language pathologists with respect to reading and writing in children and adolescents (position statement, executive summary of guidelines, technical report). ASHA, *Supplement* 21, 17–27.

American Speech-Language-Hearing Association. (2004). Knowledge and skills needed by speech–language pathologists providing services to infants and families in the NICU environment. ASHA, *Supplement* 9(8), 159–165.

Anderson, J. (1986). Sensory intervention with the preterm infant in the neonatal intensive care unit. *American Journal of Occupational Therapy*, 40(1), 9–26.

Anderson, N., & Battle, D. (1993). Cultural diversity in the development of language. In D. Battle (Ed.), *Communication disorders in multicultural populations* (pp. 158–185). Boston: Andover Medical Publishers.

Anderson, R. (1994). Cultural and linguistic diversity and language impairment in preschool children. *Seminars in Speech and Language*, 15(2), 11–124.

Applebee, A. N. (1978). *The child's concept of story: Ages two to seventeen.* Chicago: University of Chicago Press.

Aram, D., Ekelman, B., & Nation, J. (1984). Preschoolers with language disorders: 10 years later. *Journal of Speech and Hearing Research*, 27, 232–244.

Attride-Stirling, J., Davis, H., Markless, G., Sclare, I., & Day, C. (2001). "Someone to talk to who'll listen": Addressing the psychosocial needs of children and families. *Journal of Community and Applied Social Psychology*, 11, 179–191.

Backus, A. (1999). Mixed native languages: A challenge to the monolithic view of language. *Topics in Language Disorders* 19(4), 11–22.

Bailey, D. B. (1987). Collaboration goal setting with families: Resolving differences in values and priorities for services. *Topics in Early Childhood Special Education*, 7(2), 59–71.

Bailey, D. B. (1991). Issues and perspectives on family assessment. *Infants and Young Children*, 4, 26–34.

Bailey, D. B. (2000). The federal role in early intervention: Prospects for the future. *Topics in Early Childhood Special Education*, 20(2), 71.

Bailey, D. B., et al. (1996). Critical events checklist. *Journal of Early Childhood*, 10(2), 156–171.

Bailey, D. B., & Simeonsson, R. (1985). *Family project.* Frank Porter Graham Child Development Center. University of North Carolina: Chapel Hill.

Bailey, D. B., & Wolery, M. (1984). *Teaching infants and preschoolers with handicaps.* Upper Saddle River, NJ: Merrill/Prentice Hall.

Bailey, D. B., Aytch, L. S., Odom, S. I., Symons, F., & Wolery, M. (1999). Early intervention as we know it. *Mental Retardation and Developmental Disabilities Research Reviews, 5,* 11–20.

Bailey, D. B., McWilliam, R. A., Darkes, L. A., Hebbeler, K., Simeonsson, R. J., Spiker, D., et al. (1998). Family outcomes in early intervention: A framework for program evaluation and efficacy research. *Exceptional Children, 64,* 313–328.

Bailey, D. B., Simeonsson, R. J., Yoder, D., & Huntington, G. S. (1990). Preparing professionals to serve infants and toddlers with handicaps and their families: An integrative analysis across eight disciplines. *Exceptional Children, 57,* 26–35.

Bailey, D. B., & Wolery, M. (1989). *Assessing infants and preschoolers with handicaps.* Upper Saddle River, NJ: Merrill/Prentice Hall.

Banbury, M., & Miller, J. (1993). *Special students: Simulations and solutions, a guide to mainstreaming.* Buffalo, NY: United Educational Services.

Baranek, G. T., Foster, L. G., & Berkson, G. (1997). Tactile defensiveness and stereotyped behaviors. *American Journal of Occupational Therapy, 51*(2), 91–95.

Barnett, D., Pepiton, A., Bell, S., Gilkey, C., Smith, T., Stone, C. et al. (1999). Evaluating early intervention: Accountability methods of service delivery innovation. *Journal of Special Education, 33*(3), 177–189.

Barnett, D. W., & Lentz, F. E. (1997). Ecological foundations of early intervention: Planned activities and strategic sampling. *Journal of Special Education, 30*(4), 471.

Baron-Cohen, S. (1995). *Mindblindness: An essay on autism and theory of mind.* Cambridge, MA: MIT Press, 1995.

Baron-Cohen, S. (1997). Mindblind: Autistic people's inability to relate to people. *Natural History, 106*(7), 62–66.

Bat-Chava, Y., & Deignan, E. (2001). Peer relationships of children with cochlear implants. *Journal of Deaf Studies and Deaf Education, 6*(3), 186–199.

Battle, D. (1996). Language learning and use by African American children. *Topics in Language Disorders, 16*(4), 22–37.

Beckman, P., & Kohl, F. (1984). The effects of social and isolate toys on the interactions and play of integrated and nonintegrated groups of preschoolers. *Education and Training of Mentally Retarded, 19,* 169–174.

Bedore, L. (2001). Assessing morphosyntax in Spanish speaking children. *Seminars in Speech and Language. 22,* 65–77.

Behrmann, J. (1993). *Ideas for inclusion: The classroom teacher's guide to integrating students with severe disabilities.* Longmont, CO: Sopris West.

Bell, R. Q., & Harper, L. V. (1977). *Child effects on adults.* Hillsdale, NJ: Lawrence Erlbaum.

Bellini, S. (2004). Social skill deficits and anxiety in high-functioning adolescents with autism spectrum disorders. *Focus on Autism & Other Developmental Disabilities, 19*(2), 78–86.

Bellis, T. (1998). *Assessment and management of central auditory processing disorders in the educational setting.* San Diego, CA: Singular Publishing Group.

Bellis, T. (2003). *Assessment and management of central auditory processing disorder in the educational setting from science to practice* (2nd ed.) Clifton Park, NY: Thomson Delmar Learning.

Benner, S. (1998). Special education and cultural diversity in America. In *Special education issues within the context of American society.* Belmont, CA: Wadsworth Publishing.

Bereiter, C. (1980). Development in writing. In L. W. Gregg & E. R. Steinberg (Eds.), *Cognitive process in writing.* Hillsdale, NJ. Erlbaum.

Bergin, V. (1980). *Special education needs in bilingual programs.* Washington, DC: National Clearinghouse for Bilingual Education.

Berk, L. E. (1998). *Development through the lifespan.* Boston: Allyn and Bacon.

Bernstein, D. (1989). *Assessing children with limited English proficiency*: Current Perspectives. *Topics in Language Disorders, 9*(3), 15–20.

Bernstein-Ratner, N. (2004). Dialect free assessment principles. *Topics in Language Disorders, 25*(1), 1.

Bertrand, J., Boyle, C., Yeargin-Allsopp, M., Decoufle, P., Mars, A., & Bove, F. (2001). Prevalence of autism in a United States population: The Brick Township, New Jersey, investigation. *Pediatrics, 108*(5), 1155–1162.

Bird, J., Bishop, D. V. M., & Freeman, N. H. (1995). Phonological awareness and literacy development in children with expressive phonological impairments. *Journal of Speech and Hearing Research, 38,* 446–462.

Birnbrauer, J. S., & Leach, D. J. (1993). The Murdoch early intervention program after 2 years. *Behavior Change 10*(2), 63–74.

Bishop, D. V. M. (1997). *Uncommon understanding: Development and disorders of language comprehension in children.* Hove, U.K.: Psychology Press.

Bishop, D. V. M. (2000). Pragmatic language impairment: A correlate of SLI, a distinct subgroup, or part of the autistic continuum? In D. V. M. Bishop & L. B. Leonard (Eds.), *Speech and language impairments in children; causes, characteristics, intervention and outcome* (pp. 99–114). New York: Psychology Press.

Bishop, D. V. M., Price, T. S., Dale, P. S., & Plomin, R. (2003). Outcomes of early language delay: II. Etiology of transient and persistent language difficulties. *Journal of Speech, Language & Hearing Research, 46*(3), 561–576.

Blachman, B. (1984). Relationships of rapid naming ability and language analysis skills to kindergarten and first grade reading achievement. *Journal of Educational Psychology, (76),* 610–622.

Blachowicz, C. (1994). Problem-solving strategies for academic success. In G. Wallach & K. Butler (Eds.), *Language–learning disabilities in school-age children and adolescents* (pp. 253–274). New York: Macmillan.

Blackman, B. (1991). Phonological awareness and word recognition. In A. Kamhi & H. Catts (Eds.), *Reading disabilities: A developmental language approach* (pp.133–158). Boston: Allyn and Bacon.

Blackwell, J., & Niederhauser, C. (2003). Diagnose and manage autistic children. *Nurse Practitioner, 28*(6), 36–43.

Blank, M., Rose, S. A., & Berlin, L. J. (1978). *The language of learning: The preschool years*. New York: Grune & Stratton.

Bloom, L. (1974). Talking, understanding, and thinking. In. R. Schiefelbusch & L. Lloyd (Eds.), *Language perspectives—acquisition, retardation, and intervention*. Baltimore: Univeristy Park Press.

Bogdan, R., & Kugelmass, J. (1984). Case studies of mainstreaming: A symbolic interactionist approach to special schooling. In L. Barton & S. Tomlinson (Eds.), *Special education and social interests* (pp. 173–191). YorkBeach, ME: Nicholas-Hays.

Boothroyd, A. (1969). *Distribution of hearing levels in the student population of the Clarke School for the Deaf.* Northampton, MA: Clarke School for the Deaf.

Boscolo, B., Ratner, N. B., & Rescorla, L. (2002). Fluency of school-aged children with a history of specific expressive language impairment: An exploratory study. *American Journal of Speech-Language Pathology, 11,* 41–49.

Boushel, M. (1998). Research review. *Child and Family Social Work, 3,* 267–276.

Bowe, F. G. (2002). Enhancing reading ability to prevent students from becoming "low functioning deaf" as adults. *American Annals of the Deaf, 147*(5), 22–27.

Boxhill, E. (1985). *Music therapy for the developmentally disabled.* Rockville, MD: Aspen Systems.

Brady, S., Fowler, A., Stone, B., & Winbury, N. (1994). Training phonological awareness: A study with inner-city kindergarten children. *Annals of Dyslexia, 44,* 26–59.

Bratter, J. L., & Eschbach, K. (2005). Race/ethnic differences in nonspecific psychological distress: Evidence from the National Health Interview Survey. *Social Science Quarterly, 86*(3), 620–644.

Brazelton, T. B. (1982). Joint regulation of neonate–parent behavior. In E. Z. Tronick (Ed.), *Social interchange in infancy: Affect, cognition, and communication* (pp. 7–22). Baltimore: University Park Press.

Brazelton, T., & Nugent, J. (1995). *Neonatal behavioral assessment scale* (3rd ed.) (Clinics in Developmental Medicine No. 137). London: MacKeith Press.

Brazy, J. E., Anderson, B. M. H., Becker, P. T., & Becker, M. (2001). How parents of premature infants gather information and obtain support. *Neonatal Network, 20*(2), 41–48.

Briggs, M. (1991). Team development: Decision-making for early intervention. *Infant–Toddler Intervention: The Transdisciplinary Journal, 1,* 1–9.

Brink, M. B. (2002). Involving parents in early childhood assessment: Perspectives from an early intervention instructor. *Early Childhood Education Journal, 29*(4), 251–256.

Brinton, B., Fujiki, M., & Higbee, L. M. (1998). Participation in cooperative learning activities by children with specific language impairment. *Journal of Speech, Language, and Hearing Research, 41,* 1193–1206.

Brinton, B., Fujiki, M., & McKee, L. (1998). Negotiation skills of children with specific language impairment. *Journal of Speech, Language, and Hearing Research, 41,* 927–940.

Bronfenbrenner, U. (1986). Ecology of the family as a context for human development: Research perspectives. *Developmental Psychology, 22,* 723–742.

Bronfenbrenner, U. (1992). Ecological systems theory. In R. Vasta (Ed.), *6th theory of child development: Revised formulation and current issues* (pp. 187–249). Philadelphia: Kingsley.

Brook, S. L., & Bowler, D. M. (1992). Autism by another name? Semantic and pragmatic impairments in children. *Journal of Autism and Developmental Disorders, 22*(1), 61–81.

Brown, L. Sherbenou, R., & Johnsen, S. (1997). *Test of nonverbal intelligence* (3rd ed.). Austin, TX: Pro-Ed.

Brown, W., & Conroy, M. (1999). Entitled to what? Public policy and the responsibilities of early intervention. *Infants and Young Children*, 11(3), 27–36.

Brownell, M., & Walther-Thomas, C. (2001). Steven Shore: Understanding the autism spectrum—What teachers need to know. *Intervention in School & Clinic*, 36(5), 293–300.

Brownell, R. (2000). *Expressive one-word picture vocabulary test* (3rd ed.). Novato, CA: Academic Therapy Publications.

Bruder, M. (2000). Family-centered early intervention: Clarifying our values for the new millennium. *Topics in Early Childhood Special Education*, 20(2), 105–116.

Bruscia, K. (1989). *Defining music therapy*. Spring City, PA: Spring House Books.

Bruskewitz, R. (1998). Collaborative intervention: A system of support for teachers attempting to meet the needs of students with challenging behaviors: Teachers, students—psychology. *Preventing School Failure*, 42(3), 129.

Buck, D. M., Cox, A. W., Shannon, P., & Hash, K. (2001). Building collaboration among physicians and other early intervention providers: Practices that work. *Infant's and Young Children*, 13(4), 11–20.

Bullard, H. R. (2004). Ensure the successful inclusion of a child with Asperger syndrome in the general education classroom. *Intervention in School & Clinic*, 39(3), 176–180.

Buschbacher, P., & Fox, L. (2003). Understanding and intervening with the challenging behavior of young children with autism spectrum disorder. *Language, Speech, and Hearing Services in Schools*, 34, 217–227.

Buysse, V., & Wesley, P. (1999). Community development approaches for early intervention. *Topics in Early Childhood Special Education*, 19(4), 236–244.

Bzoch, K. R., League, R., & Brown, V. L. (2003). *Receptive expressive emergent language scale* (3rd ed.). Baltimore: University Park Press.

Calderon, R. (2000). Parental involvement in deaf children's education programs as a predictor of child language, early reading and social emotional development. *Journal of Deaf Studies and Deaf Education*, 5(2), 140–155.

Calderon, R., & Naidu, S. (1999). Further support for the benefits of early identification and intervention for children with hearing loss. *Volta Review*, 100(5), 53–85.

Caldwell, B. M., & Bradley, R. H. (1984). *Home observation for measurement of the environment*, Little Rock: University of Arkansas.

Calloway, C. J., Myles, B. S., & Earles, T. L. (1999). The development of communicative functions and means in students with autism. *Focus on Autism and Other Developmental Disabilities*, 14(3), 140–150.

Calvert, D. R., & Silverman, R. S. (1983). *Speech and deafness* (rev. ed.). Washington, DC: Alexander Graham Bell Assignation for the Deaf.

Carr, E. G., & Blakeley-Smith, A. (2006). Classroom intervention for illness-related problem behavior in children with developmental disabilities. *Behavior Modification*, 30(6), 901–924.

Catts, H. (1989). Speech production deficits in developmental dyslexia. *Journal of Speech and Hearing Disorders*, 54, 422–428.

Catts, H., & Kamhi, A. (1986). The linguistic basis of reading disorders: Implications for the speech-language pathologist. *Language, Speech and Hearing Services in Schools*, 17, 329–341.

Catts, H. W. (2001). Estimating the risk of future reading difficulties in kindergarten children: A research-based model and its clinical implementation. *Language, Speech & Hearing Services in Schools*, 32(1), 38–50.

Cavallaro, C. C., & Ballard-Rosa, M. (1998). A preliminary study of inclusive special education services for infants, toddlers, and preschool-age children in California. *Topics in Early Childhood Special Education*, 18(3), 169.

Chandler, L. (1979). Gross and fine motor development. In M. Cohen & P. Gross (Eds.), *The developmental resource: Behavioral sequences for assessment and program planning* (Vol. 1, pp. 119–152). New York: Grune and Stratton.

Chapa, J., & Valencia, R. (1993). Latino populations, growth, demographic characteristics, and educational stagnation: An examination of recent trends. *Hispanic Journal of Behavioral Sciences*, 152(2), 165–187.

Charman, T. (2004). Matching preschool children with autism spectrum disorders and comparison children for language ability: Methodological challenges. *Journal of Autism and Developmental Disorders*, 34(1), 59–64.

Cheng, L. (1996). Beyond bilingualism: Language acquisition and disorders—A global perspective. *Topics in Language Disorders*, 16(4), IV–V.

Cheng, L. L. (1991). *Assessing Asian language performance: Guidelines for evaluating limited English-proficient students* (2nd ed.) Oceanside, CA: Academic Communication Associations.

Cheng, L. L. (1993). Asian American cultures. In D. Battle (Ed.), *Communication disorders in multicultural populations* (pp. 38–77). Boston: Andover Medical Publications.

Chess, S. (1986). Early childhood development and its implications for analytical theory and practice. *American Journal of Psychoanalysis, 46,* 122–148.

Chiat, S. (2001). Mapping theories of developmental language impairment: Premises, predictions and evidence. *Language and Cognitive Processes, 16*(2/3), 113–142.

Christenson, S. L. (1999). Families and schools: Rights, responsibilities, resources, and relationships. In R. C. Pianta & M.J. Cox (Eds.), *The transition to kindergarten* (pp. 143–177). Baltimore: Paul H. Brooks.

Church, C., Alisanski, S., & Amanullah, S. (2000). The social, behavioral, and academic experiences of children with Asperger syndrome. *Focus on Autism & Other Developmental Disabilities, 15*(1), 12–21.

Clark, D. M., & Smith, S. W. (1999). Facilitating friendships: Including students with autism in the early elementary classroom. *Intervention in School & Clinic, 34*(4), 248–251.

Clark, G. N., & Seifer, R. (1985). Assessment of parents' interactions with their developmentally delayed infants. *Infant Mental Health Journal, 6,* 214–225.

Clay, M. (1998). *By different paths to common outcome.* York, ME: Stenhouse Publishers.

Clifford, R. M., & Harms, T. (1980). *Early Childhood Environment Rating Scale.* New York: Teachers College Press.

Cobb, B., Lehmann, J., Tochterman, S., & Bomotti, S. (2000). Students with disabilities in transition: A review of four reforms. In D. Johnson & E. Emanuel (Eds.), *Issues influencing the future of transition programs and services in the United States* (pp. 3–19). Minneapolis, MN: University of Minnesota, National Transition Network, Institute of Community Integration.

Coggins, T., & Carpenter, R. (1981). The communicative intention inventory: A system for observing and coding children's early intentional communication. *Applied Psycholinguistics, 2,* 235–251.

Cohen, N., Davine, M., Horodezsky, N., Lipsett, L., & Issacson, L. (1993). Unsuspected language impairment in psychiatrically disturbed children: Prevalence and language and behavioral characteristic. *Journal of the American Academy of Child and Adolescent Psychiatry, 32,* 595–603.

Cohen, S., Thomas, C. C., Sattler, R. O, & Morsink, C. V. (1997). Meeting the challenge of consultation and collaboration: Developing interactive teams. *Journal of Learning Disabilities, 30*(4), 427–433.

Cole, L. (1980). *Developmental analysis of social dialect features in the spontaneous language of preschool Black children.* Unpublished master's thesis, Northwestern University, Evanston, IL.

Coleman, P., Buysse, V., Scalise-Smith, D., & Schute, A. (1991). Consultation: Applications to early intervention. *Infants and Young Children, 4*(2), 41–46.

Congress, E. (1994). The use of culturagrams to assess and empower culturally diverse families. *Families in Society, 75,* 531–540.

Connor, C., Heiber, S., Arts, H., & Zwolan, T. (2000). Speech, vocabulary and the education of children using cochlear implants: Oral or total communication? *Journal of Speech, Language and Hearing Research, 43*(5), 1185–1204.

Connor, M. (2000). Asperger syndrome (autistic spectrum disorder) and the self-reports of comprehensive school students. *Educational Psychology in Practice, 16*(3), 285–296.

Constable, A., Stackhouse, J., & Wells, B. (1997). Developmental word-finding difficulties and phonological processing: The case of the missing handcuffs. *Applied Psycholinguistics, 18,* 507–536.

Conti-Ramsden, G., & Botting, N. (1999). Classification of children with specific language impairment: Longitudinal considerations. *Journal of Speech Language and Hearing Research, 42*(5), 1195–1205.

Conti-Ramsden, G., & Windfuhr, K. (2002). Productivity with word order and morphology: A comparative look at children with SLI and children with normal language abilities. *International Journal of Language & Communication Disorders, 37*(1), 17–30.

Cook-Gumperz, J. (1977). Situated instructions: Language socialization of school age children. In S. Ervin-Tripp & C. Mitchell-Kernan (Eds.), *Child discourse, language, thought, and culture: Advances in the study of cognition.* New York: Academic Press.

Coplan, J. (1993). *Early language milestone scale* (2nd ed). Austin, TX: Pro-Ed.

Coplan, J., & Jawad, A. F. (2005). Modeling clinical outcome of children with autistic spectrum disorders. *Pediatrics, 116*(1), 117–122.

Craig, H., & Washington, J. (2000). An assessment battery for identifying language impairments in African American children. *Journal of Speech, Language, and Hearing Research, 43,* 366–379.

Craig, H. K., & Washington, J. A. (1993). Access behaviors of children with specific language impairment. *Journal of Speech and Hearing Research, 36*(2), 322–337.

Crais, E., & Roberts, J. (1991). Decision making in assessment and early intervention planning. *Language, Speech, and Hearing Services in Schools*, 22, 19–30.

Crais, K. (1993). Families and professionals as collaborators in assessment. *Topics in Language Disorders*, 14(1), 29–40.

Crawley, S. B., & Spiker, D. (1982). *Mother–Child Rating Scale*. Chicago: University of Illinois. (Available from ERIC Document Reproduction Service No. ED221978.)

Critchley, M. (1970). *The dyslexic child*. London: Heinemann Medical Books.

Crosbie, S., Dodd, B., & Howard, D. (2002). Spoken word comprehension in children with SLI: A comparison of three case studies. *Child Language Teaching and Therapy*, 18(3), 191–212.

Cross, T. (1977). Mothers' speech adjustments: The contribution of selected child listener variables. In C. Snow & C. Ferguson (Eds.), *Talking to children: Language input and acquisition*. London: Cambridge University Press.

Crowley, C. (2003). *Diagnosing communication disorders in culturally and linguistically diverse students*. (EDO-EC-03–11). Digest E650. Arlington, VA: Educational Resources Information Center (ERIC) Clearinghouse on Disabilities and Gifted Education.

Cummins, J. (1981). The role of primary language and development in promoting educational success for language minority students. In *Schooling and language minority students: A theoretical framework*. Los Angeles: California State Department of Education, Evaluation, Assessment, and Dissemination Center.

Cummins, J. (1984). *Bilingualism and special education*. San Diego, CA: College-Hill.

Cunningham, M., & Cox, E. (2003). Hearing assessment in infants and children: Recommendations beyond neonatal screening. *Pediatrics*, 111(2), 436–440.

Curtis, S., Prutting, C., & Lowell, E. (1979). Pragmatic, semantic development in young children with impaired hearing, *Journal of Speech and Hearing Research*, 22, 534–552.

Dale, P. S., Price, T. S., Bishop, D. V. M., & Plomin, R. (2003). Outcomes of early language delay: I. Predicting persistent and transient language difficulties at 3 and 4 years. *Journal of Speech, Language & Hearing Research*, 46(3), 544–561.

Danaher, J., Shackelford, J., & Harbin, G. (2004). Revisiting a comparison of eligibility policies for infant/toddler programs and preschool special education programs. *Topics in Early Childhood Special Education*, 24(2), 59–67.

Davis, L., & Proctor, E. (1989). *Race, gender and class: Guidelines for practice with individuals, families and groups*. Upper Saddle River, NJ: Prentice Hall.

Dawson, G., & Watling, R. (2000). Interventions to facilitate auditory, visual, and motor integration in autism: A review of the evidence. *Journal of Autism and Developmental Disorders*, 30(5), 415–421.

Dawson, P. M., Robinson, J. L., Butterfield, P. M., Van Doorninck, W. L., Geansbauer, T. J., & Harmon, R. J. (1990). Supporting new parents through home visits: Effects on mother–child interaction. *Topics in Early Childhood Special Education*, 10, 1–13.

Day, P. (1986). Deaf children's expression of communicative intentions. *Journal of Communication Disorders*, 19, 367–385.

DeGangi, G., Wietlisbach, S., Poisson, S., Stein, E., & Royeen, C. (1994). The impact of culture and socioeconomic status on family–professional collaboration: Challenges and solutions. *Topics in Early Childhood Special Education*, 14(4), 503–520.

de Halleux, C., & Poncelet, F. (2001). Not a disability. *Lancet Supplement*, p. 358.

Delack, J. B., & Fowlow, P. J. (1978). The ontogenesis of differential vocalization: Development of prosodic contrastivity during the first year of life. In N. Waterson & C. Snow (Eds.), *The development of communication*. New York: Wiley.

DeMyer, M., Barton, S., DeMyer, E., Norton, J., Allen, J., & Steele, R. (1973). Prognosis in autism: A follow-up study. *Journal of Autism and Childhood Schizophrenia*, 3, 199–216.

Dempsey, I., & Foreman, P. (2001). A review of educational approaches for individuals with autism. *International Journal of Disability, Development and Education*, 48(1), 103–116.

Denckla, M. (1972). Color-naming deficits in dyslexic boys. *Cortex*, 8, 164–176.

Denton, M., & Foley, D.J. (1994). The marriage of special and regular education through inclusion. *Teaching and Change*, 1, 349–368.

Desjardin, J. L. (2003). Assessing parental perceptions of self-efficacy and involvement in families of young children with hearing loss. *Volta Review*, 103(4), 391–410.

de Villiers, P., de Villiers, J., Schick, B., & Hoffmeister, R. (2000). *Theory of mind development in signing and nonsigning deaf children. The impact of sign language on social cognition*. Paper presented at the seventh

International Conference on Theoretical Issues in Sign Language Research, Amsterdam, The Netherlands.

Dew, D. W. (Ed.) (1999). *Serving individuals who are low-functioning deaf: Report of the Twenty-Fifth Institute on Rehabilitation Issues*. Washington, DC: George Washington University.

Dillard, J. L. (1973). *Black English: Its history and usage in the United States*. New York: Random House.

Dimes, J. H., Merritt, D. D., & Culatta, B. (1998). Collaborative partnership and decision making. In D. D. Merritt & B. Culatta (Eds.), *Limiting bias in the classroom* (pp. 37–97). San Diego, CA: Singular.

Dinnebeil, L. A., Hale, L., & Rule, S. (1996). A qualitative analysis of parents' and service coordinators; descriptions of variables that influence collaborative relationships. *Topics in Early Childhood Special Education, 16*, 322–347.

Dipipi, C. M., Jitendra, A. K., & Miller, J. A. (2001). Reducing repetitive speech: Effects of strategy instruction. *Preventing School Failure, 45*(4), 177–181.

Dobson, S., & Henderson, L. (1998). A comparison of training approaches for support assistants using the Hanen philosophy. *International Journal of Language and Communication Disorders, 33*, 515–519.

Doering, L. V., Moser, D. K., & Dracup, K. (2000). Correlates of anxiety, hostility, depression, and psychosocial adjustment in parents of NICU infants. *Neonatal Network, 19*(4), 15–23.

Done, D., & Miles, T. (1978). Learning, memory, and dyslexia. In M. Gruneberg, P. Morris, & R.. Sykes (Eds.), *Practical aspects of memory*. London: Academic Press.

Dubowitz, L., Dubowitz, V., & Mercuri, E. (1999). The neurological assessment of the preterm and full-term newborn infant. In MacKeith, E. (Ed.), *Clinics in developmental medicine* (2nd ed., p. 148). MacKeith. (Ed.), Cambridge, U.K.: MacKeith Press.

Dunn, C., & Newton, L. (1986). A comprehensive model for speech development and hearing impaired children. *Topics in Language Disorders, 6*(3), 25–46.

Dunn, L., Jugo, D., & Padilla, E. (1986). *Peabody Picture Vocabulary*. Circle Pines, MN: American Guidance Services.

Dunn, M., Flax, J., Sliwinski, M., & Aram, D. (1996). The use of spontaneous language measures as criteria for identifying children with specific language impairment: An attempt to reconcile clinical and research incongruence. *Journal of Speech and Hearing Research, 39*(3), 643–654.

Dunst, C. J. (2000) Revisiting "Rethinking Early Intervention." *Topics in Early Childhood Special Education, 20*(2), 95.

Dunst, C. J., Herter, S., Shields, H., & Bennis, L. (2001). Mapping community-based natural learning opportunities. *Young Exceptional Child, 4*(4), 16–25.

Dunst, C. J., & Jenkins, V. (1983). *Family support scale*. Western Carolina Center: Morganton, NC.

Dunst, C. J., & Trivette C. M. (1989). An empowerment perspective of case management. *Topics in Early Childhood Special Education, 8*, 87–102.

Eccles, J. S., Wigfield, A., & Schiefele, U. (1998). Motivation to succeed. In *Handbook of child psychology*. (vol. 3, pp. 1051–1075). New York: Wiley.

Ehren, B. (2006). Partnerships to support reading comprehension for students with language impairment. *Topics in Language Disorders, 26*, 42–54.

Ehren, B., & Jackson, J. (2003). Curriculum based language intervention with adolescents. ASHA Telephone Seminar, Rockville, MD.

Ehren, B. J. (1994). New directions for meeting the academic needs of adolescents with language learning disabilities. In G. P. Wallach & K. G. Butler (Eds.), *Language learning disabilities in school age children and adolescents: Some principles and applications*. Boston: Allyn and Bacon.

Ehren, B. J. (2000). Views of cognitive referencing from the pragmatist's lens. Newsletter of the special interest division 1, language learning and education, *American Speech Language-Hearing Association, 7*(1), 3–8.

Eisenberg, A. (1985). Learning to describe past experiences in conversation. *Discourse Processes, 8*, 177–204.

Eisenberg, L. (1956). The autistic child in adolescence. *American Journal of Psychiatry, 112*, 607–612.

Ekstein, R. (1983). *Children of time and space, of action and impulse*. New York: Jason Aronson.

Ellis, A. W. (1993). *Reading, writing and dyslexia*. Hove, UK: Erlbaum.

Ellis, L., Schlaudecker, C., & Regimbal, C. (1995). Effectiveness of a collaborative consultation approach to basic concept instruction with kindergarten children. *Language, Speech, and Hearing Services in Schools, 26*, 69–74.

Emmorey, K., Bellugi, U., Frederici, A., & Horn, P. (1995). Effects of age of acquisition on grammatical sensitivity: Evidence from on-line and off-line tasks. *Applied Psycholinguistics, 16*(1), 1–23.

Englert, C. S. (1992). Writing instruction from a sociocultural perspective: The holistic, dialogic, and social enterprise of writing. *Journal of Learning Disabilities, 25*(3), 153–177.

Erchial, W., Covington, G., Hughes, J., & Meyers, J. (1995). Further explorations of request-centered relational communication with social consultation. *School Psychology Review, 24*(4), 621.

Ericsson, K. A., & Kintsch, W. (1991). Memory in comprehension and problem solving: A long term working memory. *Institute of Cognitive Science Technical Report*, No. 9, pp. 1–13. Boulder, CO: University of Colorado.

Evans, J., Alibali, M., & McNeil, N. (2001). Divergence of verbal expression and embodied knowledge: Evidence from speech and gesture in children with specific language impairment. *Language and Cognitive Processes, 16*(2/3), 309–331.

Evans, J. L., Viele, K., Kass, R.E., & Tang, F. (2002). Grammatical morphology and perception of synthetic and natural speech in children with specific language impairments. *Journal of Speech, Language & Hearing Research, 45*(3), 494–505.

Farel, A., Shackelford, J., & Hurth. (1997). Perception regarding the IFSP process in a statewide interagency service coordination program. *Topics in Early Childhood Special Education, 17*(2), 234–250.

Farlow, L. (1996). A quarter of success stories: How to make inclusion work. *Educational Leadership, 53*(5), 56–59.

Farran, D. C., Kasari, C., Comfort, M., & Jay, S. (1986). *The parent/caregiver involvement scale*. Greensboro, NC: The University of North Carolina at Greensboro, Child Development and Family Relations, School of Human Environmental Sciences.

Farran D. C., Kasari, C., Yoder, P., Harber, L., Huntington, G., & Comfort-Smith, M. (1987). Rating mother-child interactions in handicapped and at-risk infants. In D. Tamir, T.B. Brazelton, & A. Russell (Eds.), *Stimulation and intervention in infant development* (pp. 297–312). London: Freund Publishing House, Ltd.

Felton, R. H., & Pepper, P. A. (1995). Early identification and intervention of phonological deficits in kindergarten and early elementary children at risk for reading disability. *School Psychology Review, 24*(3), 405–415.

Fenrick, N. J., Pearson, M. E., & Pepelnjak, J. M. (1984). The play, attending, and language of young handicapped children in integrated and segregated settings. *Journal of the Division for Early Childhood, 8*, 57–67.

Fenson, L., Dale, P. S., Reznick, J. S., Bates, E., Harting, J., Thal, S., et al. (1993). *Guide and technical manual for the MacArthur communicative development inventories*. San Diego, CA: Singular.

Fenson, L., Dale, P. S., Reznick, J. S., Thal, S., Bates, E., & Harting, J. P. (1994). *MacArthur communicative development inventories*. San Diego, CA: Singular.

Fewster, G. (2002). The DSM IV you, but not IV me. *Child & Youth Care Forum, 31*(6), 365–381.

Fey, M. E., Long, S. H., & Finestack, L. H. (2003). Ten principles of grammar facilitation for children with specific language impairments. *American Journal of Speech-Language Pathology, 12*, 3–15.

Fishback, P., & Baskin, J. (1991). Narrowing the black–white gap in child literacy in 1990: The roles of school inputs and family inputs. *Review of Economic and Statistics, 73*, 725–728.

Fitch, E. F. (2002). Disability and inclusion: From labeling deviance to social valuing. *Educational Theory 52*(4), 463–477.

Fitch, F. (2003). Inclusion, exclusion, and ideology: Special education students' changing sense of self. *Urban Review, 35*(3), 233–252.

Fitzgerald, M. T., & Karnes, D. E. (1987). A parent-implemented language model for at risk and developmentally delayed preschool children. *Topics in Language Disorders, 7*(3), 31–46.

Florian, L. (1995). Part H early intervention program: Legislative history and intent of the law. *Topics in Early Childhood Special Education, 15*, 247–262.

Foley, G. (1990). Portrait of the arena evacuation: Assessment in the transdisciplinary approach. In F. Gibbs & D. Teti (Eds.), *Interdisciplinary assessment of infants: A guide for early intervention professionals* (pp. 271–286). Baltimore: Paul H. Brookes.

Folstein, S. E. (1999). Autism. *International Review of Psychiatry, 11*(4), 269–278.

Forest, E. J., Horner, R. H., Lewis-Palmer, T., & Todd, A. W. (2004). Transitions for young children with autism from preschool to kindergarten. *Journal of Positive Behavior Interventions, 6*(2), 103–112.

Fox, A. V., Dodd, B., & Howard, D. (2002). Risk factors for speech disorders in children. *International Journal of Language & Communication Disorders, 37*(2), 117–131.

Fox, B. (2000). *Word identification strategies: Phonics from a new perspective* (2nd ed.). Upper Saddle River, NJ: Merrill/Prentice Hall.

Frederickson, N., & Cline, T. (2001). *Special educational needs, inclusion and diversity*. Buckingham, UK: Open University Press.

Freeman, B. J., Cronin, P., & Candela, P. (2002). Asperger syndrome or autistic disorder? *Focus on Autism & Other Developmental Disabilities, 17*(3), 145–152.

Freeman, S. F. N., & Alkin, M. C. (2000). Academic and social attainments of children with mental retardation in general education and special education settings. *Remedial and Special Education, 21,* 3–18.

Freund, P. J., Boone, H. A., Barlow, J. H., & Lim, C. I. (2005). Healthcare and early intervention collaborative supports for families and young children. *Infants & Young Children, 18*(1), 25–36.

Friedman, K. A., Leone, P., & Friedman, E. (1999). Strengths-based assessment of children with SED: Consistency of reporting by teachers and parents. *Journal of Child and Family Studies, 8,* 169–180.

Friend, M., & Cook, L. (1996). *Interactions: Collaboration skills for school professionals.* White Plains, NY: Longman.

Frith, U., & Happe, F. (1999). Theory of mind and self-consciousness: What is it like to be autistic? *Mind & Language, 14,* 1–22.

Fu, V., Stremmel, A., & Treppte, C. (1993). *Multiculturalism in early childhood programs.* Perspective from ERIC/EECE: A Monograph Series, No. 3. Urbana, IL: ERIC Clearinghouse on Elementary and Early Childhood Education.

Fuerstein, R. (1979). *The dynamic assessment of retarded performers: The learning potential assessment device, theory, instruments, techniques.* Baltimore, MD: University Park Press.

Fujiki, M., Brinton, B., & Clarke, D. (2002). Emotion regulation in children with specific language impairment. *Language, Speech, and Hearing Services in Schools, 33,* 102–111.

Fujiki, M., Brinton, B., Hart, C. H., & Fitzgerald, A. (1999). Peer acceptance and friendship in children with specific language impairment. *Topics in Language Disorders, 19*(2), 34–48.

Fujiki, M., Spackman, M. P., Brinton, B., & Hall, A. (2004). The relationship of language and emotion regulation skills to reticence in children with specific language impairment. *Journal of Speech, Language & Hearing Research, 47*(3), 637–646.

Furney, K. S., Hasazi, S. B., Clark-Keefe, K., & Hartnett, J. (2003). A longitudinal analysis of shifting policy landscapes in special and general education reform. *Exceptional Children, 70*(1), 81–94.

Furth, H. (1966). *Thinking without language: Psychological implications of deafness.* New York: Free Press.

Furth, H. (1973). *Deafness and learning: A psychosocial approach.* Belmont, CA: Wadsworth.

Furth, H., & Youniss, J. (1965). The influence of language and experience on discovery and use of logical symbols. *British Journal of Psychology, 56,* 381–390.

Gable, R. A, & Manning, M. L. (1999). Interdisciplinary teaming: Solution to instructing heterogeneous groups of students. Interdisciplinary approach in education. *Education Clearing House, 72*(3), 182–186.

Gallagher, J., & Desimone, L. (1995). Lessons learned from the implementation of the IEP: Application to the IFSP. *Topics in Early Childhood Special Education 15*(3), 353–379.

Gallagher, J., Harbin, G., Eckland, J., & Clifford, R. (1994). State diversity and policy implementation: Infants and toddlers. In L. J. Johnson, R. J.Gallagher, M. J. LaMontagne, J. B. Jordan, & J. J. Gallagher (Eds.), *Meeting early intervention challenges: Issues from birth to 3* (2nd ed., p. 336). Baltimore: Paul H. Brookes.

Gallagher, J., Harbin, G., Thomas, D., Clifford, R., & Wenger, M. (1998). Major policy issues in implementing Part H-P.L. *Infants and Toddlers, 99,* 452–457.

Gallagher, J. J. (2000). The beginnings of federal help for young children with disabilities. *Topics in Early Childhood Special Education, 20*(1), 3–7.

Gallagher, J. J., Scharfman, W., & Bristol, M. (1984). The division of responsibilities in families with preschool handicapped and nonhandicapped children. *Journal of the Division for Early Childhood, 8,* 3–12.

Gallagher, P. A. (1997). Teachers and inclusion: Perspectives on changing roles. *Topics in Early Childhood Special Education, 17*(3), 363–387.

Gallagher, T. (1996). Social–interactional approaches to child language intervention. In J. Beitchman & M. Konstatareas (Eds.), *Language, learning and behavior problems: Emerging perspectives* (pp. 418–435). Cambridge, UK: Cambridge University Press.

Gallagher, T. M. (1999). Interrelationships among children's language, behavior and emotional problems. *Topics in Language Disorders, 19*(1), 1–15.

Gallagher, T. M., Swigert, N. B., & Baum, H. M. (1998). Collecting outcomes data in schools: Needs and challenges. *Language, Speech, and Hearing Services in Schools, 29,* 250–256.

Garcia, E., & Gonzalez, G. (1984). The interrelationship of Spanish and Spanish/English language acquisition in the Hispanic child. In J. V. Martinez & R. H. Mendoza (Eds.), *Chicano psychology* (2nd ed). New York: Academic Press.

Gardner, W. L. (1982). Why do we persist? *Education and Treatment of Children*, 5, 369–377.

Garnett, K. (1986). Telling tales: Narratives and learning-disabled children. *Topics in Language Disorders*, 6(2), 44–56.

Garrett, J. N., & Thorp, E. K. (1998). The impact of early intervention legislation: Local perceptions. *Topics in Early Childhood Special Education*, 18(3), 183–191.

Geers, A. (2004). Speech, language, and reading skills after early cochlear implantation. *Archives of Otolaryngology Head Neck Surgery*, 130(5), 634–638.

Geers, A., & Brenner, C. (2003). Background and educational characteristics of prelingually deaf children implantation by five years of age. *Ear and Hearing*, 14, 2–14.

Gerber, S. (2003). A developmental perspective on language assessment and intervention for children on the autistic spectrum. *Topics in Language Disorders*, 23(2), 74–94.

Gibelman, M. (1998). Theory, practice and experience in the purchase of services. In M. Gibelman & H. W. Demone, Jr. (Eds.), *The privatization of human services: Policy and practice issues* (Vol. 1, pp. 1–51). New York: Springer.

Gillam, R. B., & Pearson, N. A. (2005). *Test of narrative language*. Austin, TX: Pro-Ed.

Ginsburg, G. S., La Greca, A. M., & W. K. Silverman, (1998). Social anxiety in children with anxiety disorders: Relation with social and emotional functioning. *Journal of Abnormal Child Psychology*, 26(3), 175–185.

Gitlin, A. (1999). Collaboration and progressive school reform: Educational change, school management & organization, reformers. *Educational Policy*, 13(5), 630.

Gitterman, A. (1996). Ecological perspectives: Response to Professor Jerry Wakefield. *Social Service Review*, 70(3), 472–476.

Goldin-Meadow, S. M., & Mayberry, R. (2001). How do profoundly deaf children learn to read? *Learning Disabilities Research & Practice*, 16(4), 222–229.

Goldman, R., & Fristoe, M. (2000). *Test of articulation*. Circle Pines, MN: American Guidance Service.

Goldstein, B. (2000). *Cultural and linguistic diversity resource guide for speech language pathologists*. San Diego, CA: Singular.

Goldstein, B. (2001). Assessing phonological skills in Hispanic Latino children. *Seminars in Speech and Language*, 22, 39–49.

Goldstein, B., & Washington, P. (2001). An initial investigation of phonological patterns in 4-year-old typically developing bilingual Spanish–English children. *Language Speech Hearing Services in the Schools*, 32(3), 153–162.

Goldstein, H., English, K., Shafer, K., & Kaczmarek, L. (1997). Interaction among preschoolers without disabilities: Effects of across the day peer invention. *Journal of Speech, Language, and Hearing Research*, 40(1), 33–48.

Goodman, C. C., & Silverstein, M. (2005). Latina grandmothers raising grandchildren: Acculturation and psychological well-being. *International Journal of Aging & Human Development*, 60(4), 305–316.

Goodman, K. S., Goodman, Y. M., & Hood, W. J. (1998). *The whole language evaluation book*. Portsmouth, NH: Heinemann.

Gopnik, M. (1999). Familial language impairment: More English evidence. *Folia Phoniatrica et Logopaedica*, 51, 5–19.

Goswami, U., & Bryant, P. (1990). *Phonological skills and learning to read*. Hillsdale, NJ: Erlbaum.

Gough, P., Ehri, L., & Treiman, R. (Eds.). (1992). *Reading acquisition*. Hillsdale, NJ: Erlbaum.

Greenberg, M. (1980). Social interactions between deaf preschoolers and their mothers: The effects of communication method and communication competence. *Development Psychology*, 16, 465–474.

Greene, J. C. (2000). Understanding social programs through evaluation. In N. K. Denzin & Y. S. Lincoln (Eds.), *Handbook of qualitative research* (pp. 981–1000). Thousand Oaks, CA: Sage.

Greenspan, S., & Pollack, G. (1989). The course of life, Vol. II. *Early childhood*. Madison, CT: International Universities Press.

Greenspan, S. I., & Wieder, S. (1997). Developmental patterns and outcomes in infants and children with disorders in relating and communicating: A chart review of 200 cases of children with autistic spectrum diagnosis. *Journal of Developmental and Learning Disabilities*, 2, 87–141.

Guaralnick, M. (1986). The peer relations of young handicapped and nonhandicapped children. In P. S. Strain, M. J. Guralnick, & H. M. Walker (Eds.), *Children's social behaviors: Development, assessment, and modification* (pp. 93–140). New York: Academic Press.

Guralnick, M. J. (1998). Effectiveness of early intervention for vulnerable children: A developmental perspective. *American Journal on Mental Retardation*, 102(4), 319–345.

Guralnick, M. J. (2001). A developmental systems model for early intervention. *Infants and Young Children*, 14(2), 1–18.

Gutheil, I. (1992). Considering the physical environment. An essential component of good practice. *Social Work*, 37(5), 391–396.

Gutierrez-Clellen, V. F. (2000). Dynamic assessment: An approach to assessing children's language potential. *Seminars in Speech and Language*, 21, 215–222.

Hacker, J. C. (1992). Competency-based job related basic skills training through a model partnership. *Final Report and Final Evaluation Report of National Workplace Literacy Project*.

Hadley, P., & Schuele, M. (1998). Facilitating peer interaction: Socially relevant objectives for preschool language intervention. *American Journal of Speech-Language Pathology*, 7(4), 25–36.

Hall, S., DeBernardis, M., & Reiss, A. (2006). Social escape behaviors in children with fragile X syndrome. *Journal of Autism and Developmental Disorders*, 36(7), 935–947.

Hammil, D., & Larsen, S. (1995). *The test of written language*. Austin, TX: Pro-Ed.

Hanft, B., & Humphrey, R. (1989, April). Training occupational therapists in early intervention. *Infants and Young Children*, 1, 54–66.

Hanson, M., Lynch, E., & Wayman, K. (1990). Honoring the cultural diversity of families when gathering data. *Topics in Language Disorders*, 10(1), 112–131.

Hansson, K., Nettelbladt, U., & Nilholm, C. (2000). Contextual influence on the language production of children with speech/language impairment. *International Journal of Language & Communication Disorders*, 35(1), 31–47.

Harbin, G. (1977). Educational assessment. In L. Cross & K. Gobin (Eds.), *Identifying handicapped children* (pp. 35–52). Chapel Hill: University of North Carolina.

Harbin, G., Bruder, M., Adams, C., Mazzarella, C., Whitbread, K., Gabbard, G., & Staff, I. (2004). Early Head Start: Identifying and serving children with disabilities. *Topics in Early Childhood Special Education*, 24(2), 89–94.

Harbin, G., & Danaher, J. (1994). Comparison of eligibility policies for infants/toddlers program and preschool education program. *Topics in Early Childhood Special Education*, 14(4), 455–472.

Harbin, G. L., & Kameny, R. (2000). *Early childhood organization of services*. Chapel Hill: University of North Carolina, FPG Child Development Institute.

Harbin, G. L., & Salisbury, C. (2000). Policies, administration, and systems change. In S. Sandall, M. E. McLean, & B. J. Smith (Eds.), *Recommended practices in early intervention/early childhood special education* (pp. 65–69). Longmont, CO: Sopris West.

Harn, W., Bradshaw, M., & Ogletree, B. (1999). The speech language pathologist in the schools: Changing role. *Intervention in School and Clinic*, 34(3), 163–170.

Harris, S., Handleman, L., Gordon, R., Kristoff, B., & Fuentes, F. (1991). Changes in cognitive and language functioning of preschool children with autism. *Journal of Autism and Developmental Disorders*, 21, 281–290.

Haynes, W., & Moran, M. (1989). A cross-sectional developmental study of final consonant production in southern black children from preschool to third grade. *Language Speech Hearing Services in Schools*, 21(4), 400–406.

Hazan, V., & Barrett, S. (2000). The development of phonemic categorization in children aged 6–12. *Journal of Phonetics*, 28, 377–396.

Healy, A., Keesee, P., & Smith, B. (1989). *Early services for children with special needs: Transactions for family support*. Iowa City: University Hospital School.

Heath, S. (1986). Taking a cross-cultural look at narratives. *Topics in Language Disorders*, 7, 84–94.

Hebbeler, K. M., Wagner, M., Spiker, D., Scarborough, A., Simeonsson, R., & Collier, M. (2001). *A first look at the characteristics of children and families entering early intervention*. National Early Intervention Longitudinal Study (NEILS) Services, Data Report.

Heclo, H. H. (1997). Values underpinning poverty programs for children. *Future Child*, 7, 141–148.

Hedberg, N., & Stoel-Gammon, C. (1986), Narrative analysis: Clinical procedures. *Topics in Language Disorders* 7(1), 58–69.

Hedley-Williams, A., Sladen, D., & Tharpe, A. (2003). Programming, care, and troubleshooting of cochlear Implants for children. *Topics in Language Disorders*, 23(1), 46–56.

Hedrick, D. E., Prather, E. M., & Tobin, A. R. (1984). *Sequenced inventory of communicative development* (revised). Seattle: University of Washington Press.

Henry, H. M., Stiles, W. B., & Biran, M. W. (2005). Loss and mourning in immigration: Using the assimilation model to assess continuing bonds with native culture. *Counselling Psychology Quarterly,* 18(2), 109–119.

Hick, R., Joseph, K., Conti-Ramsden, G., Serratrice, L., & Faragher, B. (2002). Vocabulary profiles of children with specific language impairment. *Child Language Teaching & Therapy,* 18(2), 165–181.

Hogan, T., Catts, H., & Little, T. (2005). The relationship between phonological awareness and reading: Implications for the assessment of phonological awareness. *Language, Speech and Hearing Services in Schools,* 36, 285–293.

Holditch-Davis, D., & Miles, M. S. (2000). Mothers' stories about their experiences in the neonatal intensive care unit. *Neonatal Network,* 19(3), 13–21.

Hopkins, H. (1988). An historical perspective on occupational therapy. In H. Hopkins & H. Smith (Eds.), *Willard and Spackman's occupational therapy* (pp. 12–19). Philadelphia: Lippincott.

Howes, C. (1980). Peer play scale as an index of complexity of peer interaction. *Developmental Psychology,* 16, 371–372.

Hresko, W., Reid, D., & Hammel, D. (1999). *Test of early language development* (3rd ed.). Austin, TX: Pro-Ed.

Hurth, J. (1998). *Service coordination case loads in state early intervention systems.* Chapel Hill, NC: National Early Childhood Technical Assistance System. Available: www.nectas.unc.edu

Hutson-Nechkash, R. (1990). *Story building: A guide to structuring narratives.* Eau Claire, WI: Thinking Publications.

Huttunen, K. H. (2001). Phonological development in 4–6 year old moderately hearing impaired children. *Scandanavian Audiology,* 30(Suppl. 53), 79–82.

Iglesias, A. (2001). What test should I use? *Seminars in Speech and Language: Communicative Assessment of the Hispanic Child,* 22, 3–15.

Individuals with Disabilities Education Act. (1993). A reaction to full inclusion: A reaffirmation of the right of students with learning disabilities to a continuum of services. *Journal of Learning Disabilities,* 26(9), 596.

Individuals with Disabilities Education Act Amendments of 1997, 20 U.S.C. Section 1400 et seq.

Ingram, D. (1981). *Procedures for the phonological analysis of children's language.* Baltimore: University Park Press.

Innes, J. (1994). Full inclusion and the deaf student: A deaf consumer's review of the issue. *American Annals of the Deaf,* 139, 152–156.

Innocenti, M. S. & Karl, R. (1993). Are more intensive early intervention programs more effective? *Exceptionality,* 4(1), 31.

Jackson, K., Ternestedt, B. M., & Schollin, J. (2003). From alienation to familiarity: Experiences of mothers and fathers of preterm infants. *Journal of Advanced Nursing,* 43, 120–129.

Jaffe, M. (1989). Feeding at-risk infants and toddlers. *Topics in Language Disorders,* 10(1), 13–15.

Jayanthi, M., & Friend, M. (1992). Interpersonal problem solving: A selective literature review to guide practice. *Journal of Educational & Psychological Consultation,* 3(1), 39–54.

Jencks, C., & Phillips, M. (1998). *The black–white test score gap.* Washington, DC: Brookings Institution Press.

Jenkins, A. (2005). Restrictiveness and race in special education: The content mastery center model. *Learning Disabilities: A Contemporary Journal,* 3(1), 45–50.

Jensema, C., & Trybus, R. (1978). Communication patterns and educational achievement of hearing impaired students. Series T2. Data from the national Achievement Test Standardization Program for Hearing Impaired Students. Washington, DC.: Galludet College Press.

Jerome, A. C., Fujiki, M., Brinton, B., & James, S. L. (2002). Self-esteem in children with specific language impairment. *Journal of Speech, Language & Hearing Research,* 45(4), 700–715.

Jewett, J., Tertell, L., King-Taylor, M., Parker, D., Tertell, L., & Orr, M. (1998). Four early childhood teachers reflect on helping children with special needs make the transition. *Elementary School Journal,* 98(4), 329–338.

Johnson, D. (1987). Disorders of written language. In D. Johnson & J. Blalock (Eds.), *Adults with learning disabilities: Clinical studies,* (pp. 173–204). New York: Grune & Stratton.

Johnson, J., & Newport, E. (1989). Critical period effects in second language learning: The influence of maturational state on the acquisition of English as a second language. *Cognitive Psychology,* 21(1), 60–99.

Johnson, J. R. (1992). Cognitive abilities of language-impaired children. In P. Fletcher & D. Hall (Eds.), *Specific speech and language disorders in children: Correlates, characteristics and outcomes* (pp. 105–116). London: Whurr Publishers.

Johnson, P. D. (1996). Reclaiming choice. ETC: A *Review of General Semantics,* 53(1), 16–19.

Johnston, R. (1999). Cognitive deficits in specific language impairments: Decision in spite of uncertainty.

Journal of Speech-Language Pathology and Audiology, 23, 1165–1172.

Johnston, T. (2004). W(h)ither the Deaf Community? Population, genetics, and the future of Austrailian sign language. *American Annals of the Deaf*, 148(5), 358–375.

Jones, L. T., & Blendinger, J. (1994). New beginnings: Preparing future teachers to work with diverse families. *Action in Teacher Education*, 16, 79–88.

Justice, L., & Kaderavek, J. (2004). Embedded-explicit emergency intervention I: Background and description of approach. *Language, Speech and Hearing Services in Schools*, 35, 201–211.

Kaczmarek, L., Goldstein, H., Florey, J. D., Carter, A., & Cannon, S. (2004). Supporting families: A preschool model. *Topics in Early Childhood Special Education*, 24(4), 213–226.

Kaiser, A. P., Fischer, R., Alpet, C. L., Hemmeter, M. L., Tiernan, M., & Ostrosky, M. (1990). *Toward a hybrid model of parent-implemented language intervention: Analysis of the effects of milieu and responsive-interaction teaching by parents*. Paper presented at the Annual Meeting of the American Association on Mental Retardation, Atlanta, GA.

Kamhi, A. (1991). Causes and consequences of reading disabilities. In A. Kamhi & H. Catts (Eds.), *Reading disabilities: A developmental language approach* (pp. 67–100). MA, Boston: Allyn and Bacon.

Katims, D. S., & Pierce, P. L. (1995). Literacy rich environments and the transition of young children with special needs. *Topics in Early Childhood Special Education*, 15, 219–234.

Kauffman, J. (2004). *Characteristics of emotional and behavioral disorders of children and youth* (8th ed). Upper Saddle River, NJ: Prentice Hall/Merrill.

Kaufman, S. S., Prelock, P. A., Weiler, E. M., Creaghead, N. A., & Donnelly, C. A. (1994). Metapragmatic awareness of explanation adequacy: Developing skills for academic success from a collaborative communication skills unit. *Language, Speech and Hearing Services in Schools*, 25, 174–180.

Kavale, K. A. (2002). Mainstreaming to full inclusion: From orthogenesis to pathogenesis of an idea. *International Journal of Disability, Development and Education*, 49(2), 201–214.

Kayser, H. (1993). Hispanic cultures. In D. Battle (Ed.), *Communication disorders in multicultural populations* (pp. 114–157). Boston: Andover Medical Publications.

Kayser, H., & Restrepo, M. A. (1995). Language samples: Elicitation and analysis. In H. Kayser (Ed.), *Bilingual speech language pathology: An Hispanic focus* (pp. 243–264). San Diego: Singular Publishing Group.

Keith, R. W. (2000). *Random gap detection test: Revised AFT-R*. St. Louis, MO: AUDITEC of St. Louis.

Kelley, E., Paul, J., Fein, D., Naigles, L. R. (2006). Residual language deficits in optimal outcome children with a history of autism. *Journal of Autism and Developmental Disorders*, 36(6) 807–828.

Kemp, C., & Carter, M. (2005). Identifying skills for promoting successful inclusion in kindergarten. *Journal of Intellectual & Developmental Disability*, 30(1), 31–44.

Kemper, A., & Downs, S. (2000). A cost effectiveness analysis of newborn hearing screening strategies. *Archives of Pediatric and Adolescent Medicine*, 154(5), 484–488.

Kim, B. S. K., & Omizo, M. M. (2005). Asian and European American cultural values, collective self-esteem, acculturative stress, cognitive flexibility, and general self-efficacy among Asian American college students. *Journal of Counseling Psychology*, 52(3), 412–419.

Kintsch, W. (1988). The use of knowledge in discourse processing: A construction–integration model. *Psychological Review*, 95, 163–182.

Kintsch, W. (1992). How readers construct situation models for stories: The role of syntactic cues and causal inferences. In A. F. Healy, S. M. Kosslyn, & R. M. Shiffrin (Eds.), *From learning process to cognitive process: Essays in honor of William K. Estes*. Hillsdale, NJ: Lawrence Erlbaum.

Kintsch, W. (1994). Text comprehension, memory and learning. *American Psychologist*, 49, 294–303.

Kirby, D., Liner, T., & Vinz, R. (1988). *Inside out: Developmental strategies for teaching writing*. Portsmouth, NH: Heinemann.

Kirst-Ashman, K., & Hull, G., Jr. (2001). *Generalist practice with organizations and communities* (2nd ed.). Pacific Grove, CA: Brooks-Cole.

Klahr, D., & MacWhinney, B. (1998). Information processing. In W. Damon (Ed.), *Handbook of child psychology* (Vol. 2, p. 1072). New York: Wiley.

Kleinhammer-Tramill, P. J., & Rosenkoetter, S. E. (1994). Early intervention and secondary/transition services: Harbingers of change in education. *Focus on Exceptional Children*, 27(2), 1–15.

Klinger, L., & Renner, P. (2000). Performance-based measures in autism: Implications for diagnosis early detection, and identification of cognitive profiles. *Journal of Clinical Child Psychology*, 29(4), 479–493.

Knoblock, H., & Passamanick, B. (1974). *Gesell and Amatruda's developmental diagnoses: The evaluation and management of normal and neuropsychologic development in infancy and early childhood*. New York: Harper & Row.

Koontz, C. W. (1974). *Koontz child developmental program: Training activities for the first 48 months*. Los Angeles: Western Psychological Services.

Kral, A., Hartmann, R., Tillein, J., Heid, S., & Klinke R. (2000). Congenital auditory deprivation reduces synaptic activity within the auditory cortex in a layer-specific manner. *Cerebral Cortex*, 10(7), 714–726.

Kramer, R. (1994). Voluntary agencies and the contract culture: Dream or nightmare? *Social Service Review*, 68, 33–60.

Kretschmer, R. (1989). Pragmatics, reading, and writing: Implications for hearing impaired individuals. *Topics in Language Disorders*, 9(4), 17–32.

Kroll, B. (Ed.). (2003). *Exploring the dynamics of second language writing*. Cambridge: Cambridge University Press.

Krug, D. A., Arick, J. R., Almond, P. J. (1980). *Autism screening instrument for educational planning*. Portland, OR: ASIEP Education.

Kuntze, M. (1998). Literacy and deaf children: The language question. *Topics in Language Disorders*, 18(4), 1–15.

Kupperman, P. (1997). Precocious reading skills may signal hyperlexia. *Brown University Child & Adolescent Behavior Letter*, 13(11), 1–4.

Labov, W. (1966). *The social stratifications of English in New York City*. Washington, DC: Center for Applied Linguistics.

Labov, W. (1998). Co-existent systems in African-American vernacular English. In S. Mufwene, J. Rickford, G. Bailey, & J. Baugh (Eds.), *African-American English: Structure, history, and use* (pp. 110–153). New York: Routledge.

Laing, G. J., Law, J., Levin, A., & Logan, S. (2002). Evaluation of a structured test and a parent led method for screening for speech and language problems: Prospective population based study. *British Medical Journal*, 325, 7373, 1152–1154.

Lainhart, J. E. (1999). Psychiatric problems in individuals with autism, their parents and siblings. *International Review of Psychiatry*, 11(4), 278–299.

Langdon, H. (1996). English language learning by immigrant Spanish speakers: A United States

perspective, *Topics in Language Disorders*, 16(4),38–53.

Law, J., & Durkin, C. (2000). The literacy skills of language-impaired children: Time for "Joined up" thinking? *Educational Psychology in Practice*, 16(1), 75–87.

Lederberg, A., Prezbindowski, A., & Spencer, P. (2000). Word learning skills of deaf preschoolers: The development of novel mapping and rapid word learning strategies. *Child Development*, 71, 1571–1585.

Lee, S-H., Palmer, S. B., Turnbull, A. P., & Wehmeyer, M. L. (2006). A model for parent-teacher collaboration to promote self-determination in young children with disabilities. *Teaching Exceptional Children*, 38(3), 36–41.

Lee, S., Potamianos, A., & Naryanan, S. (1999). Acoustics of children's speech: Developmental changes of temporal and spectral parameters. *Journal of the Acoustic Society of America*, 105, 1455–1468.

Lennon, J. E., & Slesinski, C. (1999). Early intervention in reading: Results of a screening and intervention program for kindergarten students. *School Psychology Review*, 28(3), 353–365.

Leonard, L. B. (1998). *Children with specific language impairments*. Cambridge, MA: MIT Press.

Leonard, L. B., Deevy, P., Miller, C. A., Rauf, L., Charest, M., & Kurtz, R. (2003). Surface forms and grammatical functions: Past tense and passive participle use by children with specific language impairment. *Journal of Speech, Language & Hearing Research*, 46(1), 43–56.

Leonard, L. B., Miller, C. A., Deevy, P., Rauf, L., Gerber, E., & Charest, M. (2002). Production operations and the use of nonfinite verbs by children with specific language impairment. *Journal of Speech, Language & Hearing Research*, 45(4), 744–759.

Levy, F. J. (1992). *Dance movement therapy: A healing art*. Reston, VA: American Alliance for Health, Physical Education, Recreation and Dance.

Lewis, M., & Rosenblum, J. (Eds.). (1974). *The effects of the infant on its caregiver*. New York: Wiley.

Lewis, V., & Boucher, J. (1995). Generativity in the play of young people with autism. *Journal of Autism and Developmental Disorders*, 25, 105–121.

Light, J. C., Roberts, B., Dimarco, R., & Greiner, N. (1998). Augmentative and alternative communication to support receptive and expressive communication for people with autism. *Journal of Communication Disorders*, 31(2), 153–180.

Linares, N. (1983). Management of communicatively handicapped hispanic children. In D. R. Omark &

J. G. Erickson (Eds.), *The bilingual exceptional child*, Boston: College Hill Press.

Lindsay, G. (2003). Inclusive education: A critical perspective. *British Journal of Special Education, 30*(1), 3–12.

Ling, D. (1976). *Speech and the hearing impaired child: Theory and practice*. Washington DC: Alexander Graham Bell Association for the Deaf.

Little, M. E., & Robinson, S. M. (1997). Renovating and refurbishing the field experience structures for novice teachers. *Journal of Learning Disabilities, 30*, 443–441.

Long, S. (1999). Technology applications in the assessment of children's language. *Seminars in Speech and Language, 20*, 117–132.

Lord, C., Rutter, M., Goode, S., Heemsbergen, J., Jordan, H., Mawhood, L., & Schopler, E. (1989). Autism diagnostic observation schedule: A standardized observation of communicative and social behavior. *Journal of Autism and Developmental Disorders, 19*(2), 185–212.

Lord, C., Rutter, M. L., & LeCouteur, A. (1994). Autism diagnostic interview—revised: A revised version of a diagnostic interview for caregivers of individuals with possible pervasive developmental disorders. *Journal of Autism and Developmental Disorders, 24*, 659–685.

Lovaas, O., & Buch, G. (1997). Intensive behavioral intervention with young children with autism. In N. N. Singh (Ed.), *Prevention and treatment of severe behavior problems: Models and methods in developmental disabilities* (pp. 61–86). Pacific Grove, CA: Brooks/Cole.

Loveland, K., Landry, S., Hughes, S., Hall, S., & McEvoy, R. (1998). Speech acts and the pragmatic deficits of autism. *Journal of Speech and Hearing Research, 31*, 503–604.

Lubeck, R., & Chandler, L. (1990). Organizing the home: Caregiver environment for infants. *Journal of Clinical Child Psychology, 23*, 360–372.

Lundahl, B., Risser, H. J., & Lovejoy, M. C. (2006). A meta-analysis of parent training: Moderators and follow-up effects. *Clinical Psychology Review, 26*(1), 86–104.

MacDonald, J., & Carroll, J. Y. (1992). A social partnership model for assessing early communication development: An intervention model for preconversational children. *Language, Speech and Hearing Services in Schools, 23*, 113–124.

MacLean, M., Bryant, P., & Bradley, L. (1987). Rhymes, nursery rhymes and reading in early childhood. *Merrill Palmer Quarterly, 33*, 255–281.

MacWhinney, B. (1995). *The CHILDES Project: Tools for analyzing talk* (2nd ed.). Hillsdale, NJ: Erlbaum.

Madden, N. A., & Slavin, R. E. (1983). Mainstreaming students with mild handicaps: Academic and social outcomes. *Review of Educational Research, 53*(4), 519–569.

Mahoney, G., & Bella, J. M. (1998). An examination of the effects of family-centered early intervention on child and family outcomes. *Topics in Early Childhood Special Education, 18*(2), 83.

Mahoney, G., Boyce, G., Fewell, R. R., Spiker, D., & Wheeden, C. A. (1998). The relationship of parent–child interaction to the effectiveness of early intervention services for at-risk children and children with disabilities. *Topics in Early Childhood Special Education, 18*, 5–17.

Mahoney, G., & Spiker, D. (1996). Clinical assessments of parent–child interaction: Are professionals ready to implement this practice? *Topics in Early Childhood Special Education, 16*(1), 26–51.

Mahoney, G., & Wheeden, C. A. (1997). Parent–child interaction—The foundation for family-centered early intervention practice: A response to Baird and Peterson. *Topics in Early Childhood Special Education, 17*(2), 165–187.

Mahoney, J., & Powell, A. (1988). Modifying parent–child interaction: Enhancing the development of handicapped children. *Journal of Special Education, 22*, 82–96.

Major, E. M., & Bernhardt, B. H. (1998). Metaphonological skills of children with phonological disorders before and after phonological and metaphonological intervention. *International Journal Language & Communication Disorders, 33*(4), 413–444.

Malone, D. M, McKinsey, P. D., Thyer, B. A., & Straka, E. (2000). Social work early intervention for young children with developmental disabilities. *Health & Social Work, 25*(3), 169–180.

Malone, D. M., Straka, E., & Logan, K. R. (2000). Professional development in early intervention: Creating effective inservice training opportunities. *Infants & Young Children, 12*(4), 53–62.

Mann, V., & Liberman, I. (1984). Phonological awareness and verbal short term memory. *Journal of Learning Disabilities 17*, 592–599.

Markides, A. (1970). The speech of deaf and partially hearing children with special reference to factors affecting intelligibility. *British Journal of Disorders of Communication, 5*(2), 126–140.

Martens, B. K., & Witt, J. C. (1988). On the ecological validity of behavior modification. In J. C. Witt, S. N. Elliott, & F. M. Gresham (Eds.) *Handbook of behavior therapy in education*. New York: Plenum Press.

Martin, F., & Clark, J. (2000). *Introduction to audiology*. Boston: Allyn and Bacon.

Masterson, J., & Oller, K. (1999). Use of technology in phonological assessment? Evaluation of early meaningful speech and prelinguistic vocalizations. *Seminars in Speech and Language, 20*, 133–148.

Masterson, J., & Pagan, F. (1993). Interactive System for Phonological Analysis [Computer program]. San Antonio, TX: Psychological Corporation.

Masterson, J., & Rvachew, S. (1999). Use of technology in phonological intervention. *Seminars in Speech and Language, 20*, 233–250.

Masterson, J. J., & Kamhi, A. G. (1992). Linguistic trade-offs in school-age children with and without language disorders. *Journal of Speech and Hearing Research, 35*, 1064–1075.

Masur, E. F. (1997). Maternal labeling of novel and familiar objects: Implications for children's development of lexical constraints. *Journal of Child Language, 24*, 427–439.

Mattes, L. (1995). *Spanish language assessment procedures (SLAP)*. Oceanside, CA: Academic Communication Associates.

Matthews, P. (1994). *Inclusion: Some selected key legal, legislative, and related influences*. Unpublished manuscript. Lock Haven, PA: Lock Haven University.

Mavilya, M. (1978, May). *Natural gesture language and spoken words: Mode of communication for the multiply handicapped hearing impaired infants and toddlers*. Paper presented at the American International Convention of the Council for Exceptional Children, Kansas City, MO.

Mayberry, R. I., & Eichen, E. B. (1991). The long-lasting advantage of learning sign language in childhood: Another look at the critical period for language acquisition. *Journal of Memory and Language, 30*, 486–512.

McBurney, D. (1991). *Experimental psychology* (2nd ed.). Belmont, CA: Wadsworth.

McCollum, J. A., & Stayton, V., (1985). Infant-parent interaction: Studies and intervention guidelines based on the SIAI model. *Journal of the Division for Early Childhood, 10*(2), 125–135.

McConkey R. A., (2003). Communication intervention for infants and toddlers with cochlear implants. *Topics in Language Disorders, 23*(1), 16–33.

McCormick, L., & Schiefelbusch, R. (1990). *Intervention processes and procedures in early language interven-*tion. Upper Saddle River, NJ: Merrill/Prentice Hall.

McCracken, J. (2002). Risperidone for aggressive behavior in autistic children. *New England Journal of Medicine, 314*–321.

McDade, H., & Simpson, M. (1984). Use of instruction, modeling and videotape feedback to modify parent behavior. A strategy for facilitating language development in the home. *Seminars in Speech and Language, 5*(3), 229–240.

McEachin, J. J., Smith, T., & Lovaas, O. I. (1993). Long-term outcome for children with autism who received early intensive behavioral treatment. *American Journal of Mental Retardation, 97*, 359–372.

McEvoy, M., Shores, R., Westby, J., Johnson, S., & Fox, J. (1990, September). Special education teachers' implementation of procedures to promote social interaction among children in integrated settings. *Education and Training in Mental Retardation, 25*(3), 267–276.

McFadden T. U., & Gillam, R. B. (1996). An examination of the quality of narratives produced by children with language disorders. *Language Speech Hearing with Services with Schools, 27*, 48–56.

McGregor, K., & Appel, A. (2002). On the relation between mental representation and naming in a child with specific language impairment. *Clinical Linguistics & Phonetics, 16*(1), 1–20.

McGregor, K. K., Newman, R. M., Reilly, R. M., & Capone, N. C. (2002). Semantic representation and naming in children with specific language impairment. *Journal of Speech, Language & Hearing Research, 45*(5), 998–1015.

McLaughlin, S. (1998). *Introduction to language development*. San Diego, CA: Singular Publishing Group.

McLean, J. E., & Snyder-McLean, L. R. (1978). *A transactional approach to early language training*. Upper Saddle River, NJ: Merrill/Prentice Hall.

McLean, M., & Vincent, L. (1984). The use of expansion as a language intervention technique in the natural environment. *Journal of the Division for Early Childhood, 9*, 57–66.

McLeskey, J., & Skiba, R. (1990) . Reform and special education: A mainstream perspective. *Journal of Special Education, 24*(3), 319–326.

McLeskey, J., & Waldron, N. (1996). Responses to questions teachers and administrators frequently ask about inclusive school programs. *Phi Delta Kappan, 78*(2), 150–157.

McLeskey, J., & Waldron, N. (2000). *Inclusive education in action: Making differences ordinary.* Arlington, VA: Association for Supervision and Curriculum Development.

McNaughton, D. (1994). Measuring parent satisfaction with early childhood intervention programs: Current practice, problems, and future perspectives. *Topics in Early Childhood Special Education, 14*(1), 26.

McNeill, D. (1992). *Hand and mind: What gestures reveal about thought.* Chicago: University of Chicago Press.

McWilliam, R. A., Ferguson, A., Harbin, G. L., Porter, P., Munn, D., & Vandiviere, P. (1998). The family-centeredness of individualized family service plans. *Topics in Early Childhood Special Education, 18,* 69–82.

McWilliam, R. A., Tocci, L., & Harbin, G. L. (1998). Family-centered services: Service provider's discourse and behavior. *Topics in Early Childhood Special Education, 18*(4), 206–222.

McWilliam, R. A., & Young, H. J., (1996). Therapy services in early intervention: Current status, barriers, and recommendations. *Topics in Early Childhood Special Education, 16*(3), 348–375.

Meadow, K. P. (1980). *Deafness and child development.* Los Angeles: University of California Press.

Menyuk, P. (1974). The bases of language acquisition: Some questions. *Journal of Autism and Childhood Schizophrenia, 4*(4), 325–345.

Merriman, W. E., Marazita, J. M., & Jarvis, L. H. (1995). Children's dispositions to map new words onto new referents. In M. Tomasello & W. E. Merriman (Eds.), *Beyond the names for things* (pp. 175–198). Hillsdale, NJ: Erlbaum.

Messer, D., Murphy, N., & Dockrell, J. E. (2004). Relation between naming and literacy in children with word-finding difficulties. *Journal of Educational Psychology, 96*(3), 462–470.

Meyer, J. (1997). Models of service delivery. In P. E. O' Connell (Ed.), *Speech, language and hearing programs in schools: A guide for students and practitioners* (pp. 241–286). Gaithersburg, MD: Aspen.

Mihamoto, R., Svirsky, M., & Robbins, A. (1997). Enhancement of expressive language in prelingually deaf children with cochlear implants. *Acta Otolaryngologica, 117*(2), 154–157.

Miles, T., & Ellis, N. (1981). A lexical encoding deficiency I and II. Experimental evidence and classical observations. In G. Pavlidis & T. Miles (Eds.), *Dyslexia research and its application to education* (pp. 53–89). New York: Wiley.

Miller, J. F., & Chapman, R. S. (1998). Systematic Analysis of Language Transcripts (SALT). Version 4.0 (MS-DOS) [Computer program]. Madison, WI: Language Analysis Laboratory, Waisman Center on Mental Retardation and Human Development.

Miranda-Linné, F. M., & Melin, L. (1997). A comparison of speaking and mute individuals with autism and autistic-like conditions on the autism behavior checklist. *Journal of Autism & Developmental Disorders, 27*(3), 245–265.

Mirenda, P. (1997). Supporting individuals with challenging behaviour through functional communication training and AAC: A research review, *Augmentative and Alternative Communication, 13,* 207–225.

Moeller, M. P. (2000). Early intervention and language development in children who are deaf or hard of hearing. *Pediatrics, 106,* 1–9.

Moeller, M. P., & McConkey, A. (1984). Language intervention with preschool deaf children: A cognitive/linguistic approach. In W. Perkins (Ed.), *Current therapy of communication disorders, hearing disorders.* New York: Thieme-Stratton.

Moeller, M. P., Osberger, M. J., McConkey, A., & Ecarius, M. (1981). Some language skills of the students in a residential school for the deaf. *Journal of the Academy of Rehabilitative Audiology, 14,* 84–141.

Moes, D. R., & Frea, W. D., (2002). Contextualized behavioral support in early intervention for children with autism and their families. *Journal of Autism and Developmental Disorders, 32*(6), 519–533.

Monolson, A. (1992). *It takes two to talk: A parent's guide to helping children communicate.* Toronto: The Hanen Center.

Monsen, R. B. (1978). Toward measuring how well hearing impaired children speak. *Journal of Speech and Hearing Research, 21,* 197–219.

Montgomery, J. W. (2002). Understanding the language difficulties of children with specific language impairments: Does verbal working memory matter? *American Journal of Speech-Language Pathology, 11,* 77–91.

Moore, J. (1998, August). A corporate challenge for charities. *Chronicle of Philanthropy,* 34–36.

Moran, D. R., & Whitman, T. L. (1985). The multiple effects of a play-oriented parent training program for mothers of developmentally delayed children. *Analysis and Intervention in Developmental Disabilities, 5,* 73–96.

Morris, S. E. (1982). *Pre-speech assessment scale.* Clifton, NJ: J. A. Preston.

Morris, S. E., & Klein, M. D. (1987). *Pre-feeding skills.* Tucson, AZ: Therapy Skill Builders.

Most, T., & Zaidman-Zait, A. (2003). The needs of parents of children with cochlear implants. *Volta Review, 103*(2), 99–113.

Muma, J. R. (1978). *Language handbook: Concepts, assessment, intervention.* Upper Saddle River, NJ: Prentice Hall.

Munson, B., & Babel, M. (2005). The sequential cueing effect in children's speech production. *Applied Psycholinguistics, 26,* pp. 157–174.

Munson, B., Edwards, J., & Beckman, M. E. (2005). Phonological knowledge in typical and atypical speech-sound development. *Topics in Language Disorders, 25*(3), 190–206.

Musiek, F. (1983). Assessment of central auditory dysfunction: The dichotic digits test revisited. *Ear and Hearing, 4,* 79–83.

Musiek, F. E., & Rintelmann, W. F. (1999). *Contemporary perspectives on hearing assessment.* Boston: Allyn and Bacon.

Musselman, C., & Kircacli-Iftar, G. (1996). The development of spoken language in deaf children: Explaining the unexplained variance. *Journal of Deaf Studies and Deaf Education, 1,* 108–121.

Myles, B. S., Cook, K. T., Miller, N. E., Rinner, L., & Robbins, L. A. (2000). *Asperger syndrome and sensory issues: Practical solutions for making sense of the world.* Shawnee Mission, KS: Autism Asperger Publishing.

Myles, B. S., & Southwick, J. (1999). *Asperger syndrome and difficult moments: Practical solutions for tantrums, rage, and meltdowns.* Shawnee Mission, KS: Autism Asperger Publishing.

Nancollis, A., Lawrie, B., & Dodd, B. (2005). Phonological awareness intervention and the acquisition of literacy skills in children from deprived social backgrounds. *Language, Speech and Hearing Services in Schools, 36,* 325–335.

Naremore, R. (1997). Making it hang together: Children use of mental framework—to structure narratives. *Topics in Language Disorders, 18,* 16–30.

National Institutes of Health, National Institute on Deafness and Other Communication Disorders (NIDCD). (1997). Available at www.nih.gov/nidcd

Nelson, J. R., Benner, G. J., & Gonzalez, J. (2003). Learner characteristics that influence the treatment effectiveness of early literacy interventions: A meta analytic review. *Learning Disabilities Research & Practice, 18,* 255–267.

Nelson, J. R., Benner, G. J., & Gonzalez, J. (2005). An investigation of the effects of a prereading intervention on the early literacy skills of children at risk of emotional disturbance and reading problems. *Journal of Emotional and Behavioral Disorders, 13*(1), 3–12.

Nelson, N., & Van Meter, A. (2002). Assessing curriculum-based reading and writing samples. *Topics in Language Disorders, 22,* 35–59.

Nelson, N. W. (1986). Individual processing in classroom settings. *Topics in Language Disorders, 6,* 13–27.

Nelson, N. W. (1989). Curriculum-based language assessment and intervention. *Language, Speech and Hearing Services in Schools, 20,* 170–184.

Nelson, N. W. (1998). *Childhood language disorders in context.* Boston: Allyn and Bacon.

Nelson, N., & Van Meter, A. (2002). Assessing curriculum-based reading and writing samples. *Topics in Language Disorders, 22,* 35–59.

Nevins, M. E., & Chute, P. (1997). *Children with cochlear implants.* San Diego, CA: Singular Publishing Group.

New York State Department of Health. (1998). *Clinical practice guidelines for autism/pervasive developmental disorders. Quick reference guide for parents and professionals.* Albany: Author.

New York State Department of Health. (1999). *Clinical practice guidelines for communication disorders. Quick reference guide for parents and professionals.* Albany: Author.

Nientemp, E. G., & Cole, C. L. (1992). Teaching socially valid social interaction responses to students with severe disabilities in an integrated school setting. *Journal of School Psychology, 30*(4), 343–354.

Nippold, M. A. (1993). Developmental markers in adolescent language: Syntax, semantics, and pragmatics. *Language, Speech, and Hearing Services in Schools, 24,* 21–28.

Nippold, M. A. (2002). Stuttering and phonology: Is there an interaction? *American Journal of Speech-Language Pathology, 11,* 99–110.

Nittrouer, S. (2002). From ear to cortex: A perspective on what clinicians need to understand about speech perception and language processing. *Language, Speech, & Hearing Services in Schools, 33*(4), 237–252.

Njiokiktjien, C., Verschoor, A., de Sonneville, L., Huyser, C., Op het Veld, V., & Toorenaar, N. (2001). Disordered recognition of facial identity and emotions in three Asperger type autists. *European Child & Adolescent Psychiatry, 10* (1), 79–90.

Nober, H. (1968). *Air and bone conduction thresholds of deaf and normal hearing subjects before and during the elimination of cutaneous-tactile interference with anesthesia.* Syracuse, NY: Syracuse University Press.

Nolan, K. W., Young, E. C., Herbert, E. B., & Wilding, G. E. (2005). Service coordination for children with complex healthcare needs in an early intervention program. *Infants & Young Children,* 18(2), 161–170.

Nordoff, P., & Robbins, C. (1971). *Therapy in music for handicapped children.* London: Gollancz.

Nugent, T., & Shipley, K. (1991). *Spanish test for assessing.* Provencio, CA: Academic Communication Associates.

Nyquist, K., Rubertsson, C., Ewald, U., & Sjoden, P. (1996). Development of the preterm infant breast-feeding behavior scale (PIBBS). A study of nurse–mother agreement. *Journal of Human Lactation,* 12(3), 207–219.

O'Connor, R. E., Notari- Syverson, A., & Vadasy, P. (1996). Ladders to literacy: The effects of teacher-led phonological activities for kindergarten children with and without disabilities. *Exceptional Children,* 63, 117–130.

Oetting, J. B., & McDonald, J. L. (2001). Nonmainstream dialect use and specific language impairment. *Journal of Speech, Language, and Hearing Research,* 44, 207–223.

Ogle, D. (2005). *Teachers learning together.* Thousand Oaks, CA: Corwin Press.

Ogletree, B. T., & Fischer, M. A. (1995). An innovative language treatment for a child with high-functioning autism. *Focus on Autistic Behavior,* 10(3), 1–11.

Oller, D., Jensen, H., & LaFayette, R. (1978). The relatedness of phonological processes of a hearing impaired child. *Journal of Communication Disorders,* 11, 97–105.

Oller, D. K. (1980). The emergence of the sounds of speech in infancy. In G. A. Yer-Komshian, J. F. Kavanagh, & C. A. Ferguson (Eds.), *Child phonology* (Vol.1, pp. 93–112). New York: Academic Press.

Oller, D. K. (1986). Metaphonology and infant vocalization. In B. Lindblom & R. Zetterstrom (Eds.), *Precursors of early speech* (pp. 21–35). New York: Stockton Press.

Oller, K. (1991). Computational approaches to transcription and analysis in child phonology. *Journal for Computer Users in Speech and Hearing,* 7, 44–59.

Oller, K. D., & Kelly, C. A. (1974). Phonological substitution processes of a hard-of-hearing child. *Journal of Speech and Hearing Disorders,* 39(1), 65–74.

Olney, M. F. (2000). Working with autism and other social–communication disorders. *Journal of Rehabilitation,* 66(4), 51–57.

Omark, D. R., & Erickson, J. G. (1983). *The bilingual exceptional child.* San Diego, CA: College Hill Press.

Ornitz, E. M. (1973). Childhood autism: A review of the clinical and experimental literature. *California Medicine,* 118, 21–47.

Orr, R. R., Cameron, S. J., & Day, M. (1991). Coping with stress in families with children who have mental retardation: An evaluation of the double ABCX model. *American Journal on Mental Retardation,* 95, 444–450.

Orsolini, M., Sechi, E., Maronato, C., Bonvino, E., & Corcelli, A. (2001). Nature of phonological delay in children with specific language impairment. *International Journal of Language & Communication Disorders,* 36(1), 63–90.

Osberger, M. J. (1983). Development and evaluation of some speech training procedures for hearing-impaired children. In I. Hochberg, H. Levitt, & M. J. Osberger (Eds.), *Speech of the hearing impaired: Research, training, and personnel preparation.* Baltimore: University Park Press.

Osborne, S., Garland, C., & Fisher, N. (2002). Caregiver training: Changing minds, opening doors to inclusion. *Infants and Young Children,* 14(3), 43–53.

O'Shea, D., Williams, A., & Sattler, R. (1999). Collaboration across special education and general education: Preserve teachers' views. *Journal of Teacher Education,* 50(2), 147.

Owens, R. (1999). *Language disorders: A functional approach to assessment and intervention* (3rd ed.). Boston: Allyn and Bacon.

Owens, R. (2002). *Mental retardation: Difference and delay in language and communication disorders in children.* In D. Bernstein & E. Tiegerman-Farber, *Language and communication disorders in children* (5th ed). Boston: Allyn and Bacon.

Ozonoff, S., & Miller, J. N (1995). *Teaching theory of the mind: A new approach to social skills training for individuals with autism.* Journal of Autism and Developmental Disorders, 25, 415–433.

Padden, C., & Ramsey, C. (2000). American Sign Language and reading ability in deaf children. In C. Chamberlain, J. P. Mortfort, & R. I. Mayberry (Eds.), *Language acquisition by eye* (pp.165–189). Mahwah, NJ: Earlbaum.

Palmer, M., Crawley, K., & Blanco, I. (1993). Neonatal oral-motor assessment scale: A reliability study. *Journal of Perinatology,* 13(1), 28–35.

Parke, T., & Drury, R. (2001). Language development at home and school: Gains and losses in young bilinguals. *Early Years: Journal of International Research & Development*, 21(2), 117–128.

Parks, P. L., & Smeriglio, V. L. (1986). Relationships among parenting knowledge, quality of stimulation in the home and infant development. *Family Relations*, 35, 411–416.

Pashley, N. R. T. (1984). Otitis media. In J. Northern (Ed.), *Hearing disorders* (pp. 103–110). Boston: Little, Brown.

Paul, P. V. (1998). *Literacy and deafness: The development of reading, writing and literate thought*. Boston: Allyn and Bacon.

Paul, R. (2000). Predicting outcomes of early expressive language delay: Ethical implications. In D. V. M. Bishop & L. B. Leonard (Eds.), *Speech and language impairments in children: Causes, characteristics, intervention and outcome* (pp. 195–209). Hove, UK: Psychology Press.

Pearson, L. J. (2003). Understanding the culture of poverty. *Journal of the American Academy of Nurse Practitioners*, 28(4), 6.

Peña, E., Iglesias, A., & Lidz, C. (2001). Reducing test bias through dynamic assessment of children's word learning ability. *American Journal of Speech Language Pathology*, 10, 138–154.

Peña, L. (2002b). *Solving the problems of biased speech and language assessment with bilingual children*. Short course presented at the New York State Speech Language Association, Rochester, New York.

Peppé, S., McCann, J., Gibbon, F., O'Hare, A., & Rutherford, M. (2006). Assessing prosodic and pragmatic ability in children with high-functioning autism. *Journal of Pragmatics*, 38(10), 1776–1791.

Perera, K. (1984). *Children's writing and reading: Analyzing classroom language*. Oxford, UK: Basil Blackwell.

Perez-Pereira, M. (1991). The acquisition of gender: What Spanish children tell us. *Journal of Child Language* 18, 571–590.

Perfetti, C. (1985). *Reading ability*. New York: Oxford University Press.

Perkins, M. R. (2001). Compensatory strategies in SLI. *Clinical Linguistics & Phonetics*, 15(1), 67–71.

Persampieri, M., Gortmaker, V., Daly III, E. J., Sheridan, S. M., & McCurdy, M. (2006). Promoting parent use of empirically supported reading interventions: Two experimental investigations of child outcomes. *Behavioral Interventions*, 21(1), 31–57.

Piaget, J. (1952). *The origins of intelligence in children*. New York: International Universities Press.

Pien, D. (1985), The development of language functions in deaf infants of hearing parents. In D. Martin (Ed.), *Cognitive, education, and deafness* (Vol. 2, pp. 30–34). Washingtion, DC: Galludet College Press.

Pinter, R., Eisenson, J., & Stanton, M. (1941). *The psychology of the physically handicapped*. New York: Crofts.

Pinter, R., & Patterson, D. (1916). A measurement of the language ability of deaf children. *Psychological Review*, 23, 413–436.

Pinter, R., & Reamer, J.F. (1920). A mental and educational survey of schools for the deaf. *American Annals of the Deaf*, 65, 451–472.

Ploof, D. L., & Feldman, H. M. (1992). Organizing early intervention services in a hospital setting: The developmental support project as a parallel organization. *Infants and Young Children: An Interdisciplinary Journal of Special Care Practices*, 5, 28–39.

Polowe-Aldersley, S. (1994). Human resources and full inclusion of students who are deaf. *American Annals of the Deaf*, 138(2), 162–163.

Ponton, C., Don, M., Eggermont, J., Waring, M., Kwong, B., & Masuda, A. (1996). Auditory system plasticity in children after long periods of complete deafness. *Neuroreport*, 8(1), 61–65.

Power, D. J., & Quigley, S. P. (1973). Deaf children's acquisition of the passive voice. *Journal of Speech and Hearing Research*, 16(1), 5–11.

Prelock, P. A., Miller, B. E., & Reed, N. L. (1995). Collaborative partnerships in a language in the classroom program. *Language, Speech, and Hearing Services in Schools*, 26, 286–292.

Prendeville, J., & Ross-Allen, J. (2002). The transition process in the early years: Enhancing speech-language pathologists' perspectives. *Language, Speech, and Hearing Services in Schools*, 33(2), 130–136.

Prinz, P., & Strong, M. (1998). ASL proficiency and English literacy within a bilingual deaf education model of instruction. *Topics in Language Disorders*, 18(4), 47–60.

Prior, M., & Hoffmann, W. (1990). Brief report: Neuropsychological testing of autistic children through an exploration with frontal lobe tests. *Journal of Autism and Developmental Disorders*, 20, 581–590.

Prizant, B. (1983). Language acquisition and communicative behavior in autism: Toward an understanding of the "whole" of it. *Journal of Speech and Hearing Disorders*, 46, 241–249.

Prizant, B., & Wetherby, A. (1987). Communicative intent: A framework for understanding social–communicative behavior in autism. *Journal of the American Academy of Child and Adolescent Psychiatry*, 26, 472–479.

Prizant, B. M., Audet, L., Burke, G., Hummel, L., Maher, S., & Theadore, G. (1990). Communication disorders and emotional/behavioral disorders in children. *Journal of Speech and Hearing Disorders, 55,* 179–192.

Prizant, B. M., & Rydell, P. (1984). Analysis of functions of delayed echolalia in autistic children. *Journal of Speech and Hearing Research, 27,* 183–192.

Proctor, A. (1989). Stages of normal noncry vocal development in infancy: A protocol for assessment. *Topics in Language Disorders,* 10(1), 26–42.

Quigley, S. P., & Kretschmer, R. E. (1982). *The education of deaf children.* Baltimore: University Park Press.

Quigley, S. P., Smith, N. L., & Wilbur, R. B. (1974). Comprehension of relativized sentences by deaf students. *Journal of Speech and Hearing Research, 17,* 325–341.

Quigley, S. P., & Steinkamp, M. W. (1977). Assessing deaf children's written language. *Volta Review,* 79(1), 10–18.

Quinn, M. A., & Tomblin, J. B. (1985). *A comparison of comprehension strategies in normal, language impaired and hearing impaired children.* Paper presented at the Sixth Wisconsin Symposium on Research in Child Language Disorders, Madison, Wisconsin.

Radziewicz, C., & Antonellis, S. (2002). Considerations and implications for habilitation of hearing impaired children. In D. Bernstein, & E. Tiegerman-Farber (Eds.), *Language and communication disorders in children.* (5th ed., pp. 565–598). Boston: Allyn and Bacon.

Readence, J., Bean, T., & Baldwin, R. (1995). *Content area reading: An integrated approach.* Dubuque, IA: Kendall/Hunt.

Reese, R. M., Richman, D. M., Zarcone, J., & Zarcone, T. (2003). Individualizing functional assessments for children with autism: The contribution of perseverative behavior and sensory disturbances to disruptive behavior. *Focus on Autism and Other Developmental Disabilities,* 18(2), 87–92.

Reid, D. K., Hresko, W. P., & Hammel, D. (1999). *Test of early language development* (3rd ed). Austin, TX: Pro-Ed.

Reid, R., Epstein, M. H., Pastor, D. A., & Ryser, G. R. (2000). Strengths-based assessment differences across students with LD and EBD. *Remedial & Special Education,* 21(6), 346–356.

Reilly, J. S., Bates, E. A., & Marchman, V. A. (1998). Narrative discourse in children with early focal brain injury. *Brain & Language* 61, 335–375.

Reisler, J. (2003). Technology: Improving sound, easing fury. *Newsweek,* 141(8), 16.

Rescorla, L. (1989). The language development survey: A screening tool for delayed language in toddlers. *Journal of Speech and Hearing Disorders,* 54, 587–599.

Rescorla, L. (2002). The language and reading outcomes to age 9 in late-talking toddlers. *Journal of Speech Language and Hearing, Research,* 45, 360–371.

Rescorla, L., Alley, A., & Christine, J. B. (2001). Word frequencies in toddlers' lexicons. *Journal of Speech, Language & Hearing Research,* 44(3), 598–610.

Reynolds, S. M., & McGrath, P. J. (2006). Predictors of parent training efficacy for child externalizing behavior problems: A meta-analytic review. *Journal of Child Psychology & Psychiatry,* 47(1), 99–111.

Richards, G. (2001). *The source for processing disorders.* East Moline, IL: Linguisystems.

Richardson, E., & DiBenedetto, B. (1985). *Decoding skills test.* Parkton, MD: York Press.

Riding, R. J. (1997). On the nature of cognitive style. *Educational Psychology,* 17, 29–49.

Riding, R. J., & Chema, I. (1991). Cognitive styles—An overview and integration. *Educational Psychology,* 11, 193–215.

Riding, R. J., & Rayner, S. (1998). *Cognitive styles and learning strategies: Understanding style differences in learning and behavior.* London: David Fulton Publishers.

Rist, R. C. (2000). Influencing the policy process with qualitative research. In N. K. Denzin & Y. S. Lincoln (Eds.), *Handbook of qualitative research* (pp. 1001–1017). Thousand Oaks, CA: Sage.

Roach, C. (1989). *Mother/infant communication screening (M/ICS).* Schaumburg, IL: Community Therapy Services. (Available from Community Therapy Services, P.O. Box 68484, 975 East Nerge Road, Suite 130, Schaumburg, IL, 60168–0484.)

Roberts, R. N., Akes, A. L., & Behl, D. D. (1996). Family-level service coordination within home visiting programs. *Topics in Early Childhood Special Education,* 16, 279–301.

Roberts, R. N., Innocenti, M. S., & Goetz, L. D. (1999). Emerging issues from state level evaluations of early intervention programs. *Journal of Early Intervention,* 22(2), 152–163.

Robertson, C., & Salter, W. (1997). *The phonological awareness test.* East Moline, IL: Lingui Systems.

Romer, E. F., & Umbreit, J. (1998). The effects of family-centered service coordination: A social validity study. *Journal of Early Intervention,* 21, 95–110.

Roseberry-McKibbin, C. (1995). *Multicultural students with special language needs.* Oceanside, CA: Academic Communication Associates.

Rossetti, L. (1990). *Infant toddler language scale.* East Moline, IL: Linguisystems.

Roth, F., & Spekman, N. (1991). Higher order language processes and reading disabilities. In A. Kamhi & H. Catts (Eds.), *Reading disabilities: A developmental language prespective.* Boston: Allyn and Bacon.

Roth, F., & Troia, G. (2005). Collaborative efforts to promote emergent literacy and efficient word recognition skills. *Topics in Language Disorders,* 26, 24–41.

Rowley v. Board of Education of the Hendrick Hudson Central School District (1982). The U.S. Supreme Court 458 US 176.

Rozin, P., Bressman, B., & Taft, M. (1974). Do children understand the basic relationship between speech and writing? The mow–motorcycle test. *Journal of Reading Behavior,* 6, 327–334.

Russell, J., Mauthner, N., Sharpe, S., & Tidswell, T. (1991). The "window task" as a measure of strategic deception in preschoolers and autistic subjects. *British Journal of Developmental Psychology,* 9, 331–349.

Russo, C. (2000). *A quasi-experimental study of the effects of fast-forward and recipe for reading on central auditory processing and phonological processing deficits among hearing disabled and language disabled reading students in grades 1 through 6.* Oakdale, New York: Dowling College.

Rutter, M. (2004). Incidence of autism spectrum disorders: Changes over time and their meaning. *Acta Paediatrica.* doï: 10.1080/08035250410023124.

Rutter, M., & Rutter, M. (1992). *Developing minds.* Harmondsworth, Middlesex: Hammond Books.

Sachs, J. (1988). Teacher preparation, teacher self-efficacy and the regular education initiative. *Education and Training in Mental Retardation,* 23, 327–332.

Sack, J. L. (2000). Study shows early intervention can avert special education needs. *Education Week,* 19(22), 26.

Safran, J. S. (2002a). A practitioner's guide to resources on Asperger syndrome. *Intervention in School & Clinic,* 37(5), 283–292.

Safran, J. S. (2002b). Supporting students with Asperger syndrome. *Teaching Exceptional Children,* 24(5), 60–66.

Salameh, E., Hakansson, G., & Nettelbladt, U. (2004). Developmental perspectives on bilingual Swedish-Arabic children with and without language impairment: A longitudinal study. *International Journal of Language & Communication Disorders,* 39(1), 65–91.

Salend, S. (1994). *Effective mainstreaming: Creating inclusive classrooms.* Upper Saddle River, NJ: Merrill/Prentice Hall.

Salend, S. J., Garrick, L, M., & Montgomery, W. (2002). A comprehensive approach to identifying and addressing issues of disproportionate representation. *Remedial & Special Education,* 23(5), 289–300.

Salisbury, C. L., Magino, M., Petrigala, M., Rainforth, B., Syryca, C., & Palombaro, M. M. (1994). Promoting the instructional inclusion of young children with disabilities in the primary grades. *Journal of Early Intervention,* 18, 311–322.

Salvia, J., & Ysseldyke, J. (1991). *Assessment* (5th ed.) Boston: Houghton Mifflin.

Sandall, S., McLean, M. E., & Smith, B. J. (2000). *DEC recommended practices in early intervention/early childhood special education.* Longmont, CO: Sopris West.

Sattler, J. M. (1988). *Assessment of children* (3rd ed) San Diego, CA: Jerome M. Sattler.

Scarborough, H. S., & Debrich, W. (1990). Development of children with early language delay. *Journal of Speech and Hearing Research,* 33(1), 70–83.

Scardamalia, M., & Bereiter, C. (1986). Research on written composition. In M. C. Wittrock (Ed.), *Handbook of research on teaching* (3rd ed). New York: Macmillan.

Schaefer, E. S. (1989). Prediction of child competence from maternal beliefs and behaviors during infancy. In C. Doxiadis (Ed.), *Early influences shaping the individual* (pp. 257–268). New York: Plenum.

Schank, R. C., & Abelson, R. P. (1977). *Scripts, plans, goals, and understanding.* Mahwah, NJ: Lawrence Erlbaum.

Shannon, P. (2004). Barriers to family-centered services for infants and toddlers with developmental delays. *Social Work,* 49(2), 301–309.

Schopler, E., Reichler, R. & Renner, B. (1988). *Childhood autism rating scale* (CARS). Los Angeles: Western Psychological Services.

Scott, C. (1994). A discourse continuum for school age students: Impact of modality and genre. In G. P. Wallach & K. G. Butler (Eds.), *Language learning disabilities in school age children and adolescents: Some underlying principles and applications* (pp. 219–252). Boston: Allyn and Bacon.

Scott, C. M. (1988). A perspective on the evaluation of school children's narratives. *Language Speech and Hearing Services in Schools,* 19 (1), 67–82.

Scott, C. M. (1989). Learning to write: Content form and process. In A. G. Kamhi & H. W. Catts (Eds.), *Reading Disabilities: A developmental perspective.* Boston: Allyn and Bacon.

Seibert, P. S., Stridh-Igo, P., & Zimmerman, C. G. (2002). A checklist to facilitate cultural awareness and sensitivity. *Journal of Medical Ethics*, 28, 143–146.

Seidenberg, P. (2002). Understanding learning disabilities in language and communication disorders in children. In D. Bernstein & E. Tiegerman-Farber (Eds.), *Language and communication disorders in children* (5th ed., pp. 388–435). Boston: Allyn and Bacon.

Seifer, R., Clark, G. N., & Sameroff, A. J. (1991). Positive effects of interaction coaching on infants with developmental disabilities and their mothers. *American Journal on Mental Retardation*, 96 (1), 1–11.

Sexton, D., Synder, P., Wadsworth, D. Jardine, A., & Ernest, J. (1998). Applying Q methodology to investigations of subjective judgments of early intervention effectiveness. *Topics in Early Childhood Special Education*, 18(2), 95–108.

Seymour, H. (2004). The challenge of language assessment for African American English-speaking children: A historical perspective. *Topics In Language Disorders*, 25(1), 3–12.

Seymour, H., Bland-Stewart, L., & Green, L. (1997). Difference versus deficit in child African American English. *Language, Speech, and Hearing Services in Schools*, 29, 96–108.

Seymour, H., Roeper, T., & de Villiers, J. (2003). *Diagnostic evaluation of language variation DELV-screening test*. San Antonio, TX: Psychological Corporation.

Shackelford, J. (1998). *State and jurisdictional eligibility definitions for infants and toddlers with disabilities under IDEA*. Chapel Hill: University of North Carolina, NECTAS, Frank Porter Graham Child Development Center.

Shanker, A. (1995). Full inclusion is neither free nor appropriate. *Educational Leadership*, 5(4), 18–21.

Shankweiler, D., & Crain, S. (1987). Language mechanisms and reading disorder: A modular approach. In P. Bertelson (Ed.), *The onset of literacy: Cognitive processes in reading acquisition* (pp. 139–169). Amsterdam: Elsevier.

Shannon, P. (2004). Barriers to family-centered services for infants and toddlers with developmental delays. *Social Work*, 49(2), 301–309.

Shapiro, T., Sherman, M., Calamari, G., & Koch, D. (1987). Attachment in autism and other developmental disorders. *Journal of the American Academy of Child and Adolescent Psychiatry*, 26, 480–484.

Sharma, A., & Dorman, M. (2005). The clinical use of P1 latency as a bio-marker for assessment of central auditory development in children with hearing impairment. *Audiology Today* (May/June) 18–19.

Sharma, A., Dorman, M., & Spahr, A. (2002). Rapid development of cortical auditory evoked potentials after early cochlear implantation. *Neuroreport*, 13(10), 1365–1368.

Sheridan-Pereira, M., Ellison, P. H., & Helgesen, V. (1991). The construction of a scored neonatal neurological examination for assessment of neurological integrity in full-term neonates. *Journal of Developmental Behavioral Pediatrics*, 12, 25–30.

Shogren, K. A., & Turnbull, A. P. (2006). Promoting self-determination in young children with disabilities: The critical role of families. *Infants & Young Children: An Interdisciplinary Journal of Special Care Practices*, 19(4), 338–352.

Shrager, J., & Siegler, R. S. (1998). SCADS: A model of children's strategy choices and strategy discoveries. *Psychological Science*, 9, 405–410.

Shriberg, L. D., Paul, R., McSweeny, J. L., Klin, A., Cohen, D. J., & Volkmar, F. R. (2001). Speech and prosody characteristics of adolescents and adults with high-functioning autism and Asperger syndrome. *Journal of Speech, Language & Hearing Research*, 44(5), 1097–1116.

Shulman, L. (1999). *The skills of helping individuals families, groups and communities* (4th ed.). Itasca, IL: Peacock Publishers.

Siegel, D. J., Minshew, N. J., & Goldstein, G. (1996). Wechsler IQ profiles in diagnosis of high-functioning autism. *Journal of Autism & Developmental Disorders*, 26(4), 389–406.

Silliman, E. R., Diehl, S. F., Bahr, R. H., Hnath-Chisolm, T., Zenko, C. B., & Friedman, S. A. (2003). A new look at performance on theory-of-mind tasks by adolescents with autism spectrum disorder. *Language, Speech, and Hearing Services in Schools*, 34, 236–252.

Simpson, R., de Boer-Ott, S., & Smith-Myles, B. (2003). Inclusion of learners with autism spectrum disorders in general education settings. *Topics in Language Disorders*, 23, (2), 116–133.

Singer, B. (1995). Written language development and disorders: Selected principles, patterns, and intervention possibilities. *Topics in Language Disorders*, 16, 83–96.

Skarakis, E., & Prutting, C. (1977). Early communication: Semantic functions and communicative intentions in the communication of the preschool child with impaired hearing. *American Annals of the Deaf*, 122, 382–391.

Sleight, M., & Niman, C. (1984). *Gross motor and oral motor development in children with down syndrome: Birth through three years*. St. Louis, MO: St. Louis Association for Retarded Citizens.

Small, R. V. (2002). Collaboration. *Teacher Librarian*, 29(5), 8–12.

Smith, C. R. (1975). Residual hearing and speech production in deaf children. *Journal of Speech and Hearing Research*, 21, 197–219.

Smith, J., Downs, M., & Mogford-Bevan, K. (1998). Can phonological awareness training facilitate minimal pair therapy? *International Journal of Language Communication Disorders*, 33, 463–468.

Smith, P. (1989). Assessing motor skills. In D. B. Bailey & M. Wolery (Eds.), *Assessing infant and preschoolers with handicaps* (pp. 301–338). Upper Saddle River, NJ: Merrill/Prentice Hall.

Smoot, S. L. (2004). An outcome measure for social goals of inclusion. *Rural Special Education Quarterly*, 23(3), 15–23.

Smrekar, C., & Cohen-Vogel, L. (2001). The voices of parents: Rethinking the intersection of family and school. *Peabody Journal of Education*, 76(2), 75–101.

Snow, C. (1986). Conversations with children. In P. Fletcher & M. Garman (Eds.), *Language acquisition* (2nd ed.). New York: Cambridge University Press.

Snow, C., Midkiff-Borunda, S., Small, A., & Proctor, A. (1984). Therapy as social interaction: Analyzing the contexts for language remediation. *Topics in Language Disorders*, 4, 72–85.

Snow, C., Scarborough, H., & Burns, M. S. (1999). What speech language pathologists need to know about early reading. *Topics in Language Disorders*, 20(1) 48–58.

Snow, C. E. (1995). Issues in the study of input: Finetuning, universality, individual and developmental differences, and necessary causes. In P. Fletcher & B. MacWhinney (Eds.), *The handbook of child language* (pp. 180–193). Oxford: Blackwell.

Snow, C. E., Burns, M. S., & Griffin, P. (Eds.). (1998). *Preventing reading difficulties in young children*. Washington, DC: National Academy Press.

Snowling, M., Goulandris, N., Bowlby, M., & Howell, P. (1985). Segmentation and speech perception in relation to reading skill: A developmental analysis. *Journal of Experimental Child Psychology*, 41, 489–507.

Sparks, R. L., & Artzer, M. (2000). Foreign language learning, hyperlexia, and early word recognition. *Annals of Dyslexia*, 50, 189–211.

Sparling, J., Berger, R., & Biller, M. (1992). Fathers: Myth, reality and Public Law 99–457. *Infants and Young Children*, 4, 9–19.

Spencer, L., Barker, B., & Tomblin, J. (2003). Exploring the language and literacy outcomes of pediatric cochlear implant users. *Ear and Hearing*, 24, 236–247.

Spencer, L., Tomblin, J., & Gantz, B. (1997). Reading skills in children with multichannel cochlear implant experience. *Volta Review*, 99, 193–202.

Spencer, P. (2004). Individual differences in language performance after cochlear implantation at one to three years of age: Child, family and linguistic factors. *Journal of Deaf Studies and Education*, 9(4), 395–412.

Spiker, D., Hebbeler, K., Wagner, M., Cameto, R., & McKenna, P. (2000). A framework for describing variations in state early intervention systems. *Topics in Early Childhood Special Education*, 20(4), 195.

Stach, B. A. (1997). *Comprehensive dictionary of audiology. The Hearing Journal*. Baltimore: Williams & Wilkins.

Stanovich, K., & Siegel, L. (1994). Phenotype performance profile of children with reading disabilities: A regression-based test of the phonological core variable-difference model. *Journal of Educational Psychology*, 86, 24–53.

Stanovich, P. J. (1996). Collaboration—The key to successful instruction in today's inclusive schools. *Intervention in School & Clinic*, 32(1), 39–43.

Staskowski, M., & Rivera, E. (2005). Speech-language pathologists' involvement in responsiveness to intervention activities. *Topics in Language Disorders*, 25, 132–147.

Stickler, K. R. (1987). *Guide to analysis of language transcripts*. Eau Claire, WI: Thinking Publications.

Stockman, I. (1986). Language acquisition in culturally diverse populations: The beach child as case study. In O. Taylor (Ed.), *Nature of communication disorders in culturally and linguistically diverse populations* (pp. 117–155). San Diego, CA: College Hill Press.

Stoel-Gammon, C. (1987). Phonological skills of 2-year-olds. *Language, Speech, and Hearing Services in Schools*, 18, 323–329.

Stoel-Gammon, C. (1998). Sounds and words in early language acquisition: The relationship between lexical and phonological development. In S. F. Warren, J. Reichle (series Eds.) & R. Paul (vol. ed.) *Communication and language intervention series:*

Exploring the speech-language connection (pp. 25–52). Baltimore: Paul H. Brookes.

Stone, D. A. (2002). *Policy paradox: The art of political decision making.* Boston: W. W. Norton.

Storkel, H., & Rogers, M. (2000). The effect of probabilistic phonotactics on lexical acquisition. *Clinical Linguistics & Phonetics,* 14(6), 407–425.

Stout, K., & McPhail, B. (1998). *Confronting sexism and violence against women: A challenge for social work.* New York: Longman.

Strong, M. (Ed.). (1988). *Language learning and deafness.* New York: Cambridge University Press.

Strong, M., & Prinz, P. (2000). Is American sign language skill related to English literacy? In C. Chamberlain, J. P. Morford, & R. I. Mayberry (Eds.), *Language acquisition by eye* (pp. 13–41). Mahwah, NJ: Erlbaum.

Subtelny, J. D. (1983). Patterns of performance in speech perception and production. In I. Hochberg, H. Levitt, & M. J. Osberger (Eds.), *Speech of the hearing impaired: Research, training, and personnel preparation.* Baltimore: University Park Press.

Svaib, T. (1994). "Once a time . . .": A *deaf child's development of narrative skills.* Unpublished doctoral dissertation. Stanford University, Stanford, CA.

Swan, W., & Morgan, J. (1994). *Collaborating for comprehensive services for young children and their families: The local interagency coordinating council.* Baltimore: Paul H. Brookes.

Swigert, N. (1998). *Source for pediatric dysphagia.* San Diego, CA: Singular Publishing Group.

Switlick, D. (1997). Curriculum modifications and adaptations. In D. F. Bradley, M. E. King-Sears, & D. M. Tessier-Switlick (Eds.), *Teaching students in inclusive settings: From theory to practice* (pp. 225–251). Boston: Allyn and Bacon.

Tager-Flusberg, H. (1999). A psychological approach to understanding the social and language impairments in autism. *International Review of Psychiatry,* 11(4), 325–335.

Tager-Flusberg, H. (2001). A reexamination of the theory of mind hypothesis of autism. In J. A. Burach, T. Charman, N. Yirmiya, & P. R. Zelazo (Eds.), *The development of autism: Perspectives from theory and research* (pp. 173–193). Mahwah, NJ: Erlbaum.

Tallal, P. (1987). Developmental language disorders. In *Learning disabilities: A report to the U.S. Congress.* Washington, DC: Interagency Committee on Learning Disabilities.

Tannock, R., Girolametto, L., & Siegel, L. S. (1992). Language intervention with children who have developmental delays: Effects of an interactive approach. *American Journal of Mental Retardation,* 97, 145–160.

Taub, J. (2001). The effects of parent empowerment on adjustment for children receiving comprehensive mental health services. *Children's Services: Social Policy, Research, and Practice,* 4(3), 103–122.

Taylor, O. (1986). *Nature of Communication Disorders in Culturally and Linguistically Diverse Populations.* San Diego, CA: College Hill Press.

Taylor, S. (1988). Caught in the continuum: A critical analysis of the principle of the least restrictive environment. *Journal of the Association for Persons with Severe Handicaps,* 29(4), 41–53.

Teitelbaum, P., Teitelbaum, O., Nye, J., Fryman, J., & Maurer, R. (1998). *Proceedings of the National Academy of Sciences of the United States of America,* 95, 13982–13987.

Terpstra, J., Higgins, K., & Pierce, T. (2002). Can I play? Classroom-based interventions for teaching play skills to children with autism. *Focus on Autism & Other Developmental Disabilities,* 17(2), 119–128.

Terrel, S., & Terrel, F. (1993). African-American cultures. In D. Battle (Ed.), *Communication disorders in multicultural populations* (pp. 3–37). Boston: Andover Medical Publications.

Terrel, S. L., Arensberg, K., & Rosa, M. (1992). Parent-child comparative analysis: A criterion-referenced method for the nondiscriminatory assessment of a child who spoke a relatively uncommon dialect of English. *Language-Speech-Hearing Services in the Schools,* 23, 34–42.

Thal, D. J., & Katich, J. (1996). Predicaments in early identification of specific language impairment: Does the early bird always catch the worm? In K. N. Cole, P. S. Dale, & D. J. Thal (Eds.), *Assessment of communication and language* (pp. 1–28). Baltimore: Paul H. Brookes.

Thomas, A., & Chess, S. (1977). *Temperament and development.* New York: Brunner/Mazel.

Thomas, K. R., & Weinrach, S. G. (2004). Mental health counseling and the AMCD multicultural counseling competencies: A civil debate. *Journal of Mental Health Counseling,* 26(1), 41–43.

Thompson, C., Craig, H., & Washington, J. (2004). Variable production of African American English across oracy and literacy contexts. *Language, Speech, and Hearing Services in Schools,* 35(3), 269–282.

Tiegerman-Farber, E. (1995). *Language and communication intervention in preschool children.* Boston: Allyn and Bacon.

Tiegerman-Farber E., & Siperstein, M. (1982). *Communication training: Changing mother–child interaction*. Paper presented at the meeting of the New York State Speech and Hearing Association, Ellenville, New York.

Tiegerman-Farber E., & Siperstein, M. (1984). Individual patterns of interaction in the mother–child dyad: Implications for parent intervention. *Topics in Language Disorders*, 4, 50–61.

Tiegerman-Farber, E. (2002a). Autism spectrum disorders: Learning to communicate in language and communication disorders in children. In D. Bernstein, & E. Tiegerman-Farber, *Language and communication disorders in children* (5th ed., pp. 510–564). Boston: Allyn and Bacon.

Tiegerman-Farber, E. (2002b). Interactive teaming: The changing role of the speech-language pathologist in language and communication disorders in children. In D. Bernstein & E. Tiegerman-Farber (Eds.), *Language and communication disorders in children* (5th ed.). Boston: Allyn and Bacon.

Tiegerman-Farber, E., & Radziewicz, C. (1998). *Collaborative decision making: The pathway to inclusion*. Upper Saddle River, NJ: Merrill/Prentice Hall.

Tolson, J. (1999). Can the quietest war be brought to an end? U.S. *News & World Report*, 126(8), 58–60.

Tomasello, J. (2002). Things are what they do: Katherine Nelson's functional approach to language and cognition. *Journal of Cognition & Development*, 3(1), 5–19.

Tomasello, M. (2002). Not waving but speaking. *Nature*, 417, 791–793.

Tomasello, M., & Brooks, P. (1999). Early syntactic development: A construction approach. In M. Barrett (Ed.), *The development of language* (pp. 161–190). Hove, UK: Psychology Press.

Tomblin, I., Spencer, L., Flock, S., Tyler, R., & Gantz, B. (1999). A comparison of language achievement in children with cochlear implants and children using hearing aids. *Journal of Speech, Language, and Hearing Research*, 42, 497–511.

Tonge, B., Brereton, A., Gray, K., & Einfield, S. (1999). Behavioural disturbance in high functioning autism and Asperger syndrome. *Autism*, 3(2), 117–130.

Torgesen, J. (1985). Memory processing in reading disordered children, *Journal of Learning Disabilities*, 18, 350–357.

Torgesen, J., Alexander A., Wagner, R., Rashotte, C., Voeller, K., & Conway, T. (2001). Intensive remedial instruction for children with severe reading disabilities: Immediate and long-term outcomes from two instructional approaches. *Journal of Learning Disabilities*, 34, 33–58.

Tough, J. (1981). *Talk for teaching and learning*. Portsmouth, NH: Heinemann.

Tractenberg, R. (2002). Exploring hypotheses about phonological awareness, memory, and reading achievement. *Learning Disabilities*, 35(5), 407–424.

Tracy, E., & Whittaker, J. (1990). *Social treatment: An introduction to interpersonal helping in social work practice*. New York: Aldine deGruyler.

Trask, R. L. (1996). *A dictionary of phonetics and phonology*. London: Routledge.

Tronick, E. Z., & Ganino, A. (1986). Interactive mismatch and repair: Challenges to the coping infant. *Zero to Three*, 6(3), 1–6.

Trout, A. L., Nordness, P. D., Pierce, C. D. and Epstein, M. H. (2003). Research on the academic status of children with emotional and behavioral disorders: A review of the literature from 1961 to 2000. *Journal of Emotional and Behavioral Disorders*, 2(4), 198–210.

Tyack, D., & Gottsleben, R. (1975). *Language sampling analysis and training: A handbook for teachers and clinicians*. Palo Alto, CA: Consulting Psychology.

Tyler, R., Davis, J., & Lansing, C. (1987). Cochlear implants in children. *American Speech-Language Hearing Association (ASHA)*. 29, 41–49.

U.S. Department of Education. (2002). To assure the free appropriate public education of all Americans: *Twenty-fourth annual report to Congress on the implementation of the Individuals with Disabilities Education Act*.

Uzgiris, I. C., & Hunt, J. (1975). *Assessment in infancy: Ordinal scales of psychological development*. Urbana: University of Illinois Press.

Van Dijk, T.A., & Kintsch, W. (1983). *Strategies of discourse comprehension*. New York: Academic Press.

Van Kleeck, A., Gillam, R. B., & Davis, V. (1997). The relationship between middle class parents' book-sharing discussion and their preschoolers' abstract language development. *Journal of Speech, Language and Hearing Research*, 40(6), 1261–1272.

Van Kleeck, A., & Gillam, R. B., & McFadden, T. U. (1998). A study of classroom based phonolgical awareness training for preschoolers with speech and/or language disorders. *American Journal of Speech, Language Pathology*, 7, 65–76.

Van Kleeck, A., Gillam, R. B., Hamilton, L., & McGrath, C. (1997). The relationship between middle-class parents' book-sharing discussion and their preschoolers' abstract language development.

Journal of Speech, Language, and Hearing Research, 40, 1261–1271.

Vassallo, P. (2000). More than grades: How choice boosts parental involvement and benefits children. *Policy Analysis* (Report No. 383). Washington, DC: Cato Institute.

Vaughn, S., Bos, C. S., and Schumm, J. S. (2003). Special education and inclusive schooling. In *Teaching exceptional, diverse, and at-risk students in the general education classroom* (3rd ed.). Boston: Allyn and Bacon.

Vaughn, S., & Klingner, J. (1999). Teaching reading comprehension through collaborative strategic reading. *Intervention in School and Clinic*, 34, 284–292.

Vellutino, F. R., Harding, C. J., Phillips, F., & Steger, J. A. (1975). Differential transfer in poor and normal readers. *Journal of Genetic Psychology*, 126(1), 3–19.

Vellutino, F. R., Scanlon, D., & Tanzman, M. (1994). Components of reading ability: Issues and problems in operationalizing word identification, phonological coding, and orthographic coding. In G. R. Lyon (Ed.), *Frames of reference for the assessment of learning disabilities: New views on measurement issues*. Baltimore: Paul H. Brookes.

Vernon, M. (1967). Relationship of language to the thinking process. *Archives of General Psychology*, 16, 325–333.

Voltz, D. L. (1994). Developing collaborative parent–teacher relationships with culturally diverse parents. *Intervention in School and Clinic*, 29, 288–291.

Voltz, D. L. (1995). Learning and cultural diversities in general and special education classes: Frameworks for success. *Multiple Voices for Ethnically Diverse Learners*, 1(1), 1–11.

Wachs, T. D., Francis, J., & McQuiston, S. (1978). Purdue home stimulation inventory, psychological dimensions of the infant's physical environment. *Merrill-Palmer Quarterly*, 24, 3–41.

Wallach, G. P., & Miller, L. (1988). *Language intervention and academic success*. New York: Little, Brown.

Watkins, B. (1999). Family-centered early intervention. *Bilingual Review*, 24(1/2), 19–35.

Watkins, R. V., & Bunce, B. H. (1996). Natural literacy: Theory and practice for preschool intervention programs. *Topics in Early Childhood Special Education*, 16, 191–212.

Watson, C. (1993). *Making Hanen happen: The Hanen progamme for parents*. Toronto: Hanen Centre Publications.

Washington, J., & Craig, H. (1994). Dialect forms during discourse of poor, urban African American preschoolers. *Journal of Speech and Hearing Research*, 37, 816–823.

Washington, J., Craig, H., & Kushmaul, A. (1998). Variable use of African American English across two language sampling contexts. *Journal of Speech and Hearing Research*, 38, 1115–1124.

Webster-Stratton, C., & Reid, M. J. (2004). Strengthening social and emotional competence in young children—The foundation for early school readiness and success. *Infants & Young Children: An Interdisciplinary Journal of Special Care Practices*, 17(2), 96–114.

Weinrach, S. G., & Thomas, K. R. (1998). Diversity-sensitive counseling today: A postmodern clash of values. *Journal of Counseling & Development*, 76(2), 115–122.

Weisler, A., & McCall, R. B. (1976). Exploration and play: Resume and re-direction. *American Psychologist*, 31(7) 492–508.

Weismer, S. E., & Evans, J. L. (2002). The role of processing limitations in early identification of specific language impairment. *Topics in Language Disorder*, 22(3), 15–29.

Weiss, A. L. & Nakamura, M. (1992). Children with normal language skills in preschool classrooms for children with language impairments: Differences in modeling styles. *Language, Speech, and Hearing Services in Schools*, 23, 64–70.

Welch, M. (1996). Teacher education and the neglected diversity: Preparing educators to teach students with disabilities. *Journal of Teacher Education*, 47(5), 355.

Wesley, P. W., Buysee, V., & Tyndall, S. (1997). Family and professional perspectives on early intervention: An exploration using focus groups. *Topics in Early Childhood Special Education*, 17(4), 435–456.

West, J. J., & Weber, J. L.(1973). A phonological analysis of the spontaneous language of a four-year-old, hard-of-hearing child. *Journal of Speech and Hearing Disorders*, 38(1), 25–35.

Westby, C. (1989). Assessing narrative competence. In R. Van Dongen & Z. Maggart (Eds.), *Seminars in Speech and Language*, 10, 63–76.

Westby, C. E. (1984). Development of narrative language abilities. In G. P. Wallach & K. G. Butler (Eds.), *Language Learning Disabilities in School Age Children*. Baltimore: Williams & Wilkins.

Whitehead, A. D. (1996). Service coordination and models of coordination. In P. Rosin, A. D. Whitehead, L. I.

Tuchman, G. S. Jesien, A. L. Begun, & L. Irwin (Eds.), *Partnerships in family-centered care: A guide to collaborative early intervention* (pp. 205–222). Baltimore: Paul H. Brookes.

Whitehurst, G., Fischel, J., Arnold, D., & Lonigan, C. (1992). Evaluating outcomes with children with expressive language delay. In S. Warren & J. Reichle (Eds.), *Causes and effects in communication and language intervention* (pp. 273–313). Baltimore: Paul H. Brookes.

Wiig, E. (1992). *Language intervention for school age children: Models and procedures that work.* Buffalo, NY: Educom Associates.

Wiig, L. (1997). The autistic spectrum. *Lancet*, 350(9093), 1761–1767.

Wilbarger, W. (1984). Planning an adequate "sensory diet"—Application of sensory processing theory during the first year of life. *Zero to Three*, 5(1), 7–12.

Wilbur, R. (2000). The use of ASL to support the development of English and literacy. *Journal of Deaf Studies and Deaf Education*, 5(1), 81–104.

Wilcox, M. J., Kouri, T. A., & Caswell, S. B. (1991). Early language intervention: A comparison of classroom and individual treatment. *American Journal of Speech Language Pathology*, 1(1), 49–62.

Wilhelm, J. (2001). *Improving comprehension with think-aloud strategies.* Peterborough, NH: Scholastic Professional Books.

Willems, E. P. (1977). Steps toward an ecobehavioral technology. In A. Rogers-Warren & S. E. Warren (Eds.), *Ecological perspectives in behavior analysis.* Baltimore: University Park Press.

Williamson, G. (1988). Motor control as a resource for adaptive coping. *Zero to Three*, 9(1), 1–7.

Wing, L. (1997). Editorial: Asperger's syndrome: Management requires diagnosis. *Journal of Forensic Psychiatry*, 8, 253–257.

Wing, L. (2005). Problems of categorical classification systems. In F. Volkmar, A. Klin, & R. Paul (Eds.), *Handbook of autism and developmental disorders* (3rd ed., p. 583). New York: Wiley.

Woodcock, R., McGrew, K., & Mather, N. (2001). *Woodcock–Johnson III.* Itasca, IL: Riverside Publishing.

Woods, J. J., & Wetherby, A. M. (2003). Early identification of and intervention for infants and toddlers who are at risk for autism spectrum disorder. *Language, Speech, and Hearing Services in Schools*, 34(3), 180–194.

Yanok, J. (1986). Free appropriate public education for handicapped children: Congressional intent and judicial interpretation. *Remedial and Special Education*, 7, 49–53.

Yanow, D. (2000). *Conducting interpretive policy analysis.* Thousand Oaks, CA: Sage.

Yell, M., & Espin, C. (1990). The Handicapped Children's Protection Act of 1986: Time to pay the piper? *Exceptional Children*, 56, 396–407.

Yell, M., & Drasgow, E. (2000). Litigating a free appropriate public education: The Lovaas hearings and cases. *Journal of Special Education*, 33, 206–215.

Yoder, P. J., & Davies, B. (1992). Children with developmental delays use more frequent and diverse language in verbal routines. *American Journal on Mental Retardation*, 97, 197–208.

Yoshinaga-Itano, C. (2003). From screening to early identification and intervention: Discovering predictors to successful outcomes for children with significant hearing loss. *Journal of Deaf Studies and Deaf Education.* 8(1), 11–30.

Yoshinaga-Itano, C., & Apuzzo, M. R. (1998a). The development of deaf and hard of hearing children identified early through the high-risk registry. *American Annals of the Deaf*, 143, 416–424.

Yoshinaga-Itano, C., & Apuzzo, M. R. (1998b). Identification of hearing loss after 18 months is not early enough. *American Annals of the Deaf*, 143, 380–387.

Yoshinaga-Itano, C., & Gravel, J. (2001). The evidence for universal newborn hearing screening. *American Journal of Audiology*, 10, 62–64.

Yoshinaga-Itano, C., Sedey, A. L., Coulter, D., & Mehl, A. (1998). Language of early and later-identified children with hearing loss. *Pediatrics*, 102, 1161–1171.

Zhang, D., & Katsiyannis, A. (2002). Minority representation in special education. *Remedial & Special Education*, 23(3), 180.

Zigmond, N. (2001). Special education at a crossroads. *Preventing School Failure*, 45(2), 70–75.

Zigmond, N., & Baker, J. M. (1995). Concluding comments: Current and future practices in inclusive schooling. *Journal of Special Education*, 29(2), 245–250.

Zimmerman, I., Steiner, V., & Pond, R. (2002). *Preschool language scale* (4th ed.). San Antonio, TX: Psychological Corp.

Zwolan, T., & Heavner, K. (2005). Measuring and monitoring progress with cochlear implants. *ASHA Leader*, 10(6), 8–9, 28.

Websites

Association of Women's Health, Obstetric, and Neonatal Nurses, 1990. Systematic assessment of the infant at breast (SAIB). Retrieved November 13, 2006, from www.awhonn.org

The Supreme Court Rowley Case. Retrieved November 9, 2006, from www.specialeducation.ws/supreme_court_rowley_case.html

New cochlear implant could improve hearing. (2006, Feb. 6). University of Michigan News Service. Retrieved October 23, 2006, from www.umich.edu/news/index.html?Releases/2006/Feb06/r020606a

Name Index

Subject Index